Technology Strategies for the Hospitality Industry

Peter D. Nyheim
Drexel University

Francis M. McFadden
Drexel University

Daniel J. Connolly
University of Denver

with
A. Joseph Paiva

PEARSON
Prentice Hall

Upper Saddle River, NJ 07458

Library of Congress Cataloging-in-Publication Data

Nyheim, Peter D.
   Technology strategies for the hospitality industry / Peter D. Nyheim, Francis M.
McFadden, Daniel J. Connolly.
      p. cm.
   Includes index.
   ISBN 0-13-030504-9
   1. Hospitality industry—Data processing. 2. Information technology. I. McFadden,
   Francis M. II. Connolly, Daniel J. III. Title.
TX911.3.E4N95 2004
647.94'0285—dc22

                                                              2003064979

Editor in Chief: Stephen Helba
Executive Editor: Vernon R. Anthony
Executive Assistant: Nancy Kesterson
Editorial Assistant: Ann Brunner
Director of Manufacturing and Production: Bruce Johnson
Managing Editor: Mary Carnis
Production Liaison: Adele M. Kupchik
Creative Director: Cheryl Asherman
Manufacturing Manager: Ilene Sanford
Manufacturing Buyer: Cathleen Petersen
Production Editor: Melissa Scott, Carlisle Publishers Services
Senior Cover Design Coordinator: Miguel Ortiz
Interior Design and Formatting: Carlisle Publishers Services
Senior Marketing Manager: Ryan DeGrote
Marketing Assistant: Elizabeth Farrell
Senior Marketing Coordinator: Adam Kloza
Printer/Binder: R.R. Donnelley and Sons, Inc./Harrisonburg, VA
Cover Printer: Phoenix Color

Pearson Prentice Hall™ is a trademark of Pearson Education, Inc.
Pearson® is a registered trademark of Pearson plc
Prentice Hall® is a registered trademark of Pearson Education, Inc.

Pearson Education LTD.
Pearson Education Singapore, Pte. Ltd.
Pearson Education Canada, Ltd.
Pearson Education—Japan

Pearson Education Australia PTY, Limited
Pearson Education North Asia Ltd.
Pearson Educación de Mexico, S.A. de C.V.
Pearson Education Malaysia, Pte. Ltd.

10 9 8 7 6 5 4 3 2 1
ISBN 0-13-030504-9

Contents

Preface

Hospitality organizations, like all others, have gone digital. Whether it is with a customer, supplier, or co-worker, our industry is expected to operate to a large degree "digitally." In an industry where presentation is everything, this must be accomplished seamlessly, even though numerous boundaries and multiple parties are involved. Take heed that if along the way it breaks down, it is the property where the customer is located that suffers. If it works properly, well that was expected in the first place. *Technology Strategies for the Hospitality Industry* not only takes away the confusion surrounding technology in our industry, it also gives you the tools to succeed.

Obviously, information technology (IT) or information systems' (IS) role is an important and challenging one for managers today. From daily operations to future planning, it is hard to find a process where some form of technology is not involved. Do you wish to understand it?

Ours is a fast moving industry, where serving the customer right away often takes precedence over all other considerations. For this and other reasons, oftentimes the uses and advantages of technology are not employed to their fullest potential. Given the competitive nature of our industry and the fact that technology will not go away (regardless of the "dot.com" crash), today's manager has no choice but to understand it. Simply put, technology is part of doing business in the new millennium.

Information technology (IT), information systems (IS), management information systems (MIS) . . . just what is the difference? The first two are often used interchangeably in this book and elsewhere; however, MIS is very different. The M in MIS stands for management. Managers are concerned with getting things done through other people. Managers are also evaluated on revenue and expenses. Although IS and IT are used, their purpose is to lead the reader in understanding technology within a management context, or MIS.

From a human resources perspective, those managers with this information technology understanding find themselves with a "leg up" on their competition and often a brighter career path. Whether your role or career aspirations focus on food and beverage (F&B) management, asset and space management, marketing and sales, consulting, or perhaps even MIS, your specialty will only be enhanced with the right MIS knowledge base resulting in your becoming a coveted "knowledge worker."

Changing Roles in Hospitality Management

Past day-to-day operations in our industry involved pens, paper, and files. Although they are obviously still used, the focus has shifted towards technology. Managers find themselves using technology daily. Almost all departments have department-specific software and systems through which an organization is managed. Take, for example, the purchasing environment. Today, e-commerce has enabled hospitality organizations to purchase needed items from a vendor or supplier over the Internet. Other examples include the systems and applications used in a restaurant or catering environment. No longer is a stand-alone cash register or paper seating chart enough. Now, enterprise, meaning companywide, systems have been put in place to take advantage of data collection and collaboration across different locations. On the lodging side, properties are now managed by entire systems that track the status and charges of specific spaces and allocate costs and supplies accordingly, all the while interfacing with the outside world. The use of the Internet plays a large role in *Technology Strategies for the Hospitality Industry*.

Audience

If you are a current hospitality management student or a hospitality professional wishing to better your MIS knowledge, you can use this text. With an eleven-chapter layout and specific emphasis on aligning technology to business strategy, this text presents both specific and conceptual themes.

Layout/Unique Features

This text is a collaboration among three academics and one industry professional who keeps us honest. Further, the "living" world of hospitality technology is incorporated via interviews at the beginning of each chapter with leaders in our industry. They include Bill Fisher, the former president of the American Hotel and Lodging Association (AH&LA) and now Eminent Scholar at the Rosen School of Hospitality Management at Florida International University, and Bob Bennett, one of the few members in the Hospitality Technology Hall of Fame, currently senior vice president—property systems and services for Pegasus Solutions. Through these interviews, we take a look at hospitality technology from two main vantage points. From Microsoft to Micros, we first seek to understand *Technology Strategies for the Hospitality Industry* from a vendor's perspective. Second, we look at it from the view of those who purchase and use these systems and applications every day in hospitality, be they a general manager or a director of technology for a specific property. Through these two views, the reader is able to fully capture the function and use of technology in the hospitality industry.

Entrepreneurial

Regardless of the "dot.com" crash, the drive and execution of innovative ideas play a vital part in our industry and are presented throughout the book. From the ability to make a restaurant reservation over the Internet from companies such as Open Table Inc. to new phone systems using the same medium such as bConvergent Inc., new technologies are giving both managers and customers more capability.

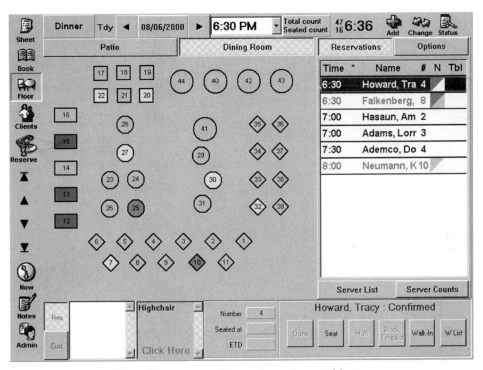

A "digital" restaurant layout from Open Table, Inc.

After the opening interview, the subject matter is detailed in the chapter itself, with a case study and learning activity at the end. After reading the chapter, we recommend that you reread the interview with your newly gained knowledge.

The text opens with a foreward written by Richard G. Moore, Professor Emeritus at Cornell University. The eleven-chapter text itself is divided into two parts. Chapters 1 through 4 form Part I and constitute *fundamentals* of knowledge and usage. Chapters 5 through 11 make up Part II and look at specific software and systems in hospitality.

Time	Name	#	Tbl	N	Time	Name	#	Tbl	N	Time	Name	#	Tbl	N
11:30	Blocked	0			12:00	Aberg, Roland	5			12:30		6		
11:30	Blocked	0			12:00	Sakai, Kent	5			12:30		6		
11:30	Blocked	0			12:00		2			1:00	Abington, Rob	2		
11:30	Blocked	0			12:00		2			1:00	Naito, Arinobu	6		
11:30	Blocked	0			12:00		4			1:00		2		
11:30		2			12:00		4			1:00		2		
11:45	Abizad, Charl	4	65		12:15	Slusky, Alex	2			1:00		4		
11:45		2			12:15		2			1:00		4		
11:45		2			12:15		4			1:00		6		
11:45		2			12:30	Jonson, Nels	3			1:15	Kahn, Liz	2		
11:45		4			12:30		2			1:15		2		
11:45		4			12:30		2			1:15		4		
12:00	Blocked	0			12:30		4			1:30	Gale, Janelle	2		
12:00	Blum, Richard	2			12:30		4			1:30		2		
12:00	Falkenberg, P	2			12:30		4			1:30		2		
12:00	Blocked	0			12:30		4			1:30		4		
12:00	Takaga, Yosh	4			12:30		4			1:30		4		

Electronic reservation management from Open Table, Inc.

The first chapter welcomes you to the world of hospitality information technology, and Chapter 2 shows how we can use it for competitive advantage. These two chapters set the tone for the rest of the book, while presenting to the reader what career and business opportunities are available through technology understanding and usage. These points are reinforced throughout the book and serve as its major themes. Rounding out the fundamentals section are Chapters 3 and 4 with a description of computing essentials and networks, requisite knowledge for the next section.

Chapter 5 begins Part II with a detailed discussion of e-commerce and the way in which the Internet has changed the way we do business. Chapters 6 and 7 detail operational-specific applications for both the food and beverage and lodging sides. Chapter 8 is our most detailed chapter and is a thorough analysis of the global distribution system, where and through which much of our customer data originates and travels. Chapters 9 and 10 round out the text with a discussion of databases and customer relationship management (Chapter 9) and the efficient usage of information through such systems as executive information systems (Chapter 10). Today's front line managers often purchase technology directly, just as they would food or uniforms. They are expected to shop competitively, apply it to their department, and provide a return on investment (ROI). For this reason, we end the book with the investment and implementation chapter (Chapter 11).

Appendices

The appendices of the book contain further detailed analysis on four important themes. The first appendix expands on the case study from Chapter 3, it is the **HITIS** initiative from the AH&LA for hospitality information technology industry standards. This organization is concerned with the interoperability of technology used in our industry.

The second appendix comes from an established professional, Cindy Estis Green, and is a more detailed analysis of revenue and yield management from Chapter 7 and customer relationship management (CRM) from Chapter 9.

The third appendix offers more detail on the global distribution system from Chapter 8.

The fourth appendix contains a sample request for proposal (RFP) from Chapter 11, providing a working example of the content presented in the chapter.

Companion Web Site

The companion Web site *www.prenhall.com/nyheim* to the text provides hands-on problem solving. Interactive "how to" solutions are presented to the reader. Topics include return on investment (ROI) and labor cost spreadsheet exercises, a customer database problem, and an e-commerce exercise on implementation and marketing. The Web site also contains updated materials and industry news and links.

Career

For those seriously considering hospitality technology as a career, the authors encourage the reader to pursue the industry's certification, Certified Hospitality Technology Professional (CHTP). This certification is offered from the Hospitality and Finance Technology Professionals (HFTP). More information can be found at *www.hftp.org*.

Biographies
and Acknowledgements

Peter D. Nyheim is an instructor of technology in Drexel University's Department of Hospitality Management and would like to thank the following people:

"Leading this charge has been quite an endeavor and aside from my co-authors many deserve praise. I would like to thank all the many companies and individuals who helped in this endeavor—Paul Manley from Cendant, Bill Fisher from the University of Central Florida, Gary Cooke from the Microsoft corporation, Bill Bennett from Pegasus, Alan Hayman from Micros, the American Hotel and Lodging Association, Edward F. Nesta, the Union League of Philadelphia, Michael J. Benjamin from GuestWare, Open Table, Inc., Nicholas Porretta, Jerry Reece of Dimension Data, and Mike Dileva from Unisys. I would also like to thank President J. Michael Adams of Fairleigh Dickinson University, Dr. Lynn Hoffman of Drexel University, Dr. Julio Aramberri of Drexel University, and President Constantine Papadakis of Drexel University. My editor, Vern Anthony of Prentice Hall, and Monica Ohlenger and her team deserve much credit for all their help and support. Finally I would like to thank my wife, Stephanie and all the Nyheims out there for their love and support!"

Francis M. McFadden is an associate professor in Drexel University's Department of Hospitality Management and would like to thank the following people:

"The writing of this book was to a great extent made possible by the help, kindness, and generosity of many people. First, my wife Kim McFadden, who encouraged my complete devotion to the project. I could not have imagined undertaking this project without her support, intelligence, and assistance. To my friends and colleagues at Drexel University: Donna, Julio, Chuck, Peter, Will, Corinne, Alan, and Lynn to whom I owe a deep debt of gratitude for their encouragement. To Anna Chrulkiewicz for her tremendous help with the e-commerce research. And the many other friends and professional acquaintances for their help in reading the manuscript and providing feedback. Finally, I thank my parents, Francis and Dolores, and my brothers and sisters, Mary, Lynda, Michele, Krissy "Cookie," and Danny for always believing in me."

Daniel J. Connolly is an assistant professor in Hotel, Restaurant, and Tourism Management, and Information Technology and Electronic Commerce at the University of Denver and would like to thank the following people:

"I wish to thank Paul Manley of Cendant, Elizabeth Lauer Ivey of HVS International, Doug Anderson of Hotwire.com, and Mike Goldenberg of Statability for their participation in this book and their invaluable contributions and critiques of the chapters in which they are featured. I would also like to thank Jerome Staverosky for serving as a sounding board and for the many suggestions he shared that have helped in the development of this book. I must thank the faculty, staff, and administration at the University of Denver for allowing me the opportunity to work on this book and for supporting me and encouraging me during the process. A special thanks goes to my bosses Dr. Peter Rainsford, director of the School of Hotel, Restaurant, and Tourism Management, and Dr. Stephen Haag, chair of the Department of Information Technology and Electronic Commerce. I am forever indebted to my mentors Professor Richard Moore of Cornell University and Dr. Michael Olsen of Virginia Tech. I also wish to recognize my co-authors and the unsung heroes of this process— the publishers, reviewers, editors, and production team. Prentice Hall put together an all-star team to help turn an idea into an entire book. Lastly, and most importantly, I must thank my friends and family who have inspired me and challenged me to tackle what seemed to be the impossible. I cannot acknowledge enough my wife, Sarah Connolly, my parents, George and Natalie Connolly, and my siblings. You are the best. To all, thank you!"

Foreword

A chief information officer (CIO) of one of the major hotel chains once told me that IT has two functions. The first is to drive revenues, and the second is to contain or reduce costs. However, the use of information technology (IT) in the hospitality industry has dramatically changed over the past four decades, shifting from a back-of-the-house support role to one of strategic significance. It has also become a key means by which we interact with our guests. IT is now requisite in all aspects of any hospitality business. It is an important consideration in most business decisions and a key element in delivering exceptional guest service. IT has evolved from a focus on performing manual processes more cost effectively to an emphasis on knowledge-based systems that can help drive revenues and create competitive advantage. We could argue that early IT had more focus on cost containment while today's IT focus is more on revenue generation and strategic enablement.

To help put things in context and understand the present state of the industry with regards to IT, it is important to take a historical perspective. Within the hotel industry, hospitality IT usage has followed two major paths: (1) the use of technology to distribute hotel "products" or rooms through as many channels as possible and (2) the use of technology to automate specific processes and tasks. Because of the relative high cost of early technology, initial applications focused on business opportunities where the costs of IT could be spread over many hotels or many hotel rooms to create economies of scale. The HOLIDEX reservation system developed by Holiday Inns in the mid 1960s was a prime example. This landmark reservation system was developed before the "free" 800 number system proved that existing IT could be used to process reservations in a cost-effective manner. One could also argue that HOLIDEX was not only a reservation system but also a marketing system to sell Holiday Inn franchises. Every major chain soon realized that a central reservation system (CRS) was critical to their survival and success. Today, the hotel chain's CRS is the major component in a highly complex distribution system that encompasses the global distribution systems developed by the airlines and the World Wide Web (WWW).

Initial in-house hotel automation projects focused on large hotels—those with 1,000 rooms or more. In the mid 1970s, the number of hotels that had a property management system (PMS), the heart of most hotel property technology, could be counted on both hands. These systems were justified mainly because of personnel reductions and better accountability for reservations and room inventory. A personal digital assistant (PDA) today has many times the processing capability of these early million-dollar systems—and at a mere fraction of the cost, which goes to show how much technology has progressed. As technology became more affordable, companies developed systems that focused on automating the many manual, repetitive tasks found in hotel operations to create efficiencies and reduce overhead costs. Examples ranged from in-room mini-bar management to managing the food and beverage inventory. As systems were developed for narrow and specific tasks, the need to pass on information to other systems or get information from other systems was discovered. This introduced another complexity in managing IT in a hospitality organization. The guest who viewed a pay-per-view movie needed to have the charge posted to his/her folio. Interfaces were built to connect systems. These early interfaces were custom designed and required constant tweaking. They were expensive to buy and costly to maintain, something which is still true today. A diagram of the many systems in a typical hotel today looks like a large bowl of spaghetti and meatballs, with the meatballs representing systems and the strands of spaghetti between the meatballs representing interfaces. There have been partially successful initiatives to develop interface standards, but more progress is needed. Standards would lower the costs of technology and reduce the barriers to upgrading or replacing technology.

Hotel operations can be highly complex, involving far-reaching and multifaceted decisions. IT has evolved to where we can make better business decisions; for example, a centralized revenue management system helps us answer "what rate should we set for our hotels in a city for a specific market segment on a particular date?" IT has also developed so that we can process more complex tasks. For example, a customer planning a last minute sales meeting might ask, "I need a meeting room for 30 people and 25 sleeping rooms for the night before at a major airport hotel two days from now. What do you have available?" IT has also evolved to help us know our customers better. Each customer has a different lifetime value to us. Our customer relationship management (CRM) systems allow us to tailor a unique experience for each customer or guest to maximize that value. IT is the enabler that allows us to recognize a customer from one property in the chain to another and provide amenities and service that make his/her stay unique.

IT issues facing managers continue to expand and now largely involve embracing the Internet, creating the enabling infrastructure which powers the technology, addressing security, integrating systems, taking on large-scale projects like CRM and enterprise resource planning (ERP), and more. The list of issues and the many considerations one must take into account are growing, requiring every manager to have a keen sense of what IT can and cannot do and when it should be used and when it shouldn't.

One could argue that IT has contributed to a change in the structure of the hospitality industry. IT has been an enabler of the consolidation of the industry into a few mega brands. If we use a "store" analogy, we can say that the mega brands present a different storefront to each market segment based on the price and service preferences of the customers. However, when one looks at the back-of-the-house infrastructure, one can see the same reservation system, the same purchasing system, the same CRM system, etc. driving all the brands. Revenue (yield) management on a regional basis across brands is possible because of common reservation and revenue managements systems. The ability to cross-sell and up-sell from one brand to the next is IT based, "I'm sorry rooms aren't available at the property you requested, but our sister property across the street has rooms available."

Why is this book needed? We have reached a point in time where IT as a discipline is growing up. Competition in the industry is increasingly driven by IT. With most hospitality companies dependent on IT, it is incumbent upon all managers and managers in training to understand IT, how it ties to the business, and its ramifications on various business decisions. It is also capital intensive. Thus, managers must know how to wisely pick and choose the appropriate solutions given the needs of their businesses.

Non-IT technology in hotels is stable and well understood. Elevators, HVAC (heating, ventilation, and air-conditioning) systems, plumbing and electrical systems, while also very capital intensive, need little more than routine maintenance, and if well cared for, can last for decades. IT, conversely, evolves in a much more rapid fashion, and the decisions facing today's manager are more complex and far-reaching. The wiring network selected two years ago is probably technologically obsolete today. What is the impact on guest service and in-house system performance? Should you select a new property management system, and if so, should you consider an application service provider (ASP) model? How do you prevent a hacker getting into your systems and stealing all of your guests' credit card numbers? These are some of the many concerns presently facing industry leaders.

IT is an investment, and like any other asset, it requires continual upkeep and ongoing expenditures to sustain its useful life. Today's manager needs to have fundamental knowledge about hardware, software, databases, networks, and security. He/she does not necessarily need to be a technical expert but does need to be IT literate to understand how systems work and their implications on the business. Today's manager needs to be able to understand the technical person, but more importantly, he/she needs to understand the business and customer impact of technology decisions.

This book gives the reader the skills and perspectives necessary to thrive in a competitive and ever-changing environment, one in which IT will greatly determine or contribute to an organization's and an individual's success. This book covers the key topics that should be foremost on any manager's mind and does so in a way that is easy to understand and relevant to industry practice. It blends theory and strategy with application and how-to. It raises awareness for important investment considerations that must be asked by chief financial officers, asset managers, and property owners to ensure their organizations are deriving the maximum value from IT. It also opens the doors to many career opportunities within the industry involving IT.

In short, this book is a must-read for all hospitality professionals and students of the industry, even if IT is not the primary career focus. One can no longer afford to ignore the impacts of IT or delegate responsibility for this important function to others. IT must be part of anyone's core competencies who wishes to be an industry leader.

Professor Richard G. Moore

Emeritus
Cornell University's School of Hotel Administration

CHAPTER ONE

Welcome to the World of Hospitality Information Technology

CHAPTER CONTENTS

INTERVIEW

Paul Manley is a senior project manager for Cendant Corporation's Lodging Division in Parsippany, New Jersey. He provides project management and business support for large-scale hospitality technology initiatives such as customer relationship management (CRM, Chapter 9), central reservation systems (CRS, Chapters 7 and 8), and property management systems (PMS, Chapter 7).

Q: Paul, thank you for taking this opportunity to discuss your career in hospitality information technology (IT). Please give us a brief history of your career.

A: For nearly 30 years, I have been working in hospitality IT, implementing and supporting a variety of computer systems (including front office, back office, restaurant and gift shop point-of-sale, sales and catering, time and attendance, and revenue management) for leading hospitality firms and technology vendors. Prior to joining Cendant in 2002, I was a technology consultant for four years, leading software development, system selection, and customer relationship management projects.

Q: Could you share with us some examples of some of the projects in which you have been involved thus far?

A: I've been involved in establishing property system strategies, standards, and user requirements for major hotel companies; managing the development of the customer relationship management strategy for Carnival Cruise Line; serving as project manager for a $20 million custom software development project that addressed all sales, marketing, and customer fulfillment activities for a timeshare company; providing customer support for various hospitality systems and technology; creating systems training programs for vendors and hotel companies; overseeing the quality assurance processes for various software releases; defining and implementing the request for proposal (RFP) processes for various companies; re-engineering the business processes of a software supplier resulting in the first ever ISO9002 quality service certification in the industry; and managing the design and development of a customer-focused, logical data model at Walt Disney World.

Q: How did you decide upon a career in hospitality IT?

A: I think the career chose me. After receiving my undergraduate degree with majors in statistics and math, I found a position as a systems manager with the Innisbrook Resort in Tarpon Springs, Florida. I developed specifications for application enhancements, staff training, and business process re-engineering.

Q: What do you consider to be your most significant career accomplishment to date and why? What was your most gratifying moment?

A: If I have to pick just one thing, I guess it would be the development of a computer training course for general managers at Hilton International in New York City. It was significant because, at the time, IT in hotels was seen more as a necessary evil and not as an enabler for increased revenue, guest service, or employee satisfaction. Within Hilton International, this course changed the way hotel general managers viewed IT and IT managers; it gave them an understanding of how to truly leverage their technology investment and work with their IT team.

Q: What courses did you take that have provided the most value to you in your career? If you could take courses again, what would you study?

A: I would have to say typing. Early in my career, I made opportunities for myself by volunteering to type minutes, reports, or anything else I could in order to understand the business around me. Basic concepts from my accounting and other business courses, including business algebra and BASIC programming have also been helpful. If I could redo my course load based on what I know now (remember, my majors were statistics and math), I would learn more about computer networking, data warehousing, and marketing. I would also take hospitality management courses like food and beverage.

Q: IT is ever changing. How have you managed to stay abreast of the latest trends and avoid obsolescence?

A: It is important to follow the industry through leading trade magazines, university research, publications by leading consulting firms, and Internet sites. It is also helpful to read hospitality books that provide a historical perspective, for example, Conrad Hilton's *Be My Guest.*

Q: What do you consider to be the most important skills and knowledge for someone who is interested in pursuing a career in hospitality IT? How will these skills likely be used in one's career?

A: In addition to the need to understand the big picture, there are three types of skills for success—content, learning, and people skills. Content is the ability to deliver tangible results based on your role. For example, a software developer on a project team is involved in one or many aspects of application development. A chief information officer (CIO), chief technology officer (CTO), or director of IT must have a range of systems knowledge, from networks to implementation and support. Learning is the ability to absorb new information and put it into the context of the job and how it will benefit your employer. People skills is the ability to develop long-term relationships with people, whether they are subordinates, peers, managers, or anyone in the industry. Finally, the big picture is that you must understand the drivers of the industry and hotel companies, owners, and hotel units.

Q: To pursue a career in hospitality IT, is it more important to understand the business or the technology?

A: That is a great question! Today, I would have to say both, but the answer has changed since I first started working in the industry some 30 years ago. Then, everything was about hospitality. Over time, however, both the business and technology have matured. The constant enhancement of technological capabilities has led to the implementation of many types of technologies at property, regional, and corporate levels. These systems require a broad range of skills and perspectives to develop and maintain them, a complete understanding of the business, and how to use technology to achieve solid business results—especially financial performance and value creation. As one develops a hospitality IT career from employee to manager to executive, there are three broad paths from which to choose. One is the CIO route. This requires the greatest combination of technology knowledge, people skills, and business acumen. A second is the project management route. This requires great IT conceptual knowledge, systems life cycle management skills, superb people and team-building skills, and some technical knowledge. A third path is that of a technologist. This can be as a software developer, hardware/network engineer, database manager, database administrator, or application specialist.

Q: Where do you see future opportunities in hospitality IT? What will be the hot technologies, skills, and industry sectors on which one should focus?

A: While it is difficult to predict the future, I think it is safe to say that network management, application development, system architecture, and data management will remain important areas of study for those interested in pursuing hospitality IT careers. If you gain deep skill sets in one or more of these, you will be an attractive candidate to work in a large chain. If, on the other hand, you develop a broad skill set, you will be a suitable candidate for smaller hospitality companies. There are also some technically challenging jobs that do not reside in a hotel company's IT department. For example, marketing, accounting, and human resources—especially in large hospitality firms, entertainment companies, and the gaming industry—require people with strong technical skills to run marketing campaigns, CRM systems, call centers, e-commerce initiatives, self-service benefits, personnel systems, etc. For many positions in these areas, it isn't enough to know only the business side of the equation; one must also understand the technology and possess some important technical skills. In addition, suppliers to the industry hold many rewarding career development opportunities.

Q: What advice would you offer to anyone interested in pursuing a career in hospitality IT?

A: First, decide if you are equally excited about both hospitality and IT. If so, learn both well, especially the IT side. It is much easier to learn about hospitality operations than it is to learn about technology. Go to a good hotel school and take as many IT courses as you can. Volunteer or get a job helping to run the school's network and computer lab, and then secure summer employment working in IT systems for hospitality firms, vendors, or consultants. These jobs can be in any industry, although it is helpful to gain exposure to the hospitality industry as early as you can. Also, be sure to work in hospitality operations. It is important to understand the operations and the role technology plays. See things from all sides including the users', businesses', and the owners' perspectives. Go to hospitality companies' websites to learn about available jobs. Speak to hospitality IT professors, read, and network.

1. INTRODUCTION

At the start of each new academic term, the number of prospective candidates seeking careers in hospitality information technology (IT) is generally few. Comparing IT salaries to other types of hospitality career salaries you might be likely to pursue (e.g., management positions in hospitality operations, sales, and human resources) may entice you, but the reality is that for most careers, IT is an important, integral, and necessary component. Thanks to the convergence of various forms of technology (e.g., computers, software, and telecommunications), the rise in electronic business (e-business), and a growing number of enterprisewide technology initiatives, technology is a critical aspect of almost any job. It has become an essential element in almost every business process, disrupting functional silos and creating the need for boundary spanners. Simply put, IT changes everything—from guest expectations and needs to industry structure to how you perform your job and what skills you will need to be successful. Consequently, IT is inescapable and must be a core skill for any aspiring hospitality manager or executive. Just as management guru Peter Drucker once said that everyone in the firm is responsible for marketing the firm and ensuring customer satisfaction and is, therefore, by default, a member of the marketing team, everyone in today's organization must be responsible for IT and think and act like a chief information officer (CIO). Congratulations, you have just joined the IT team—whether you like it or not!

For example, it is tough to be a great marketer without IT. In today's high-tech era, IT is a prerequisite to marketing and must go hand in hand. You cannot make marketing decisions without in-depth knowledge about the capabilities and limitations of IT. Global distribution, supply chain management, customer relationship management (CRM), electronic commerce (e-commerce), customer segmentation, and revenue management, are all underpinned by IT applications. Thus, a good marketer must be well versed in IT.

The same could be said for every other discipline, including human resources, finance and accounting, management, and operations. Front desk managers must be intimately familiar with property management (PMS), revenue (yield) management, central reservations (CRS), call accounting (PBX), voice messaging, guest locking systems, and more. Similarly, restaurant managers must be proficient in point-of-sale (POS) technology, inventory management systems, menu engineering, and the like.

How can a hospitality executive determine how to maximize value for the firm if he/she is faced with resource constraints and must decide between, say, a new sales and catering system and the renovation and re-theming of a restaurant outlet? How can anyone possibly estimate cash flows, assess risks, assign risk premiums, and calculate returns on investment (ROI) without fully comprehending IT? It would be difficult to evaluate the pros and cons, quantify the benefits, and understand the strategic opportunities associated with each option to make a well-informed business decision without having a solid grasp of IT. From your perspective as an aspiring manager or executive, how can you lead others, make hiring decisions, and mentor and develop people without understanding the technological future of the industry?

Many are quick to say that they don't need to become proficient in a particular area because they can hire someone else to handle those responsibilities or they can outsource those functions. Generally speaking, this type of thinking is shortsighted, and when it comes to IT, it can be outright dangerous—especially considering the stakes involved. IT tends to rank among the top three expense categories of most firms. It also tends to be one of the most pervasive and enabling—or confining—resources in the firm. Therefore, every manager or executive must strive to understand how to use IT, see its strategic potential, and recognize its limitations so as not to be confused by it, led astray, or constrained by the limitations of the firm's IT infrastructure. Understanding and using IT require investment (of both time and money), commitment, and diligence. Your knowledge in this area will reduce your dependence on others and improve your ability to ask the *right* questions so you can properly lead your firm.

2. WELCOME TO THE WORLD OF IT!

IT is one of the greatest forces driving change in almost any industry, especially the hospitality industry—so get used to IT! Unfortunately, human bandwidth, that is people's ability to grasp IT and understand how to effectively use it and apply it in business, is one of the greatest barriers to a firm's ability to successfully adopt IT and realize its many benefits. The IT wave will likely continue for the foreseeable future for several reasons. First, the pace of change and the expected number of technological advances continue to grow at alarming rates. Second, the technological demands of guests continue to rise. Third, the competitive environment is growing in intensity with increased investment in and emphasis on IT. Fourth, labor issues continue to plague the industry. Both the cost of labor and the scarcity of people willing and able to fill industry positions require greater focus on technology as a viable alternative to run the business and service guests. For these reasons, IT is quickly becoming one of the most important skills industry managers and leaders need to possess and one of the most important competitive methods a hospitality firm can exploit to gain advantage in an increasingly competitive business. These advantages come in many forms including, but not limited to, differentiation, efficiency (economies of scale), resource capabilities, cost reduction, and information asymmetry. Despite their diversity, they all have one thing in common; they are all enabled by IT. Thus, whether you are interested in pursuing a career in IT or not makes little difference. The underlying premise is the same; no matter what you choose to do as a profession, you need to become proficient in IT at the personal, intraorganizational, and interorganizational levels.

By default, your career will involve IT. IT transcends today's organizations, crossing and blurring all traditional departmental, organizational, and geographic boundaries. This is especially true with large-scale initiatives such as e-business, enterprise resource planning (ERP), and customer relationship management (CRM). Enterprise resource planning involves the integration of all departmental-specific applications into one resource. Again, customer relationship management (CRM) will be detailed in Chapter 9. Figure 1-1 helps bring this reality to life. IT-related decisions require input from multiple perspectives within the organization since IT is pervasive throughout the firm's *value chain,* all of the primary and support activities of the firm required to produce products and services that generate revenues and drive profits. Consequently, if the organization is to exploit IT for competitive advantage, business leaders, regardless of the discipline they represent, must (1) focus on enterprise-wide solutions, (2) be able *boundary spanners* (people who can cross multiple disciplines or areas of knowledge), and (3) become technologically savvy. Decisions involving IT cannot be made in a vacuum, and because of their reach, cost, and strategic implications, they should not be delegated to others.

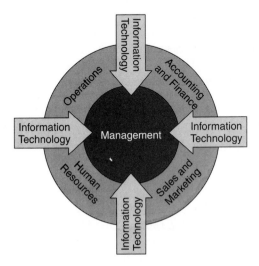

Figure 1-1. Information technology plays a crucial role in the management of all departments.

They require commitment from the top, insight from all aspects of the business, and the involvement of those possessing specific expertise in IT.

3. MANAGING YOUR CAREER

This is an exciting time to be pursuing an IT career within the context of the hospitality industry. Hospitality and tourism are among the largest and fastest growing employers worldwide and offer a rich, yet diverse, set of possibilities. IT, despite the temporary slowdown in the economy (especially in the technology sector) and the number of dot.com crashes, is also among the fastest growing areas of employment and one of the economy's great contributors, a trend expected to continue well into the future.

IT will continue to be one of the greatest forces driving transformation in almost any industry, including hospitality. Consequently, everything will continue to change—from how you work and learn to how you transact business with guests and employees, to the technological amenities and infrastructure found in establishments. With the rise in e-business, these changes have become more pronounced and more commonplace—moving the industry to new heights technologically, while at the same time expanding the globalization of the hospitality industry. Certainly for those seeking careers in this industry, exciting opportunities abound, and because of IT, many new career possibilities have surfaced. You are encouraged to explore IT-based careers for many reasons—not just for the salaries but also for the diversity of career options, the challenges and intellectual stimulation, and the overall quality of work life (i.e., better and more predictable hours than careers in hospitality operations).

To excel at your career, you need to have passion and enjoy what you do. You also need to continue to develop yourself and your skills. Learning should be a lifelong journey and a regular part of your job. The hospitality industry has become complex and continues to change at a rapid pace. Thus, you, too, need to change, adapt, and stay current—especially with IT. One of the nice things about IT is that there is a built-in mechanism or incentive that forces you to stay current if you want to stay employed.

Remember that career paths seldom resemble a straight line. They often take many twists and turns, but these twists and turns are largely up to you. It is your responsibility and obligation to manage your own career. Although others can help you with this important task, no one can do this for you in the way you can do it for yourself. After all, you know yourself, your interests, your goals, and what motivates you and gives you personal satisfaction better than anyone else does.

At this point in your career, one of the best things you can do is to conduct a self-assessment or *SWOT (strengths, weaknesses, opportunities, and threats)* analysis. Determine what you like and what you don't and inventory your skills and core competencies. Be sure to think about what you would like to do long-term and what skills will be required to achieve your goals. Where are you strong, and where is there room for improvement? What skills are you lacking, or which ones need further development? How prepared are you for the digital economy? What are the job opportunities like presently, and where will they be in the next five, ten, or fifteen years? In essence, you want to create your own personal balance sheet that identifies your assets (strengths) and liabilities (weaknesses) relative to the marketplace you will enter. Then, just as you would do if you were managing a firm's balance sheet, figure out how to improve your assets through *value creation* (adding something for which people are willing to pay that wasn't there before and will provide a noticeable advantage) while reducing, and hopefully eliminating, your liabilities. Look for jobs that will serve as springboards to new opportunities and help you progress and achieve your ultimate career dreams. Each position you take should help you acquire new skills and serve as a stepping-stone to the position you ultimately desire. When it comes time to interview for a job, be prepared to address with conviction the question "What value do you bring to the table?"

4. DECISIONS, DECISIONS, DECISIONS

One of the hard parts of planning a career is knowing what options exist. Awareness of these options allows you to better prepare and take the necessary steps to gain the skills and knowledge required for a desired career path. The beauty of IT is that it is broad and far-reaching. While attractive, these attributes often create discomfort. Because of the number of choices, the decision-making process can become overly complex and downright confusing at times. There are so many options and possibilities. Having to make such a paramount decision that can alter the course of your life seems daunting. While true, the good news is that you do have options. These are the kinds of decisions you like to have. It is this type of flexibility and diversity that many people have found attractive when developing their career paths, and it is what helps to keep them marketable today in a volatile economy.

There are many types of IT-related careers from which to choose. You may be interested in operations, consulting, web design, e-commerce or e-business, project management, system development, database management, computer programming, electronic marketing, distribution, customer relationship management, training, system management, or perhaps something more entrepreneurial. The possibilities are almost endless. Consider three basic career path options depicted in Figure 1-2. Within the hospitality industry, there are numerous possibilities for exploring a career involving IT. However, at the macro level, careers can be defined as those involving the managerial aspects of IT or the technical aspects of IT, or the career path could be for a non-IT managerial position that relies extensively on IT.

IT Managerial

If you are seeking an IT managerial position, it is important to understand both the hospitality business and IT. Although there is no definitive mix, many

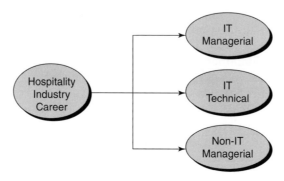

Figure 1-2.   Career Path Options

would agree that business knowledge is just as important as the technology or technical skills. The appropriate mix will likely vary with each position and set of responsibilities. You must possess the ability to develop sound strategies, make rational and informed decisions, and allocate and manage resources appropriately to generate business value (i.e., profits and competitive advantage) and shareholder returns. IT is a resource or tool that should be applied as a competitive method and aligned with the firm's strategy. Those who are able to utilize IT and its by-product, information, to solve business problems and create new business opportunities will be in a position to drive strategy and generate strong business value. Clearly, managers of today and tomorrow must be exceptional managers and users of information.

As technology becomes more pervasive and influential, it will become an underlying part of nearly every business decision, business process, and the entire value chain. Therefore, thinking is shifting away from "pure" technology projects in favor of business projects that involve IT. In effect, people assuming these roles need to be great managers and leaders. However, they must also be able to serve as liaisons between the various aspects of the business and the functional disciplines (e.g., sales and marketing, finance and accounting, human resources, operations, etc.) and the IT staff (i.e., the programmers and software engineers/architects who design and develop the applications). To do this, it is important to be able to "speak" the languages of both business and technology (yes, all those acronyms) and to do so decisively and convincingly. Being able to recognize needs, find solutions, and then develop, pitch, and defend persuasive business cases are requisite skills. Often, you must translate business requirements into technical solutions as well as have the ability to find new business opportunities using technology to drive revenues, gain market share, or reduce overhead costs. Needs analysis, business case development, and risk assessment are important and frequent aspects of the job. It is also important to understand, recognize, and balance the needs of competing stakeholders that include customers, employees, owners and investors, franchisees, suppliers, and the community. If projects are not managed well, they can quickly become derailed—over budget, late, or short on functionality. Therefore, the ability to manage projects (including resources, budgets, and functional scope) is essential. Projects involving IT can quickly become political due to the many variables, stakeholder groups, resource requirements, and the stakes (i.e., costs, risks, organizational impact, and complexity).

The position of *chief information officer (CIO)* represents the ultimate business-IT liaison and should report to the organization's chief executive officer (CEO), although this reporting relationship may vary from company to company. This individual must understand the ins and outs of the business completely and know when (and when not to) apply technology to achieve business results (e.g., higher customer retention, more market share, increased profits, decreased costs, greater employee productivity, stronger shareholder value, etc.). This person must also possess a global perspective and have a significant amount of large-scale, multinational project experience, including justification, systems design and development, rollout, implementation, and benefits tracking. Other positions, to name a few, include IT directors, managers, consultants, and business analysts.

To prepare for an IT managerial career, you must seek to understand all of the relevant business aspects of the hospitality sector you plan to enter. Strong operational experience with cross-functional exposure is an absolute must. This is an industry where people work their way up to the top. Start early to begin paying your dues and learn the nuts and bolts of the industry, both the craft or service aspects of hospitality and the business acumen and technical know-how required. Then, continue to seek more exposure and positions of greater responsibility that will enable you to strengthen and develop your management skills. While in school, enroll in classes that will enable you to develop your analytical and critical reasoning, communications, leadership, financial management, and strategic thinking skills. In addition, take classes and look for experiences that will help you master technology as a user and a person seeking ways to apply it. These include courses in programming, office applications (especially spreadsheets), database management, project management, networking, security, e-commerce, collaboration software (groupware), and IT strategy. Generally, it is a good idea to accept one or more jobs that will immerse you in the technical side in order to establish yourself and build your technical credibility. As with anything, it is easier to manage something if you are completely knowledgeable about that which you are managing.

It is important to be comfortable with technology and capable and willing to explore its outer bounds. As you understand both the business and the technology, your value-add and competitive differentiator will be your ability to marry the two to come up with creative and effective combinations that will give your firm competitive advantage. Perhaps your biggest and most overwhelming challenges will be to stay current and abreast of extremely dynamic environments. In an IT managerial capacity, you must continuously monitor and follow key trends for all aspects of your business (i.e., sales and marketing, operations, human resources, finance and accounting, and management) as well as the technology trends. You will need to know how to evaluate emerging trends and technologies, assess their impacts, and know when to embrace them and when not to. Although these tasks can be overwhelming and a lot of work, they are essential to survivability; failure to do so will render you ineffective in your job and ultimately obsolete. So, if you don't want your career to end prematurely, you must make continuous learning and trend-tracking key parts of your job responsibilities.

As you progress on your IT managerial career track, you will likely find it worthwhile to pursue a graduate degree, most notably a master of business administration (MBA) with a concentration or specialization in information technology and electronic business.

IT Technical

Those of you who are attracted to the computer science or software engineering aspects of IT may wish to pursue a technical career track. Some people love to write software applications, design databases, and deal with technology infrastructure, network topology, and data networking issues. They have no real interest in managing people per se. Instead, they prefer to deal with, develop, and manage technology. These are important people to have on staff because without them, the industry would not have the technology applications and solutions that are in use today. For people serving in these roles, it is important to understand the particulars of the hospitality business and have a keen sense of the guest and guest service. Unfortunately, being a great programmer is not sufficient due to the many complexities and nuances of the business. Some of the hospitality industry's systems are among the most complex in the world, given the number of transactions they must process, the diversity of the guests and properties, the volume of data that must be tracked, the number of disparate systems that must be integrated, and the subsecond response times required. To gain the necessary skills and competencies, you should seek training, coursework, and jobs involving computer programming, data networking, telecommunications, wireless communications, web design and development, database design and management, systems analysis and design, IT security, and enterprise architecture planning coupled with industry exposure through coursework and practical (i.e., hands-on) work experience.

The ultimate technical position is that of *chief technology officer (CTO)*. This individual typically reports to the CIO and is responsible for the firm's technology infrastructure, network typology, standards, architectural decisions, and computer operations. Having the *right* (i.e., fast, capable, responsive, integrated, stable, reliable, and secure) technology in place is the foremost responsibility of this individual. This person must possess a strong set of technical skills and in-depth knowledge of the business. However, the order of priority is reversed from that of the CIO. The technical skills take on greater priority followed closely by knowledge of the business. This person must also possess a significant amount of system development and rollout experience for large-scale, multinational projects. A graduate degree is strongly recommended. Examples of other technical positions include database manager or administrator, web master, network operations manager, data center manager, system manager, technology director, senior programmer, technology/application specialist, systems analyst, technology architect, technical writer, quality assurance, and help desk/support.

Non-IT Managerial

IT, by its very nature is multidisciplinary, and will soon become a major component of every discipline and every business process. As stated earlier, it is difficult to carry out a particular job function without understanding the opportunities of IT and recognizing its limits. Consequently, it is important to understand IT in order to spend wisely and not needlessly on IT. Thanks to many recent technological developments like customer relationship management (CRM), enterprise resource planning (ERP), and e-business, most hospitality jobs are being affected by IT, and the people filling these jobs are increasingly being required to play more active roles in technology decision making, direction setting, project development, and implementation. Moreover, employee compensation is often tied to the outcomes of IT-enabled initiatives.

In many companies, most of the major requests for technology funding are now being made and decided by the business executives who are considered to be a project's client base or primary users/beneficiaries of the system. These are typically the people who are responsible for the company's financial assets, marketing initiatives, and operations. Although the CIO, the CTO, and other IT staff provide support and guidance, make recommendations, and work closely with these individuals, it is up to these executives to develop, defend, and *own* the business cases. They must then execute the project upon successful approval and funding. They are required to take an active managerial role rather than simply to provide moral support and to hide behind the IT staff, which, in the past, has often become the scapegoat whenever a project got derailed. In fact, their compensation (i.e., bonuses and merit increases) is often based on the successful outcome of IT projects. With that kind of vested interest (or "skin in the game"), it is incumbent upon these individuals to learn about and understand IT and how it can be used, when to use it, when not to use it, and then, to subsequently promote its use and adoption throughout the organization. Thus, there is more of a partnership rather than an adversarial role developing between the business units and IT, which results in a higher success rate and greater realized benefits for all IT-related initiatives.

Because of their rank and positioning in the organization, these individuals are influential in determining the organization's culture and attitudes towards IT. They play an important role in affecting the success of initiatives involving IT. They also serve as important role models and mentors for others in the organization—seeking ways to grow and prepare for future trends, trying to grapple with change and understand IT, and looking to be more open-minded or think "out-of-the-box" to develop innovative and creative solutions that will lead to competitive advantage (and personal promotion). In short, they should be technology advocates and consider IT as an important aspect of their job responsibilities. They should also be early adopters of new technology and demonstrate by example how technology can enable individuals and the business to make great things happen.

To climb the rungs of the corporate ladder at a faster rate, you are advised to attain a graduate degree, preferably an MBA. To be successful in these positions, you must demonstrate a proven track record (i.e., string of successes) and have a strong sense of the business, a global perspective, and a good working understanding of IT, at least from a macro level. It is not necessary to know specifically which buttons to push on the computer to make something happen. Instead, it is important to be able to define and articulate needs, specify functional requirements, recognize opportunities for applying IT to achieve business success, and prepare compelling business cases to secure funding and resources to make IT happen. You must also be willing to assume risk, experiment, and think strategically and creatively. People serving in these capacities must, like their IT managerial counterparts, serve as liaisons and boundary spanners. They must seek to understand foreign ground—the world of IT—and then apply it in a given context to their specific area or areas of the business. These individuals must be strong managers able to toe the line, hold others accountable for deadlines and deliverables, and be held accountable and able to deliver projects themselves—on time and on budget according to the agreed-upon specifications.

A series of great commercials help to put all of this into perspective. In one, the setting is the conference room of a major, multinational corporation. Sitting around the table are a number of executives who are trying to troubleshoot, address the aftermath of a major system outage, and prevent such a catastrophe from recurring. The executive in charge is polling her direct reports, trying to determine what led to the calamity and to establish accountability so that appropriate disciplinary action can be taken. As she fires through her litany of questions, the shift of blame moves around the room. Ultimately, she hones in on the source and asks who was responsible. One timid member of her staff politely whispers to her that the direct responsibility for the problem rested with her. What an embarrassing realization for the manager—although humorous for the audience—to find out that she was responsible for something about which she had no knowledge.

In another, the media and Wall Street are grilling a CEO of a Fortune 500 firm regarding his company's future plans and strategy. The executive responds to inquiries about his company's technology infrastructure, a topic which, judging by his nervousness, he is ill prepared to address. Nevertheless, he makes several lofty promises that his staff, watching the televised interview in a nearby conference room, doubts can ever be realized. The interrogators take note of the promises made and indicate that they will hold the CEO accountable. When the interview is over, the CEO joins his staff in the conference room and asks one simple question: "What is infrastructure?"

Although these commercials are amusing, they represent some very serious issues and considerations that are relevant to you and your career. What can you do to save yourself from similar embarrassments and from becoming the subject of countless company jokes? Assume that there are no second chances; you have only one chance to get it right. Every job involves IT, so take action now to understand IT, how it affects your job, and what your control and responsibilities are so that you are not caught off guard, making uninformed decisions like the characters depicted in these commercials.

Unfortunately, according to the trade literature, it is generally suggested that the majority (about two-thirds) of all IT-related projects result in failure. They are late, over budget, or fail to deliver the functionality that was originally specified. This does not have to be the case and would not be the case if more people took the time to learn about and understand IT. Be sure to do your part to develop your IT skills and knowledge and contribute to your organization's IT success.

5. SUMMARY

Instructors are often asked what skills are required to succeed in the hospitality industry. There are five principal areas we always advise our students to consider, regardless of specific career focus. These include (1) developing business acumen and leadership skills, (2) establishing a strong foundation of technical skills (e.g., financial and statistics, communications, interpersonal, etc.), (3) becoming technologically savvy, (4) understanding the art of service management (the craft elements of the business), and (5) being socially and ethically responsible. The industry is highly complex and extremely competitive. Customers and investors are becoming increasingly more demanding. Keeping pace with the demands and making sound business decisions to respond accordingly require strategic thinking, strong analytical and financial skills, and a keen sense as to where the business is heading. Leadership, interpersonal, and communication skills are also essential since this is a people business. Remember, human resources are your most important strategic assets. The theory of this chapter focuses on the technology aspects and why you must master these to be a successful industry leader. Because the business is service-oriented, the customer must take center stage in all that you do and plan. In order to create unique, memorable experiences, you must also understand the dynamics of service management and how to blend high-tech with high-touch to provide the right information at the right time to the right people to create the right experience or service as required by the guest, given any circumstance. You are a solution provider. As such, it is up to you to make what is seemingly impossible possible—and with ease. In the end, leaders need to know how to use the many business tools (technology or otherwise) available to flawlessly execute their service mission in an ethical and socially responsible manner and with an eye towards profits and shareholder value—every time and with every guest. To do this, you need to be well rounded and understand as many aspects of the business as you can to know how to lead and direct. Your skills assessment and career planning are vital to your future and ensuring you are well prepared, so get started on these immediately.

Take to heart the words of two of history's greatest people: Thomas Edison and Franklin Delano Roosevelt (FDR). In the words of Thomas Edison, "If we all did the things we are capable of doing, we would literally astound ourselves." Engraved on one of the walls of FDR's memorial in Washington, D.C., is this quote from an undelivered Jefferson Day speech that he was to give within days of his death: "The only limit to our realization of tomorrow will be our doubts of today. Let us move forward with strong and active faith." These quotes are appropriate and offer many insights when thinking about and launching a career. Anything is possible if you set your mind to it.

As you go forward in your studies and your career, think of what is possible and what you are capable of doing. Channel your energies and creativity to make great things happen. IT's up to you!

Miniaturization, portability, and the convergence of powerful computers, intelligent software, and high-speed, global telecommunications networks and wireless communications are creating a new climate for conducting business throughout the world. IT is transforming virtually every aspect of the industry, from business models and value chains to customer service. Clearly, IT is not a panacea, but it is here to stay and will play an important role in both your professional career and personal life. You need to know what it can do for you and your company, recognize opportunities to apply it to gain advantages, understand how it is reshaping business processes, and know when there might be other non-IT alternatives that should be exercised instead. The new source of competitive advantage will be based on intellect rather than on assets and capital. Although the latter two resources are necessary, they are no longer sufficient in a dynamic, high-tech world where the customer is the boss (i.e., more demanding, more informed, and value conscious). To survive and thrive in the long run, the hospitality organization of the future will need to be a learning organization, one that must always reinvent itself to create value and provide the ultimate in individualized, personalized service. Knowledge will be the basis of competition in the future. The dichotomy between the "haves" and the "have nots" will be exacerbated by the bipolarization between those who know and those who know not (especially when it comes to IT) in what could be categorized as the great digital divide. In other words, it is not sufficient to have the latest in tools and technology. In order to prosper, you must know how to effectively use and deploy these tools and technologies and exploit their capabilities in such a way that competitors cannot easily duplicate.

Ultimately, the challenge will be to creatively implement new technologies to effectively and efficiently treat each consumer as an individual segment (i.e., providing a highly customized, unique experience) while simultaneously creating shareholder value. Information and communications technologies will drive these opportunities—but only if the *right* infrastructure is first established. What is right, of course, will be organization-dependent, but it is clear that the technology architecture in any organization must be flexible and capable of being upgraded to meet changing business needs and take advantage of newer technology innovations. To reach this state, a well-thought strategy must be developed; this can only be done if the events shaping the future are identified and understood. Hence, the need to focus on IT and the resulting convergence is not only timely but also essential to the industry's future. The timing is now to begin this planning effort if the industry is to proactively manage the changes that will inevitably occur and if you are to prosper in your career.

Without question, the information technology requirements of today's marketplace are raising the level of investment and level of knowledge required to compete successfully. In an information economy, everyone in the organization must think and act like a CIO—otherwise, no one is doing his/her job! IT presently ranks among the top three expenditures of most hospitality firms, is quickly becoming pervasive with its impacts spanning all aspects and levels of the firm, and is clearly becoming inescapable as it touches upon all aspects of your life, both personally and professionally. Its role has shifted from that of support or utility to that of strategic enablement. It is no longer a cost to be contained but rather a competitive lever to create strategic value. It is an investment in a firm's long-term prosperity and viability. Because of the scope, cost, reach, and strategic implications of most IT projects, it is unacceptable and inexcusable for any hospitality manager not to be involved and adequately prepared to handle such decisions. As someone entrusted with managing the firm's assets with the goal of maximizing shareholder value, it is your fiduciary (i.e., legal) responsibility to carry out your duties to the best of your abilities. You can only fulfill your obligations if you have prepared yourself properly, are well versed in what you manage, and continue to keep yourself current. In an information age, this requires knowledge of and competence in IT and continuous learning regardless of the type of career you seek. Are you ready? Go for IT—and remember it is up to you to make IT happen! Good luck to you as you explore the wonderful world of hospitality and embark on your career!

6. CASE STUDY AND LEARNING ACTIVITY

Career paths vary widely and often are discovered. Here is how Professor Daniel Connolly, assistant professor of information technology and electronic commerce at the University of Denver's Daniels College of Business, discovered his career calling. Although his career choices and interests may differ from yours, there are many relevant lessons that should benefit you in your journey. What follows is Professor Connolly reflecting on portions of his career—the decisions he made and how he came to pursue a career in hospitality IT.

Let me take a step back and share with you how and why I came to pursue a career in hospitality IT—not because I am the exemplar—but because I took a sort of serendipitous route and because many of the decisions I had to make along the way might be similar to those you presently or will soon face. Ironically, when I entered college, I wanted nothing to do with IT. My real goal was to own and operate my own family-style restaurant, much like the one I had worked in as a kid. It was this goal that led to my college selection and major. I took—or should I say struggled through—my first computer course in high school. It was a course in computer programming. Although the course was interesting and challenging, I found it to be extremely frustrating. For some reason, my programs never seemed to work properly after the first, second, or even third attempt. In most cases, I found it easier and faster to do the work myself rather than to program the computer to do the tasks for me. At the time, I could neither understand nor appreciate the power and potential of computers, but as a result of the experience, I did develop some great analytical skills.

Upon entering Cornell University's School of Hotel Administration, I once again found myself faced with having to take another computer course. Needless to say, my anxiety level was at an all-time high. However, this course became a defining moment for me, thanks in part to an instructor who inspired and challenged me to expand my thinking and comfort zone. It was during this course that I began to understand the benefits and potential time-saving applications of computers. I began to see the computer as a tool. As many of my classmates were struggling through their first computer programming experiences, I was building on what I had already learned. In fact, I was beginning to actually understand and appreciate what I had learned in my high school computer course. I was so intrigued that I was constantly looking for new ways to apply the computer in my everyday life. I would write short programs to help me carry out basic tasks more efficiently. What had previously seemed like tedious tasks became fun because I was experimenting and learning while doing my work. At the end of the term, I was convinced that computers would be an important part of the hospitality industry, and that for an aspiring manager, I would need to understand this phenomenon in order to become the industry great I had hoped to be. I then began to seek out additional courses to build my skills so that I would be well positioned for what is now known as the information age or information economy.

What really turned me on to computers and ultimately a career in hospitality IT is the pervasive nature of IT. During my years at Cornell, I was studying many subjects and developing proficiencies in key areas like accounting, finance, and operations to become a successful businessman. My problem at the time was deliberating over a question that everyone faces: "What career should I ultimately pursue?" At first, as I noted earlier, my interest lay in the restaurant industry. Over time, I had developed interests in hotels, sales and marketing, and accounting. Clearly, I could not do everything and would have to make some difficult choices.

As graduation neared, I was debating between careers in lodging, food and beverage, and accounting. With the help of a good faculty mentor and countless hours of advice from friends and family, the light started to become clearer. I realized that I did not necessarily have to give up any of my many interests. If I pursued a career in hospitality IT, I could simultaneously pursue, albeit in a different way, my interests in lodging, restaurants, accounting, and sales because IT was quickly becoming an important ingredient in each of these areas. Thus, what appeared to be a difficult choice became rather obvious.

Upon graduation, I joined the Marriott Corporation (now Marriott International) as a programmer/analyst at its corporate offices in Bethesda, Maryland—and I never looked back. Ever since then, I have found myself exposed to many different facets of the industry and always faced with a new set of interesting challenges to keep me learning and growing. My knowledge of and experience in IT have given me access to many aspects of the hospitality industry, including hotels, restaurants, institutional foodservice, healthcare, retirement communities, and, now, education—and my travels have taken me around the world exposing me to numerous cultures, technologies, and innovative applications of technology. I relish the challenges of understanding the business—identifying problems and opportunities, and then finding technology solutions. Clearly, there are great opportunities to be had for anyone interested in and willing to develop the skills and knowledge required to pursue a career in hospitality IT, but it is important to remember that IT is only a tool—an enabler—to make many things possible. To be successful, you must possess skills in three areas: business acumen, technology, and service (the craft elements of the business). A solid grasp of these three areas is requisite to becoming a strong leader and decision maker. IT is important, but by itself, it is of little value if it cannot be applied effectively in the appropriate industry contexts. To effectively apply IT, you must understand how to respond to changing business conditions, think in both strategic and financial terms, and focus on customer service and value creation.

I offer this story to help you appreciate some of the many doors IT can open for you, to get you to think about your own interests and the possibilities IT may play for you, and to focus your attention on important decisions with which you will be faced so that when the time comes, you can make informed choices that take into account your *best* and long-term interests. There are a few themes you should take away from this account regardless of the type of career you may be considering or the industry in which you seek to work. First, interests change with time, exposure to new subjects, and work experiences. Therefore, keep your mind open and be receptive to new possibilities, even if you do not readily see the fit and even if you think—or are certain as I was—that you already know what you want. Also, pursue multiple career tracks and opportunities simultaneously. That way, if market conditions change or if one possibility dries up, you will have other alternatives to pursue. Second, look for opportunities that will allow you to combine multiple interests and that will offer great flexibility long-term for you and your career. Third, just because you struggle with a subject does not mean you should give up and write it off. Be willing to give it another try and push yourself to achieve new levels. Finally, make career decisions with an eye towards the future. Look for opportunities that will offer growth and open new doors down the line. When I was in college looking to the future, I saw great potential for people well versed in IT. I also saw that it could open many doors and offer many opportunities to branch into new areas that I had not previously considered. I am so fortunate to have those who helped me along the way to recognize and begin pursuing my passion and now my vocation. As poet Robert Frost once wrote, combine your avocation and your vocation. If you do so, you will thrive and love every minute of your work.

Learning Activity

1. Give at least three examples of businesses within hospitality that rely heavily upon technology. For each example, discuss the role technology plays relative to how the business functions.
2. What are the key points you take away from Professor Connolly's story? How can you apply them to your own career?
3. Define and develop what you would consider to be the "ideal" career path for you. What steps will you need to take to achieve your goals?

7. KEY TERMS

Boundary spanners

Chief Information Officer (CIO)

Chief Technology Officer (CTO)

SWOT analysis

Value chain

Value creation

8. CHAPTER QUESTIONS

1. What does it mean to be a boundary spanner?
2. What are the different career options available within the hospitality industry for those wishing to explore a career involving IT? How do these options and the skills required vary across industry segments?
3. How would you advise someone interested in pursuing a career in (a) hospitality IT and (b) hospitality management? For each, what steps should he/she take to prepare? What schooling and coursework would you recommend? What types of work experience/jobs would you advise? What skills should be developed and why?
4. Scan industry job postings from a variety of online and offline sources for hospitality managerial positions, IT and non-IT alike. What positions are available? For each position, list and discuss the stated qualifications, skills, job duties, and IT expertise required to perform the job. Which positions are most appealing to you and why?
5. Define what the hospitality industry might be like in twenty years. How will business be conducted? What roles will technology play? What will be the hot issues keeping managers awake at night? How will you prepare for these?

CHAPTER TWO

Using Information Technology for Competitive Advantage

CHAPTER CONTENTS

INTERVIEW

Elizabeth Lauer Ivey is a senior information technology strategist for HVS International in its Boulder, Colorado office. She advises hospitality companies on the selection and application of IT. She is also a frequent contributor to *Hospitality Upgrade,* a leading hospitality IT trade journal.

Q: Liz, thank you so much for taking time to share your perspectives regarding IT strategy and the uses of IT for competitive advantage in the hospitality industry. What is your background?

A: My undergraduate studies are in hospitality and tourism management, and over the past ten years, I have worked in a variety of facets of the industry, including hotel and resort operations, technology services and support, and consulting. Before joining HVS International, I worked for The Broadmoor Hotel and Resort, Grand Heritage Hotels, MCI Systems Engineering, and Resort Computer Corporation. When I first joined HVS International, I conducted hotel feasibility studies and appraisals, but now, I am helping to lead our IT strategies practices as a senior technology strategist. Our mission is to understand the true impact of technology on the profitability and value of a hotel or hotel portfolio and to promote improvements in technology throughout the hospitality industry. These are necessary in order to help hoteliers make smarter and more informed decisions regarding the use of technology. In addition to my duties at HVS International, I write regular columns regarding IT practices, applications, and issues in the hospitality industry for *Hospitality Upgrade* magazine.

Q: How do you define *competitive advantage*? What are the necessary ingredients?

A: Competitive advantage in the hospitality industry is demonstrated through a property's (or chain's) ability to attain and maintain a strong bottom line, one with the capability of returning profits to investors and fueling sustainable expansion. Competitive advantage may result from increased room sales (e.g., efficient reservation systems), decreased costs of goods sold (e.g., less expensive distribution channels or lower operating overhead), a solid base of satisfied meeting business (e.g., efficient sales and marketing systems), strong brand awareness (e.g., effective advertising campaigns delivered through the most appropriate, cost-effective medium), brand loyalty (e.g., great service and guest recognition systems), lean expense ratios (e.g., strong cost control systems), lower employee turnover and costs associated with employee turnover (e.g., better human resources and training systems), the ability to attract and retain the best employees (e.g., by giving them a fulfilling and stimulating work environment with upward mobility), and strong decision support systems that allow timely (i.e., immediate) access to operating information for improved managerial decision making.

Q: How can competitive advantage be measured, especially when IT is involved?

A: In order for IT to create competitive advantage, it must be properly aligned with a company's overall business strategy. Too often IT is viewed as a cost center; yet, for almost every operational challenge, technology can present a possible solution. Technology that supports the components of competitive advantage discussed above can contribute to a firm's overall success. Some measures of competitive advantage include sales volume, REVPAR (revenue per available room), house profit, net income as a percentage of revenue, market penetration levels, salaries and wages as a percentage of revenues, growth in franchising fee income, share price, the ability to expand into new markets or market segments, the ability to quickly turn around or dispose of underperforming assets, and the ability to respond to adverse conditions (such as an economic downturn).

Q: Are hospitality firms using IT to create competitive advantage? If so, how? Who are the exemplars?

A: Regrettably, not enough hospitality firms are using IT to create competitive advantage. Some of the largest—and in the minds of many investors—most successful hospitality firms could be doing much more in using IT to improve profitability.

   Marriott always comes to mind when people think of an exemplary hotel company. Marriott has made significant investments in IT over the past two decades, specifically in the areas of central reservations technology and loyalty program administration. Its sheer size gives the company tremendous purchasing power and the ability to drive development initiatives from the vendor community. Its technology applications help to win management contracts and sign up new franchisees because of their capabilities and sophistication.

Q: What are the barriers to creating competitive advantage through IT?

A: Capital constraints represent one of the greatest barriers for technology investment. Despite relatively healthy bottom lines (when compared to other industries such as pharmaceuticals and airlines), hotels are real estate assets; and the business of hospitality is returning profits to the real estate owners. Typically, real estate people are not concerned with the operations of a property so long as it yields a healthy net income. IT investments are treated as costly and risky because it is difficult to estimate and measure the true value derived from IT. Therefore, hotel operators are wary of such expenditures and would rather use their financial resources for other uses.

The hospitality software marketplace represents another barrier. Traditional hospitality technology providers have held the industry hostage and inhibited innovation through the use of proprietary technology, closed architectures, obsolete programming languages and platforms, and their unwillingness to customize applications for special needs or niche properties.

Q: Is there such a thing as *sustainable competitive advantage?* What can firms do to protect their competitive advantages?

A: It is difficult, if not impossible, to achieve lasting or sustainable competitive advantage, especially with IT. The only way to do so is through constant innovation and investment in IT. Once a hotel property or hotel company begins to operate more efficiently, there are economies of scale that can be compounded over time, so long as the company continues to reinvest a portion of profits (perhaps those derived from the previous technology improvements) back into the operation. Because technology continues to evolve, no IT investment will keep a company on top indefinitely. However, the hotel or hotel company that adopts a progressive view of technology investment, makes sound technology decisions, measures results, and can demonstrate the value of previous IT investments will be able to fund future developments, making it more likely to sustain competitive advantage.

Q: What is the best way to predict the amount of competitive advantage an IT application can provide? How can the business case be made to sell an IT initiative to management?

A: Companies that get the most out of their IT investments generally follow five basic steps: analyzing market opportunities, defining and assessing strategy, allocating resources, managing investment decisions and IT projects, and measuring and communicating results. The steps are simple and logical, but all too often, IT and business executives skip one or more steps and, therefore, fail to realize value from IT implementations.

The process of capturing value begins with identifying and understanding the dynamic market forces that represent opportunities for a company to increase (or maintain) its value by reducing costs, increasing revenue, or improving capital management.

In the second step, executives devise strategies to focus the organization so it can capitalize on those market opportunities. The third step involves allocating resources (financial and people), weighing and choosing among various initiatives (such as implementing a centralized accounting system, delving into electronic commerce, or outsourcing distribution to execute the chosen strategies). Assuming value is defined in terms of business performance, investments can then be tracked—and managed—over time to ensure that the expected value is truly realized.

The fourth step, managing investments and IT projects, encompasses the hard work of actually developing and implementing the project. This stage includes designing and building systems, evaluating and selecting off-the-shelf technology, streamlining processes, training end users, and system deployment. Step four is especially critical because no value can be accrued until all of these things happen.

The fifth and final step involves measuring value derived from IT projects and communicating this value to employees, management, and shareholders.

Q: What advice would you share with those pursuing careers in hospitality IT?

A: While it is hard to perform your day-to-day duties, maintain your current systems, and plan for the future of your operation or organization, with respect to technology, you have to learn to juggle multiple responsibilities and to make IT a priority if you want to profit from its potential. Focus on the future and be proactive. If you can't do these things yourself, seek outside guidance to help you in formulating a strategic technology plan that supports the overall business objectives and responds to changing market conditions.

1. INTRODUCTION

If you are new to technology, return to this chapter after completing the rest of the text. Information technology (IT) is an important resource for any firm. Within the hospitality industry, IT represents one of the largest areas of capital expenditure. To some, it is viewed as a rather large expense, but to others, IT represents a strategic opportunity. Hospitality executives must continually look towards the strategic opportunities technology offers and use it as a *competitive method*—a tool, if you will—to differentiate and create competitive advantage.

Competitive advantage must be created, and its creation must involve multiple aspects of the firm coming together. In this chapter, you will explore the use of IT for creating—or at least contributing to—competitive advantage in a hospitality firm. If you look at history across the general business landscape, you can find many great companies that have creatively and strategically deployed IT to create competitive advantage. Some of them include American Airlines and its SABRE reservation system, FedEx and its PowerShip shipping and package tracking software, Wal★Mart and its supply chain management technology, Hertz and its system for driving directions, and Dell Computer's self-ordering system for customized personal computers.

Your challenge as a hospitality manager is to find opportunities like these great companies where IT can be used to creatively solve business problems and create new business prospects. Ultimately, you want to use technology to lower your cost structure, increase revenues and market share, create unique value propositions for guests, and create unprecedented returns for investors or shareholders. Creating competitive advantage requires creative, out-of-the-box thinking. It requires doing things that no one else has attempted or doing things better, cheaper, or faster than anyone else. It requires dedication, determination, focus, and a consistent allocation of resources. It even requires taking risks, and possibly stumbling from time to time. If creating competitive advantage were so easy, then every manager would have already thought of all the great ideas possible, and every company would have implemented them by now. Creating competitive advantage requires you to see things that others cannot or do not see and then act on these opportunities to make them happen, but it does not stop there. Once the competitive advantage has been created, the challenge shifts to sustaining that competitive advantage or destroying it and either reinventing it or replacing it with something else before anyone else has time to copy it and catch up to your lead.

2. TECHNOLOGY TAKES CENTER STAGE

One of the most significant developments related to technology over the past decade (and for the foreseeable future) is the concept of *convergence*, the coming together of numerous technologies to make great things happen. At the core of this convergence, as shown in Figure 2-1, are information technology (i.e., computer hardware, software, databases, etc.), telecommunications and telephony (i.e., voice, data, cable, and wireless networks; telephones, facsimile, and telephone answering devices), interactive, multimedia content (i.e., text, voice, graphics, digital photos, sound, and video), and broadcast media (i.e., radio and television).

This digital convergence, supported by miniaturization, portability, declining costs, push technology, and more powerful applications, is part of a trend driving computers to ubiquity in everyday life—so much so that they are deemed essential or required for survival in today's world. As such, technology

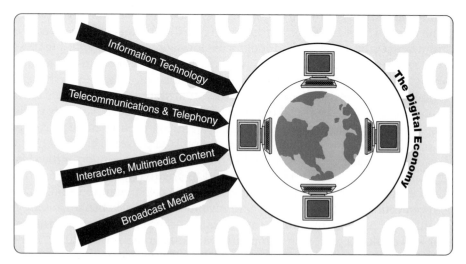

Figure 2-1. The Great Convergence Gives Rise to the Digital Economy Today businesses and consumers are finding that the lines are blurring. What were once separate entities now have many similarities and relationships within the larger digital economy.

is reshaping everything you do—including how you work, play, and learn. IT is redefining communications between employees, guests, and suppliers; changing the nature of business transactions; and increasing the technology needs and amenity expectations of guests. You must, therefore, learn to embrace technology and use it creatively to win over customers and provide employees with the appropriate tools to perform their job responsibilities. You must constantly stay abreast of the developments taking place in and outside of the market space and remain alert to signals of change and opportunity. Lack of vigilance, however brief, could allow a competitor or outsider to move in, capitalize on new opportunities, and leave you in a trail of dust.

As a result of digital convergence, the competitive landscape is drastically and constantly in a state of flux. Speed, agility, connectivity, and the ability to amass and subsequently employ knowledge are key competitive ingredients to long-term survivability, but you must seek not merely to survive but to thrive under these conditions. This calls into question the competitive nature of business, the skills required to succeed, and what this will mean to managers serving as stewards of their companies, working to guide them to prosperity and vitality. Needless to say, the effects of digital convergence are both impressive and exciting—offering new opportunities and capabilities limited only by your imagination. It is how you tap into this digital convergence that will set you apart from others and allow you to create competitive advantage.

As Porter (1985), Quinn (1988), Burrus (1993), D'Aveni (1994), and others have astutely observed, IT undermines traditional forms of competition, strategic management, organizational structure, governance, and economic policy making. The resulting environment is one of hypercompetition, where shorter transaction times, nontraditional competitors, volatility, surprise, and new alliances are the norm. For the hospitality industry, the implications are also profound: higher capital costs, more sophisticated and discriminating customers, knowledge gaps, labor shortages, more demanding investors, new competitors, and new operating paradigms. Therefore, in the new business climate, continuous change, lifelong learning, and innovation will become standard components of everyone's job responsibilities.

Bounded by Tradition

Conventional thinking suggests that services are less technologically advanced than their manufacturing counterparts. Within the hotel industry, the traditional paradigm of IT as a support mechanism has prevailed. This thinking has influenced IT spending, investment, and usage throughout the industry, placing the primary emphasis, more often than not, on tactical systems with calculable returns on investment. Until recently, seldom did strategic vision or a *preemptive* (i.e., proactive) *strategy* drive investment decisions in IT. In a study of three prominent, multinational hospitality companies, it was found that cost-benefit criteria consistently outweighed strategic preemptiveness when considering IT investment decisions. In essence, IT expenditures are typically viewed as discretionary spending and are, therefore, subjected to intense scrutiny. Moreover, pressures from Wall Street and the investment community to focus on earnings result in a short-term orientation at the expense of long-term benefits and positioning. Encumbering the implementation of information technology are management's lack of understanding of technology (i.e., its applications and capabilities) and the uncertainty surrounding the effectiveness of an organization's investment in information technology.

It seems that there are six prevailing philosophies regarding IT investment within the hospitality industry. All projects have tended to fall into one of the following six categories: (1) projects that are essential to survival; (2) projects requiring an act of faith (or gut feeling) that an investment will prove beneficial to the firm over the long term; (3) projects with an intuitive appeal and seemingly obvious outcomes; (4) projects that are required or mandated (either by law, by regulation, or by top management); (5) projects in response to moves by competitors to achieve parity or protect market share; and (6) projects that undergo intense scrutiny and analysis due to the high degrees of risk and uncertainty—either perceived or actual. Notice that none of these categories addresses innovation or the strategic capabilities of technology. These categories are a testament to the reactionary tendencies that characterize and plague the hospitality industry.

This thinking has often hindered the deployment and effectiveness of IT within the industry, especially with respect to the use of IT for competitive advantage. Shying away from preemptive strategies is further reinforced by the continuing trend toward decreasing costs for IT equipment, which encourages managers to wait or defer technology-related decisions until the technology becomes more affordable. IT capabilities have also been hampered by the lack of industry-specific applications and proven solutions. Since many applications were adapted from other industries (e.g., airlines), they are considered inadequate or clumsy because of their poor fit and their inability to address hotel-specific needs.

Enlightenment

Fortunately, the sentiment towards the application of IT is changing, although this has been a long time in coming. The foremost forces driving technology applications in the hospitality industry are the need to enhance the quality of service related to the guest stay and the desire to improve operating efficiency. The potential and value of IT for driving competitive positioning was recognized in 1985. Technological change was among the most prominent forces driving competition. It took more than a decade for this same realization to become apparent in the hospitality industry. As Palmer (1988, 26) writes:

> Pricing strategies will always be a major determining factor, but below the surface the battles in the travel business are being fought with a more subtle weapon, information technology.

Evidence suggests that the focus is beginning to shift toward more strategic applications as IT spending throughout the industry rises. Investing in technology simply to manage a hotel is no longer sufficient. Hospitality is now at a point where information becomes the catalyst for competitive advantage, not just physical assets. Hoteliers must look to deploy technology that will help them learn faster and know more than anyone else about their business, customers, and competition, and, then, use this information to compete more effectively and more aggressively than any other company out there, to create customized and personalized services and experiences that no one else can duplicate.

In an information economy, knowledge about and access to customers are critical success factors. However, these critical success factors can only be realized through IT and competent, knowledgeable workers. IT can assist with data collection, storage, and analysis, but it is up to employees to interpret the data, convert it to usable information, and then put it to work in a way that will create uniqueness. Only recently has the industry begun to proactively apply IT in the area of guest services, a necessity that has resulted from increased competition, consumer demands, and shareholders' focus on *asset optimization* (i.e., getting the most value from firm resources or assets as measured by return on assets). Traditionally, hotel executives resisted the use of IT for fear of alienating their guests. However, this trend is reversing as a result of the many technological advancements that have occurred during the past decade. The debate between high-tech and high-touch should be dead. These can and must coexist. In today's sophisticated marketplace, it is nearly impossible to achieve high-touch without high-tech. As Hansen and Owen (1995, 1) note:

> The debate over high-tech or "high-touch" is largely a thing of the past in the hospitality industry as emerging technologies drive unprecedented change in the way hotels operate and serve customers. It is clear that investments in technologies can generate greatly improved operating efficiencies, higher hotel revenues, and enhanced guest services.

Today, IT is an important resource vital to a firm's success. No longer can it be viewed simply for its support and utility roles dominant in tactical applications, which focus on the use of IT to gain efficiencies, reduce costs, decrease labor, and improve productivity. Instead, IT is increasingly playing a strategic role in organizations, where it either creates competitive advantage or enables new business opportunities. Attention is now being given to IT's ability to differentiate products and services, to create new product and service offerings, and to build and sustain core competencies—all of which lead to the creation of competitive advantage. Thus, when it comes to IT, management focus should be on value creation rather than on cost containment.

The transformation of this management thinking related to IT is summarized in Figure 2-2 that follows. Please note, however, that this shift in thinking does not diminish the importance of reducing or containing costs.

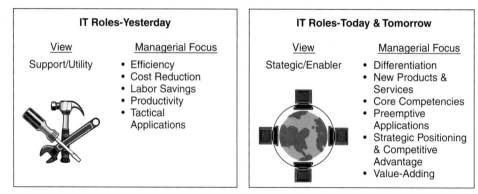

Figure 2-2. Shifting IT Roles in Organizations Information technology's role was once primarily of a supportive nature. Today, however, IT is more future oriented.

This is important, but costs can only be cut so far. Thus, to grow the business, one must look externally and strategically to create new opportunities. This mindset shift represents a transition from investing in technology as a means of surviving or maintaining competitive parity to one of thriving or creating competitive advantage. The focus must now be proactive rather than reactive, strategic versus support-oriented. Consequently, the basis of competition will shift from an asset base to an intellectual base. Increasingly, competitive advantage derived from IT will occur only when IT improves an organization's primary business functions, creates value-adding experiences that enhance customer service, and focuses on changing demand patterns to increase purchases.

Under this new paradigm, hospitality executives are positively changing their attitudes towards IT. Instead of being reactive to environmental changes and competitive thrusts, executives are now looking to IT to create competitive advantage and achieve strategic positioning through preemptive strikes. To properly prepare requires investing heavily to create a capable and secure IT infrastructure and to master the steep learning curve typically associated with IT.

Without question, IT can be value-adding. However, to realize this value, the IT function must be well-aligned with the firm's overall strategic initiatives and those of each of the core disciplines, namely sales and marketing, accounting and finance, human resources, management, and operations. IT and the strategy of the firm must be intertwined and evolve in definition together, not separately, as is often the case today. The best results from IT are usually derived when IT is viewed as an integral part of the business and the project in which it is involved. In these cases, the focus is on the business (usually the customer), not the technology itself. Technology is not the endgame, but rather, a tool or enabler to help arrive at the end goal. The fundamental question to be asked is how can IT help? Because there is a significant lead time associated with IT development and implementation, a firm must continuously focus on IT (and its capabilities and limitations) at the very inception of any business opportunity or problem assessment if it is to contribute positively to the value of the firm. The earlier IT can be brought in on a project, the greater the likelihood the organization will achieve success from IT. You must also remember that it is not the technology itself that provides the competitive advantage in a firm, but rather, how that technology is used, what it enables in the firm, and what that technology can deliver in the future that makes a competitive difference.

3. THE CONCEPT OF CO-ALIGNMENT

To understand the essence of strategy and the concept of competitive advantage, it is important to study the *co-alignment principle*, which is the theoretical underpinning of these subjects. Firms are often viewed as living organisms that must adapt to their environments to survive and thrive. This theory builds on Darwin's survival of the fittest theory. In order to survive, a person must be fit. To be fit, a person must understand the environment in which he/she operates and the forces driving change in that environment. Thus, the essence of strategy focuses on the environment in which a firm competes and the firm's (or its managers') understanding of that environment, any changes taking place, and what needs to be done to stay fit. Strategy takes a future orientation and looks to developing a game plan and competitive posture to successfully compete and build competitive advantage. In the words of Hamel and Prahalad (1994, 64):

> The vital first step in competing for the future is the quest for industry foresight. This is the race to gain an understanding deeper than competitors, of the trends and discontinuities—technological, demographic, regulatory, or lifestyle—that can be used to transform industry boundaries and create new competitive space.
> Industry foresight gives a company the potential to get to the future first and stake out a leadership position. It informs corporate direction and lets a company control the evolution of its industry and, thereby, its own destiny. The trick is to see the future before it arrives.

Many of today's failures are a direct result of an organization's inability to forecast the future. Strategists believe it is impossible for any company to succeed without a clear view of the opportunities and challenges lurking on the horizon that will shape the future. For these reasons, the co-alignment principle takes on such importance in a firm's quest for competitive advantage.

The co-alignment principle, depicted in Figure 2-3, simply states that in order for a firm to be successful, it must be well aligned, both internally and externally, with the forces driving change in its business environment. After

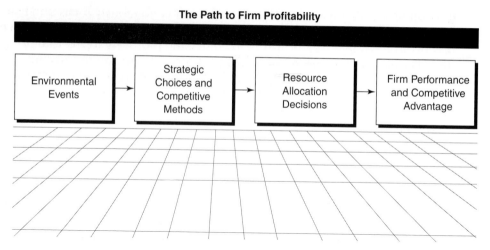

Figure 2-3. Through proper analysis and a logical approach to the steps that are undertaken, positive performance can result.

identifying opportunities and threats in the external environment, a firm can then plan, formulate, and execute strategies so as to exploit these environmental opportunities and minimize any potential or actual threats. These strategies and strategic choices should focus on the development and investment in a portfolio of products and services, competitive methods, resources, and core competencies that will competitively position the firm within the environment, while accounting for these forces driving change. This investment requires *consistent* allocation of resources to these initiatives over extended periods of time. If done well, the firm should achieve greater profitability and generate competitive advantage in its industry. In other words, if a firm can effectively identify opportunities and threats, develop the appropriate competitive methods (ways to compete), and apply firm resources (which include people, capital, facilities, and IT), financial performance will improve and competitive advantage will result. Since technological change plays such an influential role in competition, being able to forecast technological developments, select those most appropriate for a firm, and implement them in such a way that cannot be easily imitated by competitors become important skills and critical success factors for all firms.

There are multiple measures of performance that can be considered when determining the health of a company, its competitiveness, and its overall success in applying the co-alignment principle. One suggestion is that the best measure is *cash flow per share*, a measure of firm profitability. Some authors' arguments supporting this metric state that while seeking a balance between long-term and short-term earnings requirements, cash flow per share can (1) reflect the cash flows generated by investments in a complex and dynamic environment; (2) illustrate management's effectiveness with environmental scanning, choice of competitive methods, and resource allocations, and, therefore, its overall ability to compete; and (3) demonstrate how a business utilizes its assets to add value to the firm. Others also favor the use of cash flow over other accounting measures of profitability derived from the income statement because accounting practices sometimes mask cash flows with noncash expenses (e.g., depreciation, amortization, and write-offs) to create gains or losses reported on a firm's income statement. While all of these authors favor the use of cash flow over other profitability measures, they do concede, however, that not all cash flows translate directly into earnings per share.

The most popular thinking and prolific theories regarding the strategic use and value of IT come from the Harvard Business School, which is dominated by the works of Michael Porter. Porter's works are frequently cited in the IT literature as the theoretical underpinnings for studying IT and its use to create competitive advantage. Applying this school of thought, the frameworks used to measure the strategic significance of IT and identify opportunities to apply IT are value chain analysis, Porter's industry and competitive analysis (ICA) framework or *Five Forces model* (which addresses barriers to market entry, intra-industry rivalries, buyer power, supplier power, and substitute products), and Porter's *generic strategies* (i.e., low-cost producer, product differentiation, or market niche focus).

Technology strategy refers to a firm's plans, intentions, and policies regarding current and future use of IT, information, and "softer" IT-related issues such as integration with the firm and its employees. Porter (1985) suggests that technology strategy must include choices regarding the technologies in which a firm should invest, the firm's position with respect to the technologies selected (e.g., leader or follower), and decisions regarding when and how to acquire or license the technologies. A firm's IT strategy guides decisions related to its technological architecture, infrastructure, applications, and services in accordance with that firm's business strategy and objectives. Yet in today's context of rapid change and in a marketplace that is inundated with new technology products and offerings (hardware, software, and services), hospitality leaders find it difficult and even daunting to effectively evaluate these technological advancements and assimilate them into their organizations' strategies. As a result, they typically maintain short planning horizons. Although it is clear they must be judicious as to their investments and select only those that will provide value to the firm, selecting and implementing those technologies are often difficult and risky tasks, since not all of the benefits will be tangible. Porter (1985) recommends concentrating on those technologies that will lead to the greatest sustainable impact on cost or product/service differentiation, and, subsequently bestow the greatest competitive advantage. Thus, when choosing among technologies in which to invest, hotel executives must base their decisions on a thorough understanding of each technological choice and its impact to the firm's value chain.

4. ACHIEVING COMPETITIVE ADVANTAGE

Competitive advantage sounds really impressive, but what does it mean? Understanding this concept is vital to the success of future hospitality leaders, especially given the competitive nature of the hospitality industry, the high stakes of competition, and the growing trend towards commoditization of the industry—where products blur and become indistinguishable from and, therefore, interchangeable with, one another. In simplistic terms, competitive advantage is derived from one or more unique capabilities of the firm and brings value to the firm. It is these capabilities that set one firm apart from others within the industry and within its competitive set. These single out the firm for some reason, making it *different* from others competing in the same space. Typically, this differentiation comes from the firm's resources and capabilities, is established as part of the firm's strategy, and is reinforced by the firm's culture and mission statement. Competitive advantage results from doing things faster, better, or cheaper than anyone else. It can be measured in many ways, for example, in terms of product or service quality, market share, brand recognition, customer loyalty, employee loyalty, profitability, and cost structure.

Traditional sources of competitive advantage come from gaining leadership positions in one or more of four arenas: price and quality, timing and know-how, stronghold creation/invasion, and deep pockets. To properly put things in perspective, consider that everyone (employees, customers, investors, or franchisees) has a choice in today's competitive marketplace. Oftentimes, this choice can be made between multiple competing, yet similar, offerings. With more information so readily available, these people can do their homework and make more informed choices. They can be picky and extremely demanding. Are you positioned well to win their attention and to get them to select your company's offerings? What makes your firm a better choice over other options in the marketplace? What is the deciding factor, the thing that really makes the difference? This is what competitive advantage is all about.

IT provides competitive advantage if it helps a firm reduce its cost structure, generate profits, or differentiate its products and services. Competitive advantage results when a firm gains an advantage (typically in the form of economic rents, increased market share, or information asymmetries) over its competitors by exploiting its strengths relative to those of its competitors. In this context, competitive advantage from IT results when the technology itself helps a firm in achieving economies of scale, reducing costs, differentiating its products/services, creating barriers to entry, building switching costs (binding the consumer), changing the basis of competition, adding customer value, altering the balance of power with suppliers, providing first-mover effects, or generating new products.

Based on Porter's (1985) teachings, a series of questions can be raised (see Figure 2-4) to help evaluate the strategic potential and ultimate competitive advantage that can be derived from a technology-based initiative. These questions should be raised often when defining strategy and setting priorities involving IT.

- Can IT create entry barriers to keep out potential new competitors? If so, how?
- Can IT create switching costs to lock in customers and make it difficult or undesirable for them to seek out other alternatives?
- Can IT help the firm understand its customers better, use this information to provide unique experiences and customer service, and build lasting relationships that lead to loyalty?
- Can IT be used to lower the firm's cost structure, streamline operations, or to create economies of scale?
- Can IT be used to create new business opportunities and revenue streams?
- Can IT be used to differentiate the firm's products and service offerings? If so, how?
- Can IT be used to improve product or service quality or ensure consistency?
- Can IT be used to build better alliances or strategic partnerships to help the firm gain access to new markets or access to resources and skills it does not presently have?
- Can IT be used to provide an edge in dealing with suppliers or enable better negotiating leverage?
- Can IT change the nature of competition and the dynamics within the industry, shifting them in the firm's favor?
- Can IT help the firm sustain its competitive advantage in the marketplace?
- Can IT better equip employees to be more productive and capable, perhaps by providing information to them or providing faster access to information to help them do a better job and outperform the competition?
- Is IT aligned with the strategic objectives of the firm?
- How can IT be better used to help the firm achieve it strategies?

Figure 2-4   Key Questions to Ask of All IT Projects

Resource-Based View of the Firm

The assessment of competitive advantage is an important step in the IT investment decision-making process, and internal efficiency can be a significant source of competitive advantage. Two prevailing approaches to assessing competitive advantage are the following:

1. *Outcome Approach.* Places great emphasis on competitive efficiency, business value, and management productivity and uses such measures as revenue growth rate, return on investment, return on assets, profits, and net worth. This approach takes a macro-level perspective by focusing on aggregate measures that address performance of the firm.
2. *Trait Approach.* Identifies substantive attributes of an IT application known to contribute to competitive advantage. These are reflected in concepts like competitive forces, strategic thrusts, value activities, and the customer resource life cycle. This approach takes on a more micro-level view since the focus is an individual IT application and the role it plays in enhancing the firm's competitive advantage.

To assess competitive advantage derived from a single IT application, Sethi and King (1994) define a construct they call Competitive Advantage Provided by an Information Technology Application (CAPITA). *CAPITA* is defined by five dimensions: efficiency (the extent to which an IT application allows a firm to produce products/services at prices lower than its competitors), functionality (the extent to which an IT application provides the functions and capabilities required by users), threat (the impact of an IT application on the balance of power between suppliers and buyers), preemptiveness (early adoption of an IT application to usurp the market), and synergy (the degree of integration between an IT application and the firm's goals, strategies, and environment).

Because of the commoditylike nature of IT, Cho (1996) presents an alternative view of competitive advantage grounded in theory pertaining to the resource-based view of the firm as studied by Clemons and Row (1991) and Mata, Fuerst, and Barney (1995). Using this framework, a company achieves competitive advantage through the culmination and convergence of a series of events, resources, experiences, and underlying management processes. Alternatively stated, competitive advantage is the result not only of how a firm competes (or plays the game) but also of the assets it has with which to play or compete. The competitive advantage is derived collectively from a variety of firm assets that make up its resources and capabilities. These include its people (and their skills and expertise), financial assets, IT portfolio and infrastructure, corporate culture, portfolio of products and services, competitive methods, strategic alliances, etc. There is no one contributing factor but a series of ingredients or idiosyncratic resources that, when combined, provide a competitive edge in the marketplace. This hidden or *tacit* competitive edge has been termed the "X Factor." For many organizations, the integration of software applications and information technology with the organizational structure and its staff provides the source of competitive advantage. Because of its tacit nature, the competitive advantage and its contributing factors are difficult to identify and, therefore, hard to duplicate. The resulting competitive advantage can then be sustained for as long as it remains inimitable and not obsolete, a period that is becoming shorter all the time in today's hypercompetitive marketplace.

Finding sources of competitive advantage that are unique and inimitable is important, especially in the service industry where barriers to entry tend to be relatively low and where service concepts can be easily copied. One of the reasons so many Internet firms have failed is that they underestimated the ease with which their concepts could be copied. Thus, their concepts become undifferentiated and indistinguishable among their competitors. Customers spent the time shopping for the best price, causing everyone's profitability to fall. Therefore, barriers should be erected whenever possible, and sources of competitive advantage should be embedded in the organization and comprised of the firm's idiosyncratic resources. This will create tacit competitive advantage. Lastly, firms should protect their competitive advantage and discourage employees from talking with outsiders regarding the sources of competitive advantage. Doing these things will make it harder for others to copy and allow firms to prolong their advantages.

Examples of Competitive Advantage Derived from IT

Throughout the hospitality industry, there are many examples where firms are creatively using IT to create competitive advantage. What follows are some examples seen across the hotel industry in the context of global distribution systems (GDSs) (chapter 8) but whose reach goes beyond to include service delivery and customer relationship management. Although described in the context of GDS, the examples of competitive advantage derived through economies of scale, functionality, accuracy of information, and proprietary technology are readily transferable to other technology applications and areas of the hospitality industry.

Economies of scale have been among the most significant sources of competitive advantage derived from global distribution systems. Building global distribution systems is a costly, time-consuming, and difficult venture. It requires great expertise, both technical and operational. Not all companies have the resources, expertise, and wherewithal to develop a global distribution system. Traditionally, the costs have exceeded the reach of many organizations. In chains and affiliate organizations that provide reservation systems technology and services to their member hotels, the incremental cost to add new hotels is disproportional to the core investment. As such, the initial investment and fixed costs can be allocated over a wider base, thereby providing greater economic efficiencies. This efficiency appeals to franchisees that seek access to global distribution channels but lack the capital and expertise to develop their own. Efficiencies and economies of scale lead to lower deployment costs, operating costs, and transaction fees. Hence, a GDS is a primary selection criterion for companies interested in affiliating with a franchiser or a management firm. As the franchise network and number of hotels under a single umbrella grow, so do market penetration and market share. Size then becomes an important factor that can be leveraged to gain additional economies and clout with external entities.

Another source of competitive advantage comes from the functionality of the GDS, its links to external systems, and its flexibility to adapt to an ever-changing business environment. For the hospitality industry in particular, this means having the ability to control inventory and rates (including booking rules, restrictions, and selling strategies), distributing this information seamlessly and in real time to a multitude of access points (e.g., travel agents, airline GDSs, reservation call centers, sister properties or products, other member hotels, etc.), and generating instant confirmations continues to separate the capabilities of competing hotels. Access and links to external systems extend the reach of the hotel global distribution system, thereby attracting a broader audience from all over the world.

Functional advantages also include ease of use and the GDSs' role in supporting the selling process (i.e., the conversion of inquiries to bookings at the best possible rates). These advantages are typically measured in terms of the number of room-nights or revenue generated by the GDS, occupancy, REVPAR (revenue per available room), and REVPOR (revenue per occupied room). For an example of a temporary competitive advantage resulting from GDS functionality, you can turn to Marriott. In the early part of this decade when the industry was in recession, Marriott turned to deep discounting as a means to increase occupancy. Borrowing pricing strategies from the airline industry, Marriott created a twenty-one-day advance purchase promotion. In order to receive these low rates, a guest was required to meet certain conditions and comply with certain rules or restrictions (also called "fences"). In order to enforce these fences, Marriott's reservation system (MARSHA) needed to contain sophisticated functionality to manage room inventory and monitor customer purchase patterns. Since many competing chains lacked similar functionality at the time, they had difficulty in copying Marriott's promotion. Thus, Marriott enjoyed a competitive advantage until such time that other chains could modify their reservations systems to accommodate the same type of practice.

The final consideration with respect to functionality is flexibility. GDSs must be able to effectively adapt to changing market needs at a moment's notice. Cycle times are too short to tolerate long lead times. Because of the systemic nature of a GDS environment, a change in one area (which could be either functional or technical) will most likely constitute a domino affect. For example, some luxury hotels are contemplating the elimination of defined check-in and check-out times in favor of greater flexibility to offer greater convenience to their guests. This enables them to accommodate guests with atypical schedules and early morning arrivals stemming from an increase in overnight travel. These hotels are experimenting with a twenty-four-hour rental, with no extra fees for an early registration or a late departure. This will undoubtedly require major enhancements to the central reservation system, the yield management system, and the property management system as well as to the interfaces between these systems and each of the distribution channels. If implemented on a wider scale, these systems will require modification to account for the redefinition of the concept of time or room rental period and to allow for advanced room blocking so as to ensure room availability (of the room type requested) upon a guest's arrival. Because offering an early morning check-in may preclude a hotel from selling a room the night before, the appropriate checks and balances will need to be developed and incorporated into each of the major systems comprising the hotel's GDS. This will necessitate greater inventory management capability and more sophisticated yield algorithms to ensure that not only the guest's needs and preferences are met but also that the hotel can optimize its revenue potential. This example is just one of many that could be used to illustrate the need for flexibility in design and programmability of the information systems and interfaces comprising the

GDS network. In a hypercompetitive environment, changes like these will become more common and more frequent. As in the Marriott example previously cited, companies that can capitalize on these functional advantages can gain competitive advantage so long as other firms cannot easily copy or acquire the functionality.

A third source of competitive advantage is less tangible. It relates to the accuracy of the information (i.e., content) and the hotel's ability to track the guest. From a guest's perspective, a hotel's ability to meet his/her expectations and provide the correct room type, features, amenities, and services requested at the time of reservation distinguishes it from its competitors. Regardless of what channels are used to book a reservation, each guest should find convenience, hassle-free service, and reliable information. The distribution channel should convey a sense of confidence to the guest that the information being shared is indeed accurate and current and that all of his/her requests for services (i.e., location, room type, features, amenities, etc.) will be honored upon arrival. This confidence and convenience, in turn, builds guest loyalty. From the hotel's perspective, tracking the guest plays an important role in guest recognition and delivering customized services. Since each guest interaction represents an opportunity to learn more about a guest, data collection, storage, and retrieval are critical to building strong relationships, creating unique and personalized experiences, and developing customer switching costs. Being able to mine the reservations database will be a new source of value and advantage.

Another form of competitive advantage comes as the result of proprietary technologies or patents, which create barriers to entry or duplicate capabilities. Patents are common throughout the software industry, although they present challenges since they represent intellectual capital. Their presence in hotel global distribution systems is less common. Hyatt Hotels and Radisson Hotels are two companies that currently enjoy patents for functional features contained in their global distribution systems. Hyatt (U.S. Patent 5,404,291) patented an inventory control process and revenue maximization routine used by its SPIRIT CRS. Radisson's patent (U.S. Patent 5,483,444) protects the company's innovative "Look to Book" program and "World of Winners" sweepstakes program, which provide incentives to travel agents and others who provide electronic bookings at Radisson hotels. Under the "Look to Book" program, agents are awarded points or credits, which can later be redeemed for prizes, for each reservation booked. The "World of Winners" sweepstakes program randomly provides prizes or rewards to booking agents. The technology implemented by Radisson administers this program over a diverse network, where multiple computer systems and travel agencies are involved.

Although these sources of competitive advantage continue to remain viable, they are not sufficient in today's hypercompetitive world, especially since hotel products are becoming more commoditylike. In the future, as the concept of branding erodes, hotels will need to find new sources of competitive advantage.

5. SUSTAINABILITY?

There is great debate as to whether or not competitive advantage—from IT or some other source—can be sustained. In other words, how long can a firm enjoy competitive advantage? What is its life expectancy? Although there are no easy answers to these questions and even though the answers would be context-dependent, there is general consensus among management gurus and industry leaders that competitive advantage is not, by itself, sustainable for long periods of time. Some forms of competitive advantage (e.g., ones that involve patents or steep learning curves) can provide periods of sustainability. However, in all cases, competitive advantage can be lost or become obsolete with time. This is especially true with IT since it becomes obsolete so quickly. Moreover as it becomes more affordable, more standardized, and more easily copied, what once only the big chains could afford is now accessible by small chains and independents, albeit at slightly higher costs.

It is possible that, in some cases, competitive advantage can be sustained over periods of time, particularly if it is not easily copied, if it alters industry structure, or if it has some protective parameters such as a noncompete contract or a patent. Porter (1985) suggests four tests of desirable technological change that can lead to periods of sustainable competitive advantage:

1. The technological change lowers costs or enhances differentiation and provides a sustainable (i.e., inimitable) technological advantage.
2. The technological change shifts cost or uniqueness drivers in favor of a firm.
3. Pioneering the technological change translates into first-mover advantages besides those inherent in the technology itself.
4. The technological change improves overall industry structure.

Economies of scale and experience (i.e., the learning-curve phenomenon) are important but insufficient in establishing long-term success and competitive advantage; management foresight and attitudes also play vital roles and are necessary to building lasting advantages. Some agree that sustainability of competitive advantage from IT is difficult, if not impossible, to achieve. Once the competitive advantage is lost, the industry's sophistication (i.e., the minimum stakes needed to compete and maintain competitive parity) becomes greater. This, in turn, raises the costs of doing business and the complexity of competition for all players in the entire industry.

The hospitality industry has experienced this firsthand with property management and point-of-sale systems. At one time, the earlier adopters of these technologies enjoyed competitive advantages. Over time, however, as these systems became more affordable and commonplace, the advantages were minimized, and these systems went from ones that provided strategic advantage to ones of competitive parity. Today, if an operation does not have these core systems, it is at a noticeable competitive disadvantage.

An alternative recommendation is that the focus shift to *how* IT is used, rather than on the tools themselves. More specifically, Porter advocates that competitive advantage will be derived from the information collected and shared throughout the organization. Technology can always be purchased, yet this is not ordinarily the case when referring to knowledge. Therefore, competitive advantage will be a function of the ability of a firm's workforce to creatively exploit the capabilities of information technology to create new products and services that sell well; it will not be derived from the technologies themselves, since corporations today essentially have the same information technology, applications, and networking capabilities. It will come in the form of (1) innovations that result from a firm's ability to effectively leverage its unique resources, (2) competitive asymmetry or differences between firms as a result of their unique resources, and (3) the ability to preempt competitive responses and, thereby, maintain technological superiority.

To achieve sustainable competitive advantage, most scholars and industry leaders agree that a firm must continuously invest in its resources and capabilities to build core competencies and a culture that encourage learning, innovation, and risk taking so that new advantages can be created. Deep pockets, know-how, etc., are not enough to ensure long-lasting advantages. In fact, D'Aveni (1994) suggests that leading firms continually seek ways to destroy their competitive advantages (creative destruction) and create new ones before the competition does this for them. He even suggests multipronged approaches (sequential thrusts) to make it more difficult for competitors to react with counterresponses. Successful firms continuously innovate and reinvent themselves. In doing so, these leaders stay out in front while others are several steps behind trying to play catch-up with some previous initiative.

6. SUMMARY

The industry is headed for exciting but turbulent times. For the foreseeable future, the trends towards greater technological sophistication and usage will continue to dominate executive boardrooms and business strategy throughout the hospitality industry worldwide as IT continues to bring about fast-paced, continuous, and radical changes. Within the hospitality industry, many of these changes can be seen in the fundamental structure of the industry, the methods of interaction and shifts in the balance of power between buyers and sellers, and the pricing and distribution models used to sell products and services. Although industry executives may not agree as to whether digital economy represents opportunities or threats for their organizations, few would deny that the ramifications of IT are breathtaking in their pervasiveness and capital intensity.

It is no longer fruitful to resist IT and or to take a "wait-and-see" approach. The hospitality industry must overcome its reluctance to invest in new ideas and technologies that transform the organization, drive the bottom line, and generate value. In doing so, executives must formulate strategies for the development, adoption, and implementation of IT consistent with their business strategies. They must then prepare and defend compelling business cases that clearly demonstrate financial return on investment through reduced costs and/or increased revenues and IT's strategic potential (e.g., its ability to create differentiation; enhance guest service; or build lasting loyalty among customers, employees, franchisees, and suppliers). Arguments that suggest the use of technology merely to remain state-of-the-art are insufficient for winning firm resources, especially under situations involving capital rationing and internal competition for resources.

Because the impact of IT stretches across the entire hospitality enterprise, it is becoming an increasingly important component of management decisions. For most hospitality firms, IT now ranks among the largest capital expense items and will continue to remain so as these firms seek new and creative ways to exploit the growing capabilities of IT through the Internet (and sister technologies, intranets and extranets), telephony, networking, wireless communications, and portable computing devices. To succeed, companies must transition their business models, processes, and systems to the new digital economy and the world of electronic commerce. Additionally, all employees (from top executives to front line staff) must become technologically proficient to ensure the long-term viability of the enterprise.

Hospitality companies should actively seek ways to gain competitive advantage through IT. It is not enough to be first to market. Marriott International was the first hotel company to implement in-room check-out in conjunction with the now defunct Spectradyne. Unfortunately, it failed to develop this technological amenity under terms of exclusivity with its vendor. Consequently, it was not long before this functionality started to appear in its competitors. Now, it is an industry standard. Alternatively, Carlson Hospitality, parent of Radisson, has sought patents to protect some of its technology initiatives and give the company some time advantages, however slight. Everything that can be done to create an uneven playing field in your favor (so long as it is legal and ethical) should be actively explored. Think differently!

Please remember that IT itself is seldom the source of competitive advantage since it can be easily acquired and copied. Rather, it is how IT is implemented and used within a firm (i.e., what people do with it) that leads to competitive advantage. The degree to which competitive advantage can be attained will be a function of how well IT is integrated within the firm, from the culture to the business processes to the systems themselves. The specific competitive advantages derived will be based on how a firm chooses to allocate its resources to implement IT, its overall effectiveness in doing so (e.g., its ability to cost-effectively harness the capabilities provided by the IT tools and applications), its portfolio of resources and capabilities, and the employees' willingness to embrace the technology itself.

7. CASE STUDY AND LEARNING ACTIVITY

IT, when used effectively, can truly transform an organization and extend its reach and capabilities. What follows in an example of how one company is using IT to leverage its resources and create unparalleled advantages across the company. Its continuous investment in IT and innovativeness are providing sources of sustainable competitive advantage. The case is based on an actual company, but some of the names and facts have been changed to protect the identity of the company.

Today's marketplace is filled with tumult, new development, increased market segmentation, and merger mania. In other words, the environment is hypercompetitive, and in such an atmosphere, companies must continually refine their strategies and develop new competitive methods in order to survive. With more sophisticated and demanding consumers, investors seeking better returns on their investment, and a transient workforce, companies cannot rely on their traditional methods or rest on their laurels because there are no sustainable advantages and because the competition is becoming increasingly more formidable. The only constant in such an environment is change. Therefore, companies must continuously seek new methods and IT to compete and stay ahead of the competition. They must break the rules and create new ones.

One such company leading this wave of innovation is the Paris-based Hospitality Extraordinaire International. Hospitality Extraordinaire is a company that is highly revered in the hospitality industry. Often a pioneer, its operating philosophy is simple: to be the best. The company is constantly seeking new ways to apply IT to streamline its operations, increase revenue, attract and retain guests, and create competitive advantage. With over 1,200 properties and 165,000 rooms spread across most major international cities comprising some forty-five-plus countries, Hospitality Extraordinaire has a property to meet almost any guest's needs. As a global industry leader, it is exemplar in its ability to provide consistent service and maintain high service standards across its entire portfolio of products, which runs the gamut from select service to luxury hotels, not to mention time shares and short-term apartment rentals. At the heart of the company's success are its employees (including a corporate IT support team of over 700 people), a seasoned management team, a great set of products, a tight franchise network, a sophisticated portfolio of IT applications, and a very capable technology infrastructure. Each of these items and those listed in Figure 2-5 are, in and of themselves, impressive, but when combined, they create many competitive advantages, both explicit and tacit, for Hospitality Extraordinaire, which are hard to duplicate, and help to explain why the company is the envy of the industry.

With such impressive results, one might ask the question, "How does Hospitality Extraordinaire do it?" With industry maturation and performance tied to the economy, a company like this must be creative, yet cautious, regarding the technology initiatives it pursues. There is no simple answer to the company's success story, but a strong commitment, a dedicated and unrelenting focus, and a culture that supports quality service and the use of IT to accomplish its strategic objectives play important roles. The company's ability to leverage its workforce and its IT are also instrumental in creating success. IT and business strategy are carefully

- Technology infrastructure and IT portfolio
- Human capital (skills and expertise)
- Corporate structure and culture
- Financial capital (deep pockets)
- Size (critical mass) and industry clout
- Market penetration
- Geographic dispersion
- Brand recognition and reputation
- Customer loyalty
- Franchisee relationships and contracts
- Operating standards and practices
- Service delivery
- Product quality
- Value-add programs (to customers, owners, and franchisees)
- Negotiating power with suppliers

Figure 2-5 Factors Contributing to Hospitality Extraordinaire's Competitive Advantage

aligned. IT projects must be customer-centric, leverage the firm's core competencies, and focus on delivering value to the bottom line. If an IT initiative cannot demonstrate enhanced customer service or loyalty, improved employee productivity and capabilities, reduced costs, increased revenues, new business opportunities, and/or increased shareholder value, the project is not funded. For every business decision, the company's executives will do their homework to understand the competitive landscape and consumer trends. Once they understand the opportunities, competitive threats, and consumer needs, they will take calculated risks and consistently invest in the initiative to make it a success. Based on the company's performance to date, its model works—and with very few exceptions.

Hospitality Extraordinaire has long led the industry in technology initiatives. It was among the first hotel chains to implement and standardize property management systems (PMS). Its ROOMSnet reservation system has led the industry in functionality and booking capabilities and set the trend for two-way interfacing with PMS. Its RevMax yield management system also leads the industry in terms of capability and sophistication. With these systems, Hospitality Extraordinaire has been able to achieve rate and occupancy premiums over its competitors. Its Thank You Rewards loyalty/frequent travel program is one of the largest in the industry and has the most loyal following of any hotel company. Even the company's centralized payroll system provides advantages that its rivals envy. It processes payroll for employees around the world at a cost per check that others wish they could match.

Hospitality Extraordinaire's success comes largely as a result of the company's ability to redefine itself and effectively use its resources in response to changing business conditions and market needs. Pushing new limits, the company is aggressively working to create an uneven playing field that will lead to a prolonged period of unmatched competitive advantage. Over the years, the company has expanded its lodging portfolio to include Extraordinary Hotels and Resorts, Humble Inns, Simplicity Inns and Suites, Xtra-Night Stay, Efficient Inns, Corporate Touch Apartments, and Outstanding Vacation Villas. With such a diverse and complementary portfolio, the company has sought ways to eliminate duplication. Rather than have each hotel brand operate as a separate entity (or strategic business unit, in Hospitality Extraordinaire's parlance) competing with one another, the company decided to embark on a strategy that would unify its lodging initiatives to leverage its resources and capabilities and create a stronger presence in the marketplace.

To explore Hospitality Extraordinaire's new focus for competitive advantage, you will turn to a concept referred to as cluster management. The company borrowed a page from the strategy handbooks of retail marketing giants like Proctor and Gamble, Coca-Cola, and PepsiCo, each of which owns a number of competing products or brands within its respective markets. While stressing brand equity, these companies cluster their "families" of products on the same shelf in a grocery store or within geographic proximity in a market to build associations that drive market positions and opportunities and ward off competition. The premise behind this approach is to deflect consumer attention away from price competition and focus it on product/concept differentiation for products that have achieved commodity status.

Hospitality Extraordinaire has come to realize that in order to continue growth and prosperity, each product line (or lodging brand) must collaborate rather than compete with the company's other brands. Today, the company simply recognizes that each brand represents a player on the same Hospitality Extraordinaire team, not opposing teams. With this revelation, the idea is that, in highly competitive markets, it is better for a Hospitality Extraordinaire product to win business rather than to forfeit that business to a non-Hospitality Extraordinaire brand. Accordingly, the orientation shifts from optimizing individual hotel occupancies and revenues, which could lead to suboptimization for the company, to optimizing an entire cluster (or market) of Hospitality Extraordinaire hotels by managing each hotel as part of a larger entity for the benefit of the entire extended organization (including the corporate entity, franchise partners, owners, etc.). The company's reservation system (ROOMSnet), yield management system, property management systems, and INN Touch executive information system are all integrated to support this initiative.

The fundamental principle behind Hospitality Extraordinaire's large-scale organizational change effort is leveraging resources and using teamwork and technology to gain economies of scale and new-found market efficiencies. This philosophy is essential for the company's survival because it cannot hire enough resources to fuel its growth. It needs more resources and must find other ways to achieve its aggressive growth strategy without compromising service, quality, and consistency standards. Plus, things must be done faster, cheaper, different, and better than before. The mantra, especially in a tight economy, is doing more with less.

For years, Hospitality Extraordinaire has shared resources across multiple facilities in several areas including reservations, marketing, advertising, procurement, laundry, and transportation, among others, but its technology capabilities are fostering new, creative approaches to collaboration, resource sharing, efficiencies, and economies of scale. Using IT, not only are resources and costs shared across product lines but so is expertise and information. In turn, these equate to better, more consistent services across properties, a better cost structure, and new sources of revenue. Using technology effectively, Hospitality Extraordinaire can track and segment its customers, maintain brand integrity, reduce its operating overhead, and find new business opportunities. Helping to make the logistics of this possible is Project Connect, a companywide initiative as part of its PeopleSoft implementation to track the sharing of resources across all of the company's entities and bill the appropriate parties (e.g., properties and owners) for the services rendered and for their fair share of the resources consumed. This is an important initiative because Hospitality Extraordinaire is comprised of a complex ownership structure. Many of its hotels are franchised or owned by others but managed by Hospitality Extraordinaire. Since these contracts typically assess fees for services, it is important to keep an accurate accounting of these. As a result, the company can expand its management services to include consulting on a wide variety of topics and best practices and share its cost structure across all who benefit to keep individual property costs down. This provides Hospitality Extraordinaire's properties with a cost advantage over competing brands.

At the field level, total integration is the desired goal with shared data, systems, and other resources (e.g., laundry facilities, van service, etc.). By outfitting corporate, regional, and field staff with laptops and wireless personal digital assistants (PDAs) and by giving them access to electronic mail, the corporate intranet, an executive information system with a scorecard of measures, and the company's data warehouse (which culls data from such core systems as accounting, property management, guest history, central reservations, and the company's Thank You Rewards loyalty/frequent traveler database), Hospitality Extraordinaire's employees are equipped with up-to-the-minute operating results, company policies and news, and the latest in consumer trends analysis—anytime and anywhere they need such access. Armed with such sophisticated IT tools, decision makers can quickly "slice and dice" data to compare, analyze, and troubleshoot performance at a particular property, in a given market, across a specific brand, or throughout the entire chain. Using these IT tools and the company's technology infrastructure (including its ubiquitous high-speed corporate network and wireless capabilities) to gain access to key systems, management in the field and at corporate can oversee multiple departments, properties, and markets at a time; share best practices; and keep better tabs on the business. Real-time alerts and red flags notify managers of pending problems so they can intervene and seek resolutions prior to their getting out of control. They are never out of touch, regardless of where they are and what they are doing. Clearly, these systems enhance Hospitality Extraordinaire's resources and capabilities, and because many of the benefits are behind-the-scenes, it is difficult for competitors to identify the contributing factors to the company's success and copy them, thus, extending Hospitality Extraordinaire's competitive advantage. Cluster management provides the company with unprecedented opportunities through economies of scale and resource sharing to create competitive advantages that other hotel providers will have great difficulty matching or countering because they lack the structure, technology, and wherewithal to make it happen.

One example is revenue analysts who are responsible for monitoring supply and demand patterns within markets and adjusting sales strategies and room inventory controls when appropriate. Yield management is a sophisticated science that requires powerful systems and a high degree of expertise. This knowledge can now be easily shared across multiple hotels—complete with the booking patterns for each hotel in the area—so that all hotels within the cluster can more effectively manage their room inventory, rate structures, and selling strategies to avoid lost market share. Perhaps upscale hotels will be less inclined to discount their rates if they know that their sibling hotels in the economy or mid-scale sector are still projecting room availability.

Sales associates are also responsible for multiple brands. The sharing of resources here goes well beyond lead generation, referrals, and overflow business. Instead of having several sales representatives call upon the same clients in what may have appeared as a disjointed and disorganized sales strategy from the customer's perspective, one sales associate or a team of sales agents is assigned to clients or a geographic region to sell a complete portfolio of products covering all of their lodging needs: budget, extended stay, full service, meeting and conventions, or luxury. No longer are multiple properties competing for the same business and confusing the customers with multiple requests for proposal (RFPs) from the same company. Equipped with desktop and wireless sales force automation tools, these agents have instant access to rate and availability information for any hotel in the system—from almost anywhere, including the client's office. This information can then be shared through the sales system to other hotels seeking to bid on conferences that travel from year to year. Having such historical data readily at hand, sales associates can submit more accurate bids, ones that take into account actual versus projected business in prior cities, pick-up rates, special needs, etc. The system is not only a great booking resource but also a great client relationship building tool. Reservation agents are also shared across hotels in a given geographic area. Because these "mini" reservation centers are located within a given market, the agents are more qualified to answer questions regarding hotel facilities, local attractions, and upcoming events than a person sitting in a remote office trying to locate the information on a computer screen in the central reservation system. The information that they provide and the efficiency with which they provide it enhances the customer service and favorably sets a guest's initial impression for his/her upcoming stay in the area.

Just as reservations and sales staff can be shared across properties, so too can accounting and human resources staff, which allows better access to specialized resources and expertise. By sharing these resources, individual hotels no longer need to have their own accounting or human resources departments. Cluster offices, located at one of the larger hotels in the region, can provide accounting services, budgetary oversight, recruiting services, benefits administration, and other human resource functions for all properties within a cluster. The company's accounting information system provides detailed access to company expenditures. This information can then be used to tighten cost controls and negotiate better discounts with suppliers. Human resource systems aid not only in the recruitment but also the retention of employees. Capable of career tracking and progression/succession planning for the entire company, the system helps identify candidates ready for promotion: those who have completed the requisite training classes for a given position, held prior positions that serve as stepping stones, and completed stints in other product lines or functional disciplines to ensure a truly cross-functional workforce.

The preceding examples are only a small sampling. There are many others and the potential is even greater. The number of collaborative efforts such as these can only increase as groupware applications, such as Lotus Notes, become more commonplace. Furthermore, few hotel companies can match the diversity, consistency, and quality that Hospitality Extraordinaire exemplifies. It is the company's core informational technologies like ROOMSnet, yield management, PMS, Thank You Rewards, accounting, payroll, and human resources and the company's common hardware, software, and communications platforms that support data exchange and afford Hospitality Extraordinaire the opportunity to manage across product lines.

For Hospitality Extraordinaire, the competitive advantage is created by its resources (i.e., employees, capital, and technology). Complementing these resources are the relationships forged with its franchisees and the company's commitment to quality and product consistency (e.g., service delivery, cleanliness of facilities, amenities, program implementation and execution, etc.). In the end, the competitive advantage is a structural and cultural one created by innovative leadership and complementary resources and processes. Because it is difficult to duplicate, it provides Hospitality Extraordinaire with a decided and lasting advantage.

Although many leading lodging providers enjoy heavily segmented lodging portfolios, their zeal for growth and market share has resulted in loose contracts, lax standards, and blurred distinctions between their concepts by overlapping product positioning—so much so that customers cannot easily distinguish the advantages of one product over another. Confounded by low switching costs and inconsistent product quality, amenities, and service delivery within a product line, the problem of brand identity is exacerbated. Consequently, the barriers to implementing cluster management for competing chains are high should these organizations consider following or copying Hospitality Extraordinaire's lead.

For Hospitality Extraordinaire, a blurring of product lines is not much of an issue—at least not yet, though this could change as the result of recent additions to its product offerings. At present, the company maintains a unique identity for each of its brands in order to build customer loyalty and prevent such blurring from occurring. Since each brand has a distinct identity and target market, Hospitality Extraordinaire is able to uniquely position itself in any given market without the risk of cannibalization prevalent in other companies. Its use of technology and market data allows the company to select appropriate sites and determine the *right* product for that site. This is an important benefit that contributes to the success of cluster management and the acceptance by many of the company's franchise partners and outside owners.

The unsung hero of Hospitality Extraordinaire's technology capabilities that makes the cluster management concept possible and affordable is the infrastructure, which is somewhat transparent—especially to those on the outside. Its use of standardized systems (which are defined in management and franchisee contracts), common technology architecture, and a pervasive communications network makes connectivity and integration possible.

Hospitality Extraordinaire is an exciting, dynamic company. It has its act together and is well aligned with the external environment. Its IT usage is state-of-the-art and well aligned with its business strategy. Together, these create the many successes Hospitality Extraordinaire has enjoyed over the years. They will continue to create the basis of success for years to come. If Hospitality Extraordinaire is not a company you carefully track, you should be sure to put it on your radar screen. It is one to watch!

Learning Activity

1. Define Hospitality Extraordinaire's strategy. How does IT factor into this strategy?

2. Identify the core technologies being used by Hospitality Extraordinaire. Discuss the value each contributes and any competitive advantage derived.

3. If you worked for a competing hotel company, what traits would you find most admirable in Hospitality Extraordinaire and why? What would you do to compete?

4. If you worked for Hospitality Extraordinaire's IT department, what challenges might you face? What recommendations would you have for new technology initiatives or directions?

5. What are the key teaching points in this case? Why are they important, and how will you apply them in your professional career?

8. KEY TERMS

Asset optimization	Competitive method	Outcome approach
CAPITA	Convergence	Preemptive Strategy
Cash flow per share	Economies of scale	Sustainable competitive advantage
Co-alignment principle	*Five Forces* model	Trait approach
Competitive advantage	Generic strategies	

9. CHAPTER QUESTIONS

1. How do you define value in the eyes of key stakeholders, namely customers, investors, franchisees, and employees? How can IT contribute to value for each? What opportunities exist?

2. What is competitive advantage? How is it created? How can it be sustained? Be sure to consider the roles of corporate culture, firm resources and capabilities, and core competencies.

3. Define the co-alignment model. How is co-alignment achieved, and why, for a hospitality manager, is this so important to understand?

4. Can IT provide competitive advantage? If so, how? Provide some specific examples.

5. Can IT create *sustainable* competitive advantage? Support your answer.

6. Select some leading hospitality firms. Compare and contrast their uses of IT. What advantages does IT provide to them? How does IT limit or constrain these firms?

7. Conduct a brief literature search on the works of Harvard University Professor Michael Porter. What contributions has he made to the understanding of strategy and IT? How can these be applied in a hospitality industry context?

10. REFERENCES

Adcock, Ken, Marilyn M. Helms, and Wen-Jang Kenny Jih. 1993. Information technology: Can it provide a sustainable competitive advantage? *Information Strategy: The Executive's Journal* (spring): 10–15.

Andersen Consulting and American Hotel & Motel Association. 1989. *Looking forward: A management perspective of technology in the lodging industry.* Washington D.C.

Antonucci, Yvonne Lederer, and James J. Tucker III. 1998. Responding to earnings-related pressure to reduce IT operating and capital expenditures. *Information Strategy: The Executive's Journal* (spring): 6–14.

Applegate, Lynda M., F. Warren McFarlan, and James L. McKenney. 1996. *Corporate information systems management: The issues facing senior executives.* 4th ed. Chicago: Irwin.

Bakos, J. Yannis, and Michael E. Treacy. 1986. Information technology and corporate strategy: A research perspective. *MIS Quarterly* 10, no. 2 (June): 107–119.

Bourgeois, L. J., III. 1980. Strategy and environment: A conceptual integration. *Academy of Management Review* 5, no. 1: 25–39.

Brady, Tim, Ross Cameron, David Targett, and Chris Beaumont. 1992. Strategic IT issues: The views of some major IT investors. *Journal of Strategic Information Systems* 1, no. 4: 183–189.

Burrus, Daniel (with Gittines, Roger). 1993. *Technotrends: How to use technology and go beyond your competition.* New York: HarperBusiness.

Cash, James I., Jr., and Benn R. Konsynski. 1985. IS redraws competitive boundaries. *Harvard Business Review* (March/April): 134–142.

Chandler, Alfred D. 1962. *Strategy and structure: Chapters in the history of industrial enterprise.* Cambridge, MA: MIT Press.

Cho, Wonae. 1996. A case study: Creating and sustaining competitive advantage through an information technology application in the lodging industry. Ph.D. diss., Virginia Polytechnic Institute and State University.

Clemons, Eric K., and Steven O. Kimbrough. 1986. Information systems, telecommunications and their effects on industrial organizations. *Proceedings of the Seventh International Conference on Information Systems, San Diego, CA* (December): 99–108.

Clemons, Eric K., and Michael C. Row. 1991. Sustaining IT advantage: The role of structural differences. *MIS Quarterly* 15, no. 3 (September): 275–291.

Cline, Roger S., and Louis A. Blatt. 1998. Creating enterprise value around the customer . . . Leveraging the customer asset in today's hospitality industry. *Arthur Andersen Hospitality and Leisure Executive Report* 5, no. 1 (winter): 2–11.

Cline, Roger S., and Lalia Rach. 1996. *Hospitality 2000—A view to the next millennium: A study of the key issues facing the international hospitality industry in the next millennium.* Arthur Andersen.

Copeland, Duncan G., and James L. McKenney. 1988. Airline reservations systems: Lessons from history. *MIS Quarterly* 12, no. 3 (September): 353–370.

D'Aveni, Richard A. (with Gunther, Robert). 1994. *Hyper-competition: Managing the dynamics of strategic maneuvering.* New York: The Free Press.

Feeny, David F., and Blake Ives. 1990. In search of sustainability: Reaping long-term advantage from investments in information technology. *Journal of Management Information Systems* 7, no. 1 (summer): 27–46.

Hamel, Gary, and C. K. Prahalad. 1994. Seeing the future first. *Fortune* 64 (5 September): 66–68.

Hanks, Richard D., R. Paul Noland, and Robert G. Cross. 1992. Discounting in the hotel industry: A new approach. *Cornell Hotel and Restaurant Administration Quarterly* (February): 15–23.

Hansen, Erik Lars, and Raymond M. Owen. 1995. Evolving technologies to drive competitive advantage in hospitality industry. *Hotel Online*, fall. http://www.hotel-online.com:80/Neo/Trends/Andersen/tech.html.

Hensdill, Cherie. 1998. Hotels technology survey. *Hotels* (February): 51–76.

Hitt, Lorin M., and Erik Brynjolfsson. 1996. Productivity, business profitability, and consumer surplus: Three different measures of information technology value. *MIS Quarterly* 20, no. 2 (June): 121–143.

Hopper, Max D. 1990. Rattling SABRE—New ways to compete on information. *Harvard Business Review* (May/June): 118–125.

Ives, Blake, and Gerard P. Learmonth. 1984. The information system as a competitive weapon. *Communications of the ACM* 27, no. 12 (December): 1193–1201.

Luxury hotels consider round-the-clock concept. 1997. *The Orlando Sentinel,* 12 January, L-6.

Mata, Francisco J., William L. Fuerst, and Jay B. Barney. 1995. Information technology and sustained competitive advantage: A resource-based analysis. *MIS Quarterly* 19, no. 4 (December): 487–505.

McFarlan, F. Warren. 1984. Information technology changes the way you compete. *Harvard Business Review* (May/June): 98–103.

Murthy, Bvsan. 1994. Measurement of the strategy construct in the lodging industry, and the strategy-performance relationship. Ph.D. diss., Virginia Polytechnic Institute and State University.

Negroponte, Nicholas. 1995. *Being digital.* New York: Vintage Books.

Ohmae, Kenichi. 1992. *The mind of the strategist: Business planning for competitive advantage.* New York: Penguin Books.

Olsen, Michael D. 1996. *Into the new millennium: A white paper on the global hospitality industry.* Paris: International Hotel Association.

Olsen, Michael D., Joseph J. West, and Eliza C. Tse. 1998. *Strategic management in the hospitality industry.* 2d ed. New York: John Wiley & Sons.

Palmer, Colin. 1988. Using IT for competitive advantage at Thomson Holidays. *Long Range Planning* 21, no. 6 (December): 26–29.

Parsons, Gregory L. 1983. Information technology: A new competitive weapon. *Sloan Management Review* (fall): 3–14.

Plimpton, George. 1990. *The X factor.* Knoxville, TN: Whittle Direct Books.

Porter, Michael E. 1980. *Competitive strategy: Techniques for analyzing industries and competitors.* New York: The Free Press.

———. 1985. *Competitive advantage: Creating and sustaining superior performance.* New York: The Free Press.

Porter, Michael E., and Victor E. Millar. 1985. How information gives you competitive advantage. *Harvard Business Review* (July/August): 149–160.

Post, Gerald V., Albert Kagan, and Kin-Nam Lau. 1995. A modeling approach to evaluating strategic uses of information technology. *Journal of Management Information Systems* 12, no. 2 (fall): 161–187.

Quinn, James Brian. 1988. Service technology and manufacturing: Cornerstones of the U. S. economy. In *Managing innovation: Cases from the service industries,* edited by Bruce R. Guile and James Brian Quinn, 9–35. Washington, DC: National Academy Press.

Segars, Albert H., and Varun Grover. 1995. The industry-level impact of information technology: An empirical analysis of three industries. *Decision Sciences* 26, no. 3 (May/June): 337–368.

Sethi, Vijay, and William R. King. 1994. Development of measures to assess the extent to which an information technology application provides competitive advantage. *Management Science* 40, no. 12 (December): 1601–1626.

Tapscott, Don. 1996. *The digital economy: Promise and peril in the age of networked intelligence.* New York: McGraw-Hill.

Thompson, James D. 1967. *Organizations in action.* New York: McGraw-Hill.

Venkatraman, N., John C. Henderson, and Scott Oldach. 1993. Continuous strategic alignment: Exploiting information technology capabilities for competitive success. *European Management Journal* 11, no. 2 (June): 139–149.

Venkatraman, N., and John E. Prescott. 1990. Environment-strategy coalignment: An empirical test of its performance implications. *Strategic Management Journal* 11, no. 1 (January): 1–23.

Weill, Peter. 1991, November. The information technology payoff: Implications for investment appraisal. *Australian Accounting Review* 1(1): 2–11.

Zuboff, Shoshana. 1988. *In the age of the smart machine: The future of work and power.* New York: Basic Books, Inc.

CHAPTER THREE

Computing Essentials

CHAPTER CONTENTS

INTERVIEW

William P. Fisher is the Darden Eminent Scholar Chair in the Rosen School of Hospitality Management at the University of Central Florida and is the former president of the American Hotel and Lodging Association.

Q: Thanks for taking time to talk, Bill. First, can you tell me about your background and career path?

A: I went to the School of Hotel Administration at Cornell University, then went into the air force through ROTC. I received an MBA in finance and a Ph.D. in educational administration, and taught in the School of Hotel Administration at Cornell for seven years. I left teaching to become the executive vice president of the National Restaurant Association headquartered in Chicago. Later, I became the executive president of Finance and Administration for Service Systems Corporation, which was purchased by Marriott, and came back to the restaurant association. Finally, in 1996 I became president of the AH & LA here in Washington.

Q: What changes have you seen in technology?

A: When I first started teaching, I was teaching accounting and finance. The textbooks required that everything be solved by hand. From there we moved to calculators, then to spreadsheets and computer analysis. The technology has really changed.

Q: What sort of skills are hospitality companies looking for in a recent college graduate?

A: I think companies hiring a recent graduate of a hospitality related program are first and foremost looking for a good attitude. Experience is another factor employers look for to show interest as well as knowledge of some of the particulars such as occupancy rate and ADR, all too important in understanding the business aspects and performance. After that you need to know who the players and publications are in our industry so you can do research. Specialization is important, but so is having a broad understanding since employers look for broad-based people who have the knowledge to complement the skills learned in their major. The industry is looking for people who can be productive right away in their role within the organization but who also see the big picture. Technology is important to understand whether you use it as a tool in an operational role or it's your primary focus.

Q: Have you seen any change in profitability in hotels due to technology?

A: I think the world of technology has changed so rapidly that hotel organizations have had to "get with it" as a defensive measure or the competition will run away with their customers. I think a lot of people from the customer service side want to make customers happy, and customers are demanding the same technology they have at work when they travel. On the internal side, technology has led to more timely information, which can reduce costs in both materials and labor. If you separate your customer technology from your overhead technology and compare them to different time periods, then you can get some real answers. I think we are seeing the beginning of that analysis being performed now.

Q: Can you tell me a little about the HITIS initiative?
(HITIS stands for hospitality industry technology integration standards.) Their mission statement is as follows:

> To direct a non-proprietary, consensus based process to develop voluntary standards for the integration of evolving computerized system and sub-system transactions in the hospitality industry. The process will seek to synthesize and disseminate previous and current efforts to resolve such issues and allow hospitality operators and vendors alike to save on costly retrofitting solutions and enable faster technology adoption and evolution within the various segments of the hospitality industry.

A: When I came here in 1996, there was a meeting of some of the IT people. They invited me, and asked me if the AH & LA would be interested in adopting industry standards. My feeling was that it was probably overdue in the industry, and the association seemed to be the perfect environment for setting standards since its interests are aligned with the industry as a whole rather than just one entity. Standards were set thanks to the hard work of some good people such as Bob Elliott in areas such as central reservations. Oftentimes in technological development, a great system is created in security and operates great until the point where it needs to connect or talk to another system such as environmental monitoring or property management. In hotels you would often see more than 40 types of computer systems, and if you wished to be efficient and have timely and reliable information, the systems had to be able to "talk" to one another. In the worst case scenario, no system was talking to another system; then you moved to gerrymandering one system to communicate with another. New product sales often suffered due to the fact that the hotelier did not want to go though the process of making the systems communicate and the downtime needed to make the systems communicate. For this reason, the technology vendors for the industry were very supportive of standards. With this, I believe there are greater opportunities for customer satisfaction. For example, in the old days when I was a front desk clerk one summer in Atlantic City, people would come down at 10:00 in the morning and say "I'm checking out" and see that the breakfast that they had that morning was not on there since the dining room system and the front office system did not communicate. This resulted in the customer waiting for the operation to square things away. You don't have to worry about that now if standards are in place that allow the systems to communicate. I think from that standpoint things have gotten better. This serves as a great example on why we want to have standards. We are actually working on a suite of standards and seeing interest from the gaming and golf industries in what we are doing.

Q: A college senior is graduating tomorrow with a hospitality degree, what advice would you give him or her?

A: Number one, make sure you stay on the cutting edge. One of the reasons a graduation ceremony is called a commencement is because it is a beginning and not a conclusion. Therefore, keep learning and stay abreast of what is going on in the industry and your field within that industry, be it technology, human resources, or accounting. Next, volunteer for something outside of the organization, whether it is coaching little league baseball or small fry football. I say that because that is part of a student manager's maturation process. When you are dealing with youngsters who are 9 or 10 years old, and there is the kid who is always crying, or the kid who is always trying to get recognition, or the kid who always gets the job done, well this is what you find as a manager in a professional environment. Conversely, volunteer for something inside your organization that you do not know anything about. Many organizations have committees, whether it is a customer service committee or the Christmas committee.

1. INTRODUCTION

Bill Fisher has provided a great overview of how technology has evolved, how it can be used, why it should be understood, and why systems need to work together. Now you need to establish a technological knowledge foundation. This chapter will cover the basics of computing.

Before you can make accurate and timely decisions, you first need to know and understand the foundation. What is a computer? How does it work? Does it think as I do? What's under that cover? These and others are questions that anyone new to computing may have. From a review of systems and binary code, to system hardware and software, to the operating system and programming languages, this chapter provides you with the necessary foundation.

This chapter contains many key terms, several of which you probably have seen before. At the end of the chapter, you will revisit the AH & LA's HITIS initiative in the case study and learning activity.

2. SYSTEM

Before you learn about computers, you must first understand the system behind them. Just what is a system? You see this word all the time with regard to computing: management information systems, systems analysis, the systems department, etc. Put simply, a *system* is a way of doing things. Right

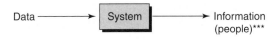

Figure 3-1.

now you may be writing notes about what you are reading in the margin of the book or somewhere else. Maybe you read a definition twice, or say it out loud to help you remember it. Whichever the case, you have your own system. One of the first endeavors hotel managers make when they start a new job is to evaluate the old system of their particular department (how was it done before?) and to adopt their own system (i.e., having more front desk clerks on duty at certain hours). That is how they handle busy periods, which is "a way of doing things." So in order to take the fear out of the word system, and hopefully computers as a whole, think of computers as a part of *your* way of doing things.

You might already have an ideal way of doing things, so how does a computer fit into your system? First off, a computer needs data, which is simply raw facts made up of words, numbers, etc. Data is input into the system, processed, and transformed, by you, into information (Figure 3-1). Here is a simple example: I bought a stock for $10 and sold it for $15, giving me a profit of $5 or a 50 percent return. A computer can do the operation 15-10 or 5/10 and give you an answer, but it is up to you to interpret the answer as good or bad. For example, you might ask, "How does this compare to other stocks?" Information is simply data to which people have given meaning and shape. An expanded definition of information can be found in Chapter 11.

How does this apply to someone in hospitality management? Well, besides the obvious systems, such as managing rooms or seats and food and beverage consumption (which will be covered later), managers often use computers to handle their budgets. You input all the numbers, tell the computer what to add, subtract, divide, etc., and the computer supplies a number. It is the manager's duty to interpret that number. In other words, you give the data shape and meaning, turning it into information. Maybe the number will tell the manager that she/he is over budget when it comes to labor and therefore needs to schedule fewer people during certain shifts. The manager is using the data and the system, and with a computer **application,** is getting information to make a managerial decision. This is a prime example of computer use in the hospitality industry helping managers make accurate and timely decisions.

The raw facts in the definition of data come in a specific form. This form is known as *binary code. Bi* comes from the Latin word for two. In binary code, the data can be presented in two options, a 1 or a 0. It makes words or letters by stringing together these 0s and 1s in a particular order. The order 01000001

Figure 3-2.   Using IBM ViaVoice, which translates speech into text, Peter Corrales,
the owner of a New York catering company, checks inventory.

represents the character A in Figure 3-3. This binary code is how a computer
counts, whereas our own counting system is in base 10 (see Table 3-1).

In the decimal system, you go up to 10 digits and start over. Binary counting is a little different. Look at Table 3-1. Can you see the pattern? Start with a
0, and from the left, each new number is where a 0 from the previous number
is replaced with a 1. Can you see how the 1s seem to be moving to the left?
When all 1s have replaced the 0s, a new number is started with a 1 in the beginning and more 0s than in the last set. These 0s and 1s are known as bits.

Bits, short for binary digits, make up the smallest form of data storage.
Put eight of them together and you get what is known as a *byte*. A byte represents one standard character or number. Again, the letter A is represented by
the following bits: 01000001. The next vowel, E, is represented by its unique
combination of 1s and 0s: 01000101.

Table 3–1. Base 10 versus binary counting

Base 10				
1	11	21	91	101
2	12	22	92	102
3	13	23	93	103
4	14	24	94	104
5	15	25	95	105
6	16	26	96	106
7	17	27	97	107
8	18	28	98	108
9	19	29	99	109
10	20	30	100	110

Binary

0
1
10
11
100
101
111
1000
1001
1011
1111
100000

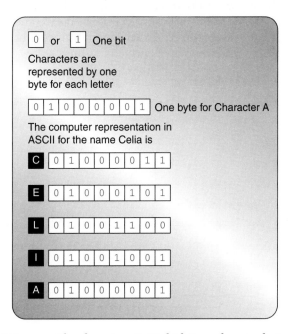

Figure 3-3. Bits can either be a 1 or 0. Eight bits make up a byte or a standard character. The word *CELIA* is made up of the depicted bytes.

Bits and bytes make up the beginning of data storage and measurement. They are followed by *kilobytes, megabytes, gigabytes,* and *terabytes.* Remember that eight bits make up a byte.

1024 bytes = 1 kilobyte

1024 kilobytes = 1 megabyte

1024 megabytes = 1 gigabyte

1024 gigabytes = 1 terabyte

The number 1024 is the one to remember. You can make up your own mnemonic device for the letters **K** for kilobyte, **M** for megabyte, **G** for gigabyte, and **T** for terabyte (a common one is **K**eep **M**y **G**iant **T**ree).

To understand how a computer "sees" whether a bit is a 1 or a 0, you must first understand how it travels. Remember electricity and Ben Franklin? Electricity is actually defined as "the class of physical phenomena arising from the existence and interactions of electronic charge." So *electricity* is a phenomenon and *voltage* measures its potential. If you vary these two in a consistent manner, then you have a *signal.*

A signal can travel down a wire or even through the air. Signals come in two general categories, analog and digital. *Analog* signals travel as a wave that has many points or states as seen in Figure 3-4.

It has a high point in B and a low point in D with points A, C, and E in between. A *digital* signal does not have points in between such as A, C, and E. It only has high and low points and varies instantaneously with no points in between. These high and low points are called high states and low states, which are just voltage levels. Look at Figure 3-5.

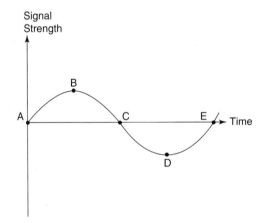

Figure 3-4. Sine waves have many levels. Here the sine wave has a high point B, a low point D, and points A, C, and E at the beginning, middle, and end.

Signal Intensity

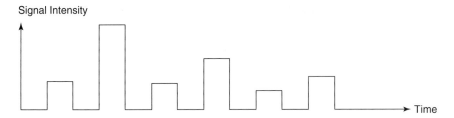

Time

Figure 3-5. In contrast to sine waves, digital signals have just a high and a low point.

In a digital signal there are only two states. The high voltage level represents a 1 and a low voltage level represents a 0, which is precisely how it identifies bits.

Analog signals are older than the new digital signals that computers use. Analog lines are found today in phone lines generally from your house to the first phone company's building. From there, the majority of carriers use digital signals. It is important to know that analog signals are used for data requiring continuous states such as voice and video and that the two types of signals can be used in conjunction with one another for greater efficiency. In daily usage, an analog signal can be converted into a data signal whereby it can be "cleaned up" and then converted back into an analog signal with no background noise. You will see how signals can be converted in the networking chapter (Chapter 4).

3. HARDWARE

Keep in mind that signals inside a computer are digital. Lets take a look inside a typical desktop computer to see where those signals go, Figure 3-6. Desktops serve as great examples for computing devices in general. Although they may differ in size and shape, general composition and principles remain constant.

Hardware is something physical you can touch and feel such as your computer screen. If you take off a cover of a computer, you would see a green board with circuitry and extensions. This is known as a printed circuit board (PCB) as well as a motherboard. This is the foundation of the computer where all of the connections take place. On this foundation sits the *central processing unit (CPU)*. This is the brain of the computer and will be discussed later. Attached to the motherboard is memory. There are two kinds of memory: *RAM* and *ROM*. RAM stands for "random access memory" and is where your applications such as word processing or solitaire run when they are used. RAM is temporary, meaning that once you turn your computer off, it is erased like a blackboard. That is why you need to save your work. When people add more memory (RAM) to their computers, they are able to have more applications open at once. Today, RAM, more often than not, is DRAM, short for dynamic random access memory, which means that the CPU can

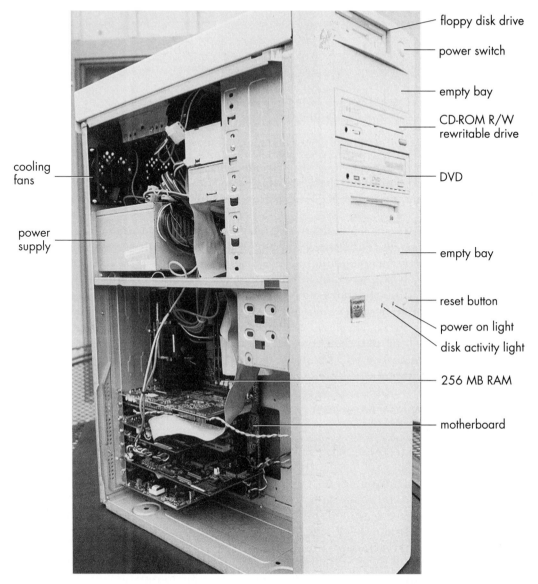

floppy disk drive

power switch

empty bay

CD-ROM R/W
rewritable drive

DVD

cooling
fans

power
supply

empty bay

reset button

power on light

disk activity light

256 MB RAM

motherboard

Figure 3-6.   Study this photo of a cutaway of a computer including the motherboard, disk
drives, and expansion slots.

access exactly which part it needs without having to go through the parts it
does not (known as sequential). This DRAM comes in 64 bit chip form
known as DIMMs (dual in-line memory module), which plugs into the motherboard. DIMMs are more capable than their predecessor, 32 bit SIMMs
(single in-line memory module). ROM, on the other hand, stands for "read
only memory." This memory is permanent and contains basic instructions

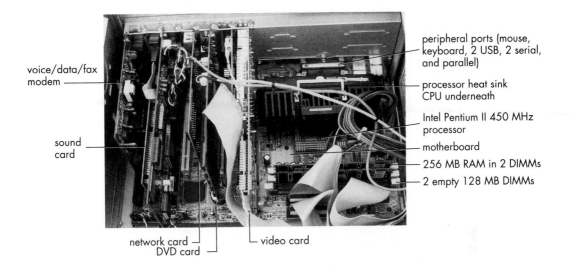

voice/data/fax modem

sound card

network card
DVD card

video card

peripheral ports (mouse, keyboard, 2 USB, 2 serial, and parallel)

processor heat sink CPU underneath

Intel Pentium II 450 MHz processor

motherboard

256 MB RAM in 2 DIMMs

2 empty 128 MB DIMMs

Figure 3-7. The motherboard serves as the foundation for the various Computer Components.

for the computer to follow upon start-up. When the power is shut off, ROM retains what is in it. Handheld and other devices use a specific type of memory named *flash memory,* which is connected to a battery and can only be erased in blocks, allowing for storage and functionality of the unit. Also attached to the motherboard, are expansion slots. When computers are purchased, they do not necessarily come with printers and scanners or other *peripherals* (external devices connected to the computer). Expansion slots provide a ready connection for devices that need to communicate with your computer. Returning to the computer example, you see the power supply. Next is a *disk drive.* This is where *floppy disks* are inserted. The *hard drive,* usually located above or below the floppy drive, is sealed in an airtight metal container. This is to prevent any dirt or other particles from entering and corrupting the data. These disk drives are where data is stored and retrieved. Disks are divided into sectors and tracks, with the *operating system,* which will be discussed shortly, keeping track of which sector contains what data. The hard disk also contains an area that is used for memory known as a *cache.* This part of the disk works with RAM in storing and retrieving frequently used data such as web pages or files.

Next is the CD (compact disk) drive. It used to be that you could only read from CDs, and they were referred to as CD-ROMS, with ROM standing for

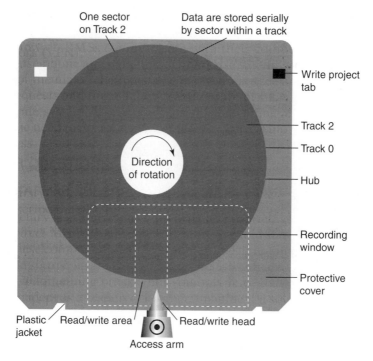

Figure 3-8. The access arm of this 3.5" floppy disk is positioned at Track 2.
Within a given sector, data is read or written serially in tracks.

"read only." Now you are able to both read and write to CDs. This is done a bit differently than our hard and floppy disks that receive direct contact. CDs are read and written to by a laser that sends out a beam and either gets absorbed or reflected (again binary). That 16x, 24x, or 32x you see when you buy a computer refers to the transmission speed (measured in multiples of 150 kilobits) of your CD. So the bigger the number, the faster it moves the data. DVDs, or digital versatile disks, which are quickly replacing the way we rent movies, can hold 4.7 gigabytes of data. DVDs are expected to replace the CDs in use now.

What you look at when you work on computers or with computer technology is known as either a *monitor* or a *display*. These units, whose names can be used interchangeably, are responsible for projecting images. The image can be projected by a cathode ray tube (CRT), a liquid crystal display (LCD), or gas plasma, among others. Monitors, which are separate from the CPU, use a cathode ray tube. This technology requires a set amount of distance from the projecting source to the screen, which is one of the reasons it is so big compared to a laptop, which uses a liquid crystal display. LCD technology uses liquid crystals and less power than CRTs but is difficult to view at angles other than straight on.

Personal digital assistants (PDAs), which are small handheld mobile computers, use a touch screen that reacts to electrical charges. Where you touch sets off a charge at the surface point that reacts to your tap and sends the CPU the location information.

The sharpness of the display—no matter what the projection technology used—is dependent on three main elements. First is how many colors (measured in bits) the computer is able to display (*display mode*), which is numbered in the millions. Second is the *dot pitch* (the size of the dots placed next to each other that make up your display), which is how sharp the image is and is measured in millimeters. The term *dots per inch (DPI)* is a common one that means the more DPI, the finer the picture. Finally, **pixels,** short for picture elements, determine how many dot pitches are used. The sizes of the dots (dot pitch) and the number of them within a square inch (DPI) are the two main factors when we talk about resolution. Any projected image needs to be constantly refreshed to keep its presence. Think of a movie projector being turned off. That is an example of an object not being refreshed. In motion, however, the object is continuously "repainted." How many times this happens per second is known as the *refresh rate.*

"Input devices translate our data and communication into a form that the computer can understand" (Long and Long 1998, p. 130)

Besides the mouse and keyboard, computing devices can receive data from other input devices. In addition to the following such devices, what others can you name?

Touch screens

Joysticks

Barcodes

Track pads

Digital pens

Voice

Output devices, on the other hand, take the processed data from the computer and translate them back into a form that we, as managers, can understand. In addition to the following examples of output devices, what others can you name?

Printers

Monitors

Projectors

Next is the Central Processing Unit.

The **central processing unit** (CPU) is divided into four main parts:

1. *Register.* Temporarily stores the pieces of information being processed
2. *Arithmetic Logic Unit (ALU).* Carries out math and logic functions

3. *Control Unit.* Coordinates the work of the register and ALU

4. *Data Storage.* Stores the results

These four parts of the CPU correspond *roughly* to the four steps of computer operation. Everyone does things in a certain order. For instance, before you drive a car, you open the door, start the car, put it in gear, and then go. When computing devices operate, they follow these four basic steps:

1. Get instructions

2. Decode instructions

3. Execute instructions

4. Store results

How fast a computer can go through these steps over and over again in one second determines its processor speed, which is measured in megahertz. For example an 800-megahertz processor can go through the preceding four steps 800 *million* times in one second! So the higher the number of the processor, the higher its computational speed. Processors operate so fast that a cooling unit is needed. On top of the processor sit either cooling rods or a fan to disperse the heat from working so hard and fast. That humming you hear is often the cooling unit.

The final piece of hardware is the *bus*. A bus in computing terminology refers to the data path. The motherboard has different components attached to it such as the hard drive, CPU, or expansion cards. The bus is the path between these units through which data travels. Think of it as the internal highway system connecting the various hardware components and circuits. The width of this bus is referred to as the *data bus path*. Common widths are 64 bit and 32 bit, which relate to the word length. Think of the width as the number of lanes on a highway. The larger the number, the more lanes it has, meaning the larger the number of bits it can handle at once, equaling faster usage.

4. SOFTWARE

Software is the detailed instructions that control the operation of a computer system. "A software program is a series of statements or instructions to the computer. The process of writing or coding programs is termed programming, and the individuals who specialize in this task are called programmers." (Laudon and Laudon 2002, p. 75) Software comes in two basic categories, application software and system software. "Application software, or applications, are the programs written for or by users to apply a computer to a specific task." (Laudon and Laudon 2002, p. 173) The "off-the-shelf" productivity software such as word processing, spreadsheets, or "specific" programs written in languages such as C++ and JAVA are examples of application software. Application software is needed since the hardware only understands its own "machine language," or binary numbers. Application software is written in words, then

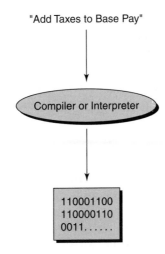

Figure 3-9. Through the use of a compiler or interpreter, familiar words are translated into machine code.

translated into machine language by a compiler or interpreter. Putting it together, a programmer writes words of code, the code is sent through a compiler or interpreter that translates it into machine code—those 1s and 0s that computers like—as illustrated in Figure 3-9.

Other examples of common "out-of-the-box" application software include database, multimedia presentation, contact management and e-mail, instant messaging, browsers, publishing, etc. Think of an industry and chances are it has software that is standard to it. "Out-of-the-box" software is convenient since thousands of common tasks have already been automated and can be accessed by pointing and clicking. The two main versions in our industry are the property management system (PMS) and the point-of-sale system (POS), which will be covered later. Today, independent software vendors (ISV) such as Microsoft and Oracle, or more specific to our industry, Micros/Fidelio, spend lots of money on research and development (R&D) to develop what is known as "a killer app" for computers, PDAs, cell phones, and whatever comes along next that requires software, and will lead to a high volume in sales.

Sometimes, however, companies need a program that does something very specific to the company or location. As noted previously, these "specific" types of applications must be written by programmers using one of the more common languages seen here.

Here is a list of some of the major programming languages and their origin dates:

FORTRAN   FORmula TRANslator. Used for Science and Math. 1956.

COBOL   Common Business Oriented Language. Used in business. Early 1960s.

BASIC	Beginners All-purpose Symbolic Instruction Code. 1964.
Pascal	Another programming language now primarily used for instructional purposes. Originally developed in the late 1960s.
C	Developed by AT&T as a language that could run on different brands of computers. Early 1970s.
C++	Developed in the late 1980s.

By design, software development has separated the procedure and the data into two different entities. In the equation 2 + 3 = ?, the numbers 2 and 3 are the data and the addition (+) function is the procedure. Object-oriented programming keeps the two together as an object, which reduces both space and processing time.

This new type of programming has led to new development environments such as visual basic where applications are made by pointing and clicking and reusing objects rather than writing code line by line.

The latest language, JAVA, developed by Sun Microsystems as a software for *devices*, not just computers, and able to run "anywhere," was developed in the early 1990s. It serves as an example of the shifting nature of programming in that it allows software to be downloaded from the Internet, known as applets, to accomplish a "specific" task. What does the word applets remind you of? If you said small applications, that's it. JAVA is an object-oriented language that is operating system independent, unlike its counterpart ActiveX, which is Microsoft's version of JAVA that can only run in a Windows environment.

Software such as this may run in a network environment, which is further discussed in the next chapter. Common presentation methods such as *HTML* for hypertext markup language and XML for extensible markup language can be used and are detailed in the networking chapter.

5. OPERATING SYSTEMS AND MORE

Between the application software and the hardware, sits the system software, one major part of which is the *operating system (OS)*. By definition, the operating system is "the system software that manages and controls the activities of the computer." (Laudon and Laudon 2002, p. 173) Further, it serves as the "middle person" between the application software and the hardware components. It is the operating system that manages the computer hardware and software while making sure that all tasks are executed correctly. It is the boss.

An operating system has seven main functions:

1. It starts the computer. Here, the operating system works in conjunction with the system *BIOS* (basic input output system) found in ROM. BIOS is a lower level operating system found in personal computers that contain basic start-up functions. It is at this stage where

a power-on self-test, POST, is performed in which the OS reaches out and tests the computer hardware and all its peripherals.

2. It insulates the user from direct hardware contact. Instead of lifting the cover and messing around with all the various components, we are able to make the hardware accomplish tasks via the operating system.

3. It provides a graphical user interface (GUI) to the user. Those icons, folders, files, and words that you are able to point and click on are the points of interaction provided by the operating system.

4. It manages the processing of programs efficiently. Every time an application is opened it uses a certain amount of RAM. Other system software likewise requires memory. Some applications use more memory than others. Computing devices have a finite supply of memory. It is up to the operating system to allocate each application or system software the memory it needs. It is also up to the operating system to allocate and track the memory assigned to each application.

5. It provides advanced processing features. The operating system provides both multitasking and multiprocessing features. Multitasking is just what it sounds like, one user performing a variety of tasks. The computer does not actually do all the things at once. In reality, the operating system assigns processor time to each event in a rotating fashion. It rotates so fast that it appears to be doing many things at once. Multiprocessing is simply the management of more than one CPU. The super computers you may have heard of are moving away from the gigantic units of the past to the linking of many processors under the control of one operating system.

6. It manages input and output devices effectively. From keyboards to printers and the like, the operating system is in control.

7. It manages filing operations and storage. Moving, copying, and storing all fall under its auspices. It is also the operating system that formats a disk for file storage.

Common PC operating systems are shown in Table 3-2.

It is important to note that remnants of older operating systems such as DOS (disk operating system) are still in use today. DOS does not provide the pointing and clicking capabilities seen in today's operating systems but instead requires the user to input commands via the keyboard.

When the operating system communicates with an application or an application communicates with another application, it is done through an application program interface (API). This little known part of a computing environment is important to hospitality managers since different software is used that often must communicate with one another.

With all of the benefits of software comes a downside that warrants further discussion, *viruses*. A virus is an unwelcome piece of software that has

Table 3–2. Sample of Popular Operating Systems

Operating System	Description
Windows XP	Latest offering from Microsoft with multiuser capabilities and improved Web integration
Unix	Nonproprietary operating system popular in the scientific community, among others
Linux	Nonproprietary operating system with available code allowing modification
Mac OS	Macintosh operating system favored by desktop publishers
Palm OS	Operating system for Palm Personal Digital Assistants (PDAs)
Windows CE	Microsoft operating system used for mobile devices

There are many different operating systems in use today and they are evolving from just serving personal computers to serving other electronic devices.

unknowingly been introduced into your computing environment. Most often, it is introduced via the Internet or another network, from a disk, as an e-mail attachment, or in some other creative way. What makes viruses so dangerous is their often destructive nature. Some viruses are harmless and do little more than display a character that wishes you a happy birthday and disappears. This is an example of a macro virus most often found in word processing programs or other application software. Other viruses hide by attaching themselves to system or "boot" software until a specific date and time have been reached and then cause havoc. Damage is usually defined by corrupted files or over-whelmed RAM. More common today are viruses that spread over networks. Knowing the source of files received and having up-to-date antivirus software have been common practice since the U.S. Department of Defense fell victim to a computer virus in 1987.

In any environment security is always an issue. Battling viruses is just one aspect. Others include rights and permissions to your network, discussed in the next chapter.

Today, the computers you typically use are smart computers, meaning they have a CPU and are able to perform their own processing. It was not always this way. In the past, "dumb" terminals, which lacked a CPU, were used to communicate with mainframe computers that did all of the processing and then outputted the results to the dumb terminals. "Dumb" terminals are all but gone; however, the mainframe has remained. This is an example of a legacy system, which is simply antiquated hardware or software that is still in use mainly because the cost of replacing it is too prohibitive. Casinos are great examples. Oftentimes specific programs have been written to run on specific machines including mainframes, such as gambling logarithms and customer databases. Changing platforms would be a huge undertaking and very expensive so the old system is used. Mainframes are large and expensive computers and are still built and used today since they can perform many more tasks than an average personal computer, support thousands of users, and process huge amounts of data.

6. SUMMARY

Management, in any form, requires understanding. Since technology plays such an active role in daily operations and future planning, understanding it is critical. On this road to discovery, you have found out that computers work much the way that other things do—via a system. Data goes into a system, which (and with the aid of people) turns it into useable information. When data moves in digital signals, a computing device will read the high and low points of this signal giving you binary code. From the motherboard to DVD players, you have seen where these binary digits travel and are stored. In conjunction with this hardware, different software is used to manipulate the data and generate information without having to understand machine code. Whether an Internet browser or spreadsheet application, it is quality software that provides the value in the management of information. One type of software, the operating system, coordinates the many different interactions of all the hardware and software devices. With computing becoming more complex over time, more has been required of operating systems. However, even as new components are introduced in the industry, older ones, or legacy systems, are still in use. This chapter has introduced you to some computing essentials that any hospitality manager must understand. With this knowledge, you're ready for the next chapter on networks, where technology is studied in a wider context.

7. CASE STUDY AND LEARNING ACTIVITY

With all the different elements mentioned in this and other chapters, sometimes it is difficult for systems from different companies to work with one another. Let's take a look at how the American Hotel and Lodging Association (AH&LA) is taking on that challenge.

White Paper

Plain English Description of Standards

In years not so long past, hotel staff spent many hours tracking, transcribing, and calculating hundreds of lines of guest information by hand. Armies of night auditors toiled diligently to calculate room charges, restaurant charges, gift shop charges, and other fees, assign them to appropriate guest folios, and post the folios for the front desk staff.

The development of modern database applications, including property management, point of sale, and other systems, has dramatically increased the efficiency with which we can accomplish these tasks, and thereby decreased the labor and effort required to perform these tasks while increasing the accuracy and reliability of the results. Other new systems, such as CRS, RMS, mini-bar, telephone, and in-room-movies, have had the additional benefit of increasing revenues and operating margins.

Unfortunately, many hotels have not been able to take full advantage of these technologies to increase revenues or lower costs. One major reason for this is the significant barrier created by the time, risk, and cost involved in the acquisition and installation of such systems. What many people may not realize is how much of that risk and cost is not related to the basic hardware or software itself, but rather to the cost of developing custom interfaces between new and existing systems.

The basic problem is that no matter how inexpensive or efficient new technologies have made transferring raw data between two systems, if the two systems do not "speak the same language," communication cannot occur. Imagine if you had a French front desk manager, a German reservations manager, a Greek restaurant manager, and none of them were bilingual? This situation has been complicated even further in recent years by a proliferation in the number of systems which hotels and motels use to operate their businesses (and the fact that all of these systems speak many different languages).

Currently, the task of "defeating the language barrier" between a hotel's many systems falls to either the PMS vendor or a third party system integrator. In either case, the result is the same: expensive custom coding which delays new system roll-outs by weeks (if not months) and costs the industry untold thousands of dollars. The cost of these custom interfaces is added into the cost of every new property management, central reservation, or other system that a hotel purchases. In addition to adding tens of thousands of dollars to the cost of those systems, the coding of these custom interfaces increases the time it takes to roll out new systems by weeks, if not months, and greatly increases the risk of system failures and other problems.

Fortunately for hotel and motel operators, the lodging industry is not the first to deal with this type of problem and a ready blueprint for its solution is available in the form of "standards." Just like color television in the 60s and video recorders in the 80s, the development and adoption of standards has become critical to the development and implementation of information systems. Just like the standards which ensure your television set (whether it is a Panasonic, Sony, RCA, or any other brand) can process signals from any brand of VCR, the Hospitality Information Technology Integration Standards (HITIS) are being developed to ensure that your next PMS will be able to "process signals" from any brand of CRS, POS, or other system (as long as it's HITIS compliant).

These new standards, being specifically developed for the hospitality industry, will make the use and implementation of new information systems less expensive, less risky, and less time consuming. Just like televisions and VCRs, hospitality information systems will still not all be created equal, and various HITIS compliant systems will have different features, options, and unique capabilities. HITIS compliant systems will not "all be created equal"; however, they will all be able to be effectively integrated in a minimal amount of time, at a reduced cost, and with less risk than previous systems. A great additional benefit of this is that it will allow system developers to devote more energy toward increasing the number of features their systems provide instead of creating custom interfaces.

Learning Activity

1. Why is it important for different hospitality systems to communicate?
2. What does HITIS stand for?
3. What is the AH&LA?
4. Why are standards important?

8. KEY TERMS

Analog	Dot pitch	Operating system
Binary code	DPI	Peripherals
BIOS	Electricity	Pixels
Bit	Flash memory	RAM
Bus	Floppy disk	Refresh rate
Byte	Gigabyte	ROM
Cache	Hard drive	Signal
CPU	Hardware	System
Data bus path	HTML	Terabyte
Digital	Kilobyte	Virus
Disk drive	Megabyte	Voltage
Display mode	Monitor	

9. CHAPTER QUESTIONS

1. How do people fit into the definition of information?
2. How is data counted?
3. What are the four parts to the CPU?
4. What is flash memory?
5. What are the seven functions of an operating system?

10. REFERENCES

Biow, Lisa. 1993. How to use your computer. Emeryville, CA: Ziff-Davis.

Laudon, Kenneth, and Jane Laudon. 2002. *Management information systems.* 7th ed. Upper Saddle River, NJ: Prentice Hall.

Long, Larry, and Nancy Long. (1998). *Computers.* 5th ed. Upper Saddle River, NJ: Prentice Hall.

CHAPTER FOUR

Networks and Security

CHAPTER CONTENTS

INTERVIEW

Mr. Nicholas Porretta is Director of
Telecommunications at Atlantic City Convention Center, home of the Miss America
Pageant. Mr. Porretta's background includes over twenty years of experience in
casino management and its associated
technology in Atlantic City, New Jersey.

Q: Hi Nick. Thanks for taking the
time. Since security has increased
in importance, let's start there.
What are some of the easiest ways
to make a network more secure?

A: Network security is important. Before anything else, make sure that you
have a good lock on your door to prevent local tampering. Next, the list includes many things such as proper hardware usage and firewall software.
After a thorough analysis is done, a daily operational security plan needs
to be implemented and tested again and again.

Q: The hospitality industry is full of older computers such as mainframes.
How difficult is it managing legacy systems such as these?

A: More and more casinos are moving away from mainframes. Mini and PC-
based platforms now have the processing power to handle the workload;
however, mainframes still exist and are used today. Looking ahead, back-
ward compatibility is a major issue and the answer for most is to migrate
to newer systems.

Q: Wireless is a newer system. Is it a logical and secure option for new networks?

A: Actually no. Although it takes a lot more work, fiber optics is a more secure
option for us. Fiber does require some attention due to its delicate nature.
But if you are migrating from a hard wire network, the infrastructure already exists, so the process is more like a network retrofit and not a new
topology design.

Q: We all know to keep multiple copies of our work. However, in networks, it
is important to keep it "up." When dealing with backup network issues,
what comes to mind?

A: When a network goes "down" organizations lose time and money. For that
reason, companies should maintain redundant links, with frame-relay networks as one example, in case one should fail. Likewise, a virtual private
network over the Internet is an inexpensive alternative that can be employed in an emergency. These are only two options; however, the point remains: A backup plan must be ready and just as in security, it must be
tested and tested again.

Q: Any final thoughts or observations about the direction or importance of networks?

A: From my side of things, I think that the entire tourism and convention business needs to think about creating the seamless, wireless-enabled traveler. Wireless PDAs/cellular phones will become the de facto assistant for the traveler. With security considerations from September 11th taken into account, what we need to create is an environment that allows retransmission on all floors and in all public spaces and especially in the heart of the convention center floor. Too much commerce will be disrupted if we don't logically plan the wireless sea.

1. INTRODUCTION

The opening interview has introduced some key networking terms and concepts that warrant further investigation. The prevalence of networks in the hospitality industry may surprise you. A guest making a room reservation on the Internet, a catering manager e-mailing a client a table seating chart for an upcoming wedding, and simply using the telephone are all examples of networks in use in the industry today. How often you interact with networks, when studied in detail, not only demonstrates their ubiquity, but also their importance in communication as well as in revenue generation.

Additionally, with the ever-increasing availability of real-time information to management and staff, not to mention customer expectations of communication at the property level, network knowledge is vital to remain competitive.

The terms *networks* and *networking* refer to the broad subject of managing computer networks and the information on them. "A network is an any-to-any communication system. This means that any station can communicate with any other station on the network" (Panko 2001, p. 2). Networking is a detailed subject matter. To management, however, there are three primary interest areas.

Security, Performance, and Reliability.   Is it safe, fast, and running are three questions that beg for the answer "yes." Ensuring that the network is protected from unauthorized users while available to authorized users seems logical. In reality, it is a daily challenge. Hacking of a company's Web page or theft of customer data are often nightly news items. Mr. Porretta's comment that security must be "tested again and again" underscores the importance and attention of a secure network. Secondly, performance refers to speed. Slow networks not only lessen communication ability, but can also drive guests away to your competitors. Finally, any system that doesn't function properly or "goes down" is not an option. It has become too much of a worldwide lifeline. How upset do you get when you can't get your e-mail? This chapter will help answer those and other questions as well as acquaint you with networks within the hospitality industry.

2. SMALL NETWORKS

Remember the definition of a data bus path where data moved from one point to another inside the computer? If this is expanded to include data moving to another device such as a printer in the next room, then you have networking. If you operate in an office or school setting and your computer can communicate with other computers or computing devices, you are most likely using a *local area network (LAN)*. The most common type of LAN is based on technology developed by Xerox in the 1970s known as Ethernet for computers in small areas, such as an office or campus. Ethernet LAN technology is the dominant technology for networks at the local level. Although technology has improved, Ethernet's core principles still govern the way that data is exchanged locally. Like all advances in technology, LANs provide a business need. Specifically they do the following:

1. Allow resources to be shared. For example, instead of everyone having a printer, which would be cost prohibitive, the resource is shared by multiple end users.
2. Allow data and information to be shared. Through networks, and unrestricted by geography, all managers can have access to "real-time" company information.

Obviously networks are all about sharing. On the back of a computer you will find openings with multiple pins or sockets. These are known as ports. "A *port* is the combination of a connector plug and internal electronics . . ." (Panko 2001, p. 39). Ports include serial, parallel, and the newer more interoperable, united serial bus (USB). Ports are used mostly for local communication with peripherals such as scanners. In networks, computers need another important device. All stations on a network, such as computers, printers, and kiosks, which are ease-of-use touch screens, are known in networking terms as **nodes.** In order for nodes to "join" a network, a network interface card (NIC) is needed. *Network interface cards (NIC)* provide network access and addressing information. An expansion slot can be seen on the rear or side of most computers. This is where a NIC can be inserted. Each and every NIC has a unique 48-bit address (known as the MAC address) that the manufacturer assigns. This unique addressing allows for efficient sending and receiving of data. With a NIC, your computer is given a new name and joins a larger community.

Just as storage has its own measurement in bytes, data transfer rates have their own form of measurement in bits per second (bps). These bits are the same bits found in binary code. Remember that storage is measured in bytes and data transfer rate, or speed, is measured in bits. Measurement is similar to data storage and comes in the form of kilobits (kbps), roughly 1 thousand bits per second; megabits (mbps), 1 million bits per second; gigabits (gbps), 1 billion bits per second; and finally, terabits (tbps), traveling at 1 trillion bits per second.

What these fast moving bits travel through from computing device to computing device are known as mediums. Currently, there are four main medium options:

1. Twisted pair copper wires. Copper is a great material for signals to travel. The phone line in an average house contains two pairs of copper wires (four wires in total) twisted together and known in networking terms as RJ-11. Each pair represents a line. When you request a second phone line from the phone company, the company simply activates and assigns a number to this second line. In many LANs, a larger form of twisted pair is used. It is known as RJ-45 and contains four pairs of twisted copper wires. The wires are twisted in such a manner that points on the twist can block interference from the other pairs of wires. RJ-11 can handle up to 56 kbps and RJ-45 up to 144 mbps.

2. Coaxial cable. If you have cable television, this is the medium involved. LANs can also utilize this copper core medium with a common data transfer rate of 100 mbps and a current threshold of 2 gbps. Coaxial cable contains one heavy copper wire that is heavily insulated by three different layers to prevent interference.

3. Fiber optics. This is a medium consisting of expensive glass tubes with a protective layer. Here, instead of an electromagnetic signal, pulses of light are used. A flash of light indicates the 1 bit. Absence of light indicates the O bit. Fiber optic technology is very reliable and unsusceptible to electromagnetic interference. Its use at the local level is minimal due to its cost and a lack of expertise. However, its reliability makes it ideal for the larger networks discussed in the next section.

4. Wireless. To be fair, wireless is not a medium but rather a broadcast technology. It is not bound by wires in between points. At the LAN level, wireless technology enables users to operate digitally without being tied to a desk. It is not perfect. Brick walls can be a major obstacle. For that reason, multiple access points, which transmit and receive data for the nodes on the network, are used. Access points at the local level vary in appearance from small cones to plates and are in charge of moving the data across the wireless spectrum. Personal digital assistants, such as palm pilots and television remote controls, use infrared technology and are highly restricted by distance. Transmission speeds of wireless technologies at the local level can reach 14 mbps. We will continue our discussion of "wireless" in the next section, "Large Networks."

Choosing a medium can be both tricky and costly. In addition, certain expertise and knowledge may be required. At the local level, RJ-45, cable, and wireless continue to dominate; however, the cost of fiber optics is declining.

There are many different variations of each medium with their own characteristics and speeds. Whatever the choice, selection of mediums must take into account distance and number of nodes to be served. In fact, the standard setting organization, the Institute for Electric and Electronic Engineers, Inc. (IEEE), has set capabilities and limitations for each medium and its various subsets. This organization has thoroughly tested, studied, and even more crucial, *certified* network mediums among other network technologies. Before any network installation or adoption, you should understand the applicable IEEE standard. An example of what expertise IEEE provides deals with attenuation. *Attenuation* is the weakening of a signal. Signals, like all things moving, eventually tire. They can be cleaned up and strengthened by repeaters and sent back on their way (signal regenerators in an analog environment are called amplifiers). Amplifiers are unable to "clean" signals and often amplify noise as well, making digital transmission more attractive across hard wire mediums. IEEE standards in Ethernet LANs range from 10Base T where the length of a copper wire segment is capped at 100 meters before it needs to be repeated and able to serve up to 1,024 computers at 10 mbps, to 10Base FL where a fiber cable can be used up to 2,000 meters before needing a repeater at 10 mbps. IEEE is the Zagats (the famed restaurant reviewers) of the networking world, and its legwork and knowledge are respected by vendors and managers alike. It is vital to follow IEEE specifications in network purchase and implementation.

The topology of a network refers to its layout such as a straight line or circle. The various nodes are placed on a LAN, utilizing the aforementioned mediums, and come with their own IEEE specifications. There are three principal topologies *used in LANs* and shown in Figure 4-1.

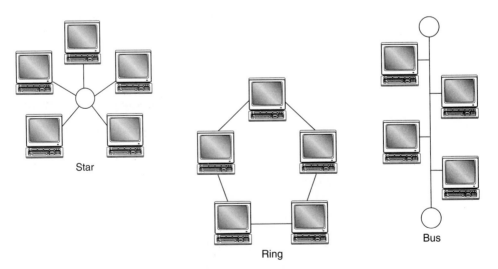

Figure 4-1. Each of the three basic LAN configurations seen here comes with its own IEEE specifications for data transfer.

1. *Bus topology.* All devices are connected to a central cable called the bus or backbone. Bus networks are relatively inexpensive and easy to install for small networks. Ethernet systems use a bus topology.

2. *Ring topology.* All devices are connected to one another in the shape of a closed loop so that each device is connected directly to two other devices, one on either side of it. Ring topologies are relatively expensive and difficult to install; however, they can span large distances.

3. *Star topology.* All devices are connected to a central hub. Star networks are relatively easy to install and manage, but bottlenecks can occur because all data must pass through the hub.

A bottleneck is a device or application that significantly degrades network performance. Bottlenecks are named, oddly enough, from the thin neck of a glass bottle through which the thicker contents from below must pass. A state-of-the-art computer with a fast CPU, abundant memory, and hard disk space accessing a network with an inadequate or slow network card is an example of a network card bottleneck.

A *hub* is a LAN hardware connectivity component that transmits data to the nodes on the LAN. Hubs are known as "chatty" or even "rude" components since they broadcast their messages such as "print" to all the other nodes on the network whether involved or not. Connectivity devices such as these serve as a data "traffic cop" in helping control data flow. Figure 4-2 displays a hub in use.

A *switch* is another hardware connectivity component through which data travels. Unlike hubs, the more expensive switches use the MAC addresses found in the network interface cards of the various nodes to keep the interaction of the involved nodes to only those needed. For example, a print job from a particular computer would only be known to the originating computer and the printer, thereby decreasing "chatty" network traffic and potential bottlenecks.

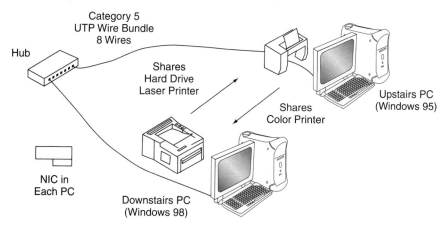

Figure 4-2. Networks allow for sharing of resources and data transfer.

These topologies can also be mixed. For example, a bus-star network consists of a high-bandwidth bus, called the backbone, which connects collections of slower-bandwidth star segments.

Networks are not just hardware. Just as the operating system runs the show of a desktop computer, another system software is the boss here. A *network operating system (NOS)* is system software that routes communications on the network and manages network resources. A NOS commonly resides on a server. A *server* is simply an expensive computer with lots of memory, hard disk space, and a fast CPU (to name a few items) that provides shared resources to the network. The NOS is the boss of the LAN. Since network outage can result in lost revenue and decreased employee productivity and since security is always a concern, often a redundant or backup NOS server is used in case the primary server fails. Additionally, a backup power supply such as diesel generators or off-site power supply arrangements made with a third party are a good idea if the electricity should fail. This is of particular concern for international properties, where infrastructure can be unreliable.

A network server is just one example of a server. Servers can be dedicated to specific tasks in large organizations. Three other servers play a crucial role in LANs and networks at large.

1. A file server is a computer and a storage device dedicated to storing files. Any authorized person on the network can store files on the server. File servers often contain commonly used templates and data for day-to-day activities. An expense report used by management is an example of a file stored here.

2. A print server is a computer that manages one or more printers. Hospitality organizations may use a large number of printers as well as make them available to guests. A large number of printers in use requires a dedicated server.

3. A database server is a system that processes database queries. Most hotel systems are server based where a search engine is integrated into the system to handle simple and complex queries. We will look at databases more closely in Chapter 9.

Today, hospitality organizations predominantly operate in this *client/server (C/S)* architecture with the client being a computing device on the network that requests resources from the server such as files, records, or services. In C/S architecture the processing is distributed, meaning that both the client and server possess a CPU; however, the server's CPU does the bulk of the work. Another architecture making a comeback is peer to peer. In a *peer to peer* architecture, processing is evenly distributed among individual computers and communication is more direct. By definition, components in a peer to peer environment possess the same potential communications capabilities and initiatives. A LAN can operate without a server.

The new kid on the block to local networks is the *private branch exchange (PBX)*. The PBX has long been a part of the hospitality world, namely hotels. For example, a hotel with 500 rooms that all contain phones needs a connection to the phone company. However, purchasing or leasing 500 phone lines plus staff lines would be cost-prohibitive, particularly since at any one time only 30 percent or less of the phone lines are utilized. Enter the PBX. The PBX is used to direct incoming calls to the larger organizational setting. An incoming call goes to the PBX, with say fifty ports, and is directed to the specific location such as a hotel room. An outgoing call is done in reverse. With phone lines already in place in many organizations, PBXs are also used in lieu of LANS. They utilize twisted pair mediums, with RJ-11 being the dominant type. In this network setup, both phones and computers can be incorporated into the local network, saving both time and money. The PBX's interface with the telephone network introduces our next network topic, large networks.

3. LARGE NETWORKS

To understand large networks as well as the evolution of small networks, you need to understand telecommunications. *Telecommunications* is simply long-distance communications. This long-distance communication involves a network you already use, the telephone system.

Alexander Graham Bell accomplished the first voice transmission in 1876. Many years later a nationwide phone network was established and controlled by one company, American Telephone and Telegraph (AT&T) until its breakup in 1984. From there, other companies such as MCI and Sprint entered the picture in competing with AT&T for the long-distance telephone market. Since a 1996 deregulation act, in theory, companies from different industries such as cable companies, broadcasters, and phone companies have been allowed to compete in each other's markets. In addition, state-by-state regulation has increased the competition between your local phone carrier or "baby bells" (the regional companies resulting from the AT&T breakup such as Verizon, Bell South, Pacific Bell, US West, etc.) and the long-distance carriers in their respective markets. Additionally, the dot.com era has brought about different organizations providing phone service known as CLECs (competitive local exchange carriers), which primarily have made their money by leasing phone lines from existing phone companies and selling this access plus additional services to the end user. Only a few CLECs have survived. The traditional carriers still rule the day, for now.

With digital signals replacing and working with analog signals, the ideal of convergence has been realized. *Convergence* is the combining of voice, video, and data into one experience and is also known as media streams. If all the signals are digital, then the vast phone network can communicate with LANs and PBXs in new and exciting global ways.

The efficiency of digital signals can be seen when contrasted to analog signals. Analog signals are still important and utilized in such forms as display and wireless transmission. However, in digital mediums using copper or glass, the digital signal takes up less space, enabling other "media streams" to use the channel. A *channel* is an instrument through which nodes on a network communicate. Think of it as part of a medium. This is accomplished by packet switching. *Packet switching* allows a digital packet to be broken up into "packets" that travel over different routes and reassemble at the end point (Figure 4-3). Packet switching is in contrast to circuit switching of the phone network of old. *Circuit switching* uses analog signals and needs a larger (64k) direct circuit that can not be shared. This 64k is the size of a standard phone line.

The "last mile" or "local loop" of the majority of the telecommunications network still uses analog technology. For instance, the phone in your house most likely uses an analog signal that is converted to digital at the first phone company's building. Conversion to data signals locally is often necessary, as done when accessing the Internet, which will be described shortly. A *modem* modulates a digital signal, converting it to an analog, or demodulates an analog signal back into digital form.

A modem is a type of connectivity device that generally aids in network transmission. Other connectivity devices include multiplexers, which allow a channel to carry multiple media streams, and concentrators, which collect multiple signals until enough are ready to be sent.

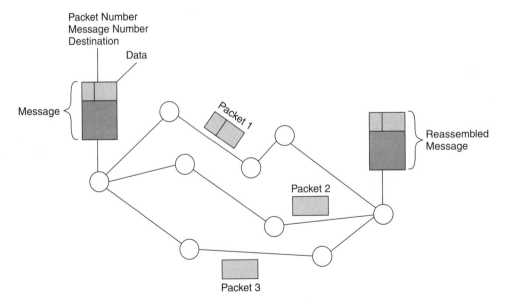

Figure 4-3. In packet communications and packed-switched networks, data grouped into small packets are transmitted independently through various communication channels and reassembled at their final destination.

With the adoption of digital signals, large networks can reap the benefits. The first type of larger networks is the *wide area network (WAN)*. A WAN is a network of larger geography than a LAN, ranging from a couple of miles to the entire world. With hospitality organizations having multiple sites or properties, connectivity and collaboration are needed. This functionality was first enabled by WANs.

Different network services are available in WAN utilization on the mediums discussed earlier. Basically these services or technologies speed up data transmission over long distances. Their transfer rate is dependent on bandwidth. *Bandwidth* is the difference between the highest and lowest point of a signal. It is this available area in between where the data flows on a channel. Remember a channel is part of a medium, and channels and mediums have specific bandwidths that can be improved upon by newer technologies presented in the next selection.

4. TRANSMISSION TECHNOLOGIES

ISDN (integrated services digital network) is popular among residential and small hospitality settings needing "dial up" (dialing) as opposed to fixed high-speed data transfer. ISDN can transmit at 128 kbps and uses existing phone lines. It costs approximately $100 for installation with a $50 per month access fee.

DSL (digital subscriber lines) also operates over existing phone lines but requires special local hardware to digitize the signal. Transmission can reach 1.54 mbps "downstream" (i.e., downloading a Web page) and 128 kbps "upstream" (i.e., sending an e-mail). DSL hardware costs around $200 with monthly fees between $40 and $50.

Cable modems use existing cable lines and can transmit up to 3 mbps downstream. Take heed, often times cable bandwidth is shared among others with cable in your area. Currently cable hardware is slightly more expensive than DSL.

A *T1* connection is a dedicated phone connection with twenty-four of those 64k phone lines. These are often referred to as trunk lines due to the number of channels, and they move the data at 1.54 mbps. A T1 costs about $1,000 a month. In the 500-room hotel example with a PBX with fifty ports, that hotel would most likely have two T1 lines.

From here, other technologies are concerned with the backbone of a network. The backbone is where the bulk of traffic is contained and is concerned with data movement between major carriers. However, the backbone is becoming more local by the day. *Frame relay* is a network service that does not utilize packet switching and uses existing LAN and WAN mediums. It offers speeds of 1.54 mbps. *Asynchronous transfer mode (ATM)* is a newer technology that can incorporate multiple voice, data, and video media streams effectively and efficiently through its structured packaging of data into packets. ATM is seen as the future in blurring the line between LANs and WANs. ATM packages media streams into fifty-three packets and can use multiple mediums (technically it is a switch technology) with speeds approaching 155 mbps over fiber. Other technologies largely used by major telecommunication carriers for intercommunication range from a T3 line with 672 64k lines moving the data at 44 mbps to the synchronous optical networks (SONET) utilizing fiber optics at speeds reaching 2.5 gbps. Larger hospitality properties offering such services as videoconferencing (which takes up a lot of bandwidth) often employ backbone technologies, namely fiber optics.

WANs can be expensive to create and maintain. For that reason, many in need of cross boundary connectivity turn to the major telecommunication carriers and lease their existing networks. Companies such as MCI and AT&T among others offer value-added networks (VAN), which can use any combination of existing mediums and technologies to link corporate and field sites.

5. THE INTERNET

Perhaps the most well-known network is the Internet. The Internet, a network that no one owns outright, links multiple networks and users around the globe. Currently, the Internet primarily uses client/server technology where servers process and provide data to clients. Please see Table 4-1 for some examples of "clients" on the Internet.

As in LANs, peer to peer networking is seen on the Internet as well, with some predicting it to become the dominant architecture. Examples of such networks include music sharing programs such as Kaza.

Like anything else, in understanding the Internet, you first need to understand the rules. In networks, communications between nodes require certain procedures and regulations known as protocols. When you send a letter by standard mail, you follow certain protocols. You place the address of the recipient in the center of the envelope, your return address in the upper left or rear, and the postage in the upper right. This protocol for standard mail is used

Table 4–1.   Examples of Internet Clients

Device	Description
PDA	Personal digital assistants, such as Palm Pilots, with browsers and other applications such as e-mail.
Laptop or PC	General use computers.
IP Telephones	Internet protocol telephones that are being used more frequently.
Game Machine	Game box with Internet access and specific controls.
Television boxes	Uses a television set and wireless keyboard to access the Internet (i.e., WebTV).
Paging/email devices	Devices such as BlackBerrys which facilitate e-mail on the go.

the world over and facilitates communication. Specifically, network protocols are concerned with four main objectives:

1. The type of error checking to be used
2. Data compression method, if any, utilized
3. How the sending device will indicate that it has finished sending a message
4. How the receiving device will indicate that it has received a message

The Internet has its own protocol that is quickly becoming the dominant small and large network protocol worldwide. This protocol, known as *TCP/IP (transmission control protocol/Internet protocol)*, was established by the department of defense in the 1970s. The Internet's foundations lie with the U.S. military. The thought process is that a decentralized network would make any nuclear attack upon the network less significant since network control and storage is not in one place. If the server at your location "goes down," it has almost no impact on the Internet at large. With this "spread out" network in mind, the military came up with the TCP/IP protocol to ensure common practices in communication. TCP/IP has "layers" that govern data flow through the software and hardware of the sending and receiving computing devices.

TCP/IP is not the only network protocol in use today. Different network protocols such as NetBui and IPX are still used. For that reason, hardware devices known as gateways are needed. *Gateways* bridge networks using different protocols.

Today the Internet has been embraced by multiple organizations with quasi-governmental organizations overseeing its operation and address allocation. When you use the Internet, you access it through an Internet service provider (ISP), which has its own servers and IP addresses (provided to them) to be given to customers. IP addresses provide the location of a node or network. An IP address like 198.4.159.10 is a "static" address and is the IP address of *www.prenhall.com*, the publishers of this book. In contrast, a "dynamic" address may be assigned by an ISP to a user dialing into the Internet via an ISP for a short time. It is the ISP through a *domain name server (DNS)* that assigns letters—which are easier to remember (i.e., Prenhall.com)—to IP numerical addresses, although both may be used. Just as the hub and switch controlled the traffic in LANs, a director is needed on the Internet. Communication between nodes here is managed in part by routers. *Routers,* the traffic cops of the Internet, are used to move or "route" data from one node to another based on IP addresses.

The Internet offers many communication tools available to management. Three major ones are the following:

- E-mail
- Instant messaging
- File transfer protocol

Electronic mail (e-mail) has all but surpassed standard mail in communicating with guests, co-workers, and suppliers. E-mail uses software on a client that accesses an e-mail server. A DNS server is likewise used here mapping IP addresses to domain names. For example, the e-mail address of the president of Drexel University in Philadelphia, Papadakis@drexel.edu, begins with a name identifier, Papadakis—his last name—followed by the host name Drexel, and finally its function .edu, signifying an educational institution. Other functions include .gov for government agencies, .com for business, .net for network carriers, and .org for organizations. New functions such as .shop have been approved and may see larger adaptation in the future. E-mail addresses outside the United States end in location identifiers such as .it for Italy and .uk for the United Kingdom.

Instant messaging (IM) usage on the Internet is increasing every day. IM is a form of "chatting" where two or more persons simultaneously connected to the Internet with IM software can engage in live conversations. The two major competitors in the IM market today are AOL (which is an ISP) and MSN (also an ISP and part of Microsoft). Managers separated by distance can use IM for quick communications, ranging from room or table availability to medical emergencies.

File transfer protocol (FTP) is used in both data transmission and retrieval of large amounts of data between two nodes (most likely computers) on the Internet. FTP requires password authentication since a computer is to be "accessed" by another computer. FTP is often unknown to hospitality managers but could be quite useful if a large amount of customer data is needed by a soon to open property "on the fly."

6. THE WORLD WIDE WEB

The World Wide *Web* is the most recognizable communication tool on the Internet. The Web and the Internet are terms often used interchangeably, which is incorrect. The Web is *part of* the Internet. The Web likewise uses the TCP/IP protocol. A *uniform resource locator (URL)* uses the aforementioned DNS server to point to Web resources and addresses such as *www.drexel.edu*. A URL is a Web address. The Web also uses specific formats. *Hypertext markup language (HTML)* is one format of the Web that provides formatting and presentation functionality as well as navigation and search capabilities. Hypertext signifies that the text when clicked will take you to another location on the Web. Recall from Chapter 3, that *extensible markup language (XML)* is a newer form of formatting and presentation on the Web with greater emphasis on the "meaning" of the data. XML allows businesses to interact via the Web with a common understanding of what the data represents. Incorporating these and other functionalities is the vital piece of software used to "surf the net." Applications such as Internet Explorer or Netscape Navigator, which are known as browsers, open the door to Internet communication.

Finding what you need can often be a daunting task on the Web. For this reason, search capabilities on the Web are enabled by search engines that may be part of your browser's functionality or may be located on specific Web pages. Oftentimes, these Web pages are called portals, from the name of windows on a ship. It is through this portal that the Internet experience begins. Popular portals include *Yahoo.com* and *Altavista.com*. We will look at search engines in more detail in the next chapter.

7. INTERNET LAYOUT

Rounding out the earlier discussion of servers is the *Web server*. A Web server is a server in a client/server architecture that contains organizational Web pages and services and is detailed in the next chapter. How much of a company's Web or Internet resources is to be made available is a managerial decision. Oftentimes, private information such as credit card numbers needs to be kept "in house." If part of the company's Internet is used exclusively internally, it is known as an *intranet*. Intranets can harness the Web and other Internet resources to an organization's benefit. For example, if a hotel's benefit plan has changed, employees can check the human resources Web page to find out how salary deductions are affected on an individual basis in "real time." If part of this intranet is shared with outside entities, it is known as an *extranet*. Extranets can be helpful in this fast moving industry. A vendor given access to a restaurant's intranet (thereby making it an extranet) can potentially monitor consumption of a food item. If the inventory level drops below a certain point, a delivery can be initiated right away.

8. LARGE WIRELESS NETWORKS

Because of their mobile nature, wireless networks are on the rise. Wireless transmissions are electromagnetic signals sent through the air. Common wireless transmissions include microwave (The M in MCI stands for microwave) and satellites, and cellular and personal communication services (PCS).

The word microwave causes most to think of the type of oven. When an electromagnetic signal passes through water it is disrupted and generates heat as a by-product. The good–microwave ovens send electromagnetic signals that end up heating water molecules, giving us warm food and drink. The bad–satellite television in rainy Seattle can be problematic since water droplets can upset reception. Microwave usage in networks is highly efficient. In conjunction with satellites that redirect the data to a new location, wireless transmission can move large amounts of data over remote places such as oceans and deserts, making it ideal for remote sites. You will take another look at restaurant enterprise communication in the case study and learning activity in Chapter 6, Restaurant Management Systems.

Cellular technology uses geographic areas that are divided into "cells." Each cell has an antenna or tower to receive a signal transmitted by a cell phone that passes it off to an available channel in the next cell all the way to the end point. Because many antennas and towers are needed to hand off the phone call, coverage can be scarce in remote areas. Additionally, unlike European technology, U.S. cellular technology uses three different protocols hampering connectivity. Lastly, *personal communication service (PCS)* is the all-digital form of cellular technology and allows for more volume.

For obvious reasons, the Web has embraced wireless technology as well. Specifically for the hospitality industry, the technology can be used to pinpoint a potential customer's location and provide that customer with nearby restaurants, hotels, stadiums, etc.

From a managerial perspective, executives are no longer dependent on being at their desks to access information. The wireless Web in the United States uses the *wireless markup language (WML)*, which is part of the larger protocol suite *wireless application protocol (WAP)*. Through a microbrowser or minibrowser on a PDA, cell phone, or other wireless Web-enabled device, the World Wide Web can be accessed in a scaled down version. Japan and, to some degree, Europe use the I-Mode protocol for the wireless Web, again raising the issue of compatibility.

9. OTHER NETWORK USAGE IN THE ENTERPRISE

Information access, communication and collaboration, and e-commerce are all vital components of networks. E-commerce is discussed in detail in Chapter 5. Aside from the aforementioned benefits, networks also provide organizations with standard communication services such as faxes, voice mail, and *electronic data interchange (EDI)*. EDI technology came before the Web and still enables companies to electronically conduct business over networks, resulting in lower transaction costs and paperwork. Currently, much of the bulk purchasing and aggregate financial transactions in hospitality use EDI. EDI provides a structure that the parties involved understand and is used primarily over private networks due to the sensitivity of the financial transactions. With the advances and common structure of such Web technologies as XML, EDI is moving to the Internet platform.

10. SECURITY

Security issues are a great concern when using networks and the Internet. Meeting this need, newer classes of networks using Internet technology have sprung up providing businesses with a secure way of conducting transactions in such a public environment. Currently, Internet service providers offer *virtual private networks (VPN)*. A VPN provides a secure connection to different sites of an enterprise over the Internet. Specific protocols are used that "wrap" data transfer, inhibiting penetration from unauthorized users. With innovations such as this, secure transmissions are further enabled. Now companies can offer telecommuting options to their workers. A popular example is telecommuting. This allows off-site workers comparable access to the same data and network speeds while at home or away from the office.

The degree of access, if at all, given to others using a network can be a tough situation. Granting and restricting access to Internet resources is a piece of software known as a firewall. *Firewalls* prohibit unauthorized users from accessing Internet/intranet/extranet resources through user verification and passwords. Advanced firewalls also monitor Internet intrusions and attacks. A popular form of attack is a "denial of service attack" where routers and other devices on the Internet are co-opted and directed to a specific Web site. The volume overwhelms a Web server and prohibits other users from accessing its resources, rendering it useless. Due to the Internet's designed public nature, oftentimes the Web server is put out in front and separated from other network resources. The area between the Web server and the rest of the network is given a military sounding name, the demilitarized zone (DMZ). Use of firewalls and placement of servers often dictate how remote workers can and cannot access company resources such as files and e-mail.

Firewalls play an important role in virus protection. Recall from Chapter 3 that a virus is an unwelcome piece of software that has unknowingly been introduced into your computing environment. Good network administrators will update their firewalls daily against the malicious pieces of software. Smaller hospitality organizations with network connections provided by DSL or cable modems do not realize that their connection is continuous, making their computer vulnerable. Firewalls must be used. It is often surprising to organizations that use advanced firewalls with monitoring capabilities how often an attempted or successful intrusion happens on their network.

Communication between different networks has its own security issues, particularly when the Internet is used for such privileged data as credit card numbers. In addition to the methods used by VPNs, scrambling of messages, known as *encryption,* is often necessary to keep transmissions private. Encryption involves a mathematical operation that assigns different values to a key. Given the discussion of 8 bits representing a specific key, encryption assigns more 1s and 0s algorithmically to each key to mask the actual keys used, and thereby the entire message. The number of additional 1s and 0s used represents the strength of the encryption method used. Common cost-effective encryption methods used today are 128 bit. Luckily, there comes a point where it is cost-prohibitive to attempt to crack higher encryption methods. It simply takes too much processing power and time. Unfortunately, technological advances in encryption are also taking place in the nefarious encryption cracking software realm.

Security issues are more local than one might think. Studies show that most breaches or thefts of company data are done internally. Remember the opening interview? A locked door and restricted access can solve many problems. On the other hand, external threats are often at a lower level than you may think. They are enabled by telephone tricks where one party calls another and tricks that party into giving access information. This is an example of so-cial engineering. Oftentimes, hackers, or those who penetrate a network, use social engineering methods to get in the door of a network and wreak havoc on Web sites or illegally obtain data. For these reasons, network administrators concern themselves daily with a host of issues. The first issue deals with user authentication. Currently, user identifications and passwords are commonly used. Other tools include rights and permissions of data. For example, a house-keeper is not given access to sales data, nor is a member of the wait staff given client home phone numbers. By restricting who has access, many problems can be avoided. In the age of employee empowerment, data access must be studied constantly by all levels of management.

Advanced identification technology such as iris (eye) and fingerprint scanning along with facial recognition take away many of the vulnerabilities of password and user IDs. Unfortunately, cost continues to be a factor in a labor-intensive industry such as hospitality. That cost is expected to drop, and given the new need for security, you should see wide implementation of a range of new security measures and systems.

11. FORWARD LOOKING ISSUES IN HOSPITALITY

In addition to teleconferencing, other network technologies beneficial to other industries present opportunities and challenges to hospitality. For one, video-conferencing allows distant and mobile workers the opportunity to interact with each other from afar. *Videoconferencing* enables individuals to communi-cate visually via a camera attached to a computer, as well as verbally (next sec-tion). In addition, access to company resources is also in "real time" decreasing the need to travel to a specific location for meetings or conferences. In a post-September 11th environment, this presents many challenges for our industry. If one is able to communicate from afar, then the revenue-generating resources including airline seats, hotel rooms, and meals are jeopardized. Conversely, if these services are not made available to hotel guests who wish to stay in con-tact using videoconferencing technology, a competitor may steal your guests.

Wireless networks offer another challenge. Wireless networks, as dis-cussed in the interview, have a greater possibility of being breached by unau-thorized personnel. Before 9/11, wireless check-in and out via PDAs were the talk of the industry. Now, no one wants to give access to company resources to a potential terrorist.

On the same note and due to an executive order signed by President George W. Bush, organizations are forbidden from doing business with over 100 suspected terrorist organizations. Allowing anonymous individuals the ability to use resources is now no longer a possible option; it is against the law.

Future capabilities need not be all bad. Currently making its way through the hospitality industry is *voice over Internet protocol (VOIP)*. VOIP allows a prop-erty to benefit from convergent technologies, which can result in an actual cost savings. VOIP is simply the packaging and conversion of analog voice into digital signals. Much of the software and hardware in place can handle voice over IP networks, mainly the Internet. Given that these IP networks can already handle other types of digital media such as data and video, the addition of voice seems only logical. One problem exists. Circuit switching and the old reliable phone network where a 64k dedicated path is opened provide better voice quality versus the packet switching of digital networks. If an e-mail takes a couple minutes to reach its destination over multiple paths and routers, it is okay. If parts of a voice conversation arrive late or not at all, the conversation is compromised. When this happens in the VOIP world, it is known as *jitter*. Likewise VOIP, also known as telephony, is dependent on high-speed Internet access. Voice digitized packets cannot operate efficiently in slow or unreliable mediums or transmission technologies. Current assumptions place ATM (asynchronous transfer mode) as the transmission technology that carries IP packets on its back across the world as the solution. However, the "local loop" or "last mile" proves to be the Achilles heel to VOIP success. This problem is currently being solved by local upgrades and its widespread adaptation is only years away and needs to be understood by management. Luckily, since it is digital, this chapter's content applies 100 percent.

12. SUMMARY

Network understanding is now a required tool for any hospitality manager. From small networks, found in a restaurant, to larger global hotel communication systems, network knowledge is a must. When a network "goes down" or is not used properly, lost revenue and unhappy customers can result. Executives meet this challenge by first applying the right combination of network topography, mediums, and transmission technologies to their organization. With the proper foundation in place, Internet offerings such as e-mail, Instant Messaging, and the World Wide Web can be used to their fullest potential. Other networks, such as Telephone, Electronic Data Interchange, and Wireless systems are equally important, and can be used to benefit the organization and guest alike. Growing in importance by the day is network security. Up to date firewall software and data encryption are a good start, particularly when considering that customers' personal information and credit card numbers make up much of the network data. A true security strategy including employee policy and procedures, which is tested often, serves as a true complement to any hardware or software. No matter what organization you are in, networks require constant attention.

13. CASE STUDY AND LEARNING ACTIVITY

Cracker Barrel

Cracker Barrel implements VSAT technology for improved customer service, cost-effective employee training, and quality communications. When the first Cracker

Barrel Old Country Store opened in 1969, it included a restaurant, a retail store, and a gas station. Almost thirty years later, the restaurant chain no longer sells gas, but has added satellite technology to better serve its guests, cost-effectively train its employees, and reliably facilitate quality communications between headquarters and its 365 nationwide stores.

The company previously relied on a standard dial-up network to process credit card and personal check payments. However, as new stores opened and the number of guests grew annually, Cracker Barrel quickly realized the need for a communications network to better address speed and bandwidth capacity. The company decided on satellite technology and implemented a very small aperture terminal (VSAT) network. VSAT satellites have small antennas that are able to broadcast to wide regions. During the evaluation process, Cracker Barrel discovered that VSAT networks could more quickly facilitate credit card and personal check authorizations than could other networking alternatives. At the same time, VSATs could also satisfy the company's bandwidth requirements for exchanging data between all 365 stores and corporate headquarters in Lebanon, Tennessee.

"We kept going back to the VSAT technology during our search because we looked at it from our guests' point of view," says Mike Matheny, Cracker Barrel's CIO. "Our stores are almost exclusively located on Interstates, so the majority of guests are traveling. They don't want to stand around and wait longer than necessary at the checkout counter."

Basing its ultimate decision on cost as well as bandwidth capacity and quality of network reliability, Cracker Barrel has implemented Hughes Network Systems' (Germantown, Maryland) VSAT technology at its headquarters and at each of the corporate-owned stores. The simple VSAT network architecture includes an HNS personal earth station located at each store and a hub earth station at corporate headquarters.

Cracker Barrel's previous concerns about a reliable communications network were laid to rest with the VSAT technology. "Some of our stores are located in rural areas and we were concerned about being dependent on the local telephone company for our connections," says Matheny. "The fear of busy signals, line breaks, and natural disasters all played a part in the decision to move to a satellite-based solution. With our VSAT network, we get reliable service 24 hours a day."

In addition to faster payment authorizations, the VSAT network established a wide area network (WAN) for Cracker Barrel, enabling it to develop an intranet and provide company e-mail capabilities. In the past, stores around the country received software updates and other important information on CDs or floppy disks mailed from the Lebanon headquarters. Today, mission-critical information is exchanged electronically in real time via the VSAT network.

Further, VSATs have the bandwidth to support interactive video broadcasting without overloading the network's capacity capabilities. By using video, Cracker Barrel brings its 40,000 employees together at the same time for meetings with key company executives, such as its president, Ron Magruder, to discuss new products, training, and other issues. Its interactive capabilities allow employees to ask questions and receive immediate responses.

The VSAT network also enables Cracker Barrel to cost-effectively address its training needs. To demonstrate special preparation procedures for new menu items, the company uses the video broadcast to train the chefs, rather than send a trainer out to each store. The company plans to expand its use of video in the future to combat the high turnover in the restaurant and retail industry with an increased interactive training program.

"VSAT technology has enabled Cracker Barrel to consolidate and manage its communications network into one resource rather than a variety of vendors," says Matheny. "Cracker Barrel will continue to provide its down-home country cooked meals, but it will also continue to expand the use of VSAT technology to better serve guests and employees."

Learning Activity

1. What is VSAT?
2. Cracker Barrel said it designed the network with the guest view as a priority. How important is the end user in the selection of technology?
3. How will VSAT technology better serve employees?
4. Do you see any security issues with satellite based computer networks? Explain.

14. KEY TERMS

ATM	Firewall	Network
Attenuation	Frame relay	Packet switching
Bandwidth	FTP	PCS
Bus topology	Gateway	Peer to peer
Cable Modems	HTML	Port
Cellular	Hub	Private Branch
Channel	Intranet	Exchange (PBX)
Circuit switching	ISDN	Ring topology
Client/Server (C/S)	Jitter	Router
Convergence	Local Area Network	Server
Domain name server	(LAN)	Star topology
(DNS)	Modem	Switch
DSL	Network interface	T1
EDI	card (NIC)	TCP/IP
Encryption	Network Operating	Telecommunications
Extranet	System (NOS)	Uniform Resource
	Networking	Locator (URL)

Videoconferencing   WAP   WML

Virtual Private   Web server   World Wide Web
  Network (VPN)   Wide Area Networks   XML
VOIP   (WAN)

15. CHAPTER QUESTIONS

1. What is the difference between a hub and a switch?
2. Describe the different mediums used in data transmission.
3. What is the main difference between client/server and peer to peer networks?
4. What is an extranet and how can it be used advantageously in hospitality?
5. How is FTP used?
6. What is social engineering?
7. How can management make a network secure?
8. What ramifications does videoconferencing have on our industry?
9. What network issues should small organizations consider?
10. How is network understanding related to hospitality management?

16. REFERENCES

Davidson, Johnathan, and James Peters. 2000. *Voice over IP fundamentals.* Indianapolis: Cisco Press.

Laudon, Kenneth, and Jane Laudon. 2000. *Management information systems.* 6th ed. Upper Saddle River, NJ: Prentice Hall.

Panko, Raymond R. 2001. *Business data communications and networking.* 3d ed. Upper Saddle River, NJ: Prentice Hall.

Weisman, Carl J. 2000. *The essential guide to RF and wireless.* Upper Saddle River, NJ: Prentice Hall.

CHAPTER FIVE

E-Commerce

CHAPTER CONTENTS

INTERVIEW

Jerry Reece is the managing director of Travel and Transportation Practice for Dimension Data, and is responsible for the practice's engagements. His clients include Marriott International, Cendant Corporation, United Airlines, *USA Today*, Walt Disney World, Carlson Wagonlit Travel, Travel Planners, Quikbook, American Express Travel, Eurostar, and Railtrack.

Prior to joining Dimension Data, Jerry spent eight years with Andersen Consulting (now known as Accenture), where he worked primarily with clients in the Transportation and Travel Services practice. He also spent three years working with the U.S. federal government, with a primary focus on system integration and reengineering initiatives.

Q: Hi Jerry. Can you describe your company's existing technologies, platforms used, and philosophies?

A: Dimension Data is technically agnostic and looks to implement the tools and technologies that are right for each client. The Dimension Data Process™ integrates business strategy, leading-edge technology, and creative design services into a formal methodology. We use this methodology to guide our clients and the Dimension Data teams through a project from planning to deployment, including the selection of tools and technologies needed. The process is used to define schedules, establish resource requirements, speed development time, and ensure that all stakeholders buy-in throughout the process. Our process is a synergistic method of translating business goals into a quality solution, and it is geared toward minimizing the risk of technical or competitive obsolescence faced by companies using the Internet.

Q: Is there a generic strategy for e-business or is each company that unique?

A: We focus on identifying the "right" strategy for each client, given their unique needs. Our technology consultants work alongside our creative and strategy disciplines to architect solutions. Utilizing a "fit-for-purpose" framework, we work with our clients to determine the appropriate technical architecture and channels necessary to meet their e-business goals and requirements. Our technology-agnostic approach and deep understanding of emerging communications channels provide our clients with a flexible and scalable multichannel solution, delivering sustainable competitive advantage.

Q: That's great. Switching gears, what is the next wave of this Internet revolution?

A: The "next wave" is one that most companies feel they should have provided more focus on originally: namely, interacting with customers in a consistent method across all available channels. While most companies do a good job of interacting with customers on their Internet sites, some companies still have a long way to go. Of course, most do a very poor job of providing consistent information across their channels, including call centers and onsite (e.g., hotels, airports, rental stations, etc.). Full customer interactive solutions that touch the customer everywhere the customer requires and that integrate information across channels is not necessarily a new idea, but one that most companies are finally waking up to. Everyone must remember that customer service can be a true differentiator. From a purely technical standpoint, many people still look at wireless technologies as the next big thing. While wireless can be an important channel, especially in the travel industry, we consider this to be one channel that must be implemented as required by customers. Other advanced technical channels such as interactive TV and IP telephony also have potential value, and need to be examined as well.

Q: Okay, let's talk a little bit about the evolution of e-commerce. We are starting to see a lot of alliances being formed. Are e-business relationships shifting from commerce to collaboration? And if so, why?

A: The fragmented and intermediary nature of the travel industry made it a prime candidate for early adoption of Internet technology. Today, the Internet has successfully manifested itself as a critical tool for conducting everyday travel transactions, putting consumers closer together with suppliers than ever before, so yes we are moving to collaboration. Yet those same requirements for online information availability and delivery have also raised the bar for customer service, further solidifying that in the travel industry, the customer is king. To remain competitive, travel suppliers and online agencies alike must streamline back-end systems and reduce costs in order to refocus their organizations on customers' needs.

Q: After all of the bells and whistles found in e-commerce such as personalization, cross selling, and up selling, what can hospitality organizations expect from e-commerce such as yours?

A: Innovation and speed-to-market. Dimension Data maintains relationships with industry leaders, best-of-breed software and hardware companies, and premier communication vendors to gain access to the latest technologies, premier technical support, advanced training opportunities, product certifications, and co-marketing efforts.

Q: Sounds good. However, given a cost-cutting atmosphere, why should companies pay attention to e-commerce?

A: Travel companies are protecting themselves from future economic downturns by focusing on acquisitions, watching reserves, and ensuring that core businesses stay profitable. Yet, applying Internet, wireless, and other advanced technologies to core businesses remains imperative for increasing efficiency, decreasing cost, growing revenue, and cultivating customer relationships. More than ever, companies need outside professionals with industry acumen and a deep understanding of technology to prioritize e-business initiatives and to help them attain the ultimate vision for their online and offline services, the ability to deliver "everything to everyone everywhere."

Q: Thanks Jerry. In closing, what are the keys to e-transformation success?

A: One, plan. Identify project goals and objectives and create a roadmap for meeting them. It is imperative that client stakeholders understand and buy into these goals and objectives. Lack of alignment within a client organization is a common reason for project failure. Two, clearly understand the client's requirements. Three, design. Invent a solution of components to deliver those requirements. Four, develop. Build and test solution components. Five, deploy. Install applications and implement processes. Six, conclude. Hand over the project to the client, celebrate success, and close the project.

1. INTRODUCTION

E-commerce transactions are merely adopting the latest and greatest communication tool—the Internet. Just as the invention of movable type and the telephone revolutionized the way people communicated and conducted business, so too does the world's network (Internet). In another generation, the Internet will be taken for granted as it is absorbed into society's expectations. This exciting creation of a new way of doing things is being improved upon every day. Electronic commerce is the newest wave of this enhanced communication paradigm. It improves guest satisfaction in hotels, increases sales in restaurants, and helps hospitality organizations manage costs. E-commerce, e-business, e-bids—the Internet is a powerful tool for our times.

The interview with Jerry Reece of Dimension Data shows how important the hospitality industry views e-commerce. Details of how Dimension Data helped Marriott will appear later in the chapter. Doing business online is becoming a necessary tool in the quest for higher profits and lower expenses. Unfortunately, just posting your hospitality unit to the Web is not enough to succeed in the highly competitive world of e-commerce. From room nights to restaurant equipment, corporate buyers and consumers will concentrate their spending on where they can find what they want and need in the most efficient and satisfying ways. Along with the logic and systems behind e-commerce, this chapter will detail how to satisfy the wants and needs of any customer successfully on the Internet.

From a management perspective, the newness of the Internet presents a challenge. Its speed, reach, and operability can be both confusing and intimidating. Basically, *e-commerce* is doing business over the Internet. It is now a management tool, and you are required not only to understand it, but also to apply it to your daily working life.

2. BEGINNINGS

The ubiquity of the Internet has changed the way we do business forever. The Web, platform-independent media, and browsers are making communication easy. This has enabled the Internet to become a powerful new channel for marketing and purchasing. With the maturation of e-commerce, businesses and individuals have already taken advantage of a global, low cost, and efficient environment to conduct business and communicate.

At its core, electronic commerce is divided into two basic types. The first, *business to business (B2B)*, is simply defined as businesses dealing with their counterparts over the Internet. Online bulk purchasing and payments are examples of B2B. On the other side, when an individual buys a book or makes an airline reservation, this is an example of *business to consumer (B2C)* commerce where a customer purchases a product or service "online" from a business.

Initial e-commerce applications began with online advertising, catalog, and retail order fulfillment systems. As one of the first industries to embrace Internet technology, the travel industry continues to evolve through online booking, travel personalization, and customer self-service. Further, travel and transportation companies are now looking to the Internet for improved communication and cross-enterprise collaboration with partners, suppliers, and even competitors— otherwise known as *collaboration commerce* (c-commerce). Two very important technology trends, the proliferation of wireless devices and the emergence of XML (extensible markup language), will ease the way in which information is delivered to consumers and will have a greater and even more rapid impact on the travel industry than did the World Wide Web. As e-commerce applications mature, other hospitality units (food and beverage, lodging, and culinary) can look forward to good bottom-line results due to two factors loved by any shopper— lower prices and higher availability. The online market now embraces this dynamic commerce—the buying and selling of goods and services through flexible pricing mechanisms that change in real time with supply and demand. With these advantages, the hospitality industry is moving towards a more frictionless, efficient, and worldwide market due to e-commerce.

Past Obstacles

For corporations, the new online e-commerce world mitigates three obstacles:

1. Geographic fragmentation
2. High cost of information exchange
3. Excessive inventory and purchasing

Commerce Fragmented By Geography.   Previously, due to geographic dispersion, many hospitality organizations found their markets limited to those areas in which they had physical offices. Customers outside coverage areas did not know about those properties and/or units, nor were they easily able to conduct business, such as making reservations, with those firms. On the B2B side, without the Internet many buyers (purchasing agents) and sellers were not easily able to acquire the product information needed to make purchasing decisions. With the Web's worldwide reach, that information is now at the agent's fingertips. Eliminating geographic and market fragmentation as a barrier to hospitality commerce is a key catalyst in facilitating online B2B and B2C commerce. Geography is no longer a limiting factor, which may mean more work for the sales department but higher commissions.

Expensive Information Exchange.   Most interactions between businesses are complex as well as labor- and information-intensive. Getting the right information to the right entity at the right time is a challenge in any small or large hospitality organization, let alone between multiple franchise or complex chain enterprises.

As you know from the networking chapter, e-mail, instant messaging, wireless blackberry devices, and Palm Pilots with Internet connections among others, have eased this burden. Now if your boss, a customer, or a colleague 3,000 miles away wants to find you, he or she has even more options. With the lower costs of Internet communications as compared to standard and express mail, businesses are seeing the cost savings every day. The Internet offers this efficiency for both B2B and B2C interactions in addition to collaboration opportunities. The Internet is the "killer platform" of information exchange and therefore e-commerce. It enables separate organizations or business units to function as vertically or horizontally integrated virtual enterprises, while providing the benefits of economies of scale and specialization.

Excessive Inventory and Purchasing.   The last obstacle is the challenge of finding other revenue sources for excess inventory. Supply chains are often bloated with excess volume due to the difficulty in predicting demand for the right quantity and mix of products. Previously, food and beverage suppliers had little information about when, how, and why their customers used their products. Production was based on history and "gut feeling." Buyers had difficulty quickly finding alternative sources during shortages. Now, purchasing agents with the ability to harness the power of the Internet can take advantage of the information it provides to both the property and the end customer, and they can "purchase better." Data can be used to collect and share information. Further, it facilitates the adjustment to changing market conditions further discussed in the database chapter (Chapter 9).

"Without a doubt hospitality organizations that 'log on' can immediately see the results. With 39 percent of restaurateurs using online services, e–procurement in the food and beverage sector of hospitality is up 28 percent from the year 2000, and overall average food costs are dropping 3 percent for new users of e-commerce."*

---

*"First Restaurant Industry Technology Study," *Hospitality Technology Magazine* (2000).

Just what kind of hospitality products are bought online? Here are the top eleven most purchased items, by category, by organizations using online procurement.

Kitchen equipment	45%
Paper disposable products	40%
Tabletop supplies	39%
Canned /Dry goods	37%
Frozen goods	31%
Chemicals	29%
Beverages	25%
Fresh meat, fish, and poultry	23%
Fresh produce	23%
Bakery products	22%
Dairy products	19%

3. CATALYSTS FOR ADAPTATION

What brought on e-commerce? According to the Goldman Sachs Survey 1.0, conducted in August, 1999, there are five catalysts stimulating adoption of the B2B/B2C solutions:

1. Increasing experience with Web technologies
2. Consolidation of industry standards
3. Simplification of application technologies
4. Increasing stickiness in B28 solutions
5. Cost savings and revenue opportunities

Increasing Experience with Web Technologies

The Web has gone from a curiosity to a commonplace tool with most hospitality entities now having a presence on it. Further, many hotel, franchise, and chain businesses use the Web to disseminate information and conduct internal company business. Using the Web is now a part of the business world. "Everyday" applications such as word processing and spreadsheet software are now joined by Web browsers.

Consolidation of Industry Standards

Industry standards are an important ingredient in unlocking the full economic potential of any technology. The *Organization for Advancement of Structured*

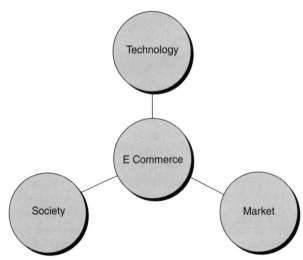

Figure 5-1. E-commerce at its most basic level is often seen as a synthesis of society, the market, and technology.

Information Standards (OASIS) adopted extensible markup language (XML) to support the business-to-business paradigm. XML was designed from the start as a markup language that combines power and flexibility with an easy-to-learn syntax. Developed as an open, extensible, self-describing language, extensible markup language is a standard that allows data sharing across different applications and platforms. Applications come from many different sources, so a common link is advantageous. XML uses good design techniques, and interfaces directly with other XML-enabled applications, Web applications, and database systems. With extensible markup language standards in place, business-to-business technology is likely to fully penetrate e-commerce markets and hospitality units in particular.

Simplification of Application Technologies

Early entrants to e-commerce had to internally build applications to support their e-business initiatives. Now, the evolution of standards has enabled companies to purchase various customizable Web applications (aside from browsers) to address their e-commerce needs. As most vendors are on version 6 or 7 of their software, maturation of application technologies has already occurred, giving businesses another easy to use Internet tool.

Increasing Stickiness in B2B Applications

Stickiness is the ability of a business to retain customers. Customer retention is everything in hospitality. As e-markets become more tightly integrated with e-infrastructure, they become an integral part of day-to-day operations. The goal of the e-infrastructure is to retain customers by affording them simplified online transactions. In fact, studies show that if you have a good experience making a restaurant reservation on a Web site, for example, you will return next time.

The perfect example of B2B stickiness is the model employed by Marriott International and Dimension Data.

Dimension Data created and developed an online branding strategy for Marriott.com to serve its customers with worldwide travel information and reservation capabilities. As a result of this alliance, Marriott International's e-commerce rollout allowed them to accomplish the following:

- Increase sales and reduce booking costs through direct online reservations for more than 1,800 properties worldwide
- Position Marriott.com as the premier e-travel resource
- Drive consumer adoption, loyalty, and use with a convenient and intuitive interface

A well-known brand name with an easy-to-use Web site is looked upon favorably by consumers using the Internet. If the customer knows the company and "likes" the Web site, more business or "stickiness" can result. With these benefits in place, Marriott is well positioned for improved customer retention and attainment.

Cost Savings Resulting from Large-Scale Implementations

Cost savings are an important driver in business and, therefore, information technology implementation. Companies are adopting business-to-business solutions because they provide a positive return on investment (ROI). ROI will be discussed more thoroughly in the final chapter.

Goldman Sachs Investment Research notes:

> Purchasing staff spend 74 percent of their time on administering transactions and only 7 percent of their time developing strategic outsourcing partners. Thus, only 35 percent of contracts are centrally negotiated, with a high percentage of purchases sourced from unauthorized suppliers. By using more B2B implementations, we estimate that B2B solutions can reduce the process costs between 10 percent and 25 percent thereby reducing total cost between 3 percent and 12.5 percent. (Joyce, 2001)

When the previous savings in food costs are combined with the additional savings in transactions, it is apparent that significant bottom-line benefits can result from e-commerce usage.

4. OTHER E-COMMERCE BUSINESS MODELS

Efficiency in operations and cost reductions are definite benefits of e-commerce. E-commerce also presents several opportunities for creating new revenue streams. Aside from B2B and B2C, three other major types of revenue opportunities in e-commerce—advertising, auction-driven transactions, and e-markets—provide businesses with new moneymaking opportunities.

Advertising

Perhaps the most obvious, if not distracting, aspect of e-commerce and Web sites in general is advertising. Everyday usage of the Internet yields a barrage of advertisements for a great number of products and services. Ads are presented in many ways, such as those that move and blink or those that are stationary with colorful backgrounds and logos. Often the end user is forced to acknowledge these advertisements by "clicking to clear." This form of forced engagement is not new. You must still turn past advertisements that you do not wish to see in newspapers and magazines, and even credit card companies force you to listen to advertisements before accessing account information over the telephone. Whatever your view of advertising online, companies in the advertising business are financially dependent on making sure that their advertisements are being seen.

Currently, advertising revenues are suffering, with some estimates stating that only some 2 percent of online ads are actually "clicked on." With advertising blocking software becoming more available, this particular business model has many challenges ahead.

Auctioning

The Internet created a market that brings sellers and buyers together instantly. The auction format of e-commerce is likely to become increasingly popular. Sites like Expedia.com continue to grow exponentially since they enhance efficiency while maximizing the return for the buyer and seller. Many companies that conduct auctions take a percentage of the revenues from auction-driven transactions. These "third parties," or clearing companies, usually charge the seller a commission fee based on a percentage of the total revenue generated at auction. This is exactly what e-Bay does.

E-markets

In addition to direct procurement, there also exists an opportunity to buy and sell vertically and horizontally through e-markets. E-markets provide an industry-specific site where one may purchase particular goods or services. Everyday products, such as automobiles and homes, have e-markets dedicated to them and many are experiencing tremendous growth. Within the hospitality industry, there are many e-markets, and not just in lodging. In the restaurant industry, for example, there are in fact *specific* sites dedicated to *specific* products needed by any manager. Examples include *EC Food Online,* which offers bakery goods and other kitchen products, and *FastParts,* which sells convection reflow ovens and other equipment.

5. E-COMMERCE TECHNOLOGIES

The technology behind e-commerce provides the necessary infrastructure and systems to properly enable online initiatives. At its heart is the application software. Let's discuss the key aspects.

Servers

In e-commerce, servers play an important role. The first type is the **Web server,** which primarily stores Web pages, tracks usage known as "hits," and provides the requested Web pages to the end user. It is the server software and additional functionality of the server (faster processor, more memory and hard disk space, etc.) that enable it to perform its task. Common Web server software includes Microsoft's Internet Information Server and Netscape's Enterprise Server. Dictating the size of the server is the amount of expected traffic it is to handle. In high traffic organizations, redundant servers are employed. For business transactions, **Electronic Commerce Server** software is used to handle everything from online reservations to purchasing. It is this software running on the server that provides links to payment systems such as credit card interfaces and includes "storefront" listings such as availability, price, and shipping information. Additionally, this software links to other systems and provides the user with the "shopping cart" utility seen on many Web sites.

Content Management and Performance

In the fast-moving world of the information age, keeping a Web site "current," particularly if it contains thousands of dynamic pages, can be a daunting task. Fortunately, content management software helps businesses keep up-to-date. *Content management software* gives companies the tools to manage and update their Web material. Changes can be made to the entire site through single entries rather than changing the content page by page. Other software functions include *performance monitoring software,* which is primarily concerned with how quickly a Web page is downloaded and making sure that all links to other Web sites are active.

Consumer and Business Tracking

E-commerce technology is also concerned with tracking customers' trends and behavior before, during, and after their visits. With this business intelligence, companies can adjust and personalize their offerings to each user. Popular technologies used include *collaborative filtering,* where a customer's purchases and behaviors are compared to other customers' interests to predict further purchases. Amazon.com's "Customers who bought this also enjoy . . ." is an example of collaborative filtering. Other technologies include *clickstream tracking,* which records exactly where and when a customer clicks on a Web site and what sites he or she visited before and after. Clickstream tracking has come under much controversy due to its secretive and intrusive nature. If used ethically and correctly, proper monitoring can help businesses further understand their customers' spending habits and behavior.

6. E-MARKETING

Search Engines and Strategy

E-marketing plays an important role for hospitality organizations using the Internet for business. Simply having a Web site is not enough with the thousands

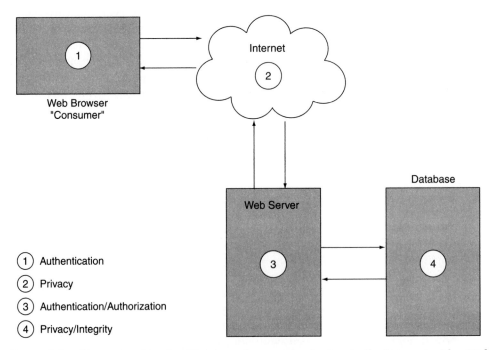

Figure 5-2. Here, a workstation Web browser communicates via the Internet with a Web server, which in turn communicates with the database server that handles authentication/authorization and privacy/integrity.

of new pages created every week. The goal is to have customers and others find your property with ease, using common Internet tools.

The agents used in finding information are known as *search engines,* which come primarily in three forms. The first are known as *crawlers,* sometimes called spiders, which are software-based searching tools that "crawl" the Internet constantly and add new sites and updates to their indexes as needed. Common crawlers include Google and HotBot. Crawler technology utilizes proprietary algorithms that rank each site as to its relevance to the topic searched. In the next section you'll learn how to best position and create your Web site so that it turns up high on the crawler index and ranking (if at all). The second type of search engine is a directory created and maintained by people. Yahoo is the best example of a *human powered directory.* In this example, a list of Web sites is updated and ranked by a staff of editors. Hybrids do exist and are in use today. In fact, Yahoo also utilizes the Google crawler technology in conjunction with its directory. The third example of search engines is *paid listings,* which use different business models focused mainly on charging by the number of "hits" a page receives. Combination offerings also exist here as payment is all too important in any e-marketing strategy since all high traffic search engine companies accept paid listings.

Web site design and implementation use HTML and XML tags to display information and describe their subject matter. In an e-marketing initiative, how a specific component is utilized can aid in high placement on the list of a search result. This item is known as a *meta-tag,* which serves as a summary of your Web site's *description* and *keywords* read by those crawlers. Other meta-tags do exist; however, these two types (description and keywords) are the most important in searches. It is important to note that crawlers read and analyze much more than just this part. The whole Web page is scanned for relevant words as are links to other Web sites. If your content and links are not consistent with the subject matter of your page, your ranking may suffer. With these components and the sacred proprietary algorithms, crawlers "size up" a Web site and rank it accordingly.

Price

It is impossible to have a successful e-marketing strategy without spending money. The four major crawlers—Google (used by Yahoo and Netscape), Inktomi (used by MSN and AOL), Fastsearch (used by Lycos), and Teoma (used by Ask Jeeves)—all charge about $30 to have your site listed right away, as opposed to waiting about a month for the crawler to find it and index it. That first month can be crucial to any business or Internet initiative. Human powered directories charge about $300 a year for listings. Besides Yahoo, the two other major ones are LookSmart and The Open Directory. Finally, the paid listing sites—Overture and Findwhat, among others—charge about $30 to join and often engage in bidding thereafter for the top spots. Pricing models change daily and need to be researched before any e-marketing initiative is undertaken.

7. SECURITY

Security of Your Electronic Transactions

In person-to-person transactions in either the B2B or B2C markets, security and fraud are rarely considered. Consumers have come to accept the risks of using credit cards in places like hotel lobbies and restaurants because they can see, touch, or consume certain products and make judgments about that specific environment. On the Internet, without those physical cues, it is much more difficult to assess the safety of a business. Also, because serious security threats have emerged, becoming aware of the risks of *Internet-based transactions (IBT)* and acquiring the proper technology solutions that overcome those risks is imperative. The major risks associated with e-commerce and its security include the following:

1. *Spoofing*—The low cost associated with Web site design and ease of copying existing pages makes it all too easy to create illegitimate sites that appear to be published by established organizations. These sites set up professional-looking storefronts that mimic legitimate businesses in the effort to obtain credit card and other information.

2. *Unauthorized Action*—A competitor or disgruntled customer can alter your Web site so that it refuses service to potential clients or malfunctions.

3. *Unauthorized Disclosure*—When transaction information is transmitted, hackers can intercept the transmissions to obtain your customers' sensitive information.

4. *Data Alteration*—The content of a transaction can be intercepted and altered en route, either maliciously or accidentally. User names, credit card numbers, and dollar amounts sent are all vulnerable to such alteration. (Verisign 2001, p.3)

Securing Your Web Site

A proven, low-cost solution to secure online transactions is a *server ID*. Server ID technology is used by virtually all of the Fortune 500 companies on the Web and all of the top 40 e-commerce sites. Server IDs work to make online transactions secure.

A server ID, also known as a digital certificate, is the electronic equivalent of a business license. Server IDs are issued by a trusted third party, called a *Certification Authority* (CA). The CA that issues a server ID is vouching for your right to use your company name and Web address.

Before issuing a server ID, a CA reviews your credentials, such as your organization's Dun & Bradstreet number or Articles of Incorporation, and completes a thorough background checking process to ensure that your organization is what it claims to be and is not claiming a false identity. Only then will a CA issue your organization a server ID. This ID provides the ultimate in credibility for your online business, which is so critical for users of hospitality resources.

Message Security

Another security concern is the actual message or content being transmitted. Message security is handled by a high-layer protocol and aided by encryption. This technology is known as SSL. *Secure sockets layer* (SSL) technology is the industry-standard protocol for secure, Web-based communications. Web servers are now configured to work with a server ID, with the server automatically activating SSL. The result is the creation of a secure communications channel between your server and your customer's browser. Any hospitality-based Web site can communicate securely with any customer who uses Netscape Navigator, Microsoft Internet Explorer, or most popular e-mail programs. Once activated by, and in conjunction with your server ID, SSL immediately begins providing you with the following components of secure online transactions:

- *Authentication.* Your customers can verify that the Web site belongs to you and not an impostor. This bolsters their confidence in submitting confidential information.
- *Message privacy.* SSL encrypts all information exchanged between your Web server and customers, such as credit card numbers and other personal data, using a unique session key. To securely transmit the session key to the consumer, your server encrypts it, with each session key used only once during a single session.
- *Message integrity.* When a message is sent, the sending and receiving computers each generate a code based on the message content. If even a single character in the message content is altered en route, the receiving computer will generate a different code, and then alert the recipient that the message is not legitimate. With message integrity, both parties involved in the transaction know that what they are seeing is exactly what the other party has sent. (Verisign 2001, p. 6)

Hospitality units that can manage and process e-commerce transactions gain a competitive edge by reaching a worldwide audience, at very low cost. But the Web poses a unique set of trust issues that hotel, restaurant, and travel groups must address at the outset to minimize risk. Customers submit information and purchase goods or services via the Web only when they are confident that their personal information, such as credit card numbers and financial data, is secure. The solution for hospitality companies that are serious about e-commerce is to implement a complete e-commerce trust infrastructure. These solutions provide the authentication, data integrity, and privacy necessary for e-commerce.

Table 5–1.   Significant Cyber Attacks 1999–2000

Date	Attack	Description
March 1999	Melissa	The Melissa was a Microsoft Word macro virus that was spread as an e-mail attachment. It arrived with the words, "Here is the document you asked for . . . don't show it to anyone else;)." The virus was first posted to the alt.sex newsgroup. When opened it would e-mail itself to the first 50 addresses in the recipient's address book. Melissa was significant because it was the first time in the 10 years since the Morris worm that a virus had infected a significant portion of the Internet.
May 1999	FBI vs. Hackers	After investigating several U.S. hacker groups and seizing the computer of a teenager, a DoS attack was launched against the FBI's Web site. As a result, the site was closed down for a week.
June 1999	Explorer.Zip	Similar to the Melissa virus, this virus was spread through e-mail that, when opened, automatically mailed itself out. The virus could also be spread without human intervention through various network-sharing vulnerabilities. Explorer.Zip created substantial problems for the e-mail systems at Microsoft, Intel, and NBC.
September 1999	Hotmail hole	A Hotmail security hole was discovered by a Bulgarian hacker named Georgi Guninski that allows a JavaScript program to be injected into a user's systems via an e-mail message. The script could be used to display a take login screen that steals the user's password. In this way the attacker could read the user's e-mail and send messages of any sort under the user's name.
November 1999	BubbleBoy	This e-mail virus differed from its predecessors because it only required the recipient to preview the message, not open it, in order to infect other computers.
January 2000	CDNow Attacked	A Russian cracker named Maxum stole 300,000 credit-card records from the CD Universe Web site, demanding $100,000 ransom for their return. When CD Universe refused, he started publishing the numbers one-by-one. Maxum's ISP shut him down when they learned about his criminal activity. Both Discover Card and American Express issued new cards to any of their cardholders shopping at CDNow.
February 2000	DDoS Attacks	See the opening case in Section 13.1.
Spring 2000	Credit Card Postings	A hacker named Raphael Gray (net name Curador) broke into EC sites in five countries—United States, Canada, Thailand, Japan, and the United Kingdom—and effortlessly obtained customer credit card numbers—26,000 in all. His stated objective was to bring the security vulnerabilities to the attention of the Webmasters at the sites, which he did by posting the numbers on the Internet.
May 2000	I LOVE YOU	The VBS.LoveLetter.A virus originated in the Philippines, struck Hong Kong on May 4, and within hours had attacked computers worldwide. By the time it had run its course, it had infected 1.2 million computers in North America and caused an estimated $80 million in damage. The virus was propagated virulently as an e-mail attachment that e-mailed itself to the contacts in the recipient's address book when opened.
August 2000	Brown Orifice	A computer consultant named Dan Brumleve announced that he had found two security flaws in the Netscape browser implementation of Java. The flaws enabled the distributor of a Java applet to view the file.
October 2000	Microsoft Source Code compromised	A cracker gained access to Microsoft's networks, enabling him or her to view the source code of applications under development. The cracker was able to penetrate the network through some "semi-retired" Web servers that hadn't been fixed to correct a vulnerability in Microsoft's Internet Information Server (i.e., Microsoft's commercial Web server product). Some security experts speculated that the cracker used the QAZ Trojan to spy on Microsoft's R&D division.

8. SUMMARY

Proper e-commerce strategy and usage are quickly becoming a *must have* tool in any manager's skills set. Both B2B and B2C concepts must be understood since you will be dealing with both customers and other businesses nline. Posting a Web site to the Internet and hoping that "they will come" is far from an efficient plan and will not result in any cost savings or revenue increases. Only proper knowledge, study, and implementation of an e-commerce rollout will make it a successful one. Particular attention must be paid to e-commerce technology and marketing. Although software capabilities such as clickstream tracking may be great, ethical and privacy issues may cause your customer to feel uncomfortable about using your site. Additionally, security issues must be understood to prevent unauthorized breaches and data theft. With these components in place and a thorough understanding of e-marketing differentiating you from the rest, an e-commerce initiative can be a successful one.

9. CASE STUDY AND LEARNING ACTIVITY

Case Study: Rosenbluth International—A New Way To Compete

The Problem

Rosenbluth International (*www.rosenbluth.com*) is a major international player in the competitive travel agent industry. The digital revolution introduces the following threats to Rosenbluth and to the travel agent industry in general:

- Airlines, hotels, and other service providers are attempting to bypass travel agents by moving aggressively to direct electronic distribution systems (e.g., electronic ticketing via online booking).
- Commission caps have been reduced (from $50 to $10) and most major airlines decreased travel agents' commission percentages from 10 percent to 5 percent. Some have even been erased completely.
- Large numbers of new online companies (e.g., Expedia.com) provide diversified travel services at bargain prices in an effort to attract individual travelers. However, these online services are now penetrating the corporate travel market as well.
- Competition among the major players is rebate-based. The travel agencies basically give part of their commission back to their customers by using the commission to subsidize lower prices.
- Innovative business models that were introduced by e-commerce, such as name your own price, auctions, and reverse auctions, have been embraced by many companies in the travel industry.

The Solution

Rosenbluth International responded to these new pressures with two strategies. First, it decided to get out of the leisure travel business, becoming a pure corporate travel agency. Second, it decided to rebate customers with its entire commission. Instead of generating revenues by these commissions, Rosenbluth now bills customers according to the services provided. For example, fees are assessed for consultations on how to lower corporate travel costs, the devolvement of in-house travel policies for corporate clients, negotiations on behalf of its clients with travel providers, and for travel related calls answered by the Rosenbluth staff.

To implement the second strategy, which completely changed the company's business model, Rosenbluth now uses several innovative e-commerce applications. The company utilizes a comprehensive Web-based business travel planning technology including policy and profile management tools, proprietary travel management applications, and seamless front line service/support. These browser-based services allow corporate travelers to book reservations anytime, anywhere, within minutes. The specific tools in this system are the following:

- **DACODA (Discount Analysis Containing Optimal Decision Algorithms)** is a patented yield management system that optimizes a corporation's travel savings, enabling travel managers to decipher complex airline pricing and identify the most favorable airline contracts.

- **Electronic messaging services** allow clients to manage their travel requests via e-mail. It uses Web-based templates that permit clients to submit reservation requests without picking up the phone. Additionally, a structured itinerary is returned to the travelers via e-mail.

- **E-ticket tracking** tracks, monitors, reports on, and collects the appropriate refund or exchange for unused e-tickets. As the amount of e-ticket usage grows, so does the amount of unused e-tickets that need to be refunded or exchanged.

- **Res-Monitor,** a patented low-fare search system, tracks a reservation up until departure time and finds additional savings for one out of every six reservations.

- **Global distribution network** electronically links the corporate locations and enables instant access to any traveler's itinerary, personal travel preferences, or corporate travel policy.

- **Custom-Res** is a global electronic reservation system that ensures policy compliance, consistent service, and accurate reservations.

- **IntelliCenters** are advanced reservation centers that use innovative telecommunications technology to manage calls from multiple accounts, resulting in cost saving and personalized service for corporate clients.

• **Network Operations Center (NOC)** monitors the many factors impacting travel, including weather, current events, and air traffic. This information is disseminated to the company's front line associates so that they can inform their clients of potential changes to their travel.

From newspapers to hotels, companies across different industries have been forced to reevaluate their respective sales channels. By combining a business model shift with new value added services, Rosenbluth has transformed the way it operates as a reaction to the Internet. How well it and other enterprises in the competitive travel market embrace the Internet, rather than fight it, remains to be seen.

Learning Activity

1. Do you agree with Rosenbluth's decision to focus only on corporate travel and terminate the leisure travel division? Explain your response.

2. Would you offer any additional services?

3. Are customer authentication issues addressed in this case study? Do you see any security issues for airlines based on the technology implemented?

4. Would Rosenbluth's strategy work without a global distribution network? Why or why not?

5. Is Rosenbluth now adding "value added services," or is it just selling excess capacity airline seats?

10. KEY TERMS

Authentication	Crawlers	Information Standards (OASIS)
Business to Business (B2B)	Data alteration	Paid listings
	E-commerce	
Business to Consumer (B2C)	Human powered directories	Performance monitoring software
Certification Authority	Internet-Based Transactions (IBT)	Search engines
Clickstream tracking	Message integrity	Secure sockets layer
Collaboration commerce	Message privacy	Server ID
	Meta-tag	Spoofing
Collaborative filtering	Organization for Advancement of Structured	Unauthorized action
Content management software		Unauthorized disclosure

11. CHAPTER QUESTIONS

1. Are e-business relationships shifting from commerce to collaboration? Why?
2. Is there a generic strategy for e-business or is each company unique?
3. How is collaborative filtering used?
4. What are meta-tags?
5. What are the inherent risks associated with Internet-based transactions?

12. REFERENCES

Alix, Michael R. 2000. The new infomediaries. (September 13), http://www.mikealix.com (accessed November 2001).

Goldman Sachs Investment Research Survey 1.0 August, 1999.

Hospitality Technology Magazine and Deloitte & Touche. "First annual restaurant industry technology" study,-2000.

Joyce, Michael. "Will Online Procurement Click?" Hospitality Technology Magazine, Feb, 2001.

Laudon, Kenneth, and Jane Laudon. 2002. *Management information systems.* 7th ed. Upper Saddle River, NJ: Prentice Hall.

Moai. 2001. An introduction to dynamic commerce and negotiated e-commerce. http://www.moai.com (accessed December 2001).

Panko, Raymond R. 2001. *Business data communications and networking.* 3d ed. Upper Saddle River, NJ: Prentice Hall.

Pomeroy, Brian. 2001. There is still cream in the middle "infomediaries" find a niche on the net. 18, 10.5 (October/November/December), High Tech Careers http://www.hightechcareers.com/doc999/networking999.html (accessed May 2002).

Taulli, Tom. 2002. Oracle b2b powerhouse. (February 13), http://www.internetstockreport.com/column/article/o,1785,252161,00.html (accessed March 1, 2002).

Turban, Efraim, David King, Jae Lee, Merrill Warkentin, and H. Chung. 2002. *Electronic commerce 2002: A managerial perspective.* 2d ed. Upper Saddle River, NJ: Prentice Hall.

Verisign. "Secure your website with a Verisign Server," white paper, 2001.

CHAPTER SIX

Restaurant Management Systems

CHAPTER CONTENTS

INTERVIEW

J. Alan Hayman is the executive vice president of
MICROS Systems, Inc., Columbia, Maryland.

Q: Alan, can you tell us about your background?

A: Sure. My experience in the POS (point-of-
sale) business dates to working for my father's cash register business in the 1960s. In
1938, he built a business, Stanley Hayman
and Co., Inc., which serviced National Cash
Registers, and was the first Sweda distributor in the United States. His company became the largest Sweda dealership. He also
founded the Independent Cash Register Dealers Association in the 1940s
and served as executive director, president, COB, and life member. I attended every convention from the age of eight, so I literally grew up in the
business.

I attended Boston University and graduated with honors from the
School of Management in 1974 with a B.S./B.A. in marketing. After entering law school, I decided to "try the family business," joining my brother
and father in July 1974. I was the office manager for a period of time, had
various sales roles, and became vice president of sales for Hayman Systems, which at that point employed over eighty people. When my father re-
tired, my older (and wiser) brother and I grew the business. We became
MICROS dealers in the early 80s and an NCR distributor in the late 80s.
Sweda, once our most popular product line, ceased doing business in the
early 90s. In 1992, our company moved to Laurel, Maryland. In 1996, we
purchased MICROS of South Florida and I became the company president.
In 1998, we purchased an interest in MICROS of Colorado.

In December, 1999, Hayman Systems and MICROS of South Florida
were acquired by MICROS. Our family business then became MICROS Fidelio Direct. I joined MICROS at its corporate headquarters as regional
manager for major accounts in the North Central Region. Within a year, I
was appointed senior vice president. In 2001, I was promoted to executive
vice president and director. As the senior manager in charge of restaurant
sales and strategies, my latest role is to insure that MICROS is providing
marketing solutions and support to all major accounts based in the U.S.

Q: What are some important factors when selecting a POS?

A: The first thing an operator should do is determine his or her exact needs
including a simple or complex system, POS reporting requirements, menu
demands, labor, inventory, credit card processing, etc. The operator should
take the time to analyze how things are done now and determine a goal for
the future. Creating an RFP is the best way to get the right solution at the

right price. Other factors include architecture preference, open-system design, durability, company stability, upgrade policy, support costs, etc.

Q: Can you tell me about your core product line and some of its features?

A: MICROS offers a variety of POS solutions. Each is designed to meet a certain vertical market and architecture, rather than utilizing a "one size fits all" approach. Each application offers incredible flexibility to be parameterized to meet the exact needs of an operator without writing custom code.

Q: Can you tell me about your recent product history?

A: MICROS introduced its first DOS based solution, HMS 4700, in 1986. In 1992, the Unix-based 8700 was released and became one of the company's most successful products for large installations, including several installations in excess of 200 terminals. Our Unix business is obviously not growing at the same rate, and we have released our 9700 NT solution as a replacement in the large system environment within the past year. Our Windows NT based 3700 was released in late 1996 and has now been enhanced and renamed RES 3000. With almost 12,000 installs, this solution has become the most successful solution for table service restaurants.

Q: How about your new portal Mymicros?

A: Mymicros.net will be released at the end of 2003. It is designed to provide operators real-time data anywhere, anytime, from a laptop. Utilizing a "software agent" at store level and persistent high-speed connection, POS data is posted to a data warehouse hosted by MICROS or the end user. The suite of offerings will include a complete information portal, as well as centrally hosted applications for food cost/inventory and labor/human resources. Ruby Tuesday is our first major account to sign on for this offering.

For our independent restaurant clients we offer Ovation II, which is derivative of our full scale RES 3000 solution. The only difference, really, is the upgrade path and the ability to use certain applications such as Enterprise Management. Ovation II offers a great value for restaurants that want a powerful solution but don't have the budget. Both products currently utilize our PC workstation called Eclipse. In 2002, we will introduce a new handheld offering and a low cost Window CE workstation. Our iPOS, centrally hosted POS solution, will also be released for sale giving MICROS and its customers more choices than ever to select the "right fit" for their business. No one in the industry offers the depth of product lines for the hospitality industry that MICROS does.

Q: In closing, how is the service side of your business doing, and what will be offered in the future?

A: Our services business represents almost half of our revenues, which exceed $340 million on an annual basis. Our clients generally need some, if not all, of the services that we offer, now that they are trimming their own IT staffs and outsourcing services. MICROS will continue to expand "one stop" shopping for services and new offerings such as VSAT, hosting, project management, expanded help desk, and on-site support.

1. INTRODUCTION

Restaurant management systems (RMSs) are the crucial technology components that enable a single outlet or enterprise to better serve its customers and aid employees with food and beverage transactions and controls. Everyday examples of their application range from quick food to fine dining. When you place an order in a fast-food restaurant, the machine being used by the person in front of you is part of the RMS. The same is true when you make a reservation online for a five star restaurant. These are just two instances of RMSs in use today. This chapter's objective is to acquaint you with the many elements of a RMS and show how, through its use, current and future restaurant technology can enable management to operate a more profitable and efficient business. Restaurants are fast moving and dynamic environments with many parts that do not "play well" with the digital age. Technology is only a tool that can aid management in operating within this environment.

2. RESTAURANT MANGEMENT SYSTEM (RMS) COMPONENTS

The size and scope of RMSs vary among organizations. There are four main offerings:

- The point-of-sale system (POS)
- Inventory and menu management systems
- Reservations and Table Management
- Back office applications and interfaces

Restaurant operators are constantly looking for ways to better understand their customers in order to serve them better. They also need a centralized system to carry out the business at hand. Many now use the point-of-sale system. By definition, a *point-of-sale system (POS)* is either a stand-alone machine or a network of input and output devices used by restaurant employees to accomplish their daily activities including food and beverage orders, transmission of tasks to the kitchen and other remote areas, guest-check settlement, credit card transaction processing, and charge posting to folios (Figure 6-1). As mentioned earlier, a POS system looks much like an *electronic cash register (ECR)*. In fact, earlier POS systems were known as ECRs. Many restaurants have just a POS system in their technology solution. Whichever the case, it is these systems that collect and disseminate information about the guest and guest orders for the establishment.

Figure 6-1. Point-of-sale systems such as this from the MICROS/Fidelio Corporation aid servers and managers in a growing number of ways. Because of their proximity to food and beverages, POS systems are often built to be more resistant to spills and other mistreatment than other pieces of technology. *(Source: Courtesy of MICROS, Inc.)*

Other POS Functionality

Aside from its basic task of order handling, a POS system also provides additional functionality.

Decreased Service Time. One of the benefits of technology is the increased speed found in communication. In a restaurant setting, a POS system allows for quicker communication among all points involved. If set up correctly, an order placed at a POS station will also be seen in the kitchen, the bar, offices, the host stand, and any other necessary areas. In other words, everyone has the needed information.

Order Accuracy. With a POS system, miscommunications are minimized. Each order has a specific field assigned to it that is used by all. For example, a hamburger may have the field "HMBGR" or simply "Hamburger." Rather than input the field, a server chooses from a list of fields provided by the POS system. With this common language, all involved in the service of food and beverage are communicating with the same vocabulary and presentation methods, thereby eliminating common handwritten and oral miscommunications.

Security of Cash Transactions and Internal Auditing Functions. Many restaurants are temporarily responsible for handling cash and credit cards, and maybe even checks. Theft can be a problem. To minimize this risk, a

POS system records all orders and transactions to each employee's assigned identification number on the POS system. It is up to the employee to make sure that his/her financial totals match those recorded by the POS. If a discrepancy occurs, a POS system utilizes an auditing function that allows management, through report generation, to dissect and backtrack a particular employee's transactions during the shift(s) in question.

Reduced Training Burden.   The hospitality industry has a great deal of employee turnover. Training can become difficult with so much staff coming and going. POS design takes this factor into account. With familiar graphical user interfaces, function buttons, and help commands, a wait person is not left in the dark.

Performance Control.   Again, through report generation, a proper POS can aid management in employee performance appraisals. How much product is sold by each server and when along with other performance controls are controlled and accessed via this function.

Sales Reporting.   Lastly, what are the most profitable items? When are they being sold? Which items are not selling? How are customers paying? These and many other questions can be answered by the sales reporting functionality of the POS. Due to the importance of understanding sales, other third party vendors have targeted this aspect of the POS in their product offerings. Now, there are numerous software options for the manager who desires better food and beverage sales intelligence.

Inventory and Menu Management

To remain competitive, management can no longer reevaluate inventory and menu items on a monthly basis. Through known technologies such as bar codes and tags, inventory can be tracked. How establishments use technology to manage their inventory and menu items differs among locations. In some, the POS is used. In others, it is tracked by a system that may or may not connect to the POS. Whatever the case, inventory and menu systems are primarily concerned with three themes:

- Inventory levels and consumption
- Purchasing
- Theft

Inventory Levels and Consumption

In assuming a new role in food and beverage, a new manager is given (it is hoped) a detailed report of how much inventory of each product is to be kept on hand. This level is known as **par stock.** With a networked RMS, item removal and action can be tracked. From there, the RMS can also track consumption volume, rate, and sales price. Common inventory level functions also include the crucial *snapshot by day* operation summarizing all inventory actions for that period.

Purchasing

Restaurants are also concerned with a number of factors surrounding the purchasing of products for their site(s). Dates of purchases and delivery, quantity, and purchase price must be logged and tracked for safety and business reasons. From there, alerts may be set up to prevent dated food and beverage products from being served. However, people determine the final outcome since some items, such as fish and vegetables, are not easily tracked and managed by technology. As with the sales report generation in the POS, business intelligence plays a major role here as well. Those food costs are just too important to the bottom line and promotions not to be tracked and managed by the advancements in RMS technology.

Theft

A major problem facing restaurants today is employee theft—often called shrinkage. Controlling shrinkage significantly adds to a restaurant's bottom line and is an important cost-control measure. According to the Jan 1999 *Nation's Restaurant News* magazine, "Up to 30 percent of all restaurants fail because of employee theft," which is no surprise, given that "almost one out of every two employees will steal from an employer if given the chance."

Inventory control operations handle this task through ID association with every item removed. Item removal may occur only when an employee assigns his or her ID or pin to the product. As with possible food spoilage, the human factor plays a crucial role here.

Benefits of Inventory and Menu Management

Some may view the use of technology in inventory management as disruptive. Taking the time to input user IDs and access codes can be perceived as a burden when a customer may be waiting. Aside from the aforementioned business intelligence aspects, the inventory and menu management component of a RMS help in other ways. Nutritional aspects may be improved. In an age where demographics prove that the number of elderly will increase dramatically, nutritional aspects must be considered. Additionally, some inventory and menu management systems also have the ability to monitor the actual nutritional aspects of a particular dish—from sodium to cholesterol. More often than not, this is accomplished through third-party culinary and nutritional software such as Mastercook™. Software such as this, which may run on just a few computers in the restaurant (the chef's or the food and beverage manager's), can provide additional information including predictive modeling and variable analysis. If you want to know, for example, how much you may need of a certain food item given the average age and number of expected covers, this software outputs the answer.

Reservations and Table Management

A RMS may also contain an electronic software module for reservations. This may be a piece of software that is part of, or separate from, the POS. It is simplistic in nature. The name, number in party, date, time, etc., are inputted here. With most restaurants still using a handwritten reservation book, model usage here is limited, although is expected to increase dramatically.

Those who incorporate technology into their reservation operations and procedures may widen their potential business by moving online. Due to the increasing level of reservations being made online, restaurateurs are starting to purchase monthly services from Internet companies such as OpenTable for their solutions. OpenTable is the Expedia of the restaurant world, taking reservations for many restaurants in different locations (see Figure 6-2). The Web

| | | Lunch | Tmw ◄ | 05/31/2000 ► | 1:00 PM | Total count 39 / Seated count 02:56 | Add | Change | Status |

Sidebar: Sheet, Book, Floor, Clients, Reserve, Now, Notes, Admin

Time	Name	#	Tbl	N	Time	Name	#	Tbl	N	Time	Name	#	Tbl	N
11:30	Blocked	0			12:00	Aberg, Roland	5			12:30		6		
11:30	Blocked	0			12:00	Sakai, Kent	6			12:30		6		
11:30	Blocked	0			12:00		2			1:00	Abington, Rob	2		
11:30	Blocked	0			12:00		2			1:00	Naito, Annobu	6		
11:30	Blocked	0			12:00		4			1:00		2		
11:30		2			12:00		4			1:00		2		
11:45	Abizad, Charl	4	65		12:15	Slusky, Alex	2			1:00		4		
11:45		2			12:15		2			1:00		4		
11:45		2			12:15		4			1:00		6		
11:45		2			12:30	Jonson, Nels	3			1:15	Kahn, Liz	2		
11:45		4			12:30		2			1:15		2		
11:45		4			12:30		2			1:15		4		
12:00	Blocked	0			12:30		4			1:30	Gale, Janelle	2		
12:00	Blum, Richard	2			12:30		4			1:30		2		
12:00	Falkenberg, P	2			12:30		4			1:30		2		
12:00	Blocked	0			12:30		4			1:30		4		
12:00	Takaga, Yosh	4			12:30		4			1:30		4		

Figure 6-2. Restaurants with computerized reservations systems have more options for handling current and future business. Current information is just a mouse click away. *(Source: OpenTable, Inc.)*

site *www.OpenTable.com* is a great example of a portal specific to the hospitality industry. When its reservations are interfaced with the on-site system, which may or may not be made by OpenTable, significant volume increases may be seen.

After reservations comes table management. *Table management software (TMS)* is designed to allocate the reservation/wait/walk-in list with appropriate tables or locations and services within the establishment. TMS is the "matchmaker" between a dining party and a table with its assigned server and may take the form of an application on a computer or even a kiosk. TMS is considered standard on large scale RMS systems and as an "add on" for smaller POS systems. TMS standard functionality includes the following:

- A map view of the entire front of the house seating
- Alerts on open, long duration, and dirty tables
- Reservation assignment to tables

Look at Figure 6-3, a sample TMS screen from OpenTable.

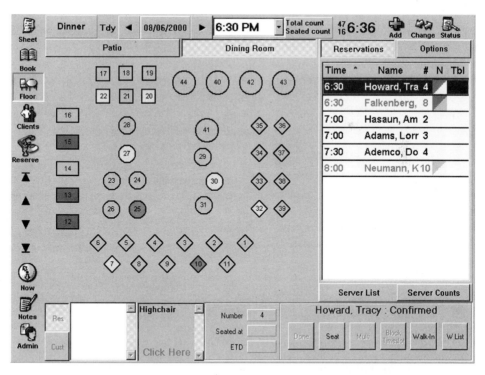

Figure 6-3. Table management systems such as this from OpenTable provide a "bird's eye" view of an establishment as well as specific details of each table. Armed with this information, management can better serve its occupied tables and have access to past table history. *(Source: OpenTable, Inc.)*

With table management systems, operational staff can better control and manage the flow of customers within a restaurant and offer timely service to the benefit of both the client and business.

Interfaces

A RMS, particularly its **POS** component, often needs to interface with other systems. If the restaurant is in a hotel environment, the system must be incorporated into the larger hotel system. Interfaces will be discussed in more detail in the next chapter.

Since a RMS is geared towards day to day restaurant operations, any back office components such as human resource and accounting software may require an additional interface. Certain technology vendors are actually offering "restaurant solutions" that take into account all offices within a restaurant—widening the definition of a RMS. You may see more of these offerings in the future.

3. OTHER RMS SYSTEMS

Fast-food restaurants use a special type of a RMS, a DRMS. The *delivery management system (DRMS)* is a software and hardware package that works with the POS and other systems with an emphasis on the delivery of orders. Since orders are not brought to you by a server, but rather "delivered" to you at the counter or drive-through window, the establishment's use of technology has a different scope. The DRMS was designed a little differently than the RMS and is divided into three major components:

- Storefront operations
- System functions
- Back office

Storefront Operations

Storefront operations in the DRMS world look much like the POS. Orders are inputted and total amounts are given. The DRMS also transmits those orders to a display system both in the kitchen and drive-through window. Aside from the order contents, approximate time of order processing is the most important item displayed here. If a manager sees an order on one of the displays over a certain amount of time allowed, action may be required.

System Functions

System functions are primarily concerned with facilitating the changes and optimizing the functionality of the DRMS as a whole. Fast-food restaurants face constant change in offerings and promotions and need the ability to change their systems just as fast. Specific system functions allow for quick item and price changes, control of all peripherals involved, backup capability, self-diagnostic tests, and training programs.

Back Office

Back office systems in quick service establishments are small. Most of the emphasis, as with most restaurants, is on the "front of the house." However, at a minimum, certain tasks need to be accomplished and measured for any business wishing to remain competitive. DRMS contain the necessary functionality for inventory control, financial transactions, and sales data. These may be accessed and manipulated from a computer in the manager's office or with a managerial ID from a storefront POS.

4. RMS SCALE

Single and multiunit operations have different technology needs. What may work for one may not for another. Let's look at both.

Small Operator Systems

Single unit establishments require a system that "does it all." These small operator systems (SOS) are designed for a single operation, allowing for the tracking and monitoring of orders, control of stock levels, and the recording of sales. Stand-alone systems are easy to configure and maintain. Other advantages include enabling small businesses to operate a state-of-the-art package without the associated expenses found in sophisticated enterprise systems.

Enterprise Systems

On the other end, enterprise systems require additional planning for proper implementation and usage. Large chains require communication among their units to gain any advantages in economies of scale. Besides obvious benefits in communications, other rewards are seen in enterprise offerings. Customer data may be captured and shared among outlets, allowing for tailored service to individual customers at all locations. Customer data will be discussed more thoroughly in Chapter 9. The RMS applications may be located off-site and accessed over data lines via a browser using software and services from an *application service provider (ASP)*. Accessing software in this fashion is a more common occurrence in all industries. Not having to worry about applications and other technology components has increased the usage and appeal of ASPs. As you learned in the interview, the leading POS vendor MICROS has released "MyMicros," which is its browser-based POS. Many predict the ASP model will have a wider customer base in the hospitality industry, freeing people to better concentrate on customers.

How do RMSs communicate with their counterparts in other locations? Many use phone and data lines. Others use satellites. If you look at the roofs of some of the major chain restaurants, you may see a satellite dish. Here, inventory requests and financial transactions are primarily transmitted to the wider corporate system. The medium used is becoming less and less relevant. However, the need to operate on an enterprise level is more than relevant—it is good business.

5. PROPRIETARY VERSUS NONPROPRIETARY RMS

Proprietary is synonymous with private. Proprietary systems come from a single source. Mixing and matching software and hardware from other vendors with these components can be troublesome, if not impossible. Purchasing from a single source has both advantages and disadvantages. You may know whom to call if something breaks, but you only have that one company and its service providers as a resource. Further, imagine if a solution comes out tomorrow from a competing company. It may not be possible to integrate the new product with your system. Decisions such as these are common in technology. In the hospitality industry, they are most applicable to POS systems. There are some superior proprietary vendors. It is up to the restaurateur to weigh the good with the bad in making a purchase.

6. ADVANCEMENTS IN RMS TECHNOLOGY

Although some solutions such as ASPs are already here, others have just appeared but are expected to see wider implementation.

Advanced Touch Screen Technology

When you use a kiosk, you are using an example of touch screen technology. This solution is ideal for the messy restaurant business that can wear down machine life. It is also easier to use. The operator touches icons of products rather than entering characters and numbers. McDonald's incorporated this ideal long ago into its machines. Pictures have replaced words. Touch screen technology uses software and hardware that dictate what a particular part of a screen is to represent. Picture a piece of invisible graph paper that is superimposed on various screens in an application. On one screen, a certain location may indicate the letter *a*, on another, a large soda. Touch screen technology warrants a detailed discussion due to its growing usage in the industry. It comes in the three forms explained in the following paragraphs.

Resistive capacity touch screens are made up of two thin layers of plastic that cover two layers of indium tin oxide (ITO). The plastic layers keep the tin layers apart. When pressed together, by say a pencil, the tin layers touch. Then an electric charge is engaged at that location and the component registers what letter, picture, sound, etc., is represented by that location.

Capacitive touch screens have a common amount of voltage flowing throughout the device. When touched, voltage is disrupted and reduced. Capacitive technology registers where the technology was disrupted and identifies what entity is to be represented by the specific area disrupted.

Infra red (IR) touch screen technology identifies a particular area of a screen in much the same way as capacitive, only an "always on" light source is interrupted at a specific location rather than a current.

Which one is best? All are viable solutions. The key is durability of the product and the technology used. Product history and current usage, along with warranties, are the key to selection here.

Personal Digital Assistants

Personal digital assistants (PDA) use touch screen technology and should likewise see wider implementation in the restaurant industry. Although limited in screen size, these applications may still be used for remote order taking and other tasks. Price is the only limiting factor here. Restaurateurs are not yet convinced that, on average, a $300 PDA with a $50 network card makes sense financially for servers who can use a much cheaper "pen, paper, and a couple of footsteps to the POS" solution. Using PDAs is being embraced by mobile managers who, with a PDA, have much needed information and capability at their fingertips.

Smart Cards

Although not seen every day, smart cards are poised to change the industry. Essentially, a *smart card* is a credit card-sized identity card with either an embedded microchip base or magnetic-strip system. Data stored in either the strip or chip may contain personal, medical, or financial facts, along with loyalty programs.

Smart cards were developed and first used in France during the 1970s. Several types exist and are undergoing rapid refinement, with current chip-based models containing 500 times as much information as a traditional magnetic-strip type card. Smart card information is secured by similar encryption methods discussed in Chapters 4 and 5.

Distribution of smart cards, and their acceptance by consumers, has been slow, especially in the United States. Adoption elsewhere has been driven in part by telecommunications infrastructure and policy. In this country, low cost, large infrastructure, abundant (by comparison to Europe) bandwidth, and rapid database access (Chapter 9) have made central database applications preferable. Behind the scenes in the United States, we access databases regularly for everyday transactions. Credit card authorizations, reservations, purchases, and applications may all access different databases. However, in other countries it is often expensive and difficult to "get through" to central databases in order to conduct instant authorizations. Chip-based cards elimi-nate this need by carrying the information and authorizations right in the chip in the card. U.S. businesses and consumers have been reluctant to embrace chip card technology, but trends show a continued rise in usage and adapta-tion. Special readers are needed to unleash the advancement associated with the cards, and many merchants have not wanted to deal with the technological requirements. Now RMS/POS systems offer "add on packages" that read and scan information in order to generate custom sale and *patron data reports (PDRs)* that detail customers and their financial relationship with a business. With their added convenience and increasing adaptation, chip cards mean that many restaurants have little choice but to add chip card accessibility to their businesses. Smart cards are discussed further in this chapter's case study.

7. SUMMARY

Restaurant management systems (RMSs) are a critical tool used by man-agement in restaurant sales and operations. If studied and used properly, RMSs will enable different locations and employees to join together in a more profitable business. Their importance, however, must be placed in a wider management setting. A RMS is a tool used by people. While this is true of technology in general, it is even more applicable here. A study of any restaurant will reveal numerous items that are not, and need not be, touched by technology. Sometimes in hospitality, more art than science is needed. In restaurants, this is particularly true. Nevertheless, a RMS, with its primary components, can give management more control over spending and sales. With these controls, owners must also reevaluate customers' tastes and ex-pectations regarding technology. If your clientele expects a certain amount of technology, it must be provided. This rings true for the future. Of partic-ular note is the increase of smart cards and the Internet. Smart cards are de-veloping into a new form of currency along with debit and credit cards. Not accepting them is bad for business. Additionally, the online medium is being used for both restaurant research and bookings. Any restaurateur must in-corporate this foresight into his or her operations. With proper knowledge and application of the various RMSs, along with a keen eye to the future, RMS technology can help grow the single site or enterprise business.

8. CASE STUDY AND LEARNING ACTIVITY

A major fine-dining restaurant chain, with twenty sites in the United States, was seeking to implement a frequency program for its customers. The company's ob-jective was to reward those who purchased a minimum of $75 at any of their lo-cations. Someone who spent that amount would receive $5 off a future meal. When a customer accumulated $150 in dining expenditures, that person was credited with $10 off future dining costs. The restaurant wished to track any re-ward via a smart card solution.

Chip Based or Magnetic-Strip Card?

The upscale restaurant chain was unsure of whether to base the program on cards that used chips or magnetic strips. It requested an analysis and comparison of both technologies. In the proposed smart card program, customers are issued frequency cards when they pay for a meal. The customers' points, reflecting the amount spent, are stored directly on the card. This smart card is always up-to-date and can be used at any location, at any time, with a current, up-to-the-minute point total stored on the card. The question was which technology to use?

Chip Cards

A chip card is tamper-proof, which hampers duplication. There is no lag time in redeeming earned awards since they are a direct function of the customer's point total, stored directly on the customer's card. Likewise, there is less of a possibility of fraud with a chip card since a customer's entire point total is not resident in any terminal or hard drive, but rather right on the customer's card. With their advanced technology and storage capability, chip cards cost almost four times as much as the common strip cards.

Magnetic-Strip Program

Magnetic-strip technology has been in use for some time. Credit cards use magnetic-strip technology. The crucial difference with strip cards is where the information is stored. In magnetic-strip cards, the customer's point total is stored in a central database and can be accessed from any location. Similar to a chip card system, there is a very limited possibility of fraud since a customer's points are resident on a central database and can be accessed only through a credit card terminal with proper access codes.

Learning Activity

1. Why should chip based cards be considered?
2. Why should strip based cards be considered?
3. Which option would you recommend?
4. Is the case study missing any critical information that would make your decision easier?

9. KEY TERMS

Application Service Provider (ASP)	Delivery Management System (DRMS)	Infra Red (IR) Touch Screens
Capacitive Touch Screens	Electronic Cash Register (ECR)	Patron Data Report (PDR)

| Point-of-Sale System (POS) | Restaurant Management System (RMS) | Snapshot by day |
| Resistive Capacity Touch screens | Smart cards | Table Management Software (TMS) |

10. CHAPTER QUESTIONS

1. What are the four main components of a RMS?
2. Why is integration so important among the various RMSs?
3. Explain proprietary versus nonproprietary purchasing decisions.
4. Why is touch screen technology so important to the restaurant industry? What are its three types?
5. How will the Internet change the way restaurants attract and serve customers?

11. REFERENCES

Laudon, Kenneth, and Jane Laudon. 2000. *Management information systems.* 6th ed. Upper Saddle River, NJ: Prentice Hall.

Panko, Raymond R. 2001. *Business data communications and networking.* 3d ed. Upper Saddle River, NJ: Prentice Hall.

Rubenstein, Ed "High-Tech systems look to head off restaurant shrinkage" National Restaurant News magazine, Jan, 1999, p. 20.

CHAPTER SEVEN

The Property Management System and Interfaces

CHAPTER CONTENTS

INTERVIEW

Gary Cooke is the industry manager for Hospitality and Food Service at Microsoft. He holds a B.S. degree from Miami of Ohio and a M.B.A. from the University of Chicago. He's been with Microsoft for seven years and before that worked for Lexis-Nexis for fourteen years.

Q: Thanks again, Gary, for taking time to talk. Microsoft, as an independent software vendor (ISV) sells software, obviously. How can software vendors differentiate themselves even though there is a movement towards having open systems that would make their products less unique?

A: ISVs who embrace standards like XML free themselves and their customers to focus more of their efforts on automating and integrating industry-specific business processes instead of building and rebuilding common infrastructure processes or making different software products work together. When software developers adhere to standards, they are able to focus on their core competencies and leverage the core competencies of other developers. And when a company is able to focus on what it does best, it can differentiate itself from the competition.

Q: We are hearing more and more about application service providers (ASP). How will they be utilized in the hospitality industry?

A: A key element of our vision for the future is that software can become a subscribeable, Web-accessible service. This applies to a business application, or a database, or even a "tool," like a calendar or a notification function. All of these can now be turned into services that live somewhere on the Internet and that are rentable. An approach like this can create an important role for the ASP. As an example, we are seeing Web-based property management and point-of-sale systems where key components of the applications will live somewhere outside the hotel or restaurant. So software is evolving from something the hotelier or restaurateur buys in a shrink-wrapped package to a service he or she can subscribe to. These are just some reasons why ASPs could play important roles in the future.

Q: I'm concerned that we are taking the people out of "the people business" with all kinds of technology. Would you say that automation in the hospitality industry automatically improves the guest experience?

A: There are cases where technology has not been particularly helpful to hotel patrons. An example might be the early versions of high-speed in-room Internet access products that required users to reconfigure their laptops to use the service. Technology either has to be transparent to users or broadly understood by them. When technology meets these criteria—when people understand it and can use it, as is the case with cellular phones or office productivity software, for example—it clearly can enhance the guest experience.

Q: Some have gone to the extreme and claimed that certain vital functions will be done by machines. For example, do you think the front desk is going to disappear?

A: I think technology will create options for hoteliers with respect to the front desk. Some might choose to make it less obtrusive, possibly by performing some traditional front desk tasks with handheld wireless devices or through kiosks or in-room devices. Approaches like this will reduce the number of times that guests need to go to the front desk during their stay. Other hoteliers might decide to do different things at the front desk. For example, maybe the front desk could become the place to get technical assistance, like a loaner PC, a modem cable, or a network card.

Q: Thanks Gary. In closing I need you to gaze into your crystal ball. What do you see down the road?

A: When I think about the future, I think about hotel and restaurant patrons interacting with people and organizations anytime and anyplace, using virtually any device they choose. The fact that they are away from home or the office does not keep them from doing many of the things they need to do or enjoy doing. I see people using smart wireless mobile devices and voice recognition to enhance their travel or dining experience, or to transact business even though they're traveling. I see people being able to access important data, like their calendars or their contact lists or their e-mail inboxes via an airport kiosk, or the terminal device, or a TV in their hotel room, or their pocket PC in a restaurant enabled with a wireless network. I visualize people being able to shop and do their banking electronically because the authentication data necessary for such activities is securely available electronically. I see travelers and diners expecting the hotels and restaurants they patronize to enable and support these kinds of activities—and rewarding those that do with repeat business. And I see forward-thinking hoteliers and restaurateurs supporting these capabilities as a way to differentiate themselves in a competitive global market.

1. INTRODUCTION

Gary Cooke brings up some great points about technology in the hospitality industry. At the center of the hotel world, for now, lies the property management system. This chapter will detail the interworkings of this system and its future within a hotel environment.

The views expressed in this article are the opinion of Gary Cooke only and do not necessarily reflect the position of Microsoft. No representations whatsoever are made with respect to the accuracy or completeness of the content provided by Mr. Cooke and any liability with respect to any potential claims (whether in law or in equity) that might arise with respect to any statements made by Mr. Cooke quoted in this article is expressly disclaimed.

Property management systems, or PMSs, started as basic systems used to replace manual methodologies for managing rooms and guest charges, but quickly became the software centerpiece of hotel information systems at the unit level. While multiple property owners, managers, and franchises relied on central reservation systems to monitor, manage, and facilitate the sale of room inventory across multiple properties, individual hotel managers and staff relied, and continue to rely, upon the property management system to manage almost all aspects of a single property's business.

From a single property management perspective, the world is often depicted as "PMS-centric" as shown in Figure 7-1, which was originally developed by Professor Richard Moore of Cornell.

As this chart aptly reflects, almost every information system within a single hotel is reliant upon the property management system for something.

PMSs have undergone dramatic changes during the past twenty years. During the 1980s, the move from "green screen" command line interfaces to almost friendly DOS-based systems was a heralded move in the right direction, but by the 1990s, inherently user-friendly Windows applications stole the day. During each of these migrations, the main concern was always the comparable functionality of newer systems versus the older ones.

Several things have contributed to a delay in technology adoption in the hotel industry. As in any organization or industry, there is always the concern that results from people's general trepidations relative to change. This is particularly true for the PMS. Workers may be accustomed to the system already in place to service guests' needs. Even some vendors may share the same view. Rather than present any new offerings, they point out the shortcomings in others' products. But in the end, the real issue delaying implementation of these systems has been the complexity of modern PMSs.

It often takes vendors years of development to finely tune a system to meet the needs of a certain target market (be it a particular chain or type of hotel/resort). It often takes a year or more after a new product is released before the vendor can incorporate 100 percent of the detailed functionality that existed in previous versions of the same application.

Almost all of the software vendors supporting the hospitality industry are moving as rapidly as possible toward the general release of browser-based versions of their existing PMSs. The majority of these systems will use XML formatted documents as a means of transferring data between the PMS's database and other systems. As you know from Chapters 4 and 5, XML is a more descriptive form of data display on the Internet. While vendors are moving in this direction as rapidly as possible, several other changes are occurring that will potentially have a much greater impact on these systems than their adaptation for the Internet.

One such movement is peer-to-peer computing. As you learned in the networking chapter, peer-to peer computing is between two "peers" or parties communicating with the same operational capabilities. Napster and Aimster, the music sharing programs, and other such programs are illustrations of peer-to-

Hotel Automation

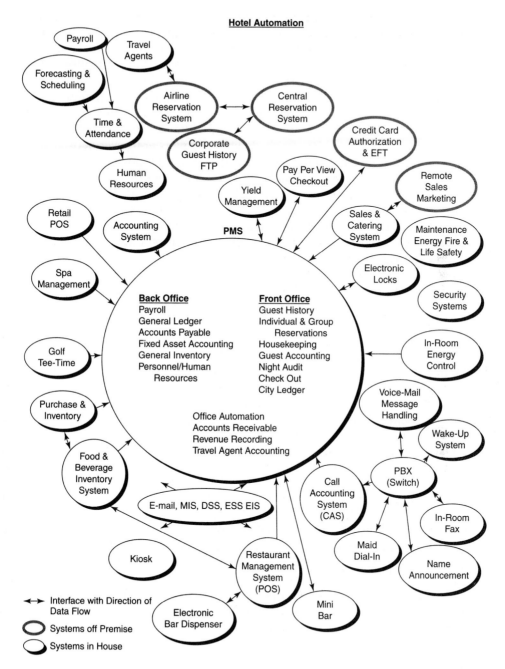

Figure 7-1. This figure by Professor Richard Moore of Cornell University shows the vast number of systems and processes that are found within many hotel systems. Each has its own particularity and the vital integration between them continues to challenge the industry.
(*Source: Professor Richard G. Moore, Cornell University, School of Hotel Administration*)

peer computing. Users have the same application installed on both computers and share access to their respective hard drives. In the evolution of computer technology and communication, peer-to-peer networking is actually making its second appearance. In the early days of the Internet, communication was from point to point. One person communicated directly with another. There was no World Wide Web; rather the military, scientists, and, later, academics communicated with their counterparts peer-to-peer. Today with faster networks, users are able to share files directly with co-workers. Unlike client server networking, this is done without a server. By simply downloading a peer-to-peer networking program and supplying an IP address of the other computer possessing the same program, you can begin the session. Pertinent applications of this technology to the benefit of the property management system not only include file sharing, but also include the ability of one hotel to check a guest into the system of another hotel, or corporate headquarters to log into a remote PMS and send via that hotel's room service, a VIP amenity, for example. Control of the mechanism is handled by user passwords, rights, and permissions.

2. PMS FUNCTIONALITY

While it is easy to underestimate the complexity and detailed functionality of a modern PMS, it is equally easy to get bogged down in a detailed discussion of specific functionality and methodologies at the cost of "not seeing the forest through the trees."

In its most basic form, a PMS must be able to provide six basic functions:

- Enable guests to make reservations
- Enable guests to check-in/register when they arrive and check-out/pay when they leave
- Enable staff to maintain guest facilities
- Account for a guest's financial transactions
- Track guests' activities for use in future sales efforts
- Interface with other systems

Each of these important functions will be discussed in the following sections. Where necessary, details will be included so that you can fully appreciate how PMSs perform certain functions.

Enable Guests to Make Reservations

The first thing you should note is that this does not say "enable a reservation agent to reserve rooms." Years ago, when PMSs and CRSs were first introduced, the only way to reserve a room in a PMS was to know a lot of text-based codes used in a command line interface (which many of you may have never seen). As a result, reserving a room in the system required a specially trained operator to gather information verbally from a guest and use that information to check availability and enter a room reservation into the system.

Enable Guests to Check-In/Register When They Arrive and Check-Out/Pay When They Leave

Whether guests have a reservation or not, this essential function of the PMS includes not only check-in when guests present themselves at the front desk, but also the ability to interface with any self-check-in/check-out or remote computers such as PDAs. Study the check-in screen and all of the information captured in the Opera PMS from Micros/Fidelio, Inc. (Figure 7-2)

Enable Staff to Maintain Guest Facilities

What have become known as the housekeeping functions of a property management system enable staff and management of a hotel to access some basic necessities when managing rooms:

- Room type, room number, king, double, etc.
- Room status—clean, dirty, departing today, etc.
- Information on the occupant of the room—name, likes extra pillows, etc.

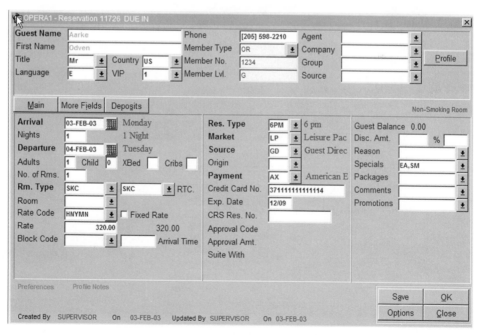

Figure 7-2. This reservation screen of the Micros/Fidelio Corporation Opera property management system contains many necessary pieces of guest information for various hotel departments. (*Source: Micros/Fidelio, Inc.*)

- Internal operational information—inspections, maintenance issues, history, etc.
- Report generation, for example–discrepancies departments

Discrepancies occur when the housekeeping department's definition of the status of a room differs with the front desk's status. This can result from many things. An example is a guest checks out a day early without going to the front desk. A housekeeper will clean the room and report it as vacant/clean. However, since the room has not been checked out by the front desk, that department will display it as occupied. Managing discrepancies is a daily ritual in hotels. The property management system generates reports such as these to aid management in solving such problems. Figure 7-3 is a screen shot, again from the Opera PMS, by Micros/Fidelio, of a housekeeping screen and a field that displays the front office (FO) status. If the two differ, there is a discrepancy. Study some of the other fields to get an idea of the various aspects of any room.

Account for a Guest's Financial Transactions

Billing information such as credit card number, home and/or business address, and the specific type of room rate are accounted for here. Typically, a front office

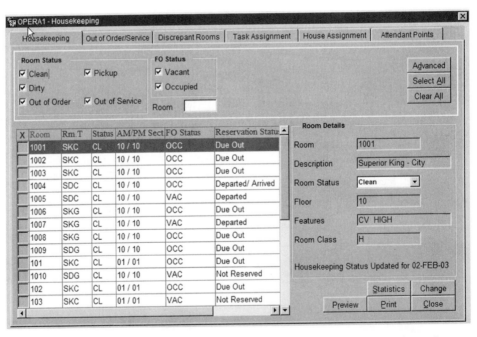

Figure 7-3. The management of hotel rooms can be a daunting task. With many different and constantly changing characteristics, organizations can benefit from department specific modules of a property management system such as housekeeping from Micros/Fidelio. (*Source: Micros/Fidelio, Inc.*)

is divided into three eight-hour shifts with the overnight shift left to "turn over the day." It is here where room and tax and all other applicable charges are "posted" to each room. This overnight shift is known as the night audit. This part of the PMS generates daily records of hotel activity such as total occupancy, total American Express charges, total cash taken in on a particular day, and so on.

Track Guests' Activities for Use in Future Sales Efforts

It is important that the PMS capture any and all information about a guest that is relevant and beneficial to future sales efforts. This information can also be accessed by the central reservation system and any CRM applications (Chapter 9) for sales and marketing initiatives. Figure 7-2 of the PMS is important. If staff members don't enter complete information on this screen, data from a critical touch point or location where a guest is provided service (for example, the restaurant or front desk) will be incomplete and future sales and analysis potentially hampered.

Interface with Other Systems

As important as the seamless integration and interoperability of different architectures and applications of all systems in the industry are, the property management system <u>must</u> interface with, if not incorporate within the property management system itself, at a minimum, the global distribution system (GDS) and the central reservation system *(CRS)*.

If the PMS and GDS/CRS come from different vendors, the two must communicate seamlessly. If not, duplicate data and mistakes, and therefore unhappy guests, may easily be encountered. Additionally, original PMSs (and most of their successors for many years afterwards) did not have real-time interfaces to either GDS/CRS or various management applications. As a further result, the available rooms in hotels were often undersold (or in some cases oversold) when agents and franchises failed to sell their entire "allotment" of a hotel's rooms. Also, when a guest called to make reservations for a vacation or meeting event, he or she would often have to be transferred between multiple operators and repeat the same information several times in order to make reservations for different activities associated with the same stay (i.e., meeting space, restaurant reservations, golf tee times, tennis court times, etc.). The Global Distribution System will be covered in detail later and also in the next chapter.

Sales and Catering Applications.   Banquets and meetings are all part of a hotel's operation and must be included in any revenue reporting of the night audit function of the PMS.

Point-of-Sale System (Food and Beverage).   As the main system on the food and beverage side, the importance of this interface cannot be understated. In the past, the lack of an interface resulted in lost revenue and poor service due to the fact that these two systems did not communicate directly.

Guest charges were sometimes processed *after* the guests checked out, resulting in lost revenue, or guests were made to wait while a charge was manually added to a folio. Secondly, if a guest wished to dispute a restaurant charge and no data appeared on the front desk screen, the front office was at a loss and often deleted the charge at checkout to speed things along.

Hotel Retail Points.   If a hotel contains other retail shops such as gift shops or pharmacies that allow room charges, their systems must interface with the PMS to ensure that purchases appear on the room bill.

HVAC or EMS Systems.   The heating, ventilating, and air-conditioning systems *(HVAC)* as well as the energy management system *(EMS)* need to be accessed by various departments in the efficient operation of any facility. For example, during the slow season, parts of a hotel may be closed and the lights and heat turned off to conserve energy and cut costs. Therefore, the PMS needs to integrate with this component and ensure that guests are placed in the proper "open" sections of the hotel.

In-Room Amenities.   Whether it's pay-per-view, printing services, the minisafe, or the minibar, all in-room purchases must be tracked.

Messaging.   If a hotel does not have voice mail, the PMS must allow for messages to be taken and applied to individual rooms.

Security.   With the advent of key cards replacing traditional key systems and through the interface with the PMS, greater *security* is available. As with the housekeeping function where report generation helps management in operations and analysis, in electronic key systems, reports can be generated with the PMS on the date, time, and individual key access to specific rooms.

The Call Accounting System.   Posting costs from any calls guests may make from their rooms is done by the PMS. The *call accounting system* is an interface between the hotel's PBX (private branch exchange), which transfers calls to specific rooms or offices, and the PMS. Newer hotels are expected to embrace voice over IP where voice is put over data lines and a router, switch, and software are used in place of the PBX. Either way, an interface is needed between the PMS and the phone system.

3. FOUR KEY INTERFACES

Due to their need for real-time data, three other important interfaces along with the GDS/CRS warrant further discussion. They are:

- Real-time interface with the GDS/CRS
- The activities management systems

- Built-in revenue and yield management tools
- The enterprise

Real-Time Interface with the GDS/CRS

While the integration between PMSs and GDSs/CRSs is rapidly evolving, this interface has traditionally been the single most important element in multi-unit operators' and brands' decision about which PMS and/or CRS to implement. While brands, owners, and agents all have the same general goal—to generate as much revenue as possible from the sale of as many room nights as possible—the different business models and the varying relationships between these entities have historically made the integration of GDS/CRS and PMS data complicated in many ways.

In short, most hotels want to sell as many of their own room nights as possible so they do not have to pay commissions or booking fees, but the hotel does not want to leave any room empty that could have been otherwise filled by any booking source. Almost everyone else wants to sell as many of the hotel's room nights as possible so they can collect commissions or booking fees. In the past, and even today in many situations, hoteliers were/are forced to decide (relatively far in advance) how many rooms they were going to allocate to various third party booking agents.

In a situation where there is no real-time integration between systems, rooms allocated to third-party booking agents, known as "blocks of rooms," are essentially removed from the hotel's inventory.

As a result, the hotel can not sell those rooms to potential guests, even if those guests would be willing to pay a higher rate per room than was given the third-party booking agent for the block. This situation may or may not benefit the third party depending on the circumstances, but it always acts to limit the hotel's ability to manage or maximize its own revenue. In recent times, with the development of large, Internet-based third party booking agents, there is even some concern that such situations may result in a single third party having the ability to negatively affect average room rates for an entire geographic area by controlling too large a percentage of the available inventory.

Real-time integration between the PMS and the GDS/CRS (and other booking engines), provides hoteliers and brands with much greater ability to manage their room inventory in real time in addition to providing a number of benefits relative to revenue management *(discussed in a following section).*

Because many GDSs/CRSs in use today rely on the collection of room inventory data from individual properties' PMSs, a brand's CRS could not function properly if the hoteliers did not install a PMS that could be integrated with the brand's CRS. As a result, large hotel chains have spent millions of dollars developing robust (and often proprietary) interfaces between their brand's CRS and hotel PMS systems. You will study the interaction of the PMS with the GDS and CRS in depth in the next chapter.

Integration with Activities Management Systems

A majority of hotels in the world have fewer than 100 rooms and do not have a great many additional activities that need to be managed within the hotel's systems. Larger hotels and resort properties, however, generally have a myriad of nonroom facilities that guests use such as restaurants, banquet rooms, meeting rooms, golf courses, and tennis courts. Additionally, guests in these properties may desire to reserve specific hotel services at predetermined times, many of which require preplanning by the hotel such as Internet access, spa treatments, or golf lessons.

Many large and resort style hotels have entirely separate systems for managing nonroom hotel resources. These systems often include (golf) tee time management, spa management, sales and catering, and other systems. It is not uncommon for hotels with older PMSs to require guests to schedule various hotel activities in these completely different systems with different staff members within the hotel. All too often, guests are forced to resupply all of the same information provided to the original room reservation clerk to each of these different system operators.

Guest service issues aside, using separate and nonintegrated systems for this purpose decreases revenues and increases expenses. Hotels lose significant potential revenues when room reservation agents fail to sell all available hotel services to guests when they call to book their rooms. Additionally, hotels lose even more potential revenue when guests cancel room reservations in a PMS that is not integrated with other hotel systems because the cancelled room reservation does not automatically result in cancellation of the spa treatment, restaurant meal, or athletic facility use. Staff may be scheduled or other guests denied reservations for various hotel amenities and resources based on false availability information in spa, tee time, and other systems because they are not integrated with the PMS.

Modern PMSs designed for use in large hotels and resort properties have integrated functionality that allows users, staff, or guests to reserve multiple hotel resources either in conjunction with or independent from an actual room reservation. Therefore, when a guest makes a reservation, reservation clerks (or the application itself in a direct guest system) have the opportunity to "upsell" additional hotel services to the guest without forcing the guest to enter the same information twice. Also, when a guest cancels a room reservation, the staff member providing the cancellation is prompted to ask the guest if he or she would also like to cancel other activities at the hotel.

Integration of the PMS with other activities management systems, therefore, drives additional hotel (nonroom) revenue and saves the hotel money by decreasing the incidents of "false no-shows" for various hotel resources.

Built-In Revenue and Yield Management Tools

In general, the hotel's goal (relative to rooms) is to maximize revenue. Contrary to what you might instinctively believe, maximizing room revenue does not necessarily mean selling as many rooms as possible. Since *Total Room Revenue*

= *Average Dollars per Room Night* × *Room Nights Sold,* maximizing revenue requires hoteliers to consider both the number of rooms they sell and the price at which they sell those rooms. Modern PMSs provide the hotelier with tools for managing room sales so as to maximize revenue and profits. These functions are generally called either revenue management or yield management tools.

While yield and revenue management are often used interchangeably, they actually mean two very different things. The process of calculating potential maximum revenue and making projections about occupancy levels and pricing is referred to as *revenue management.* The more complicated process of calculating potential maximum operating margins and making projections about types and levels of room sales and pricing based on potential profitability is referred to as *yield management.*

Just like airlines, oil companies, and bakeries, hoteliers, in order to maximize revenue or profits, must continually calculate and recalculate potential revenue models based on a number of variables. Although a completely accurate projection of potential maximum revenue requires the development and processing of complicated equations with many variables, basic calculations can be performed using historic sales and pricing data in conjunction with information that the hotelier can reasonably predict (such as major convention bookings, sports events, special groups, holidays, etc.). Modern PMSs provide this basic functionality.

Modern PMSs use a weighted historic average determined by the user along with the systems calendar (for holidays) and any additional information supplied by the user to set rates and predict availability for future room nights. While the functionality supplied by most PMSs in this regard is currently not extremely complicated, it is fast and easy to use compared with stand-alone yield management systems that generally require a significant financial and labor investment that is often not realistic for a small property.

The Enterprise

An *enterprise* is any business that uses computers. You need to look at the development of the property management system within the hotel computing environment as a whole. One final and important system with which the PMS needs to interface is the applications used by other departments such as finance and human resources. These applications are sometimes referred to as the back office since they are behind the scenes. Whereas the PMS is involved with the day to day operations of the hotel, back office systems handle other actions such as payroll or purchasing. The enterprise refers to all the systems—front and back. (*Front* and *back end* have different meanings in different contexts. In the networking world, *front end* refers to the client and *back end* to the server. In computer industry terms, *front end* refers to applications that a user deals with directly such as a Web site, and *back end,* to the applications that support them such as databases.) *Enterprise application integration (EAI)* is part of the enterprise system's evolution. EAI involves the incorporation of this technology at the application level with an end goal of fewer redundancies and

1. ERP ——————→ 2. EAI ——————→ 3. BPI

Figure 7-4.

an increase in collaborative synergy among staff members and knowledge workers. This collaboration is all too important in understanding the enterprise. With this collaboration, everyone is using the same data. EAI is the next step of its predecessor, enterprise resource planning (ERP), on the road to what has become somewhat of a holy grail for business people and technologists everywhere, *business process integration (BPI)*. Figure 7-4 shows how the enterprise has recently been transformed and developed.

Take a closer look at ERP. **Enterprise resource planning** was initially developed for the manufacturing industry for the purpose of cost reduction. ERP is made up of modules that represent and are used by specific departments. Accounting has its own software module as does human resources as does sales and so on. In the past, when a change was made in purchasing, accounting would not see that change on its computer screen or in its reports unless someone from the purchasing department let accounting know about the change through traditional channels (phone, e-mail, etc.). ERP companies saw this as an inefficiency waiting to be remedied. This led to the development of modules or department specific applications which were made to *work together*. Any change in one would reflect in the others as well. For example, if sales were increased, operations would see the need to make more products in real time and adapt accordingly. So how is this important to hospitality? Imagine a banquet doubling in size and going on longer than expected. This change would immediately be reflected in all modules, including accounting and human resources. These departments could then use this timely and identical information to account for and act upon these new costs in both food and beverage and labor. Over time and with evolution and real use of the Internet for e-commerce, EAI was the new term introduced and used when referring to the theme of the enterprise. EAI goes beyond the "in-house" enterprise collaboration to include external entities involved with the company such as customers and suppliers. Additionally, EAI incorporates newer technologies such as object-oriented programming and XML, among others. The hospitality industry is unique in that its front of the house system, the PMS (or POS in a restaurant scenario), often stands alone or contains a thicker seam in integrating with other systems such as the back office. Integration between the two is taking place; however, obstacles still remain.

Business process integration is more complicated than the previous two. Remember what a system is—a way of doing things. The definition of a process is "a systematic series of actions directed to some end." For example, think of a department using a system to complete specific departmental tasks. The controller balances the books, the housekeeping manager inspects the rooms, and the sales person entertains a client. Organizations as a whole and hotels in particular have many different departments and therefore many types of processes. This is the coveted next step of the back office or computer systems in general where such processes of sales, operations, and project management

can share and benefit from a common system and "information" once hidden–
is unearthed. This ideal currently resides in theory and not in practice. The key
is that if processes from different departments can somehow share the same
system, then more can be gained. BPI is by definition the real-time integration
of information, processes, and projects in a real-time setting. In another example, imagine a hotel being built, a new management team being formed,
supplies ordered, payments made, reservations taken, and so on. Today different systems handle these different actions and are integrating through such initiatives beginning with ERPs and now EAIs to what is hoped is something
much more efficient and intelligent—business process integration. Why is this
so important? In the future the property management system will be one piece
of a larger BPI system. BPI may not happen overnight, but the further integration and tightening up of data collaboration at a minimum will be highlighted.
With this improved internal communication, multilevel properties can share
customer and business data among other locations, expanding the enterprise.
Study the enterprise wide screen shot in Figure 7-5.

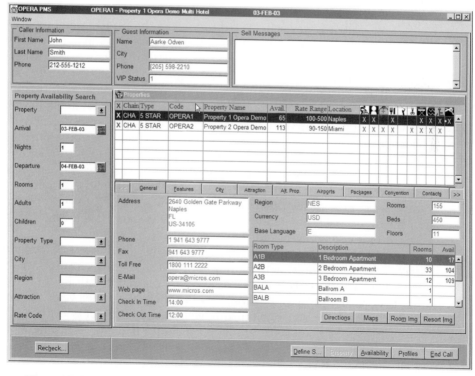

Figure 7-5. Within a brand there may be numerous hotels; therefore, systems
are used to manage a customer within the entire chain. This Micros/Fidelio
screen shows how chains are moving towards more global systems in
customer service. Here, different customer criteria may be applied to
specific member hotels around the world. (*Source: Micros/Fidelio, Inc.*)

In this example, a clerk or manager can get a companywide view of a chain or multiproperty hotel to further serve guests and obtain business intelligence. Through this screen, questions such as "does your Miami property have a golf course?" can be answered and cross property business improved.

The PMS is maturing at a faster rate than before. Spending in the year 2000 and new security measures implemented after September 11, 2001, have resulted in new demands by the industry upon the vendors. However, the biggest leap the PMS may have made is to a graphical user interface.

4. GRAPHICAL USER INTERFACE

You have probably never used anything but an intuitive *graphical user interface*. In addition, as college students, you probably have a higher level of literacy and cognitive capabilities than the general population. As a result, many of you probably take the concept of being able to "point and click" your way through any application for granted. The screen shots already presented in this chapter are perfect examples of modern PMS interfaces.

You probably never bothered to look at the user manual or instructions for the vast majority of computer applications you use on a daily basis. This is because almost all consumer-based information systems such as MS Word, Napster, Real Player, MS Explorer, Netscape, etc., have been developed with inherently user-friendly, or "intuitive," graphical user interfaces. It is important to remember though that consumer-based information systems have been designed by huge companies that derive billions of dollars in revenue from the widespread use of these systems. On the other hand, specific business-based applications, such as PMSs, have been developed by much smaller companies (with fewer resources) and are required in many cases to perform much more complicated tasks than their consumer-based cousins. So it should come as no surprise that the development and implementation of intuitive user interfaces for business-based applications, such as PMSs, have taken much longer than they did for consumer-based applications.

For hospitality professionals employing a PMS, however, there may be no single element of the system more important than the user interface. Not only must modern PMS user interfaces support the rapid training of a workforce that historically turns over almost two to three times per year, but going forward, the PMS interface will also have to support direct guest usage without the assistance of hotel staff. Whenever a choice is made regarding which PMS to use, study the interfaces. Are there other fields you wish to see? Can someone be trained on the system in a short period of time?

Modern PMS user interfaces must be almost "training free." People have to be able to ascertain how to use them as easily as they would a popular Web site. From an internal staff perspective, the issues are easy to understand. Every time an employee quits, a new employee must be trained to use the system. During the new employee's training period, the hotel must pay for additional labor (the trainee and the trainer). During the first several days of an employee "working the system solo," there are customer service slowdowns and decreased worker productivity. As a result, by the time you calculate the average number of people a typical hotel must hire and train during any given three- to seven-year period (the life of a typical PMS), it inevitably will cost more to train new staff in the use of a PMS then it does to purchase and install the system itself.

People (i.e., guests) have grown accustomed to self-service, and many guests will prefer to enter their own reservation information via a browser or "self-register" and make their own reservations, as opposed to relaying information through a hotel operator. Consumers have grown to expect business applications to have the same type of easy to use graphical user interfaces they are accustomed to in consumer products and Web sites. Direct guest interface also means much more than just accepting room reservations from computer literate people with sophisticated educational backgrounds. Educated consumers are not the only people in the world who have money and stay in hotels, so user interfaces must be intuitive even for guests who are not computer literate or lack high-end cognitive capabilities.

Direct guest interface in a rapidly shrinking world also means much more than just accepting room reservations from computer literate people who all speak the same language. Thanks to many advances in translation technologies during the past several years, people have become accustomed to viewing Web pages in their native language. Both guests and staff now expect to be able to use a PMS in multiple languages.

As a result, modern PMSs must have robust user interfaces that are extremely intuitive and user friendly. Luckily, most do. However, many still do not and telling the difference between the two is almost impossible for the average person sitting through a sales demonstration. There is an entire field of endeavor referred to as "human factors engineering" and a science associated with the development and testing of all those intuitive interfaces people take for granted in their favorite consumer applications. In a sales demonstration of a system, a professional salesperson can make almost any graphical user interface look easy to use. To actually determine the difference in "levels of intuitiveness" between two systems, however, requires somewhat extensive testing that generally is only affordable at the brand, chain, or multiproperty level.

You should understand, however, that the intuitive nature of a PMS user interface is probably one of the most critical elements there is relative to the system's ability to enable a guest to make reservations. If potential guests, either via hotel staff or directly, cannot make reservations in the system quickly, efficiently, and easily, they will ultimately find a different hotel where they can. Hence, the intuitive nature of a PMS user interface is a critical success factor relative to a hotel's obtainment of its gross revenue goals.

The terrorist strikes against the United States have pushed the need for security at the property level to the forefront. Possible new interfaces may include eye scanning, finger, and facial recognition software for individual identification. Whichever interface a property chooses, the system must be reliable.

5. SUMMARY

The property management system and its interfaces with the user as well as with other systems are vital to success in managing hotel or hotel-like organizations. Housing, feeding, and entertaining people along with providing other services can at times be a daunting task. Not only are different staffs used but different systems as well. Since managers are primarily judged by controlling costs, generating revenue, and guest satisfaction scores, any system that can serve as a focal point for data collection and management is welcomed. Whether this critical tool becomes part of a larger enterprise system or just "betters" its interface is less important to the manager as long as its role is understood. Any hospitality manager must understand its function and its development, as well as its interfaces with other systems.

6. CASE STUDY AND LEARNING ACTIVITY

The Union League of Philadelphia

Challenges and Solutions

The Union League of Philadelphia is one of the oldest clubs in the nation with 67 guest rooms, 12 meeting rooms, and a staff of 150. Clubs can provide a great example of the challenges faced in technology and its evolution since oftentimes they are found in very old buildings that make major changes difficult. In going behind the scenes, you can appreciate the knowledge and energy needed in working with technology in the hospitality industry. Under the general management of Jeff Mc-Fadden, Robert Hencinski, the MIS manager, was faced with the task of bringing the club into the future. Upon his arrival four years prior, and bringing over sixteen years of experience to the job, Robert faced numerous challenges. An environment with multiple brand personal based computers running with an antiquated DOS-based operating system on a dated Club Management System (a PMS particular to clubs), with different departments using proprietary software and hardware was only the tip of the iceberg of his challenges. The staff was using different systems that did not communicate and the building was full of "mysterious" data and analog wires with no way of allocating costs to any phone calls made. Lastly, a look in the files revealed unnecessary and costly service and purchase agreements.

Encounters such as these are all too common in the industry. With ownership or management of the fixed assets, such as the building itself, changing many times over, continuity is lost or forgotten. The result is a building with disparate, outdated systems that is not administered properly. A tour of the property shows a setup all too common in large holdings today. The phone system switch and interface is in one part of the building, the data network and servers centralized in another, and the cable and entertainment systems on another floor. With each system requiring its own dedicated space and possessing its own product evolution and life cycle, integration and consolidation are an obvious challenge. Cost considerations and building structure often hamper solutions and only allow for stopgap measures to be implemented. Further, with "back of the house" space always losing out to "front of the house" space, an MIS director's job is always a battle.

Besides staying current and solving any technology issues arriving hourly, the Union League faces the task of dealing with a number of outside vendors and service providers. A brief list of some of its technology dealings—an Internet service provider, a Web page management company, a company managing the pay phones, a different company providing local and long-distance calling, a high speed (2 T-1's and DSL) hardware company, and of course the multitude of software vendors—exemplifies how many different entities (and their related costs) can be involved in any operation utilizing the latest technology.

The leadership of the league through Robert has met these challenges head-on. Due to the historic nature of the building and the need for more meeting space, major systems have stayed in their dedicated places; however, their operational efficiency has been streamlined. Outdated wires and interfaces have been removed while the infrastructure has been updated to Category V cable for standard Ethernet network architecture. The PC of choice is now coming from one vendor—Dell, and the printers from Hewlett Packard, resulting in bulk discounts and easier to maintain hardware. A state-of-the-art club management system from Gary Jonas Ltd. was purchased for use in the restaurant, hotel, and back offices, allowing for staff and management to share and retrieve information from the different departments in real time. The League Web page has been outsourced to a specialty vendor, allowing the staff to concentrate more on daily operations. Finally, the operating system was moved to Windows NT and the productivity software to Microsoft Office, enabling knowledge workers to operate within the same framework and aid in software training.

Current projects in the works include upgrading to digital cable and the purchase of another T-1 for additional phone lines. Additionally, September 11th has resulted in increased security concerns. Some possible new ventures include the purchase of member identifier cards small enough to fit on a key chain that could track members interaction with the club and allow for secured access. The cards would be aided by the installation of additional cameras to confirm that the person in possession of the card is indeed the proper one.

With the proper system now in place, the Union League is now moving towards becoming a truly digital club.

Learning Activity

1. With all the different problems faced by the League, how do you think it did? Why?
2. Of the major changes made, which one should have taken first priority? Why?
3. List the next four priorities in order. Justify your answer.

4. Given all the new improvements in the League, what demands or improvements are needed in its club management system?

5. Can you think of any aspects unique to clubs that may make their property (club) management system unique?

7. KEY TERMS

Business Process Integration (BPI)

Call accounting system

CRS

EMS

Enterprise

Enterprise Application Integration (EAI)

Graphical user interface

HVAC

Revenue management

Security

Yield management

8. CHAPTER QUESTIONS

1. What are the broad areas of functionality that a property management system must provide?

2. What is an intuitive user interface and why is it important to a PMS?

3. Why is it important to integrate a PMS to spa management, golf tee time, and other activity management systems?

4. What is the difference between yield management and revenue management?

5. What other hotel information systems rely on the PMS for information?

6. What is an ERP?

7. Why is business process integration so important?

8. When purchasing a PMS, what are some major considerations?

9. Aside from the chapter content, can you think of any other future PMS requirements?

10. Who on your staff should be trained on PMS usage?

9. REFERENCES

Gray, William S. 1996. *Hospitality accounting.* Upper Saddle River, NJ: Prentice Hall.

Laudon, Kenneth, and Jane Laudon. 2000. *Management information systems.* 6th ed. Upper Saddle River, NJ: Prentice Hall.

Vallen, Gary K., and Jerome J. Vallen. 2000. *Check-in check-out.* 6th ed. Upper Saddle River, NJ: Prentice Hall.

CHAPTER EIGHT

Hotel Global Distribution Systems and Channels

CHAPTER CONTENTS

INTERVIEW

Mr. Doug Anderson is a hotel analyst with San Francisco-based Hotwire.com, an *opaque pricing* service that provides discount travel for airlines, hotels, and rental cars via the Internet. Prior to joining Hotwire.com, Doug served as a revenue management analyst with Hilton Hotels. He is a graduate of Michigan State University's School of Hospitality Business in East Lansing, Michigan.

Q: What challenges exist in managing hotel distribution and maximizing revenues?

A: The main challenges are the problem of *onward distribution* and the inability to yield many Internet distribution channels. Hotel revenue managers hate the fact that they frequently give a rate to one *Internet distribution system (IDS)* channel, and then, that rate is subsequently proliferated and appears in numerous other channels unbeknownst to them. This is what has become known as onward distribution. It is when a distributor of hotel room inventory (i.e., rates and availability) resells its inventory (that which was given to it from hotels and hotel companies) to other distributors or affiliates for them to sell as well. The positive side is that more entities are selling a particular hotel's inventory. The negatives, though, are many. First, it is difficult to track the actual source of a reservation, making it harder to segment customers and distribution channels. Second, onward distribution introduces new intermediaries, taking away invaluable customer relationship building and learning opportunities. With more entities involved in the process, there are more opportunities for breakdowns in communications and for others to influence customers to patronize other hotels. Finally, it makes *revenue (yield) management,* the goal of which is to offer specific differential pricing through different channels, extremely difficult, if not impossible, to accomplish. Because many IDS channels require guaranteed allotments of inventory and net rates, hotel yield management is greatly restricted. An IDS channel negotiates rates with hotel suppliers. These rates are termed *net rates.* It then can mark up the rates when it sells the inventory. Since it maintains some discretion in setting published rates and defining where those rates will be published, it can easily undercut prices being offered by the hotel or many of its other distribution channels. Consequently, control of a hotel's room inventory shifts from the hotel to the onward distributing IDS channels, and hotel revenue runs the risk of getting diluted. These are not good things for hotels trying to maximize their revenues and maintain control over their own inventory. Thus, the message to hoteliers is very clear: when choosing distributors and distribution channels, find out what affiliate distributors will be used and the policies for managing inventory and rates.

Q: How can a hotel company achieve and sustain competitive advantage in the areas of hotel distribution and the information technology used to support and enable the distribution function?

A: To achieve competitive advantage in hotel distribution, a property or hotel company must strive for the intersection of two points. The first is to gain access to the largest number of potential and targeted guests as possible through the strategic selection and usage of IDS and GDS distribution channels. The second is to leverage those relationships to gain exposure to the guests. To sustain competitive advantage, hotels must maintain their physical products and service levels and build strong relationships between the revenue management, sales and marketing, reservations, and operations functions. The goal is to make any first-time guest gained from an IDS or GDS channel a repeat guest. This requires wowing the guest and meeting or exceeding his/her expectations. Developing guest loyalty will allow a reduction in customer acquisition costs. When it comes to IT, continually invest in systems to make sure they are current, serve the organization's needs, and help staff to meet guest expectations. Where possible, maintain openness and flexibility in order to adapt to changing market needs and seamlessly connect to each distribution channel in which you elect to participate.

Q: What do you see as the key developments and trends in hotel distribution that one should watch, and why do you feel these are important?

A: Most of the key developments in hotel distribution are happening on the Internet front. Right now, guests are moving away from the traditional travel sources like travel agencies and seeking out IDS channels. With the evolution of Web travel resources, we have seen increased demand and usage of the Web to not only shop for but also book travel and accommodations. In fact, usage is doubling each year, putting these services in the mainstream. Guests are becoming more aware of and more comfortable with using online technologies. These are important trends. Hotels now have more cost effective options to sell their inventory and more direct access to their potential guests. This will help hotels by reducing customer acquisition costs, making for more attractive bottom lines. Hotel guests also benefit. They now have more choices and more information at their fingertips so they can make better or more informed choices, find better deals, and more. Certainly, the Internet has changed the competitive dynamics of the industry.

Q: What do you think will be the next developments in e-commerce? Where and in what sorts of functionality or features will companies likely invest?

A: The next developments in e-commerce have to be in the area of open connectivity between key hotel systems. In terms of features and functionality for a hotel, one must have a core set of tightly integrated applications, including central reservations, revenue management, property management, and sales and catering systems to allow for real-time exchange of data, seamless inventory management, and single-image inventory (i.e., all

systems are interconnected so they can see the same data at the same time).
If this integration does not exist, a hotel will not be able to take full advantage of its distribution channels or its revenue management system. A revenue management system must be able to know at every second of the day
how many rooms and at what rates are in inventory for the next 365 days
or more. In addition, this integration will allow the revenue management
system to set real-time rate changes, selling restrictions, etc., and simultaneously communicate these changes to all systems and channels that are
impacted by them. A hotel should also be able to track lost business and re-
gret (or turndown) statistics to determine whether or not strategies are successful or damaging. Having an integrated set of core applications makes
it easier to ascertain such data. Finally, many group hotels should maintain
some sort of technology that allows them to monitor how a piece of business progresses and its booking pace, from pitch to checkout.

Q: What is the role of discount services like Hotwire, priceline.com, and auc-
    tion Web sites? How do they work, and how can hotel companies take full
    advantage of them? Are there risks to a hotel company that competition
    will be based on price rather than demand?

A: Generally speaking, discount travel sites like Hotwire are meant to drive in-
    cremental business, that is, supplemental revenue and new guests. The busi-
    ness that Hotwire delivers is not the core business for most hotels. We are
    meant to help hotels sell rooms that would typically perish, or go unused,
    each night. One element of a service like Hotwire or priceline.com is some-
    thing called *brand shielding* or opaque distribution. These services help sup-
    pliers (hotels) discount and distribute that inventory without eroding the
    value of their brands. In effect, a hotel or hotel company can discount with-
    out letting its consumers know it is doing so. This helps to preserve *rate in-
    tegrity*. In the case of Hotwire, for example, we do not reveal a hotel's name
    or address prior to purchase. While we do provide some selection criteria
    such as a rating (star category), location (city/market areas), and price, the
    consumer's decision is mostly blind; it is devoid of the actual hotel or hotel
    brand. On average, the rates available are discounted between 40 percent
    and 70 percent of a hotel's transparent or published rates. Transparent rates
    are found on IDS channels like Orbitz, Expedia, and Travelocity, where the
    hotel name and address are readily displayed and are typical of what one
    might find in other distribution channels used by the hotel.

    To take full advantage of discount sites, use them when you need them.
    Hotwire and priceline.com do not require allotments or fixed rates from
    hotels; therefore, hotels can turn them on and off like a light switch. They
    generally do not charge commissions; they make their money by marking
    up net rates, the pre-negotiated rates with participating hotels. They attract
    customers who generally are not brand loyal and at no additional cost to
    the hotel. They represent incremental business. Therefore, the risks asso-
    ciated with these channels are minimized. If a hotel is looking to capture

some incremental business or sell some distressed inventory, services like Hotwire and priceline.com can help and are worth exploring. They can also help you provide trial service or usage for new guests, ones that have never before visited your property. When this happens, it is up to your hotel and its employees to brand the guest and win his/her loyalty for life.

Q: Going forward, what do you think will be the role of Internet-based reservation services? What about application service providers (ASP)?

A: IDS channels will be all but a total replacement of today's human based *central reservation systems (CRSs)* and *travel agents.* This will allow many hotels that currently staff a reservations department on property to out-source some of these functions to the Internet. Internet-based reservation services will allow smaller hotels to discontinue many expensive contracts with human based reservation services and become even more competitive—and we see this happening today. ASPs will also continue to expand into the hotel arena. Many of the big brands are already using them to re-duce their technology overhead costs, expedite rollout, and simplify main-tenance. ASPs, in effect, provide hotels access to high-tech without the large investment capital typically required. With this approach, there is no need for expensive hardware at the property level. Through a standard Web browser (e.g., Internet Explorer or Netscape), hotels can access informa-tion and data housed in an off-site server, database, or data warehouse. The ASP model will have the biggest impact on smaller properties because they typically do not have the capital resources to begin investing in a lot of technology. Therefore, ASPs will give them access to new hospitality sys-tems with the click of a mouse—just as easy as it is to change URLs.

Q: How do you think guests will book hotel accommodations twenty years from now? What will be the distribution channels and booking methods of choice and why? What evidence do you see to support this vision?

A: I envision that most guests will book hotel accommodations through either a self-serve IDS or GDS channel. Whether the user interface (i.e., front end) is a PC, hybrid Web-TV, or some new personal digital assistant (PDA) or *wireless application protocol (WAP)* phone-like device, IDSs and GDSs will continue to be the primary booking engines. The power, however, will shift in favor of the consumers, and away from the suppliers and distributors. These will be the booking methods of choice because they have access to most of the supply (availability and rates), because they provide consumers with choices, and be-cause they are easily accessible via the Internet. As Internet access, usage, and information grows, so, too, does consumer power. Consumers can now make more informed shopping decisions, comparison shop, access feedback from other consumers, and more—all with the click of a mouse. We also see trends indicating that the supply of rooms continues to grow and outpace demand. In the present economy, hotels are lucky if they do above 70–75 percent occupancy per year. Thus, consumers will have considerably more leverage and more tools to help them negotiate better deals or find bargains.

1. INTRODUCTION

Since the early stages of commerce, merchants have wrestled with determining the *best* approach for delivering their products and services to the marketplace for purchase and consumption. This can be defined as attaining the broadest possible reach to the largest available audience meeting a company's target market segments at the most affordable cost and with the highest potential for winning conversions (i.e., bookings). In short, there are a series of tradeoffs between reach, richness, cost, and effectiveness or conversion. The challenge of finding the best distribution methods for each targeted customer segment still exists, but what a difference there is in today's distribution process and global economy. Complicated by the many advances in information technology (IT) and the growing shift from the physical world to the virtual one (e.g., electronic marketing), the ways in which companies interact with and conduct business with their customers is radically changing and, thus, requires a new mindset and skill set to achieve success.

Until recently, hotel distribution was characterized by philosophies like "location, location, location" or "if you build it, they will come." Unfortunately, these tend to overshadow more rational approaches to selecting distribution channels and applying IT to broaden visibility and win market share. Moreover, they are, by themselves, no longer sufficient in attracting today's sophisticated and demanding consumers. Within the hotel industry, distribution systems and channels have become far too complex to be treated with such simplicity. The thrust of today's distribution systems is about having the *right* product in the *right* place at the *right* time at the *right* price and under the *right* set of conditions or circumstances, as defined by the consumer (Stein and Sweat 1998, p. 36). Applying this thinking in a hotel context, a company's *global distribution system (GDS)* must support two primary objectives. First, it must provide distribution channels that give customers the ability to easily and quickly search for products and services they are willing to purchase with full disclosure of rates and availability (what is often termed seamless, *single-image inventory*), and second, it must provide a means to conduct the transaction on the spot, with immediate confirmation that the transaction has been successfully completed. (Castleberry, Hempell, and Kaufman 1998)

To achieve these objectives, a hotel GDS requires a clear strategy, dedicated resources, effective management, and a sound information technology infrastructure if it is to provide competitive advantage—and it can with access to new customers, better and faster service, sophisticated rate and inventory management, economies of scale, reduced overhead, lower transaction costs, enhanced buyer and supplier relationships, *cross-selling* and *up-selling*, unique capabilities, and superior channel performance.

Generally, a GDS is the first point of all guest contact and it serves as the initial and primary source of data collection. Without it, business would be next to impossible to ascertain. Therefore, it is one of the most important technologies in a hotel company's IT portfolio. It is also one of the most complex components of a hotel firm's IT portfolio due to its technological prowess, the complicated business logic and rules, the numerous interfaces that must be supported to connect heterogeneous systems together to share data (both within the company and with the outside world), the volume of transactions and speed by which they must be processed, the uniqueness of room inventory and attributes across a hotel chain, individual guest needs, and the sophistication of the underlying database and search engine that powers it.

Within the hotel industry, distribution channels are being reshaped as the result of technological advancements, new and emerging players, and a shift in the balance of power between suppliers, buyers, and intermediaries. At the same time, the corresponding costs associated with technological investment and transaction processing are rising due to the complex networks and technological infrastructure (e.g., two-way interfaces) that must be in place to support seamless, single-image inventory across the spectrum of distribution channels that exist today and that will exist in the future. Complicating matters, executives have few tools and little guidance to help them determine when to invest, how much to invest, and how to assess or gauge the business value to be gained from the investment. Consequently, this is an important area of study requiring shrewd and decisive decision making due to the strategic positioning implications and the high costs of doing business in today's competitive environment. It is important for hoteliers to consider the strategic implications of using certain distribution channels while avoiding others. Moreover, the corresponding costs associated with technological investment and transaction processing (which are on the rise due to the complex networks and technological infrastructure required to support seamless, single-image inventory) necessitate greater focus on better, proactive distribution channel selection and management. This chapter will discuss the strategic significance of a hotel GDS. It will explore the many components of a hotel GDS, developments and trends in the distribution arena, and the importance of developing a *distribution strategy* to create competitive advantage.

2. IMPORTANCE OF GDS

In simplest terms, the objective of a GDS is to distribute a company's products (in this case, hotel room inventory or meeting space) to as broad an audience as possible in the most effective and cost-efficient means available so that they can be purchased. More specifically, the roles played by a hotel GDS have evolved over time—from one of transaction-based emphasis to one of strategic value—but at any one point in time, a hotel GDS fulfills five important roles, as illustrated in Figure 8-1.

The first role of a hotel GDS is one of simple utility: transaction processing and maintaining, controlling, and reporting room inventory levels and hotel rates. Initially, a hotel GDS provided a simple accounting of rooms available versus rooms sold at predetermined rates, generally set by each hotel for some

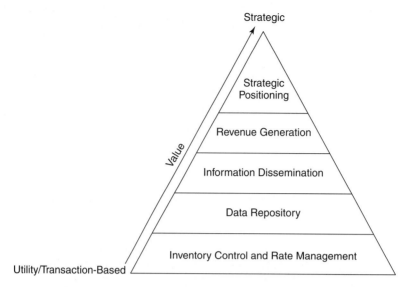

Figure 8-1.   A properly used global distribution system serves many roles from inventory
control and rate management to strategic positioning.

defined period of time (e.g., seasonal rates). Over time, this function has expanded in complexity and strategic importance as more emphasis has been
placed on yield management to maximize a hotel's total revenue. Now, this
function is responsible for the definition of *room pools* and *rate categories,* the
allocation of rooms, and the rules and restrictions that govern the sale of these
rooms. The system must support all decision making regarding the setting of
rates, the allocating of rooms, and the rules and restrictions. The system must
then communicate this information to all points of distribution in real time,
enforcing all the rules when a room is reserved or cancelled.

In its second role, a hotel GDS plays an important function as a data
repository and a learning system for guest history, preference, profiles, and
buying patterns. This system is one of the primary collection points of valuable
guest-related information and preferences. The value of the stored data increases with each subsequent guest encounter[1] and from data mining used to
help a company in developing, positioning, and marketing its products and
services. Because of the data collected, this system becomes an important feed
to other core systems, including a company's property management system
and data warehouse, which then enable a company to improve guest recognition, customize guest experiences, position products, and develop new service
and product offerings.

Its third function is that of a communications vehicle. It disseminates vital information regarding inventory availability, rates (including rules and re-

[1] Kirsner (1999) terms this interactive, iterative learning process "progressive profiling."

strictions), and hotel information as well as guest profile data to various points of distribution and service delivery in real time for access by all service associates to allow them to better perform their jobs, recognize their guests, and personalize the guest experience.

Fourth, a hotel GDS represents a source of revenue, not just in terms of room nights or meeting sales generated and revenue maximization through yield management but also through fees charged for participation and for transactions processed. An effective hotel GDS and skilled *channel management* will be key success factors, provide competitive advantage, and influence firm profitability. In room reservations, channel management is the oversight and coordination of the many different ways a reservation can be made, whether over the Internet, by phone or fax, in person, or some other means. Since the cost of hotel distribution can easily reach 20 to 30 percent of a room's daily rate, effective management is essential to containing overhead. Mismanagement of hotel distribution channels will only accelerate the profit margin erosion that results from agent commissions and transaction fees.

Finally, a hotel GDS is a strategic weapon. It plays an important role in a company's positioning, provides access to markets, allows a company to implement unique functionality and selling strategies, builds strategic alliances through *inter-organizational systems,* and provides a product that is used to sell to and attract franchisees and management contracts.

GDSs play a critical role in the sales process of any product or service. In the hospitality industry, significant advances in global distribution systems have raised the stakes of competition by providing access to more markets, creating new sources of revenue, and enhancing guest service while changing the overall economics of the booking process. More importantly, the methods of booking hotel accommodations and meeting space have shifted to alternative approaches that are cheaper to operate and require greater involvement from the customer, thereby freeing up traditional booking channels to process more complicated scenarios. As they continue to evolve, global distribution systems will reshape how travelers plan and arrange accommodations for personal vacations and business trips and how hotel companies interact with their customers. Without question, a hotel's GDS is a mission-critical application, and quite possibly the lifeline of the organization. Any disruptions in service can severely inconvenience, if not cripple, a hotel or entire lodging company. For a more detailed understanding of the complexities, inner workings of hotel GDS, and managerial issues involved, please refer to Appendix 3: Understanding the Complexities of Hotel Global Distribution Systems and Channels.

It can be said that a hotel's global distribution system is the cornerstone for the service delivery process in a hotel and for all hotel-based technology. Yet, you should not consider a global distribution system as a single system or entity. Rather, it is a collection of systems, technology, telecommunications, people, and strategies, that, when combined, provide an effective means of marketing and selling a hotel's guestrooms, meeting space, and other facilities. In most cases, it is the initial and principal data collection point that, in turn, feeds information to all other aspects of the organization and all subsequent processes in the *guest life cycle* (namely registration, in-house services, guest history, post-stay follow-up, and ongoing marketing efforts). Without a well-integrated GDS, functions like marketing, customer relationship building, data mining, revenue (yield) management, and labor forecasting, to name a few, would be severely handicapped—if not impossible to do.

The world of GDS is highly complex and requires that hospitality organizations master a number of competencies if they are to be successful in this arena. Some stress the strategic importance of *core competencies* and competency building to achieve competitive advantage. The core competencies required of hotel companies with respect to distribution channels and GDS are included in Figure 8-2. Essentially, competitive advantage stems from excellence in and mastery of several key areas, including technology development and deployment, supply chain management, customer relationship building, knowledge management, electronic commerce, speed, agility, and flexibility.

3. DEVELOPING A DISTRIBUTION CHANNEL STRATEGY

Being able to successfully manage something and invest in it requires complete understanding of precisely what it is you are trying to manage and how best to allocate firm resources to it. Alternatively stated, you must fully comprehend the concept of global distribution channels in today's context and have the ability to forecast where they are headed in order to select the appropriate channels and technologies to build competitive methods. Effective management of, investment in, and resource allocations to global distribution systems and their

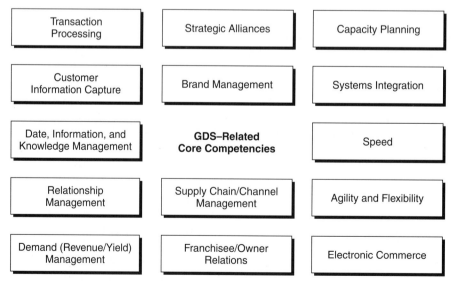

Figure 8-2. GDS-Related Core Competencies Essential for Competitive Advantage

ensuing channels will result in improvements to a hotel's profitability on two fronts: decreased costs and improved revenues. The fundamental principle at work here is that if a hotel can effectively exploit its distribution channels, it can gain market share through increased sales while simultaneously reducing overhead. Both go directly to the hotel's bottom line, thereby improving profitability and competitive advantage.

A distribution strategy does not require participation in all channels but should be able to articulate rationale for participating in those that are chosen and for electing not to participate in others. (Dombey 1997) The rising costs make participation in all channels prohibitive. One of the best illustrations in the travel industry of strategic choices and resource allocations related to GDS is Southwest Airlines. In the airline industry, it is not uncommon for airlines to list their flights and availability in competitors' systems. Just as in the hotel industry, these airlines pay a booking fee for each reservation booked in addition to ongoing fees for participation and flight listings. To reduce overhead, Southwest Airlines has consciously decided not to participate in all airline GDSs. Instead, the company participates only in SABRE and its own reservation system. Southwest is able to make this decision because it understands its customer base and knows how best to reach its targeted audience. Perhaps this is why Southwest Airlines remains one of the most profitable airlines in the industry. This is precisely the same kind of decision hotels and lodging companies must make—but only after customer booking habits, market share, and other variables are better understood.

As transactional costs continue to rise, hotels will need to determine which channels are most profitable for them and how they can yield the best results using these channels. This may mean discontinuing channels that are less productive or those that cost more to maintain in favor of channels that yield greater room revenue and require less overhead to operate. The focus will be placed on distribution share per channel (i.e., the marketing mix or the amount of volume and revenue generated by each channel in the GDS network in comparison with the others to which an organization subscribes or in which it participates). More does not necessarily mean better. Another focus will be on how the winning systems match customers with hotel providers. (Olsen 1996) With a growing number of hotel products and suitable alternatives, it becomes increasingly difficult to discern one hotel from the next. It also becomes harder to get the consumer's attention, since he/she is bombarded with an array of equally attractive options. Therefore, it will be incumbent upon leading systems and GDS providers to find ways to rise above the "noise" and convert lookers into bookers.

Finding and Competing for Electronic "Shelf Space"

Gaining a presence in multiple points of distribution is analogous to finding "shelf space" in a grocery or retail store. More is generally considered better because it improves visibility, customer access, and convenience. Yet, this is not always the best strategy due to the cost implications and support issues associated with maintaining multiple channels. When applying the principles of organizational economics theory, it is easier to see that more is not always better. Each distribution channel has associated with it certain fixed costs, which may include hardware, software, and interface development. Depending upon the channel, these fixed costs may be quite high. To achieve transactional economies of scale, the volume of transactions (reservations) must increase if the average cost per reservation is to decrease. Hence, adding a new distribution channel may destroy this relationship. It has two effects. First, it requires a fixed investment in order to make the channel operational, and second, it will likely reduce the volume of reservations processed via the other, established channels. Both consequences increase average costs and prolong the amount of time it takes to recover the initial investment. (Clemons, Reddi, and Row 1993) This is only desirable if (1) the new distribution channel is more cost-effective than other channels and can shift enough volume to recoup the initial investment, and (2) the new distribution channel attracts untapped markets and generates new demand. Otherwise, it may be more advantageous to have fewer distribution channels. What is difficult to measure in this scenario, however, is the degree to which a channel influences the booking decision, even though it may not be the actual source of the booking.

Hospitality firms must make a strategic commitment to global distribution systems. This implies defining, developing, and implementing a strategy as well as investing in the corresponding technology to support this strategy. No longer can one afford to gratuitously spend money on marketing or distribution channels without knowing the appropriate target markets and anticipating the expected returns. To help hoteliers develop a global distribution strategy and evaluate various distribution channel options, a list of criteria has been provided in Figure 8-3.

Cost Implications

For hotel companies, connectivity to airline GDSs has been costly and problematic but necessary if they want to take advantage of the travel agent market worldwide. The challenges of displaying detailed hotel information in an easy-to-use format and synchronizing databases in real time add to the administrative burdens of managing a hotel's GDS. In particular, the delays in transmission between airline GDSs and a hotel GDS, the batching of transactions, and the processing of error messages that result from incompatibilities between different systems create a cumbersome queuing process that must be closely monitored to avoid overbooking and to ensure that reservations are received at the hotel level before guests arrive. Manual and semiautomated processes also rely extensively on queues. Oftentimes, dedicated staffs are required to manage these queues. While improvements in airline GDS/hotel GDS interfaces help to alleviate the situation, they unfortunately do not completely eliminate the problems from occurring; and hence the queuing process still

Can the new distribution channel
- Gain access to new markets and new customers to drive top-line revenues?
- Strengthen customer relations and build lasting loyalty?
- Provide incremental bookings and revenue?
- Improve yield through rate lift or increases in ADR and REVPAR?
- Create switching costs?
- Build barriers to entry?
- Offer unique and sustainable advantages?
- Yield better information that can be used for competitive advantage or for creating or enhancing products and services?
- Provide easy and convenient access to single-image inventory and last-room availability?
- Be easily updated with rate changes, selling rules, restrictions, etc.?
- Be easily integrated into the company's global distribution network and managed on an ongoing basis?
- Streamline or simplify the technological complexity or management of existing distribution channels?
- Reduce the number of distribution channels required?
- Eliminate potential points of failure and third-party intermediaries?
- Provide economies of scale?
- Reduce customer acquisition costs?
- Reduce operating costs or transaction fees and shift traffic to a channel of lower cost?
- Eliminate duplication?
- Change the balance of power in customer or supplier relationships?
- Alter the basis of competition or change the nature of intra-industry competitive rivalries?
- Enable new business opportunities?
- Track sources of origination for each reservation?
- Protect customer data and ensure privacy?
- Allow the hotel to maintain the locus of control over room inventory and rates?
- Support multiple formats of content (i.e., text, graphics, sound, video, etc.)?

Figure 8-3. Distribution Channel Evaluation Criteria

exists. Despite these shortcomings, hotels are dependent upon the airline GDSs because of their extensive market reach, not only to travel agents but also to Internet booking channels. Airlines recognized early on the value of the travel agent network. To maximize travel agent bookings, airlines helped automate travel agents by providing easy access to their mainframe-based reservation systems. These relationships proved fruitful for the airlines and quickly became a source of competitive advantage. For hotel companies to realize some of the same benefits as airlines in terms of access to the travel agency networks, they must list their properties in each of the major airline GDSs.

To participate in this listing service is not an inexpensive endeavor. Hotels must pay listing fees and transaction costs for every reservation booked. Additionally, hotels are responsible for the information displayed about their facilities, rates, and availability. To maintain this information, the large hotel chains invested heavily in the development of interfaces between their GDSs and the airline GDSs. These interfaces are not only costly to develop but also costly to maintain. They require constant updating due to the dynamism of the airline GDS market and recent changes in the hotel industry. For example, the implementation of yield management systems in many of the large chains resulted in thousands of price updates each day to the airline GDSs. Needless to say, the high costs and complexity of these interfaces put them out of reach of the smaller chains and independent hotels. This resulted in a definite disadvantage with respect to their representation in the marketplace by external sales agents (e.g., travel agents). The gap between the technology "haves" and the "have-nots" became evident.

Hoteliers should consider the role IT can play in building and supporting distribution channels and the subsequent economics of these channels, which include the total cost of ownership (TCO), operation, and maintenance for each point of distribution. Understanding and controlling this cost structure can be a valuable source of competitive advantage.

Many of the interfaces between systems are costly to develop, maintain, and operate—especially for small hotels, which cannot achieve the same economies of scale of their larger competitors. Initial interface development can cost as low as a few thousand dollars to as much as tens of thousands of dollars (U.S.) per interface, depending on the system's architecture, complexity of the interface, and functionality. Since these costs are not trivial, hoteliers must estimate the value and strategic importance of each interface before embarking on its development. The ongoing support and maintenance costs must also be factored into the decision. Because the core technologies comprising the GDS environment are subject to frequent modification to keep up with market demands, these interfaces require constant monitoring and updating. Many hotels and small hotel companies cannot afford the dedicated resources and lack the technical knowledge base to make these enhancements and modifications. Instead, they either choose not to participate in certain distribution channels, compromise the degree of integration, or outsource these services and become subject to the terms and service levels of their contractual arrangements with a chosen vendor. All of these decisions have strategic consequences.

While the Internet, universal switches, open systems, and improved standards alleviate some of these cost pressures and competitive disadvantages, they do not remove them entirely. The industry is still a long way from offering truly compatible or plug-and-play systems and interfaces. It does not help the small player to know that these same technologies are available to their larger competitors, giving them some of the same price breaks as smaller companies and hotels and further strengthening their upper hand. Therefore, automation continues to favor the larger organizations in terms of cost advantage.

The costs assigned to each channel vary and are typically based on prenegotiated volumes. Some channels require fixed fees in addition to transaction fees. Transaction fees are generally based on net bookings (i.e., reservations booked minus cancellations), but in some rare cases, a transaction may be defined as any database query or inquiry (i.e., availability check or address look-up). Average costs for a single reservation are as follows:

- Travel agent or intermediary commission: 10 percent of the total room revenue
- Airline GDS fee: $3 to $4
- Universal switch: $.25 to $.75
- Hotel CRS: $8 to $12

These costs quickly accumulate and can represent as much as 20 to 30 percent or more of a hotel's daily room rate. Consider a simple example in which a hotel room sells for $150. If the reservation is made through a travel agent accessing an airline GDS that transfers the reservation to the hotel CRS via a universal switch, the cost of the transaction could be as high as $31.75 or 21 percent of the room rate. The profit margin erosion is real. Therefore, it behooves a hotel to direct reservations traffic to those channels that are able to meet its distribution needs but at lower operating costs. Offering special incentives such as price breaks, room upgrades, or frequent travel bonus points can and often does influence consumer behavior.

Any time a cost can be avoided, the bottom-line performance can be improved. Because not all organizations operate on the same level of efficiency, opportunities exist to gain competitive advantage for those hotels or hotel companies that can optimize their distribution channels by reducing overhead.

The reservations booking process is just one type of exchange or transaction in the guest life cycle. The costs in the process are a direct result of the channels and technology used, the relationship a hotel or hotel company has with each channel provider, the support structure of the organization, and the volume of transactions. Using this paradigm, it becomes possible to rethink the booking channels using a new set of lenses. A whole new set of possibilities and implications can result. For example, in the future, an interesting dimension to the yield management equation may emerge: how to yield by distribution channel or by profitability versus yielding by revenue. The channels of distribution used by guests will depend on a number of factors including, but not limited to, familiarity and comfort level with the channel and service provider, complexity of the reservation, perceived risk, travel policies imposed by an employer, etc. If hotels can segment their customer base by channels, they can potentially eliminate channels that are unnecessary. They can also work to enhance the functionality of lower-cost channels to meet the needs of their guests.

Understanding Share of Distribution

It is important for practitioners to consider which distribution channels will be most advantageous to them and subscribe or participate in only those channels. One of the common questions raised is "To which channels should a company subscribe?" A commonly held belief is that more channels lead to higher visibility, which, in turn, generates more demand. This may not always be the case. The quality of these channels and their links to the GDS must also be considered. The question regarding which channels to offer is becoming more prevalent in light of the many new distribution channels that are forming as a result of the Internet. The answer to this question is likely to vary from company to company and market to market. Each company must understand the sources of its business and the cost to acquire business through each of the distribution channels. Each channel has distinct costs; some are easily measurable, such as transaction costs. Others are more intangible, for example, the cost to provide information to answer a guest inquiry that may or may not lead to a guest booking. To gain an advantage in this competitive marketplace, you must think intelligently about how resources are allocated so as to achieve an appropriate economic return. With respect to global distribution channels, this can only be achieved if a hotel or hotel company understands from where its business comes, how its distribution channels are used, how they contribute to the bottom line (this includes occupancy as well as profitability), and what the costs are to operate each channel.

When marketing professionals select media or places in which to advertise, they are advised to consider the medium and its targeted audience and compare them with the profiles of their customer base. The same must be done when considering investment in distribution channels. In addition, when selecting distribution channels, you should determine what reach the channel has, its visibility, the level of marketing provided by the channel operator, and the services that front-end this channel. This equates to broader distribution and visibility. For example, being part of an airline GDS has a profound reach. An airline GDS provides product representation to anyone or any service with access to that GDS, thus extending the potential audience for a given hotel. When determining which distribution channels to subscribe to and which databases to market their product(s) in, hoteliers cannot ignore the reach of each channel and the popularity of its database. If the database is front-ended by a number of services such as those found on the Internet, there is no need to join each service independently. Services such as Expedia, Travelocity, and TravelWeb provide access to numerous products and extend that access to numerous service providers. As these services promote their own Web sites, they indirectly promote the products they sell and thus increase the likelihood that consumers will find a given hotel without that hotel incurring additional marketing costs for such publicity. In summary, when selecting distribution channels, you should select them carefully and choose those that will provide the most value for the investment.

The advantage of distribution channels versus traditional advertising is that more information can be captured regarding its impact and use via booking statistics, call volumes, and other traffic or usage monitoring. These statistics are not always available for unidirectional forms of media. It is important to note that not all channels provide equal value and that some consumers use multiple channels when researching and purchasing hotel accommodations.

In some cases, distribution channels may be redundant; in other cases, they may complement one another. As such, you cannot ignore the *look-to-book ratio* (i.e., the number of people who shop versus actually make reservations). It is also important to consider the fact that channel usage can vary by market segment, accommodations needed, purpose of travel, or comfort level.

Maintaining Inventory Control: A Daunting Challenge

The challenge for hotels will be to manage and control the multiple entities that make up their GDS network, even when they do not fall under the current domain of control. In a virtual world, organizations must be willing to relinquish some of their control or sovereignty in favor of a shared destiny with other organizations comprising the Internet-worked enterprise. Working in a virtual world requires trust among the partners. Chesbrough and Teece (1996) offer an interesting discussion regarding the management of virtual organizations. In particular, they suggest understanding the relationships between each entity in the network and how they impact change and innovation. Underestimation of systemic versus autonomous innovation could stifle an organization and prevent it from making desirable changes to gain new market advantages. In cases of systemic change, hotels must maintain strategic leverage and coordination over the participating partners in their distribution network. Otherwise, the change will fail to come to fruition as planned.

Loss of capacity control is one of the biggest challenges cited by industry executives moving into the next millennium, according to research sponsored by the International Hotel and Restaurant Association. Control is shifting to those who own or manage the distribution channels and to those who can aggregate volume to secure substantial discounts. Anecdotal comments from interviews with hospitality executives suggest eight additional reasons why hoteliers feel the loss of control over their own inventory. These include (1) inadequate GDS technology infrastructure, (2) inventory and rate management issues, (3) commissions and transaction fees eroding profit margins, (4) rise in number of electronic intermediaries, (5) shift in balance of power from supplier to customer, (6) new models of distribution and pricing, (7) accelerated rates of change, and (8) relinquished control of the customer relationship. Each of these factors is discussed in turn in the following sections.

Inadequate GDS Technology Infrastructure. The first reason relates to the GDS technology infrastructure. Many hotels do not have the necessary technology and information systems in place to support the selling process from multiple locations via different channels and systems. Lacking last-room availability and seamless access to the hotel's rates and availability creates hardships and adds to the overall level of frustration. Those that are considered more advanced are still not state-of-the art. The industry's software and systems lack many of the functions required to support the industry's future directions. It is as if the software has put a stranglehold on the industry and given rise to a host of opportunities for outside players.

Inventory and Rate Management Issues. The second explanation is somewhat related to the first. It has to do with a hotel's ability to control its rates and availability using the principles of revenue (yield) management. Many hotels accept commissionable or discounted reservations when it is possible for them to fill these rooms with higher-rated and/or uncommissionable business. Because these hotels lack the systems to set the appropriate restrictions and the technology to communicate these restrictions to each distribution channel, they find themselves taking business that they would otherwise consider turning down. This business is displacing more desirable, profitable opportunities.

Commissions and Transaction Fees Eroding Profit Margins. The third interpretation as to why hoteliers feel a sense of lost control is the rise in new booking channels that require *commissions* and subscription fees from hotels. In many cases, hoteliers are not familiar with these channels and as the result of onward distribution (where airline GDSs pass on hotel information to third-party booking entities, typically found on the Internet), they cannot always track the source of origination of a reservation. (Dombey 1997) Take for example one account from a general manager (GM) of a property from a well-known hotel chain in a major metropolitan city. In his hotel's guest satisfaction surveys, 2 percent of the guests reported that they booked their reservations online. While this falls within industry averages (1 to 3 percent), it is much higher than those reported for his chain (.3 percent). Moreover, it was in excess of what his hotel's Web site had recorded. What this general manager failed to realize was the power of other Internet channels able to book his hotel because of his company's CRS link to Pegasus' UltraSwitch. Services like TravelWeb had been responsible for many of the bookings and charged his hotel appropriately (somewhere in the nature of $.30 to $.75 per reservation. In sum, the hotel's expenditures were adversely impacted without the GM even realizing it. Although these fees may appear small, they can add up quickly, and they will as volume continues to grow. For those overseeing multiple properties or an entire chain, the impact is even more consequential.

This scenario is true and provides a meaningful message to hoteliers. A hotel's Web site is not the only method of gaining an Internet presence. Any hotel or hotel company that subscribes to listing services in one or more of the airline GDSs or has access to either Pegasus' UltraSwitch or WizCom's switch can be sold by anyone or any system that is connected to these devices (e.g., travel agents, CVBs, and individual consumers). That is the beauty of the technology and the preeminent purpose of a GDS: to extend the sales force and market reach of a hotel. Because most hotels are listed in or connected to one or more of these systems, they can be sold on the Internet via one of the many travel-booking Web sites, whether they realize this or not. At issue is whether the hotel property or company is proactively managing the way in which it is being represented and sold or leaving itself to the mercy of various listing services. The implications are far-reaching, as is the incremental cost to one's overhead. The profit margin erosion is very real and can be managed if appropriate strategies and uses of technology are considered.

Rise in Number of Electronic Intermediaries.   The fourth possible explanation results from the rise in the number of intermediaries in the selling process, especially cybermediaries seen on the Internet. While it is a commonly held belief that *disintermediation* will result as new electronic paths are built between the customer and supplier to create a more direct link, this thinking only applies to travel agents. The reality is that, in this digital age, the number of electronic intermediaries is increasing, albeit seamlessly to both the customer and the supplier. These new electronic intermediaries match customer needs with products and services available for purchase. They are the information brokers, the translators between computer systems, and the switches or "go-betweens" that allow reservations traffic to transfer seamlessly to a hotel's or chain's reservation system. Oftentimes, these new intermediaries are unknown to hotel operators, just as in the case cited earlier. In such cases, how can one control something in which he/she is not aware? Sometimes, the hotel provider only becomes aware of the existence of these new intermediaries when they either ask for compensation for the sales they helped generate or when a grave mistake occurs that results in an irate guest.

It is important to remember that each link in the distribution process, human or electronic, represents a potential point of service failure and a potential expense, typically a charge per transaction. Therefore, knowledge of and management of these players is critical. However, since intermediaries fall outside the traditional span of control of a hotel provider and since they are further removed from the primary source of information, it is difficult to motivate these resources to sell a particular brand or product and to educate them on how best to sell that brand or product. There is also greater potential for service delivery errors and misinforming guests due to incomplete information or general lack of knowledge. This is especially true when these intermediaries are less familiar with the products (i.e., hotel accommodations, facilities, and destinations) they are selling. The quality and timeliness of service delivered by these intermediaries can impact a guest's overall perception of the destination hotel either positively or negatively. It is the latter situation that worries hoteliers most.

Shift in Balance of Power from Supplier to Customer.   The fifth explanation for the feeling of lost capacity control by hotel suppliers relates to a shift in the balance of power between the consumer and the hotel supplier. The balance of power is moving away from the supplier in favor of the consumer.

Consumers, armed with knowledge easily obtained from the Internet, develop greater expectations and demands and higher price-value relationships than ever before of any hotel in which they stay. The tools available via the Internet allow consumers to quickly and effortlessly shop and compare products and services from one company to the next before making a buying decision. They can instantly tap into the many comments (good or bad) of prior visitors and factor this feedback into the selection and decision-making processes. Their efforts are expedited by push technology and smart agents that help to filter out irrelevant or unwanted information, find the best travel bargains, and bring material of interest directly to the consumer's desktop in a manner that is easy to process and digest. This means consumers are now in charge, and hotels must create, package, price, and deliver the perfect experience every time. In a digital world, there is no room or forgiveness for error.

New Models of Distribution and Pricing.   Another important and related consideration resulting in the feeling of lost capacity control is that many of the newer forms of distribution are changing the model for how hotel rooms are bought and sold. As a result, the sales, marketing, and distribution models are being turned on end, creating a new set of dynamics and playing field. Consequently, hoteliers are uncomfortable because this new environment is one in which they have little or no experience and which they are slow to embrace. Consumers, on the other hand, love and embrace the new model because it is consumer-centric and affords them control of their own destiny. For example, Web sites like priceline.com, TravelBids.com, and Onsale let consumers dictate many of the terms of their purchase decisions, thereby giving them greater control over the suppliers. With the rise of smart agents and shopping "bots," this trend will only continue, resulting in higher traffic to company Web sites but not necessarily with a corresponding increase in bookings.

Accelerated Rates of Change.   The seventh factor is the pace of change. The industry has had a tendency to fear and resist change. This is especially true when the changes being introduced are coming from unfamiliar or unknown sources. As a result, it is difficult to forecast the many changes on the horizon since industry leaders may not be looking in the right places or at the right indicators. By now, the business environment is characterized by the need to do more with less, faster and cheaper than ever before. The cycle time for getting products to market and the number of competitors has heightened the complexity of competition. With technology in general and the Internet in particular growing at phenomenal rates, industry players cannot possibly keep abreast of the latest indicators or determinants of their business. The rules of the game are changing, introducing uncertainty, lack of familiarity, and even fear of the unknown. The resulting anxiety creates that sense of lost control.

Relinquished Control of the Customer Relationship.   The final explanation relates less to a hotel's inventory and more to the customer relationship. In an age of digital distribution, hotel providers are increasingly concerned about losing control over the customer relationship. At a time where one-to-one marketing is paramount to success and winning customers over, hotel providers cannot afford to relinquish any control in the sales process or in customer relationship building. Because of the many distribution channels and intermediaries available and onward booking, it is often difficult to track consumers, their identity and patterns, and the originating source of the booking. The problem is even more pronounced if the guest is part of a meeting or convention.

Control and management of the customer relationship are being involuntarily relinquished in favor of outside forces such as Microsoft, American Express, and America Online (Cline and Blatt 1998) and onward distribution suppliers like airline GDSs. Hoteliers, in general, seem to lack a vision of where the GDS market is headed and the role technology is having in determining that vision. Hamel and Prahalad (1994) made a similar observation in their research and consulting efforts to help multinational organizations prepare for the future. In the absence of such a long-range view, others from outside the industry step in and take advantage of an explosive opportunity. The result is less control over inventory, more transaction fees, and higher overhead—not to mention a new set of rules dictated by unfamiliar sources.

4. TRENDS IN HOTEL GDS

Disintermediation and Reintermediation

Until recently, travel agents had near-exclusive access to information, thus creating an appropriate niche in which to operate. However, the value they provide is diminishing as new, user-friendly tools become available to the general public that offer many of the same capabilities of travel agents. These new tools are providing the general public with full access to information that once only travel agents had previously enjoyed. At one time, travel booking systems were complex and difficult to use. Users required special training to operate them and interpret the screens and cryptic codes. Today, this is no longer the case. Graphical user interfaces and easy look-up tables have negated the need for specialized knowledge, making it possible for consumers to book their own reservations without relying on travel agents.

Automation of the GDS enterprise gives rise to the notion of disintermediation (i.e., the elimination of intermediaries) and the thought that a flatter, less complex network could exist. Disintermediation reduces the value chain to its most efficient state. Do-it-yourself technologies are making the elimination of intermediaries possible and are bringing consumers and service providers closer together. In the words of media consultant John Berry:

> We will one day dance to the death knell of the middleman, that distorter of market efficiency and end-user pricing who stands in the way of a tighter producer-consumer relationship and the promise of lower prices. (1997, p. 39)

For the hospitality and travel industries, the focus has been on the elimination of travel agents and the role that they play as intermediaries. Instead, these services can be replaced by information technology. While it is true that automation can eliminate the role of intermediaries in many cases, what Berry describes is a bit idealistic. Sometimes, these intermediaries provide invaluable services and provide them cheaper than they can be done internally. This is why outsourcing many functions has become so popular.

Additionally, the new model of business created by the automation gives rise to neoteric intermediaries. Under the new paradigm, these intermediaries are information brokers, or "cybermediaries" (Berry 1997) bearing little resemblance to those of the past regime (Electronic commerce 1997). A good example within the hospitality industry of modern-day intermediaries are Pegasus and WizCom, the electronic switches or clearinghouses that translate, covert, and pass information between disparate systems.

The Internet, as vast as it is, is creating just as many intermediaries as it displaces. For example, buyers need help in finding sellers and wading through the vast amount of information available. Search engines came to the rescue to provide this service. Through increased competition and greater consumer needs, these engines will be refined and become more focused and more powerful. As markets become more segmented and specialized, new players emerge to fill in and bridge gaps. Future intermediaries will add value and save time through their adeptness at transforming information into usable knowledge and subsequently providing services and convenience as a result of the knowledge gained. In an information world, it will be this new knowledge that will provide the currency of tomorrow. Megaportals formed through intra- and inter-industry alliances for one-stop shopping and aggregators will provide value through brand recognition, trust, convenience, and access to specially discounted rates that can only be provided through them.

Digital Divide

Because of the many facets of GDS and the complexities involved, hoteliers must consider GDS as more than just the reservations booking process or the company's CRS. As the model depicts, it is much broader in scope with far-reaching implications. Competitive advantage will be derived less from the gap between the technology "haves" and the "have-nots" and more from the bipolarization that results between those who "know-how" versus those who "know-not." This distinction is far less subtle than might appear.

True, there will be gaps in what one company can afford versus another, with economies of scale favoring the larger chains. However, with many facets of the GDS technology readily available on the open market at affordable prices or accessible via outsourcing, the gap between the technology "haves" and the "have-nots" becomes very small. Therefore, the advantage will be in knowing how best to make use of this technology. This includes finding cost-effective uses as well as creating new ways to grow market share and build customer loyalty. The ultimate value will be in converting information into knowledge that then results in improved business performance, as demonstrated by the company's financials and market statistics. This can only be realized if the *right* GDS infrastructure is in place. What is right is subjective and variable by organization because each organization fills unique market needs and sets different goals. There is no right answer, but there are some definite wrong ones. Furthermore, what is right today will likely change tomorrow, so hoteliers must be flexible and ready to adapt to meet the demands of tomorrow. As *The Economist* writes, "The core competence of tomorrow's e-commerce successes will be the ability to change quickly, perhaps even more valuable than knowledge of any particular market." (Electronic commerce 1997, S18)

Transparency: A Hope for the Future

There may come a time when focus on the individual components of a GDS is less important. For example, when a person uses the telephone to place a call, he/she does not consider the many linkages and systems that are required in order for that call to be completed with an acceptable level of voice quality. The behind-the-scenes components are completely transparent during the course of the conversation. Within the hotel industry, the service levels and reliability are not to a point in which the various components can be treated as transparent as in the telephone example. Complicating the situation is the number of customer interface options. Since each customer interface represents a critical incident, hotels must fully understand how to safeguard these opportunities and guarantee unblemished service delivery. Failure to do so will result in a tainted experience for the customer and a blemished image for the organization. The transactional economics of the GDS and its various components and linkages provide another reason that this level of attention and detail is warranted. As long as intermediaries are involved, require remuneration for services rendered, and influence or control the process, the components will remain the subject of interest.

Bypassing Airline GDSs

Bypassing traditional airline GDSs during the electronic booking process is becoming more appealing due to the cost-savings that can result. The technology linking travelers directly with suppliers without always having to go through a GDS now exists. Feeling pressure, GDS systems like Galileo are reacting to some of the new distribution systems available in today's marketplace. The company admits that it is sensitive to its customers demands for more cost-effective distribution systems and is taking a cautious approach to raising prices in hopes that its customers will not seek other alternatives. (Rosen 1997) To help boost traffic, Galileo is targeting self-managed frequent travelers by outfitting them with software that provides direct access to its GDS. The software allows users to bypass the Internet, thus avoiding some of the reliability and response time issues typically experienced when surfing the Web. (Rosen 1997)

Lowering Distribution Costs Through the Internet and Other Technology Advances

FedEx (*http://www.fedex.com*) represents one of the best documented examples of how use of the Internet can save money while simultaneously improving customer service. The company estimates that it has saved $4 million in overhead by using the Web to help customers ship and track packages, locate drop boxes, and provide other forms of support. (Moeller 1996) FedEx estimates that there are as many as 400,000 users each month who use the Web to track and ship packages rather than contacting FedEx's customer service representatives through a toll-free number. Since each call would cost the company between $2 and $5, the cost avoidance is estimated at $200,000 per month. (Moeller 1996) Customer service representatives have been freed up to work on other tasks or handle more complicated consumer issues. To FedEx, this is just the beginning. The company believes that long-term the savings will be much more significant, not to mention the possibility of a potential increase in business.

American Express, American Airlines, and Alamo Rent A Car are examples of companies deploying voice recognition systems that allow customers to make reservations by speaking in a normal conversational tone with "robots." Using this technology, the companies hope to cut transaction costs per reservation in half and boost reservations productivity by as much as 5 percent without corresponding increases in staffing levels. (Thyfault 1997) The quality of voice recognition systems is improving and the prices of the hardware and software required to support them are declining, making them attractive and viable alternatives for the travel industry and other services such as UPS and Charles Schwab. Several products are currently available on the marketplace from companies like IBM, Nuance Communications, Dragon Systems, Lernout & Hauspie, Registry Magic, and Vocollect, Inc. (Thyfault 1997)

The hotel industry can benefit from electronic commerce and customer service technologies like each of the companies just mentioned. Processing reservations through the Internet can be cheaper than processing those booked through other channels, particularly when a travel agent is involved. According to industry averages, it costs a company $1 for every minute of talk/hold-time on a toll-free number. (Frook 1996) According to Thyfault (1997), the average talk-time per reservation is seven minutes. Thus, $7 are skimmed off the top for each room booked just for the phone call. This does not take into account the cost of information inquiries and cancellations. Add travel agent commissions and labor, and you can see the costs quickly grow. If hotel companies can employ technologies to reduce hold time and talk time or shift some of the current volume to the Internet for booking travel, they stand to save a considerable amount of money, changing cost structure and improving profit margins.

Shopping Bots

As technology becomes more advanced, smarter and more user-friendly shopping tools will become available. Many of these tools will function as shopping bots, which will be powered by smart agent technology. These tools will have the capability to read a traveler's profile and shop for available travel services and accommodations that match a person's needs and preferences with little to no involvement from a user—and all within a fraction of a second. They will then present a short list of options to the traveler or, if authorized, proceed directly with the booking process. Developments such as these will drastically reshape marketing and how hotels reach consumers. After all, how can one sell to a robot, a device with no emotion or human feeling? It cannot appreciate the unique attributes and sensual qualities that are presently sold by many hotels. The challenge will be to attract these devices, appeal to the criteria they are seeking, create matches, and win the business.

5. SUMMARY

A hotel GDS is one of the most important strategic applications in a hotel's IT portfolio due to its revenue-producing potential, its role in building customer relationships and serving customers, and the need to focus on reducing costs. It is the cornerstone on which most other hotel applications and services depend. Therefore, hotel executives must focus on this technology, monitor the emerging trends, and carefully chart an appropriate course of action. The rapid change of technology, the capital intensity of IT required to support a hotel GDS, and the number of new distribution options being introduced to the marketplace make managing in this environment difficult, confusing, and seemingly in a constant state of flux. For more information regarding the complexities of hotel distribution systems and channels, please be sure to refer to Appendix 4: Understanding the Complexities of Hotel Global Distribution Systems and Channels at the end of this book.

   With tomorrow's leaders aggressively jockeying for position, the hotel GDS arena is clearly in transition. The landscape is vastly changing as a result of consolidation, new technologies, distribution paths, and attempts to restructure the existing channels of distribution (e.g., bypass theories) to reduce the high fixed and variable costs associated with distribution. The future is likely to see major paradigm shifts for the hotel industry, such as yield management programs that seek to implement dynamic or real-time pricing models (Davis and Meyer 1998) and optimize by profit rather than by revenue, as is the case today. If hotels can channel reservations through services that allow them to yield greater contribution margins, they can improve their operating results and enjoy a competitive advantage over those unable to effectively manage their distribution channels.

With rising distribution costs, new channels entering the marketplace, and additional intermediaries gaining access to important customer information, hotel companies must carefully evaluate distribution options, select appropriate partners and channels, and measure and monitor effectiveness (i.e., contributions in terms of *incremental* room nights and revenues). Where possible, the number of channels should be simplified to ease the management and maintenance of them, to reduce the overlaps, and to reduce overhead costs associated with them.

Hospitality firms must begin to develop a comprehensive distribution strategy. The marketplace is getting too complex with its distribution channel offerings and too costly for companies to serendipitously choose channels to which they should subscribe. Likewise, they cannot leave these decisions to chance or defensive responses to competitors' moves. Gaining representation in as many channels as possible is a noble goal, but at what cost and at what value?

The dynamics of distribution have changed drastically over the years as a result of segmentation, greater competition, more demanding customers, and now, newer forms of technology. How a hotel company uses a GDS to win sales and marketing advantages, to gain access to new markets, and to build and strengthen customer relationships and how a company ensures effective representation (i.e., presentation of rates, availability, product amenities, etc.) in each channel using the prevailing technologies should become top priorities. The ultimate goal of a GDS strategy should be to fully automate the entire booking process to create a cost-effective, streamlined, and hassle-free guest service that cannot be duplicated by anyone else.

6. CASE STUDY AND LEARNING ACTIVITY

Understanding distribution—knowing the channels and technology in which to invest and how to effectively use and manage them—is critical to a hotel organization's competitive positioning. This is a complex undertaking that requires constant management and oversight. What follows is an example of how one company is using IT and its distribution channels to gain market advantages. The case is based on an actual company, but some of the names and facts have been changed to protect the identity of the company.

Company Overview

Hotel Eleganté is a global leader and technology innovator in the lodging industry. Its success and reputation, revered by all, are widely chronicled throughout the industry and in the trade literature. Hotel Eleganté has received numerous accolades for its programs, operations, and facilities, including high industry rankings for its use of and investment in IT. The company enjoys a strong brand image. To many, its name is synonymous with quality, consistency, and attention to detail. Moreover, its employees' commitment to service has become a hallmark of the company's culture and core values, providing a distinct competitive advantage. These tributes notwithstanding, Hotel Eleganté's market position and distribution—in terms of globalization, location, breadth, and size—are esteemed by its competitors.

Hotel Eleganté's customers exhibit a high degree of brand loyalty, due in part to the company's highly successful, multibrand frequent travel (guest loyalty) program. Through an aggressive segmentation strategy, Hotel Eleganté's lodging portfolio spans the entire gamut of the lodging industry's segmentation (i.e., from luxury to limited service) and, with more than a dozen brands, is one of the broadest in the industry. The company likes to think it has the right product for any market location in the world, although some critics would accuse the company of oversegmenting the market to the point where brands converge and confuse consumers. Hotel Eleganté's portfolio consists of over 2,000 hotels with more than 330,000 rooms in 55 countries. The company's products typically rank top in their segments in industry surveys, and its growth in earnings per share surpasses the industry. In almost all of the segments in which Hotel Eleganté competes, it outperforms the industry when it comes to sales, occupancy rates, and customer preference. The rate premiums the company commands allow its properties to earn higher REVPAR and ADR than industry averages and outpace inflation rates.

Distribution Strategy

Hotel Eleganté was one of the early players in the industry to embark on electronic distribution. Today, Hotel Eleganté's hotels rank among the most booked properties in each of the major airline GDSs. Since the company introduced its first centralized reservation system in the early 1970s, it has witnessed many changes over the years in electronic distribution and in how hotel companies deliver their products and services to the marketplace. The industry is quite different in terms of the dynamics, competitive threats, and industry cost structure as the result of computers and global distribution systems. Reminiscing about Hotel Eleganté's original strategy, one company executive remarked of its genuine simplicity and intuitiveness: "In the early days, the goal was obvious: to put inventory in front of as many people as possible to sell it." At the time, an open and close approach to inventory management worked well for managing room inventory in multiple distribution channels with little need for sophisticated interfaces. Last-room availability and single-image inventories were not even imagined then, but over time, these concepts have evolved as the company grew and as the logistics became more complex for managing room inventory across multiple properties around the world. They are now critical in today's competitive marketplace and require complex, sophisticated, and costly interfaces.

In the early years, interfaces were reportedly easy to develop, relatively inexpensive, and fairly easy to justify, making it feasible to enter almost any distribution channel used in the industry. Hotel Eleganté first developed interfaces to SABRE and APOLLO (now Galileo), the two largest airline GDSs. These interfaces provided Hotel Eleganté with competitive advantage through first-mover advantages based on evidence collected by the company's marketing department. Over time, however, other hotel companies began copying Hotel Eleganté's moves. This required Hotel Eleganté to invest more to stay ahead of the competition and protect its lead. As the functionality of these interfaces became more complex and as airline GDSs and the company's CRS changed with time, maintaining these interfaces became more challenging and costly.

Hotel Eleganté's philosophy concerning distribution has always been to provide methods or channels that people want to use to book rooms and to provide a set of choices or options so that customers can select the channel best suited to their needs or convenience. In other words, Hotel Eleganté takes a consumer-centric approach. According to one marketing executive at Hotel Eleganté, distribution channels must be driven by two key considerations:

1. How customers want to book with Hotel Eleganté
2. The revenue upside versus the costs of creating, maintaining, and using a distribution channel

Thus, Hotel Eleganté will enter any distribution channel that is indicative of how its customers want to buy its products rather than try to dictate how its consumers buy its products and services. To this end, Hotel Eleganté will continue to fund distribution channels of higher cost so long as there is sufficient volume to justify their existence. For example, one executive at Hotel Eleganté indicated he would like to eliminate the company's toll-free reservation call centers because they are so costly to operate. However, since a significant number of people prefer this service and channel to others, Hotel Eleganté will continue to offer reservation call centers as a distribution channel, but it will make them as operationally effective as possible.

Over the years, Hotel Eleganté has successfully pursued a two-pronged distribution strategy that involved building relationships and developing loyalty with both consumers and travel agents (or other influencers such as secretaries/ administrative assistants). Hotel Eleganté's competitive positioning today can largely be attributed to this strategy. Going forward, Hotel Eleganté's overarching distribution strategy continues to be "To make it as easy as possible to do business with the company by putting its products and services on as many shelves as possible." It accomplishes this objective by offering the following:

- A customer-centric sales force capable of selling multiple brands
- A strong loyalty program and detailed customer profiles to recognize repeat customers and speed the reservations process
- Superior worldwide toll-free reservation services and event booking centers
- Easy access to a fast, reliable reservation system through the highest level of connectivity presently available to each of the major airline GDSs

- Real-time, two-way, seamless links to all its hotels, with single-image inventory and access to last-room availability
- Cross-selling capabilities between properties and brands
- A fully functional Web site and presence in most Internet booking sites
- Help desks and special service counters offering support and assistance to customers and travel agents
- Strong ties to the travel agent community

The company's reservation technology and distribution channels support infrastructure and rational pricing strategy, simplify the shopping process, and add to the guest convenience. Through a simple menu of rates, Hotel Eleganté maintains that there is "a logical and rational reason for every rate offered at every hotel." This approach reduces rate "haggling," improves rate integrity, and virtually guarantees that customers will be offered the best available rate given their qualifications, dates of travel, affiliations, and room requests. Rational pricing also ensures that the same rates are offered through any booking channel used by the company.

Protecting Relationships with the Travel Agent Community

Recognizing the important contributions of travel agents in influencing and stimulating travel, Hotel Eleganté has spent years developing and fostering good relationships with the travel agent community. Programs to boost travel agent relations include special service desks, centralized travel agent commissions, familiarization programs, double commission guarantees, access to single-image inventory, last-room availability, and more.

Travel intermediaries presently deliver about 25 percent of all of Hotel Eleganté's room nights, chainwide. In 1998, Hotel Eleganté reported paying a record high of $150 million in travel agent commissions. The company attributed this volume to its reservations and global distribution system capabilities, its commitment and strong ties to the travel agent community, the quality and breadth of its lodging portfolio, its strong customer service, and its single-image inventory with last-room availability. Because of the significant contributions from the travel agent community, Hotel Eleganté continues to foster relations and develop programs that include, rather than preclude, travel agents. As one executive put it:

> Even if travel agents influence only 5 percent of the company's business, this is still a significant chunk of business that cannot be overlooked.

Therefore, Hotel Eleganté is overly cautious about doing anything that might jeopardize relationships or be perceived as a threat or an attempt to undercut travel agents out of fear of losing their business. While the Internet may threaten the role of travel agents, Hotel Eleganté does not see them disappearing—at least not any time soon. Moreover, Hotel Eleganté believes that further consolidation in the travel agency marketplace will create mega-agencies that will carry significant clout, especially in corporate travel where they help companies control travel and entertainment expenses. Thus, building and maintaining healthy travel agent relationships will continue to be important.

While Hotel Eleganté could benefit financially from steering customers away from travel agents in favor of cheaper distribution channels like its Web site, Hotel Eleganté will not promote its Web site in this way or do anything that could be construed as an overt attempt to direct bookings away from travel agents. Instead, it will assume the role of a cautious follower. It would prefer to see some other companies challenge travel agents much in the same way that Delta Air Lines has done in the airline industry. Its efforts, according to one executive, will be covert so as not to "put the mother load at risk." Hotel Eleganté will continue to monitor booking patterns, and as booking volumes shift over time with travel agents—or any other distribution channel, for that matter—Hotel Eleganté will reinvest its resources accordingly to optimize customer access, booking volumes, and revenue and work to facilitate bookings through channels of lower cost.

Future Developments

Moving forward, Hotel Eleganté will continue to explore innovative approaches that make it easier, faster, and cheaper for guests to book rooms at each of its brands. It will continue to look for ways to leverage its size and expertise to build unparalleled competitive advantages while maintaining an interminable commitment to its customers. It will also focus on exploiting Internet, *intranet*, and extranet technologies to lower costs of distribution and increase booking volumes.

Future developments for hotel GDSs will concentrate on functional enhancements, advances in yield management, graphical user interface development for ease-of-use, sales force automation, decision support tools, and further centralization of meeting space reservations. Additionally, capabilities will be expanded to incorporate electronic requests for proposal, better group handling, Internet integration, geo-coding, and cross-selling of properties and brands. Ultimately, the growing number and complexity of distribution channels will require "one-button" rate loading and updating for ease of administration and management.

Learning Activity

1. Critically evaluate Hotel Eleganté's distribution strategy. Is it appropriate? Can you think of any other GDS strategies that Hotel Eleganté might embrace?

2. How customer centric is Hotel Eleganté's approach towards distribution?

3. How can Hotel Eleganté evaluate each distribution channel and measure its contribution to its bottom line?

4. Which distribution channel needs the most attention and why? Does Hotel Eleganté need to be concerned with *channel conflict* (i.e., one or more channels cannibalizing or taking business away from other channels)?
5. Are travel agents still important to Hotel Eleganté? Going forward, what type of relationship should Hotel Eleganté have with travel agents? What role should they play? Should Hotel Eleganté continue to pay travel agent commissions? Why or why not?

7. KEY TERMS

Brand shielding

Central reservation system (CRS)

Channel conflict

Channel management

Commission

Core competencies

Cross-selling

Disintermediation

Distribution strategy

Global distribution system (GDS)

Guest life cycle

Internet distribution system (IDS)

Inter-organizational system

Intranet

Look-to-book ratio

Net rate

Onward distribution

Opaque pricing

Rate categories

Rate integrity

Revenue (yield) management

Room pools

Single-image inventory

Travel agents

Up-selling

Wireless application protocol (WAP)

8. CHAPTER QUESTIONS

1. Discuss the many roles a hotel GDS plays and why it is so important for a hotel company from strategic and marketing perspectives. How can it be used to achieve competitive advantage?
2. Why is a hotel GDS considered to be a mission-critical application?
3. What are the key technologies and hotel applications that comprise a hotel distribution system? Discuss the roles and importance of each.
4. Should a hotel company strive for representation in any and all distribution channels? Describe and justify your response.
5. How is the Internet reshaping hotel distribution and the ways in which hotels interact with their customers?

6. If a CEO of a major hotel chain hired you as a consultant to help develop a distribution strategy for his/her company, how would you go about getting started? What sorts of advice would you provide?

7. What are the advantages and disadvantages of having hotel room inventory and meeting space sold by intermediaries?

8. Why do many hotel executives feel they are losing control over the distribution process and over their inventory? What can they do to win back control?

9. Is it a good idea to participate in discount services such as Hotwire.com and priceline.com? Why or why not?

10. Where should you turn to study future technology developments and innovations in hotel distribution? Who are the leaders and innovators?

11. Discuss the latest trends shaping hotel distribution. What do you consider to be the most important changes on the horizon and why? How will these reshape the way business is transacted in the hotel industry?

12. How do you think guests will book hotel accommodations and meeting space ten years from now?

9. REFERENCES

American Express and Microsoft form alliance to provide Internet/intranet travel services. 1996. *PR Newswire*, 29 July.

Berry, John. 1997. Death of a middle man. *Internet World* (March): 39–41.

Castleberry, Jay A., Christian Hempell, and Gretchen Kaufman. 1998. The battle for electronic shelf space on the global distribution network. *Hotel Online,* Summer. http://www.hotel-online.com/Neo/Trends/Andersen/1998_GDNShelf Space.html.

Chesbrough, Henry W., and David J. Teece. 1996. When is virtual virtuous? Organizing for innovation. *Harvard Business Review* (January/February): 65–73.

Clemons, Eric K., Sashidhar P. Reddi, and Michael C. Row. 1993. The impact of information technology on the organization of economic activity: The "move to the middle" hypothesis. *Journal of Management Information Systems* 10, no. 2 (fall): 9–35.

Cline, Roger S., and Louis A. Blatt. 1998. Creating enterprise value around the customer . . . Leveraging the customer asset in today's hospitality industry. *Arthur Andersen Hospitality and Leisure Executive Report* 5, no. 1 (winter): 2–11.

Connolly, Daniel J., and Richard G. Moore. 1995. Technology and its impact on global distribution channels in the hotel industry. *Proceedings of the Decision Sciences Institute, USA* 3: 1563–1565.

Copeland, Duncan G., and James L. McKenney. 1988. Airline reservations systems: Lessons from history. *MIS Quarterly* 12, no. 3 (September): 353–370.

Crichton, Elaine, and David Edgar. 1995. Managing complexity for competitive advantage: An IT perspective. *International Journal of Contemporary Hospitality Management* 7, no. 2/3: 12–18.

Davidow, William H., and Michael S. Malone. 1992. *The virtual corporation: structuring and revitalizing the corporation for the 21st century.* New York: HarperBusiness.

Davis, Stan M. 1987. *Future perfect.* Reading, MA: Addison-Welsey Publishing Company, Inc.

Davis, Stan M., and Christopher Meyer. 1998. *Blur: The speed of change in the connected economy.* New York: Warner Books.

Dombey, Alyson. 1997. *Onward distribution of hotel information via the global distribution systems: The HEDNA White Paper.* Pittsburgh, PA: The Hotel Electronic Distribution Network Association.

Electronic commerce: In search of the perfect market. 1997. *The Economist,* 10 May, S1–18.

Evans, Philip, and Thomas S. Wurster. 2000. *Blown to bits: How the new economics of information transforms strategy.* Boston: Harvard Business School Press.

Fairlie, Rik. 1994. Apollo, System One expect to retain their market shares. *Travel Weekly,* 9 (May): 90.

Frook, John Evan. 1996. The ABCs of one-to-one marketing. *CommunicationsWeek* 628 (16 September): 63.

Hamel, Gary, and C. K. Prahalad. 1994. *Competing for the future.* Boston: Harvard Business School Press.

Kirsner, Scott. 1999. Very truly yours. *CIO Web Business* (Section 2) (1 November): 30, 32–33.

Moeller, Michael. 1996. FedEx adds shipping to the web. *PC Week* (1 July): 100.

Olsen, Michael D. 1996. *Into the new millennium: A white paper on the global hospitality industry.* Paris: International Hotel Association.

Rosen, Cheryl. 1997. CRS targets unmanaged. *Business Travel News Online Edition,* 3 March, http://www.btnOnline.com:80/db_area/archives/1997/03/97030312.htm.

Shapiro, Benson P., and John Wyman. 1981. New ways to reach your customers. *Harvard Business Review* (July/August): 103–110.

Stein, Tom, and Jeff Sweat. 1998. Killer supply chains. *InformationWeek* (9 November): 36–38, 42, 44, 46.

Tapscott, Don, and Art Caston. 1993. *Paradigm shift: The new promise of information technology.* New York: McGraw-Hill.

Thyfault, Mary E. 1997. Voice recognition enters the mainstream. *InformationWeek* (14 July): 146.

Weill, Peter. 1991. The information technology payoff: Implications for investment appraisal. *Australian Accounting Review:* 2–11.

CHAPTER NINE

Databases

CHAPTER CONTENTS

INTERVIEW

Robert S. Bennett serves as senior vice president of property systems and services for Pegasus Solutions, a leading worldwide provider of hotel industry reservations transaction processing and electronic commerce services. With more than twenty-five years of experience, Bennett is primarily responsible for developing, directing, and launching Pegasus' Web-based property technology ASP initiatives.

He most recently worked at Pricewaterhouse-Coopers where he directed the technology practice of the company's hospitality and leisure management consulting services. His career also includes serving in senior management positions in the area of technology with Micros/Fidelio, Inc.; Marriott International, Inc.; and Hilton International Co.

Bob Bennett is also a Hall of Fame member of the Hospitality Finance and Technology Professionals. We spoke with him about customer relationship management (CRM).

Q: Thanks for taking the time, Bob. First, how do you define CRM?

A: In the hospitality industry, customer relationship management (CRM) is *not* the same as a frequent guest or loyalty program, although these programs can be a component of a CRM strategy. To execute a frequent guest program a hotel does not need to know much more than a name, address, membership number, and number of nights stayed. The program itself does not improve the guest's experience during a stay or generate new room night demand.

A true CRM program needs to reward loyalty but is much more concerned with recognition than rewards. The CRM program should identify the guest's special needs and desires, make the guest feel like a valuable individual traveler, and generate new room night demand through targeted marketing. A successful CRM program will weave the information stored on a guest into actions that take place throughout the guest's experience. This includes reservations, check-in, room service, housekeeping, leisure activities, and follow-up marketing.

Q: What are some important aspects of CRM?

A: A CRM program must have all data about a guest available at all points where a guest interacts with a hotel or a hotel chain. Therefore, a central database full of guest information that is not accessible at a front desk or during a reservation call will not be effective. Data must also be up-to-date in all guest interaction locations. A guest will know if he or she just had a transaction yesterday and all guest service employees must have the same knowledge available.

Q: What are some of the problems facing CRM initiatives?

A: Given the infrastructure of many hotel chains today, it is difficult to achieve this universal distribution of timely data. Most legacy PMSs do not have the ability to store all the desired data on a customer and they are difficult to interface with newly built centralized systems. With the growing acceptance of network computing, however, this issue is being addressed. Network computing allows the central storage in a master database of all desired customer information. This information is always current and can be accessed in an affordable manner from any location because of common Internet-based technologies.

A hotel chain that owns or manages all of its properties has an important advantage over a franchised hotel chain in the implementation of a CRM strategy. This is because it is essential that information from all guest experiences be stored and then made available to all properties. In a franchised environment it is often forbidden, or properties are unwilling, to share detailed guest information with another franchised property. The franchiser, or brand owner, must establish strong regulations in this regard in order to deliver a competitive guest experience.

1. INTRODUCTION

You can't have CRM without a database. Databases are playing an ever increasingly important role in the information age. In the hospitality industry, their effective usage can help every department better manage assets, expenses, and sales. This chapter will acquaint you with client server databases and their usage in the hospitality industry.

2. DATABASE BASICS

From check-in, to food purchasing, to targeting customers, effective and efficient management of large quantities of data requires a database. You might keep a folder or notebook with different pages containing information. These papers have no apparent structure potentially linking them. When looking for specifics, you must go through each piece and extract it. In other words, they stand alone. Have you ever come across a phone number and forgotten whose it was? You are almost forced to go through a personal or business address book name by name. Companies that, even to this day, only keep paper records or noninterrelated computer systems face difficulties in data management. These are referred to as flat files. *Flat files* are usually text files that have no structured interrelationship. In the end, time and energy are wasted retrieving data with redundancies, while unseen relationships and potential couplings go undiscovered.

Today, hospitality organizations take advantage of the structural benefits provided by databases. A *database* is an organized, centralized collection of data serving applications. Databases are a key element of most mission-critical applications and represent the most common type of back-end software in client/server (C/S) systems. A property's databases store data on such things as its transactions, products, employees, guests, and assets. Such databases must be efficiently organized and easy to access. They must also provide data integrity and ensure the reliability of stored data.

The database world is a large one and client/server databases are quickly replacing and interacting with mainframe databases. Mainframe databases are still used and are often superior to other databases due to their greater processing power. However, management, extraction, and display of the data is largely done via the platforms we use daily, be it client/server, the Web, or peer-to-peer. From here on, assume that a database is not in a mainframe platform.

The structure a database takes is important to later usage. Different databases were constructed by different people in different ways. There are four basic types of structured databases.

Hierarchical databases utilize parent/child relationships among data. A child can not exist without a parent. This database looks like an inverted tree when depicted on paper, and it is hard to change this structure once you have begun. Hierarchical databases are useful for cost effectively storing large amounts of data, but are less dynamic than some others.

Network databases have circular relationships defined by the user where new fields (which will be defined later) cannot be added later. As opposed to hierarchical databases, their structure on paper looks less orderly. Their usage is less and less common.

Relational databases are the most popular type of database and will be emphasized in this chapter. Relational databases organize data in tables consisting of rows (or records) much like graph paper. This form of organization allows flexible data organization and access and use of the Structured Query Language (SQL) database language.

Object oriented databases are the newest type of structured databases and are in their infancy. It is believed that they will one day replace relational databases since they are better equipped to handle multimedia or graphics-based data commonly found on the Web. Currently, object oriented databases are manipulated through relational databases. In object oriented databases, the data and methods (actions upon the data) are encapsulated into objects. Classes of objects are used and are capable of inheriting attributes of other objects. Think of combining a noun and a verb into one entity with the noun (there are more nouns than verbs) getting more attention than the verb. The end result is a more dynamic database since the data are the focus rather than the action upon them.

Database Management Systems (DBMSs)

Whichever structured database is used, an important software component is needed. A *database management system (DBMS)* is that critical piece of software that provides users and database administrators with the ability to access and manipulate data. It is through this piece of software, with all the common software features such as menus and places to click, that most managers will interact with the database. Therefore, this section also discusses commercial databases, especially those used by contemporary C/S applications.

Many microcomputer and workstation DBMSs are available for prices comparable to word processing and spreadsheet packages. However, full-feature C/S databases can cost half a million dollars just for enterprise software. DBMSs perform several key functions:

- Provide links between different files that are used together
- Allow the storage, updating, and retrieval of data in the database
- Apply data integrity, data security, and control constraints to the data
- Coordinate multiuser database access
- Support data reliability through backup and recovery features

The DBMS provides an intervening level of software between database users (and applications) and the data storage. Figure 9-1 shows where the DBMS works within a hospitality environment. The view of the database from the user's perspective is the *logical view*. There can be many logical views since different departments need to see data in different ways. The makeup and organization of the data on the storage device is the *physical view*. There is only one physical view. The database management system takes the data from the physical view and presents it in the logical view.

The two views (logical and physical) of the data are used by the DBMS to provide data independence. This allows data models to be resistant to changes in the database's physical structure. This is convenient for system developers, who can easily change storage devices and data access methods.

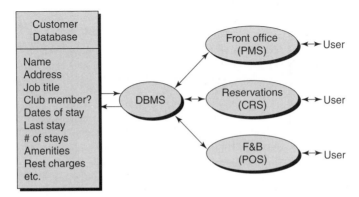

Figure 9-1. The DBMS serves as the link between departmental or user-specific requests and the database.

Your knowledge of bits and bytes is expanded into more forms found in databases. Bytes form words and numbers that form fields. A *field* is a collection of bytes or data with specific meaning such as a "Last Name." Next is a *record*, which is a collection of fields such as a customer's "Last Name," "First Name," "Address," and "Credit Card Number." A collection of records is a *file* such as "Customers," "Vendors," and "Employees," and a database is a collection of those files.

Just what provides that structured linkage lacking in flat files? It is how the rows of data are identified and related to the other rows in other files (sometimes referred to as tables). Since a database is made up of files, something connecting all of the files to one another is needed. The key here is linking files that have a field in common. Let's use an example of a simple database with only three files—Reservations, Front Office, and Housekeeping. At times, each department may be concerned only with its data. At other times, data from the other departments "in relation to" its department may be needed. In reality, each file would contain many more fields. Look at Figure 9-2. Each file has one or two fields that *uniquely* identify a record. In the Reservation file, it is the reservation number. In the Front Office file it is the combination of the Last Name and Street Address. Two fields are used together here to uniquely identify a record in cases of guests with the same last name. Finally, in the Housekeeping file, the room number is the field that uniquely identifies that record since there are no rooms with the same number. These fields that uniquely identify a record are called *primary keys*. If two are used together as in the Front Office file, they are called a *composite key*. The files are linked together where a primary key from one file is linked to a "like" field in another file. This "like" field is called a *foreign key*, which is just a primary key in another relation. In Figure 9-2, reservation number is seen as a primary key in the Reservation file and as a foreign key in the Front Office file. When the Reserva-

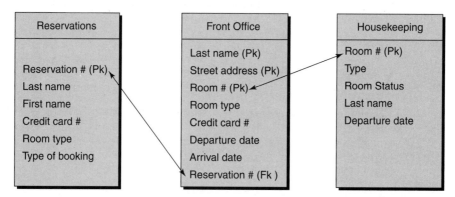

Figure 9-2. The valuable aspect of relational databases is the linkage of files. By connecting the files, you can make complex searches of the database as a whole rather than just the individual files. Here the three tables are joined by like fields—a primary key (pk) in one field and a foreign key (fk) in another. Primary keys uniquely identify a record. When two fields are used to uniquely identify a record, it is called a composite key. Foreign keys are primary keys in another relation.

tion file is linked with the Front Office file, which in turn is related to the House-keeping file, all three files are linked, which allows the "whole" database to be utilized when needed.

Through the DBMS, an important language is utilized. Using a data manipulation language or DML, users can manipulate the data in a relational database in various ways. For example, rows in a relation may be inserted, deleted, updated, displayed, or printed. For example, an airline cancels a contract with your organization. Without having to search name by name in your "active corporate client list," you can search the database via a query for the airline's name and delete the related last names in a block. Other relational operations are used to extract answers to a user's queries. One example is the "Select" operation, which returns a new relation with a subset of the relation's rows. You'll look more closely at the "select" query in use in the most widely used DML in the next section.

Functions of a DBMS

Both large and small DBMSs provide the same general features, although they vary in sophistication. They include the ability to create and manipulate new files and records using DBMS commands. For example, a DBMS should allow the user to set up a (relational) reservation database with RESERVATION # and ROOM TYPE relations by defining the fields and field types, as in Figure 9-2. Subsequently, it should allow the user to populate the files by typing in new records, or by "importing" or reading the data from another application (e.g., a word processed document or spreadsheet).

Another DBMS function minimizes redundancy among data elements to ensure database consistency. The fields shown in Figure 9-2 are stored just once. In a paper flat-file system, the reservation name may be found on many different documents. The ability of the DBMS to link and use files together eliminates this inefficiency and redundancy. DBMSs also support data independence, relieving the user of the need to know exactly how the data (e.g., supplier records) in the database is physically stored.

Data Extraction and Information Gathering

Once all the data is in place, you need to be able to extract it in a dynamic and structured way using a data language. While some DBMSs use their own proprietary DMLs, the data language of choice is *Structured Query Language* or *SQL*, the most widely used relational DML, originally developed by IBM. Queries allow a manager to extract specific data from a database. Structured Query Language (SQL), pronounced *sequel*, is used in products ranging from Access to Oracle. To find out which food items are at or below their reorder levels, for example, a food and beverage director might issue a SQL query:

> ***SELECT ITEM_#, ITEM_NAME***
> ***FROM INVENTORY***
> ***WHERE ITEMS_IN_STOCK <=REORDER_LEVEL***

This query uses the INVENTORY relation and returns item numbers and names for inventory items that should be reordered.

DBMSs also provide security features to protect files and records from unauthorized access or modification. In conjunction with network security measures discussed in Chapter 4, through the DBMS, files can be protected by passwords to completely deny access to certain users, to provide read-only access, or to allow unlimited access. For example, the supplier file may have read-only access restrictions, protected by a password, to prevent possible fraud (e.g., rerouted payments).

DBMSs also allow users to create interactive programs that manipulate database data to support the user's business applications. For example, a program might be developed in PowerBuilder, a software building application, to present a set of packaged procedures through menus to the user. Each menu option could activate a group of DBMS commands that create, access, or print data from the database, or even perform analyses of this data. Sales and marketing departments are big users of custom applications created in conjunction with DBMS manipulated data. Applications created here allow these departments to understand more definitively both current and future customers. This theme will be more thoroughly covered in database usage and in Chapter 10, The Power of Information.

Multiuser DBMSs are more sophisticated than the single-user variety and allow concurrent database access by tens or hundreds of users. If the inventory database described previously were implemented using a multiuser DBMS, two users *on different terminals* would be able to access multiple supplier records at the same time. However, problems occur in a multiuser context. The first is data integrity. For example, imagine a situation where two banquet managers retrieve an inventory record of fifty wine bottles, withdraw forty and thirty items each, and both end up with twenty bottles, potentially causing operational and security problems. Such problems are handled using file locks and record locks to restrict access to records in use. These locks are an important part of multiuser DBMSs.

Another problem multiuser DBMSs must handle is "deadly embrace," or deadlock, a situation that occurs when two processes require resources (e.g., records) held by the other. The result is that they would wait for each other, possibly indefinitely, if the ability to detect and break deadlock were not incorporated into multiuser DBMSs.

Database Servers and Distributed DBMSs

As computer networks have become more widespread, the need for database servers has grown. In non-C/S systems, requests for data from a central database in a multiuser setting would result in whole files sent by the DBMS to be processed at the user's terminal, creating heavy network traffic. For example, a request for suppliers in a certain city may result in the entire

SUPPLIERS relation being sent to the user's terminal and the request processed there. Database servers process queries on the server, greatly reducing communications overhead and returning only the query results to the requesting terminal.

Distributed databases are becoming more and more common in this network age. The DBMS supports location transparency, relieving the user of the need to know where files are physically located. If, on the other hand, different properties use different databases, then problems can result. This is what is known as disparate databases. As Bob Bennett stated, ownership is fragmented in the hospitality industry. Properties of the enterprise may be franchised and owned locally. Each property makes its own decisions regarding technology. A solution to this problem is *data-warehousing*, which is a collection of all the data from the entire enterprise centralized in one location. Its ultimate goal is "to integrate (this) enterprise-wide corporate data into a single repository from which users can easily run queries, produce reports, and perform analysis." (Connolly, Begg, and Strachan 1999) A subsection of a data-warehouse is a *data mart*, which is a departmental-specific section of a data-warehouse created to simplify tasks and improve processing time. Data marts were created so each department could analyze and query only "its" data.

3. DATABASE USAGE

You have already seen some of the uses of a database through queries and commands. Much of what has been covered detailed database usage in daily operations such as inventory management. With a good number of data captured on customers, databases can also provide the foundation for forward looking events such as sales and marketing initiatives.

Analysis

Companies with a database could find themselves with large amounts of data. At times it can be overwhelming. This stored data may have previously unseen relationships that could lead to future profit. For instance, after analyzing the data, it is uncovered that 80 percent of a hotel's weekend clientele comes from within a thirty-mile radius and has an annual income of over $75,000. Marketing initiatives could then be properly targeted to the records of a database with these "same attributes" and reevaluated at a later date as to effectiveness. This creates a "profile" that can be used to help target data for a sales campaign. A *profile* is a set of attributes and relationships that classify an entity, in this case a customer. Using this profile, the organization may then spend precious dollars more accurately in targeting potential "like" customers. This is an example of data mining. *Data mining* is analysis of data for potential relationships. Most data mining is statistical and can involve model formation such as *profiling, clustering,* and *cluster mapping.* Clustering and cluster mapping involve the plotting and mapping of data with like attributes. A newer data analytical technique is *online analytical processing (OLAP).* OLAP is "the dynamic synthesis, analysis, and consolidation of large volumes of multi-dimensional data." (Connolly, Begg, and Strachan 1999) Whereas traditional queries and analytical tools output answers such as the average room rate for a "specific" property, OLAP can view a larger data set and output the average room rate for "all" properties. OLAP provides a wider view of queries and will be detailed in the next chapter.

Setting up an analytical function beforehand can help a property take preemptive measures in preventing losses. Consider a frequent customer, Mr. Morrell, who has not stayed with a hotel in some time. In data mining, a trigger could be set to alert management of loyal customers who are not recent ones. A *trigger* in database terms is something that sets off another event. In this case, an e-mail would be sent to the sales manager stating that "Mr. Morrell" is a loyal customer whose time between stays has lapsed and should be contacted. A sales representative may pick up the phone and gently state that much time has gone by since his last stay and offer a complementary amenity upon the next visit in order to retain Mr. Morrell as a customer. Customer retention is important in any industry, particularly hospitality. On the operations side, imagine a trigger set up to alert a restaurant vendor, via an extranet, when a food or supply stock for one of the restaurants to which it sells dips below a certain level. A delivery could be initiated before the supply is depleted. Given the busy nature of the business, preemptive data management such as this can be a lifesaver.

Customer Relationship Management (CRM)

Databases are also helping the industry to serve and target customers in personalized ways. One such initiative is *customer relationship management (CRM).* The concept of customer relationship management, sometimes referred to as customer experience management or other similar names, is defined by many different persons in many different ways. You will use two definitions. First, according to the respected marketing firm of Carlson Marketing Group, CRM is defined as "a comprehensive *process* in which a company fundamentally improves the quality of interaction with its customers and prospects through the use of relevant, timely, and actionable information resulting in improved profitability." (Carlson Marketing Group 2001, p. 4) Dan Connolly, a professor of Hospitality Technology and E-Commerce at the University of Denver defines CRM this way:

> CRM is a complex and multifaceted phenomenon that involves taking a customer-centric view to every process, guest touch point, and department across the entire property (or chain, if applicable) to create rich, unique, and personalized guest experiences. It is as much a way of doing business as it is a

mindset or *philosophy* that must be embodied by everyone in the organization to become an essential part of the organization's culture. It is enabled by information technology and a series of software tools and technology applications that facilitate data collection, storage, filtering, pattern recognition, guest profiling, modeling, mapping, and more. The goals are to develop a holistic, 360-degree view of each guest, to create a segment of one, and to own each guest—for life! (Connolly 2001, p. 15)

CRM in Operations

Databases are extremely important to CRM, incorporating all of the aforementioned functions. However, what these two definitions stress is the fact that CRM is not just a computer system tracking customer preferences. CRM is a *process, mindset,* and *philosophy.* Unless everyone and everything is "on board" with this initiative, it might not work. Applying knowledge from the chapter interview, we see that some CRM initiative "musts" include the following:

- All customer touch points (PMS, POS, CRS, etc.) must be engaged.
- All staff must be trained on its importance and gather data when *possible.*
- Access must be given to this data when and where appropriate.
- Staff must be empowered to "react" to data.
- The data must be centralized or warehoused at a minimum.

More often than not CRM is accomplished through specific software that accesses the database. Let's take a look at CRM at work today (Figure 9-3).

Starting with the bottom tabs, you see that, via this software from Guest-Ware, you have a number of different views of a guest. This particular screen shot shows the customer preferences from *room type* to *wine.* Armed with this kind of information, a hotel or restaurant is much better off anticipating a guest's needs. If the property is a chain, CRM can allow the organization to cater to the specific customer needs all over the world. In an industry where the guest is king, CRM can provide the data to make sure that a guest is treated like one. Figure 9-4 shows another screen shot of GuestWare's software, this time showing the "follow-up" list. With a click of a mouse, an employee or manager now has the potential to see what is and is not going on in the hotel and, more importantly, is able to react in real time.

CRM in Sales

Software such as GuestWare also aids in targeted sales and marketing efforts. Due to such new mediums as the World Wide Web, the field of marketing is undergoing a change. Figure 9-5 depicts this paradigm shift.

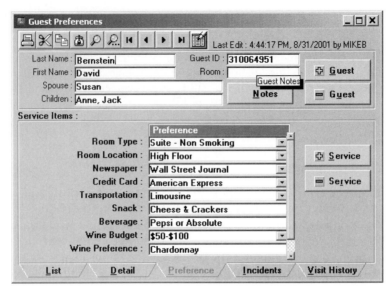

Figure 9-3. Software from companies such as GuestWare provides a user-friendly way to store and access unique guest preferences data.

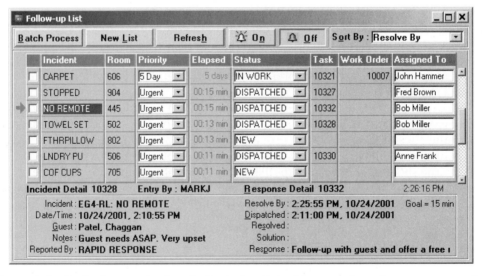

Figure 9-4. In the fast moving hospitality industry, making sure that what was supposed to get done actually got done can be very time consuming. This GuestWare "follow-up" screen aids in such efforts.

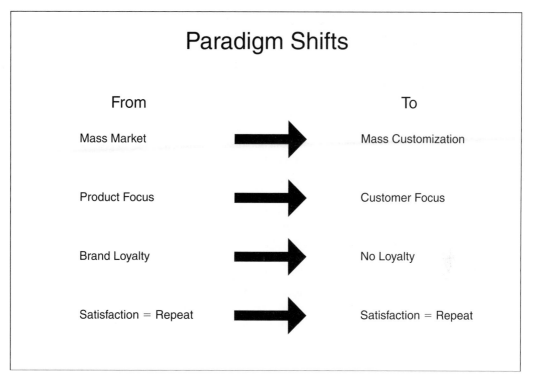

Figure 9-5. With the advances in technology, the individual has moved to the forefront in both marketing efforts and personal choices. *Source: Copyright © 2001 Carlson Marketing Group, Inc. All rights reserved.*

As this diagram shows, with CRM, marketing campaigns can now be targeted to the individual rather than to the masses. If you have ever logged on to a Web site and it personalizes a page just for you—this is an example of the paradigm shift. In hospitality, customization is needed for many types of guests. One of the most precious forms of data in a property's database is the *repeat customer list.* With the ability to purchase an item via the Internet, be it a room night or an airline ticket, guests no longer are attached to a specific chain. Keeping them is a challenge. They are concerned with price and have less brand loyalty. If management is able to show them that they really know them and can cater to their every need, guests are less likely to choose another location. CRM is meeting this paradigm shift head on.

A management team will know if it properly implemented and succeeded in CRM if the criteria listed in Figure 9-6 are met.

With these criteria met, the team can be certain that its CRM is working and should show up on the bottom line. From a database, to software, to people, successful CRM is quickly becoming a "must do" for properties wishing to stay competitive.

The Delighted Customer Experience

- The company interacts with its customers and prospects as a unified global entity.
- Customers and prospects receive messages, product/service offerings, and treatment/care as prescribed by their unique relationships.
- The message is the same regardless of interaction channel, tempered only by customer preference.
- Information is available at all customer touchpoints in a timely manner to improve mutual decision making and customer satisfaction.

Figure 9-6. The information age has led to a new customer experience that must be satisfied by the successful organization. *Source: Copyright © 2001 Carlson Marketing Group, Inc. All rights reserved.*

4. SUMMARY

Without structured organization, companies doing business in the information age can find themselves left in the dark. Databases provide that structure. Their use at first was seen as a solution to the inefficiencies found in the flat file environment. Quickly it was realized that real-time analysis could be done on data, and that initiatives such as CRM could actually help increase revenue and retention. However, moving to a database environment is not without difficulties. One of the largest impediments to organizations moving to a database is change. The old flat file environment allowed each department to control its own data. Political concerns are heightened at times when an organization is told to share. A database environment requires just that. Another problem is that the tangible benefits of databases are often years away, as is the payback period, detailed in the final chapter. The problems arising from different owners or management teams purchasing and using different technologies while serving the same customer are yet more obstacles to successful data management. Convincing management to purchase an expensive new system can be difficult. For that reason newer agreements and management contracts often stipulate the technology to be used and how the data is to be shared. The reason is simple: Shared data used effectively can increase revenue.

5. CASE STUDY AND LEARNING ACTIVITY

Take a look at how database usage and techniques can help retain and attract customers.

Golden Nugget Map for Los Angeles County by Cindy Estis Green

Hotels are utilizing new high-tech data-mining techniques such as Golden Nugget Maps™ to help identify prospects in areas that are new markets for the hotel or the chain.

The map indicates areas that have been fully penetrated (dark grey), those with a lot of potential and some penetration (medium grey), those with a lot of potential and no penetration (light grey), and those to be ignored light (white).

These so-called "golden nuggets" are the geographic markets that are ripest for prospecting. The map shows the hotel has not tapped these areas for business, but from its consumer profile, it appears that it could have a high percentage of qualified prospects. While this type of data mining technique will not guarantee success, it will greatly limit the risk of wasted promotional spending.

HOW WILL REVENUE DEVELOPMENT AND YIELD MANAGEMENT CHANGE IN THE FUTURE?

Revenue Development

Methods for revenue development will address the time-honored need to get and keep customers. This will include new techniques for prospecting, retention programs, sales extensions, and cross-selling. Hotel chains are beginning to pursue data warehousing technology to develop better customer profiles. These systems are being applied to improve prospecting so the marketing dollars spent can generate greater revenue returns. They are being used to supplement chain-wide frequency programs so unit-level customer service and local recognition programs can be employed.

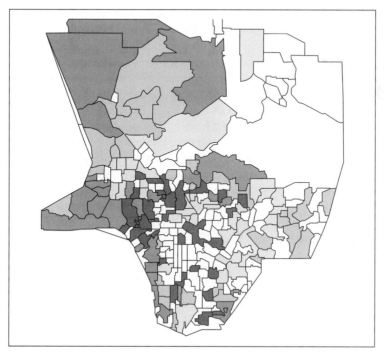

Golden Nugget Map for Los Angeles County

Recognition and improved guest service are being utilized equally by large and small chains to gain a more stable loyalty from their guests. Reward-based loyalty programs will continue to grow but the pot cannot continue to grow richer or all chains will lose the ability to cost-effectively retain their most frequent customers. Now that hotel companies have started to examine business levels hotel-by-hotel and market segment-by-market segment, it is clear that there are important types of business that are not influenced by the corporate frequency programs. The race for guest loyalty will be won by the hotel companies that have the discipline to deliver guest service consistently, not necessarily those with the richest rewards. It is an area that allows small and large companies to compete on equal footing. The bias built by reward schemes and brand name awareness can be quickly diffused by more effective use of the new distribution channels and more dedicated efforts to give personal recognition and develop dialogues with desirable customer groups.

There will be a move to more personalized marketing, not necessarily one-to-one, but rather to marketing to small like-minded clusters of customers who have similar traveling needs. Managing this effort will require technology, but this is already affordable today. Those companies that will succeed in this environment will market smarter by using information more intelligently. Developing customer clusters and planning promotions against them will be the basis of the new methods utilized. There will be less direct sales and more direct marketing through the Internet, e-mail, telephone, and more focused local media. The move will be from market segmentation to micro-segmentation. The computers will support this effort and communication breakthroughs will make this crucial customer information readily available at the point of sale or point of guest contact.

Breakthroughs in wireless technology will further enable this process. There will be a move from "broadcasting" messages to "narrowcasting" messages to a much shorter list of individuals who have indicated an interest. This is called "permission marketing" and involves asking the consumer to "opt in" to participate in a marketing program or series of customized offers.

Hotel chains will need to get full buy-in to make this approach a "way of life" in their organizations with support and understanding by operations, finance, and marketing to make it work. The building of customer relationships and the accompanying loyalty will not be "in your face" methods, but rather a series of transparent, silent, hassle-free systems that simplify reservation making, getting the room ready, and providing for special needs. The Internet will become an important part of the infrastructure in getting the information to and from customers to assure their needs are met and the process is smooth and hassle free.

Learning Activity

1. How does clustering identify potential future customers?
2. What fields would you include in your customers' profiles?
3. What marketing campaign would you use once you have identified those customers?
4. Who would lead the campaign?
5. Who would develop the customer profile?

6. KEY TERMS

Composite Key

Customer
Relationship
Management (CRM)

Clustering

Cluster mapping

Data mart

Data mining

Data-warehousing

Database

Database
Management System
(DBMS)

Field

File

Flat file

Foreign key

Hierarchical database

Logical view

Network database

Object oriented
database

Online analytical
processing (OLAP)

Physical view

Primary key

Profile

Record

Relational database

Structured Query
Language (SQL)

Trigger

7. CHAPTER QUESTIONS

1. What is the difference between the logical and physical views?
2. What is a flat file?
3. What functions does the DBMS provide?
4. What is CRM and how do you know if it is successful?
5. What is the difference between a data warehouse and a data mart?
6. What is a profile?
7. What is the difference between a primary and foreign key?
8. What is SQL and what does it do?
9. What is a trigger and how can it be used effectively?

8. REFERENCES

Carlson Marketing Group 2001, p. 4.

Connolly, Thomas, Carolyn Begg, and Anne Strachan. 1999. *Database systems.* 2d ed. North Reading, MA: Addison-Wesley.

Laudon, Kenneth, and Jane Laudon. 2002. *Management information systems.* 7th ed. Upper Saddle River, NJ: Prentice Hall.

Martin, E. Wainright, Carol V. Brown, Daniel Dehayes, Jeffrey A. Hoffer, and William C. Perkins. 2002. *Managing information technology.* 4th ed. Upper Saddle River, NJ: Prentice Hall.

CHAPTER TEN

The Power of Information[1]

CHAPTER CONTENTS

[1] The authors wish to acknowledge and thank Jerome Staverosky, CHTP and director of enterprise/CMS at SoftBrands Hospitality for his insights and contributions to this chapter.

INTERVIEW

Michael Goldenberg is co-founder of Atlanta-based Statability (*www.statability.com*), which offers Web-based reporting systems for multiunit restaurant and lodging companies. His firm specializes in collecting and consolidating data from multiple, and often, disparate systems to provide easy and fast information reporting and analysis for nontechnical professionals.

Q: Mike, thank you for sharing your perspectives regarding the importance of information capture, use, and dissemination in the hospitality industry. To start, please provide a brief overview of your career and how you came to start Statability.

A: While in college, I studied hospitality management and accounting, and upon graduation in 1987, I joined Marriott International's corporate team as a financial analyst developing budgeting models and financial reports. I spent a great deal of my time creating user-friendly budgeting and reporting tools so that busy executives could easily and quickly gain access to key performance projections, indicators, and actual results to help them make timely decisions and more effectively manage the company. I later decided I was interested in running a hotel and accepted a position as general manager for a Residence Inn. When I first started, I was shocked at the lack of tools provided to analyze the business and make decisions at the field level. I immediately began using spreadsheets to develop my own forecasting models, sales tracking reports, and other tools to help me and my management team better run the hotel.

In 1996, I left Marriott to join Homestead Village as director of financial planning and analysis. I was subsequently promoted to vice president of operations, responsible for the development of companywide budgets and reporting systems. In this capacity, I oversaw all of the systems and tools used by field and corporate personnel to analyze the company's operating results and financial performance for its 126 hotels. My responsibilities also involved the evaluation and selection of various systems for the hotels, including property management, central reservations, time and attendance, and a data warehouse. In evaluating vendor solutions, I discovered that the reporting functionality was consistently weak in each system considered, particularly when it came to having multiple views to the data (i.e., property and corporate level reports).

My experiences at Marriott and Homestead convinced me to start Statability with my partner Mike Wohl. Together, we saw a significant need in the marketplace to collect, consolidate, and report on data that are captured and stored in the many hospitality systems in use across multiunit companies. Our focus is to create reporting tools that are easy to use and that display information in an understandable and usable manner to help field, regional, and corporate staff better perform their jobs, provide better and timelier access to the information, and to enhance decision-making processes.

Q: What does Statability do? Who are some of your leading clients, and what solutions do you provide to them?

A: Statability utilizes various tools to collect and extract data from the many systems in use in hotels and restaurants. The data are then stored in a central database for querying and report generation for all levels of the organization (i.e., unit, region, and corporate). We operate as an ASP (application service provider) via the Web, which is a cost-effective tool to distribute reports to people in geographically disbursed areas. The advantage of an ASP solution is that there is no software or hardware that a client needs to purchase. To view reports, the client only needs a Web browser and an Internet connection. When enhancements are made and/or new reports are developed, they are made on a central server and immediately become available to our clients for their use. Implementation is extremely easy and hassle free for our clients.

Today, we currently provide reporting services to over 1,500 hotels and 150 restaurants in 27 countries. Our larger clients include Starwood, Marriott, Six Continents, and Candlewood. We also provide reporting applications to smaller management companies like Larkspur Hospitality and Destination Hotels and Resorts.

Q: What do you see as the primary problems of collecting quality (i.e., timely and accurate) data in the hospitality industry?

A: One of the primary problems is that most of the systems are not integrated, meaning that they don't talk to each other. This is why Statability collects data from many disparate systems and consolidates them in one central location. Another important issue is the geographic dispersion of the many systems with which we must deal. They are located in different states or countries, far removed from the central location where our database resides. While some companies have implemented effective polling systems (a process by which a central system sends out routine queries to systems in the field asking for specific data so they may be collected and consolidated on a central server) and/or take advantage of wide area networks (WANs) for real-time connectivity and data sharing, there are still many companies whose hotels are essentially acting as isolated islands, making it difficult to access and share data.

A third problem is the amount of paper-based data, which must be inputted manually. It is common for reports and forms to be sent via fax, only to be re-keyed and distributed. It astounds me that many of the challenges to create a companywide flash report are often solved the same way they were ten years ago. Issues related to the accuracy, timeliness, and completeness of data abound. Data should be captured as close to their sources of origination as possible. Rules should be encoded into each system to ensure required data are captured, validated, and error free whenever possible. The first step to turning data into actionable information requires managers and line staff to understand how data at their most basic levels can be turned into actionable information.

Q: How can managers address the issue of information overload? Is technology adding to this problem or helping to solve it?

A: According to a study conducted by the University of California at Berkeley, information production in 1999 and 2000 equaled all of the world information produced prior to 1999. To paraphrase management guru Peter Drucker, information technology can contribute to excess information, especially information of the "wrong kind." Clearly, technology is contributing to the problem, but it is also helping to solve it by giving us better tools to filter and manage data, flag exceptions or anomalies, and alert us to situations requiring our intervention. Managers who develop strong computer skills will have an advantage because they can run on-demand queries to obtain the information they need—when they need it.

Q: What kinds of things can hospitality managers do to better manage information throughout and across the organization?

A: Hospitality managers could do a better job of defining their reporting needs, that is, identifying what data they need to complete the jobs and how frequently they need the data. Better, more capable, and user-friendly querying and reporting tools will also help by allowing managers to set push and pull parameters to determine when and how information is received. In an ideal state, anyone can gain easy and fast access to the information needed at the time and place it is needed, in an easy to understand, graphical format.

Q: What do you consider to be essential information management skills for rising hospitality leaders? How does one develop these skills?

A: Hospitality leaders must have the ability to analyze information and understand what additional information may be needed to make decisions. They must have the ability to question. Good reporting, in my estimation, doesn't just provide answers; it helps you ask different questions and gain new insights. Working in both operations and IT will provide necessary experience and a technical foundation for using the tools, asking the right questions, and appropriately applying the answers.

1. INTRODUCTION

Over the past several decades, the hospitality business has steadily grown in complexity due to greater competition, more sophisticated customers, and more discriminating investors. Although the craft elements of the business remain vital to the guest experience, a new sense of focus must be placed on the strategic use of resources and the hard numbers, that is, profitability and return on investment, topics that will be explored in greater detail in the next chapter. Managing today's complex hospitality business requires effective use of information and a sophisticated business intelligence system that can gather, store, analyze, synthesize, share, and communicate information throughout the organization to those who need it, when and where they need it so that they may apply it in effective, value-creating ways. This business intelligence system operates much like the nervous system of the human body, providing important and timely information to management, the equivalent of the organization's brain, so that they and the organization can sense and respond to changing business conditions and stay out in front of competition and customers.

The present economy is often characterized as the information economy or digital economy. In such an economy, information is at the heart of all commerce, and knowledge is the basis of all competition. This is especially true in service industries like hospitality, where information becomes the essential ingredient to delivering unique, memorable, and unmatched service. Information also becomes a key competitive differentiator and can lead to competitive advantage. Differences in information, sometimes called *information asymmetry*, explain why firms respond differently and at different times to specific situations. They also explain how some firms can enter new markets or exit existing ones, launch new products and services, and respond more quickly to opportunities and threats than do their chief competitors. As seen in the previous chapters, those who use information effectively can benefit. Thanks to IT, the good news is that managers now have better and timelier access to an abundance of data regarding operations and performance. Unfortunately, this also presents challenges, as there is an overabundance of data and lack of time to wade through it all to interpret it and apply what is useful.

This chapter discusses how to effectively collect and use data to create information that can shape and guide managers' actions and decisions. It focuses on using information technology to "work smart, not hard." It explains how to funnel important information to managers to enhance their decision making, help them manage and control the business, guide the directions they set, and identify new opportunities for competitive posturing, positioning, and new product and service offerings. It presents the benefits of gathering usable information and applying it effectively and creatively to gain competitive advantage and to make it easier to manage the business.

Much of business success is determined by information and *knowledge management*—what was known, when, and by whom—and, then, how that information was put to use to outfox the competition. Good business decisions are a function of timely and accurate information in the hands of decision makers, knowledge of the context in which this information will be applied, appropriate and rigorous analysis, good common sense, experience, and speed (that is, the time to gather, interpret, and put the information to work and execute any resulting decisions). Moving forward, competition will continue to intensify in what appears to be a dog-eat-dog world. What will become important is how quickly companies can convert the reams of information they collect into knowledge that can be used for better decision making, product development, and marketing/pricing promotions. In essence, this is about how fast companies can learn, and as you know, continuous learning is the lifeline of any organization. As managers, it is important to have access to the *right* information at the *right* time to assist in making fact-based or informed decisions. This requires you to (1) constantly be in the know, (2) always have your fingers on the pulse of the organization, and (3) continually know what information is necessary to do your job and run your businesses. It also requires you to be inquisitive, to know how and when to ask provocative questions that will lead to new information and answers. Finally, you must also possess an uncanny ability to sense and respond to opportunities and threats before anyone else in the industry. These are some of the many traits of leaders in information economy. In looking at the future state of business competition, perhaps Bill Gates, chairman and co-founder of Microsoft sums it up best:

> The most meaningful way to differentiate your company from your competition . . . is to do an outstanding job with information. How you gather, manage, and use information will determine whether you win or lose. (Gates 1999, p. 3).

Leveraging information as a corporatewide asset requires a strong, capable, and flexible IT infrastructure and supportive company culture. For these systems to be effective and generate value, hospitality companies must ensure that the infrastructure in place is capable of meeting a company's needs, both now and into the future. Critical components of an organization's information foundation include management's ability to monitor performance and enforce business rules (which should be programmed into all systems), query and reporting tools, proactive reporting, comparative reporting, and analytical tools that can help to find and identify hidden meanings in the data. The tools should be easy to use so that anyone can use them without first having to speak with the IT department.

To realize value requires alignment between people, technology, and business processes. The focus must clearly be enterprisewide, that is, on the entire organization. In many organizations, enterprise application integration (EAI) (Chapter 7) initiatives are underway to connect and integrate all systems so that data can be shared and leveraged across the entire organization. The company's systems should be viewed as knowledge capture, creation, sharing, and policy enforcing devices. Collectively, they create a knowledge bank that can be shared by all employees throughout the company. In effect, these systems represent the brain trust of the organization.

2. DATA VERSUS INFORMATION

Rounding out the discussion of data and information from Chapter 3, this section now looks at these from a decision and action perspective. The terms data and information are often used interchangeably, yet they are not the same. It is worth noting the distinction. There is actually a *data hierarchy,* which is illustrated in Figure 10-1.

At the lowest level are data, the very building blocks of information; they are the raw ingredients that comprise information. By themselves, they are relatively worthless, appear random and meaningless, and can contribute to noise or distraction, but when ordered, aggregated, and put into context, they begin to take shape, develop meaning, and have a purpose. Patterns begin to emerge, and as they do, information begins to form, but information is not enough. It provides the foundation for knowledge, especially when it is coupled with experience. The more knowledge one possesses, the smarter he/she becomes. Knowledge is used in the development of insights, foresight, and judgment, which collectively lead to wisdom, the sum of knowledge over time—combined with common sense, good judgment, a wise outlook, and plan of action.

As you ascend the hierarchy, you gain more intelligence, and with that intelligence comes confidence, power, and action—the ability to make informed decisions, pursue directions that others are incapable of, and gain the upper hand in negotiating. Confidence is a prerequisite to action because it reduces risk and builds trust within the organization. By truly understanding patterns and cause-and-effect relationships, you can better predict outcomes with greater certainty. The pinnacle of the pyramid is action because your ultimate goal should be to do something impactful with the newly acquired knowledge or wisdom. If no action is taken, you must ask, "So what's the point; why did we bother with all this analysis?" It is the actions taken that will lead the firm to competitive advantage, so long as the actions taken are based on knowledge

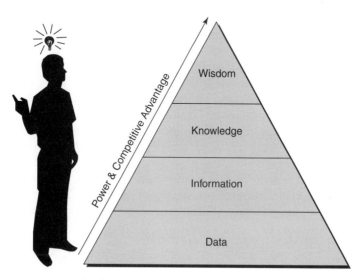

Figure 10-1. Data Hierarchy (*Source: Adapted from Professor Richard G. Moore, Cornell University's School of Hotel Administration and Michael Goldenberg, Statability.*)

that no other firm has or the actions taken apply knowledge differently or create a different path than any other industry competitor.

The keys to this ascent are capable systems, timely communications (powered by a great technology infrastructure), and inquisitive managers. Good managers ask good, tough questions and actively seek out their answers. For you to be effective as a manager, you must know how to ask the *right* questions, for that is the key to learning, but keep in mind that not all questions have answers or ones that are easily obtainable. You must often make decisions with the *best* available data, however imperfect or incomplete, and you must be comfortable with this. At times, you will be asked to fill in gaps in the data with assumptions and research and make inferences based on what knowledge is available while working within the given time frame. Although analysis is important, you must balance this with the need to take action and avoid paralysis by analysis (i.e., too much thinking, studying, and assessing of situations). To accomplish this, organizations must have in place an effective sense and response system that can tell what is and is not working. Many management consultants suggest the need for a culture within organizations that supports a bias towards action. If something is not working according to plan, intervention is required to fix it—but fix it quickly before the situation gets out of control. In order to do this, you need to have systems in place that can help you identify signals in a timely manner and correctly determine cause-and-effect relationships so that you can address the root causes of problems, not just their symptoms.

This data hierarchy calls attention to the importance of data and, in particular, the need to collect good, accurate data as close to the source of origination as possible. Second, it helps to explain the fundamental roles of all information technology (IT), which are to collect and organize data, process them while maintaining their integrity, and convert them from random bits to meaningful and usable information—as one progresses up the hierarchy—so that managers are well informed about the decisions they must make and the actions they must take in steering the business on a road to prosperity. All IT applications require data input as the raw ingredient. They then process these data and transform them into an intelligible output used to create the wisdom behind your thought processes. Ultimately, they become key repositories or the brain trust of the organization's collective knowledge or wisdom. The 6 stages of this process are represented pictorially in Figure 10-2 that follows. Although depicted in a linear fashion, the process will likely be iterative, with each stage having a recursive relationship with the one before it. Companies pursuing enterprise application integration strategies (Chapter 7) are trying to harness what this model depicts by modernizing and integrating all applications across their organizations to create a central repository and holistic view of all aspects of their businesses and customers.

As stated before, data must be collected as close to the point of origin as possible. Employees should be well trained in how to collect accurate data because these data will be used downstream in subsequent processes. Because the hospitality industry uses multiple, disparate systems and collects data from a variety of sources, it is necessary to go through a quality process of data

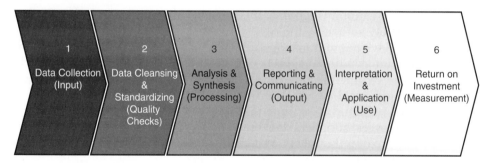

Figure 10-2. The Process of Refining and Making Sense of Data

cleansing and standardizing to ensure what was captured is usable and valid and that it can be consolidated. Once the data have been approved, the analysis and synthesis can occur. These processes will likely involve statistics, what-if analysis, scenario building, and other forms of modeling. Reporting and communication are important because these functions help to share what is known with people who can interpret or apply that knowledge to make impactful decisions; deliver better, more personalized guest service; and create value and competitive advantage. Finally, there has to be a measurement stage to provide a feedback loop and encourage organizational learning and improvements. In the end, you must be held accountable and be able to answer questions like "Was the effort worth it? Was the original investment recovered?"

3. INFORMATION AS A VALUED ASSET

Information is one of a hospitality firm's most important, yet undervalued, assets due to its intangible value. It is highly coveted, as its role is critical in every aspect of the hospitality industry, from guest services, marketing, decision making, administration, and control of the operation or organization. The digital economy is powered by an infrastructure of highly sophisticated computer systems and communications networks that collect, analyze, and share information throughout the corporation and its value chain of suppliers and allied partners to all those who need access to that information when and where their needs dictate. This economy is fueled by information and intellectual capital. To some, information might be viewed as a by-product of IT applications, but in reality, it is—or should be—the primary focus, for it is this information that gives IT its value and empowers managers and employees alike to do great things that provide them and their firms a competitive edge.

Information is a critical source of competitive advantage, but it is not just the information that contributes to a competitive advantage. It is how quickly you can act on this information after finding meaning in it through the discovery of patterns, relationships, and insights—before the competition—to do things that it cannot. Of course, this assumes that an organization is properly and effectively gathering the *right* information at the *right* time. This is why many of today's popular management theorists and consultants suggest focusing on the informational aspects of a business. When these are digitized (i.e., put in an electronic format), new things become possible. Information comes to life through graphics and multimedia and traverses faster throughout an organization, reducing cycle times and time to knowledge. People (e.g., management, employees, suppliers, customers, and partners) then have timely access to the information they need to fulfill their roles in the service delivery process and to make better, more informed decisions.

When you deal with data and information, you must remember four important characteristics. The first is the old adage "Garbage in equals garbage out." It is imperative that the data collection processes (e.g., reservations, order entry, lead development, etc.) are accurate, complete, consistent, and standardized. Accurate involves the ability to have processes in place to ensure *good* data via proper staff training and automated validation and error checking. Complete implies the ability to connect to various systems to gain all of the data needed, which is a major challenge with the systems in use today. Consistent and standardized suggest that processes, terminology, and data formats should be the same throughout the organization to allow for consolidation and interpretation. These data will be used downstream, for example, for subsequent processes such as check-in, guest profiles, function booking, data mining (defined in Chapter 9) and marketing campaigns among others. Therefore, the accuracy of these later activities is only as good as the data collected during the initial guest contact points. Achieving this level of accuracy is a function not only of the systems in place but also the training front line employees receive and the culture of the organization. All guest contact associates must understand and appreciate the important roles data play and their own importance and the contributions they make in collecting and using data to benefit guest service and the overall success of the organization. This is essential to maintaining the integrity of the data.

To avoid service failures and bad (i.e., ineffective) management decisions, you must ensure you have the appropriate procedures and systems in place, and you must train employees not only on how to collect data but also on the strategic importance of these data. In service businesses like those found in the hospitality industry, data are the raw ingredients used repeatedly in the guest life cycle for the production of service and the resulting experiences. Thus, to produce flawless service, create positively memorable experiences, and wow guests, employees require accurate and timely access to reliable data that can then be aggregated, ordered, and converted into usable information.

The second attribute to remember is that data and information can be perishable. Most data are dynamic, not static. Therefore, their lives are generally short-lived in terms of their relevance. Consequently, the value of data can shift over time, given the context and how it is being applied. Data that have surpassed their useful shelf life may have limited value in a specific situation or guest encounter, but when they are put in a historical context and used to establish trends or patterns and predict future events, their value takes on a different meaning and purpose. The opportunity costs, especially of missed opportunities, are where organizations are really vulnerable. In a time when speed wins, the opportunity costs can be rather high. Therefore, they must be carefully assessed and managed.

The third characteristic is that data and information are context-sensitive. In order to effectively use them, they must be treated in appropriate contexts for which they were collected and in which they will be applied. Finally, it is also important to remember that there is a humanistic element to data and information as well. Computers can help people organize and process data and information more quickly to find meaning in them, but humans must be able to recognize the value, see the meaning, and know how and when to apply this meaning in their jobs—from making managerial decisions to delivering outstanding guest services to developing successful marketing programs. This also implies their ethical and responsible use, which should never be overlooked.

4. WORKING SMART

Under the present economic environment, attention must be given to reducing or containing costs, which typically results in having to do more with less as financial resources are rationed and as people resources are eliminated. Under these circumstances, there are fewer staff persons and fewer managers to operate and manage the many diverse business activities associated with a hospitality enterprise. As managers' time is spread across a wider array of issues and business operations, managers are expected to oversee multiple aspects of the business without necessarily having all of the specific expertise—and certainly not all of the time—required to focus on the many important details to ensure smooth business operations, the consistent delivery of exceptional guest services, and the desired performance levels. Clearly, managers must figure out not only how to work smart if they are to be effective and productive but also how to pay close attention to the numbers while maintaining high visibility across departments. They have little time to spend in their offices reviewing reams of reports, trying to decipher meaning in the numbers, and reflecting on what could have been. The conditions of today require hospitality organizations to apply IT to extend their managers' reach and knowledge across the entire enterprise without necessarily having to have a ubiquitous physical presence to know how the business is performing.

In today's marketplace, the time it takes to acquire knowledge and subsequently act on this knowledge is critical in gaining competitive advantage. Without effective systems and a sound technology infrastructure connecting these systems to each other and to management, the reports generated provide little value. Managers must have real-time access to up-to-the-minute data and information to make informed decisions. When these are digitized, or put into an electronic format, this real-time access can happen. Not only do data and information move faster around the organization and get shared with more people, but they can also come to life through graphical and multimedia tools. Digitized data can be easily shared, graphed, manipulated, and tied to alarms to identify trends and exceptions. Thus, the computer can do most of the work while freeing up resources to spend time acting upon the results and making decisions that will positively influence the future.

In the past and in many cases even today, a corporate office provides much of the reporting for key operating statistics, financial data, and customer satisfaction surveys. This process is neither efficient nor timely and often leads to ineffective decisions. The resulting reports provide *lagging indicators* or historical operating information, making it difficult for managers to determine where and how to intervene to positively influence outcomes. By the time the reports are read, analyzed, and interpreted, the information contained within them is obsolete while the factors contributing to results are long forgotten. As properties become more automated, the local reporting capabilities increase, providing more timely information and alleviating many of the problems cited here. Yet, the number of disparate systems create difficulties in gaining access to timely, meaningful, and consolidated data. At times, administrative staff re-key data from reports into spreadsheets to create customized and consolidated *flash reports,* a daily snapshot of key performance indicators, for management. This process is prone to inaccuracies as a result of keyboard errors, and, as previously mentioned, relevance is an issue due to the time involved in preparing the reports. Unfortunately and perhaps surprising to some, these practices, as bad as they are, still exist today. With better systems and technology, these practices are changing, but the hospitality industry still has a long way to go, and the timing will be elongated due to the incompatibilities between many systems in use today and the lack of integrated solutions available for purchase.

Through advances in technology such as more open and integrated systems, greater organizational connectivity, and better reporting and analysis tools, the situation has greatly improved, giving managers access to more timely data as well as tools to help interpret the results quickly and effectively. With these tools, managers spend less time buried in reports and more time proactively managing the business.

5. TOOLS THAT CAN HELP

All hospitality systems are designed to help managers collect, manage, share, and interpret data, but since the systems in use today are many and diverse, it can be difficult to aggregate data and report on them. This is especially true when trying to aggregate data across departments, properties, and brands. Consider, for example, all of the many systems used to run a large ski resort—from the property management system and restaurant point-of-sale to the spa and ski lift ticket systems to the resort's Web site. In each case, data about guests, operational statistics, and financial performance are being collected. For a high-level executive to have to monitor and use each of the many systems to understand how a resort is performing would be time consuming. These problems are intensified when this same executive must determine performance across properties or brands or within a region where systems are not necessarily standardized.

Fortunately, there are two systems that run behind the scenes whose specific purpose is to help aggregate, analyze, interpret, and report data from multiple systems. These are the *executive information system (EIS)* and the *decision support system (DSS)*. There are components of each of these embedded in many hospitality systems. However, their functionality in these systems is limited. Therefore, managers must turn to specific tools dedicated to meeting these analytical and reporting needs of the business, tools that are more robust and powerful in their modeling capabilities and statistical assessment abilities.

An EIS is a tool that provides key operating data to managers and executives much like a car's dashboard reports important information regarding the health and status of the vehicle to its driver. Like a car's dashboard, an EIS is information central or a command center of sorts. Because the industry lacks a well-integrated system that can fulfill all of an organization's needs, hospitality operations require multiple disparate systems to operate efficiently and effectively. An EIS is a useful tool in polling these systems to collect, consolidate, and report on the various levels of activity in a single operation, within a region, and across the entire company in a common format. Because the system is intended for busy executives at different levels within the firm, the system must be easy to use, report on key performance measures with multiple units of analysis and views of the data (e.g., summary information to full details), and provide *drilldown* capabilities to explore increasing levels of detail and the individual components that comprise each of the high-level measures. The system tends to be visual (i.e., graphical) in nature, using charts to depict trends and performance over time. It also uses color and sound to call attention to key areas. The system can also be integrated with the company's electronic mail system or instant messaging system to issue timely alerts to management when specific action or intervention is required. The system is typically based on the concept of exceptions management. Assuming an executive has little time and few resources, what are the key areas (as denoted by warning signals or *red flags*) requiring immediate attention? These exceptions do not always have to highlight negative situations. They can also call attention to positive events, thereby allowing management to recognize and reward outstanding performance.

An EIS is more than a reporting and communications tool. It can be used for analysis, troubleshooting, and scenario building (e.g., what-if analysis). Because it is relatively easy to use, managers can create their own reports as needed without always having to rely on their IT staff. It gives them better control and access to the data they need to perform their jobs. Additional benefits include comparative analysis with similar properties in the chain, variance reports (actual versus budget), and event triggers or alarms. For each critical measure, management can set thresholds or acceptable ranges for performance. If the numbers shift above or below the established limits, alarms are triggered. At the press of a key or the click of a mouse, management has immediate access to real-time summary information and detailed data about its operations. For example, a district manager might be interested in knowing how performance at one particular hotel within his/her region compares with similar hotels within the region or elsewhere in the company. If it is outperforming others, one might question why and look for reasons and best practices that can be shared with the management teams at comparable hotels. Similarly, if the hotel in question is underperforming, one should also look to identify causes and then prepare an appropriate course of action. The goal is to ascertain the root cause—not just the symptoms—of problems so they can be quickly fixed.

A DSS, generally targeted for use by full-time business analysts versus executive management, has many of the same capabilities of an EIS, but it is more robust and sophisticated for more heavy duty data analysis, manipulation, and trends forecasting. A DSS is used for multidimensional analytics and multivariate statistics to find relationships and patterns in data. Recalling from the previous chapter, *online analytical processing (OLAP)* may be utilized to give users the ability to view and extract data from multiple points of view in real time. Working with multidimensional databases, OLAP allows data to be combined and analyzed through complex queries in many different ways interactively and on an ad hoc basis. Typically, users of OLAP are interested in viewing data by multiple criteria concurrently and are involved with calculation-intensive analyses. As such, the DSS analytical engine and modeling tools tend to be more powerful than those found in an EIS since the system must wade through voluminous data for mining purposes and discover patterns and trends by combining and comparing data and using these findings to predict the future. At the heart of a DSS are its statistical tools used for modeling, simulation, and *predictive analysis* (trying to forecast future trends, behavior, and outcomes). Whereas an EIS focuses more on communicating performance results, a DSS's primary emphasis is on understanding these results over time and what they mean in terms of the future. It helps to interpret these results, predict future market and buyer behavior, and troubleshoot. The system queries tend to be more ad hoc and more complex than those encountered in a typical EIS, and its use is for unveiling important cause-and-effect relationships that can enhance the performance, strategic direction, and value of the firm. A DSS query might look to identify consumers from a specific geographic region with common demographic and psychographic traits who have demonstrated similar purchasing behaviors so that an electronic mail target marketing campaign can be launched. In another query, a user might want to know how much money was spent on cleaning supplies across the organization in order to consolidate purchasing and negotiate better volume discounts. These are just a couple of the many possible questions that might be asked of a DSS. The questions can be one time or repetitive, broad or specific, cover a relatively short period or extend over multiple years, but in each case, the questions usually involve an extemporized component.

6. THE BALANCED SCORECARD

Over time, EIS systems have evolved and now focus on providing a *balanced scorecard* (an organizational report card of sorts) to top managers, a concept first popularized by Kaplan and Norton (1996). The balanced scorecard may vary from organization to organization, but the underlying premise is the same: ascertaining the health of the business. In assessing performance, organizations should not rely on any single measure but rather on a composite set of measures that take into account the various stakeholders of the firm (i.e., guests, employees, owners and investors, suppliers, franchisees, allied partners, government, and community). The goal is to assemble a comprehensive and integrated measurement system that will allow managers to monitor performance, identify problem areas, develop intervening strategies, chart the performance of the organization against its overarching strategies, and aid in the development of future strategic directions. The system must not only report historical information but also predict future outcomes.

Traditionally, almost exclusive emphasis was given to financial measures. This approach, which overlooked other key measures, has proven problematic for several reasons. These include a historical and inward focus, a tendency to concentrate on short-term results, and an inappropriate assumption that everything can be quantified. In the words of Kaplan and Norton (1996, p. 24):

> Financial measures are inadequate for guiding and evaluating organizations' trajectories through competitive environments. They are lagging indicators that fail to capture much of the value that has been created or destroyed by managers' actions . . . [They] tell some, but not all, of the story . . . and they fail to provide adequate guidance for the actions to be taken today and the day after to create future financial value.

Certainly, financial measures are important and must be included, but they only represent one view of the firm. Instead of a single measure or single category of measures, what is proposed is a composite of integrated and telling measures or key indicators (sometimes referred to as *critical success factors*) across a variety of categories tied to each stakeholder group that will provide vital information regarding the health and performance of the organization. For each measurement category, management should define strategic objectives (or drivers), appropriate measures, targets to be achieved, and key initiatives that will be undertaken to achieve the established goals. Table 10-1 provides a worksheet that can be used in the scorecard development process to help identify and document key measures and goals and align them with the firm's strategy.

The measurement categories will likely include financial considerations (e.g., financial ratios, revenues, net profit, actual versus budget variances), operational statistics (e.g., occupancy, ADR, REVPAR), competitive activity and positioning (e.g., market share, rate positioning), internal factors (e.g., efficiencies, cost savings), employee measures (e.g., turnover, overtime, satisfaction ratings), guest perspectives (e.g., repeat business, satisfaction ratings), supplier relationships and performance (e.g., quality, on-time delivery),

Table 10-1. Balanced Scorecard Development Worksheet

Measurement Category	Strategic Objectives (Drivers)	Measures	Targets (Goals)	Key Initiatives

environmental concerns (e.g., recycling programs, energy consumption), community (e.g., programs sponsored, charitable contributions), external factors (e.g., economic indicators, weather), and assessments for learning and innovation (e.g., training, experimentation, new ideas, research and development). Using the critical success factors, or key determinants of success for the organization, as measured by each stakeholder group, a snapshot of the firm is prepared indicating its overall health and preparedness as well as providing a source of tracking against the firm's defined strategy. The specific measures chosen and the weight assigned to each are important. Their selection should not be taken lightly because they will help a firm articulate its strategic objectives to all those charged with their implementation and fulfillment. The measures should be an appropriate blend of the firm's critical success factors, focus on internal and external indicators, and include actual results as well as projections and comparisons to budgets and historical results. The measures used will also help to determine how management spends its time and how resources are allocated within the firm. Finally, they provide a basis for benchmarking and can be used to compare against previous results, predetermined goals, and/or against competitors to see if the organization is improving over time. For an example of a balanced scorecard, refer to Figure 10-3.

Using such a system provides numerous advantages. First, it improves visibility and communications within the firm, letting employees and managers know how the company is performing with respect to itself, its goals, the marketplace, and the industry as a whole. Second, it allows managers to keep their fingers on the pulse, have up-to-date status information regarding the business, and identify key areas (through early warning indicators like red flags and exception reporting) that require their attention and intervention.

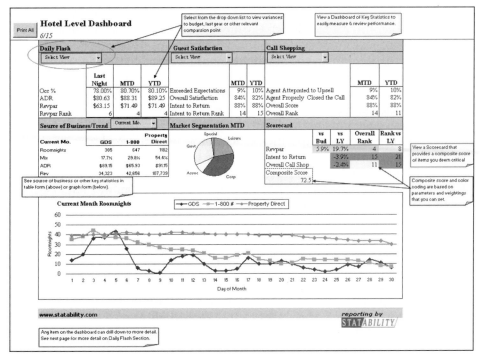

Figure 10-3. Measurement, management, and planning come together in the balanced scorecard. (*Source: Courtesy of Statability*)

Third and finally, a balanced scorecard system provides a source of accountability and control. Remember the old saying, "What gets measured gets done."

To better understand these concepts and see how to operationalize them, study the following two important examples, Toronto-based Four Seasons Hotels and Resorts and Minneapolis-based Carlson Hospitality. Four Seasons Hotels and Resorts has implemented a scorecard system referred to as the "Three P System," which comprises three very specific measurement categories: people (results of associate opinion surveys), product (service quality), and profit. The data can be collected from the systems installed in all of the company's hotels and resorts around the world and consolidated at the corporate offices in Toronto. The results can then be shared with all those requiring access via the company's intranet. This approach automates the data collection, aggregation, reporting, and dissemination processes, making the information accessible on an as-needed basis. Through the Three P System, Four Seasons carefully monitors its business and maintains the quality and high service standards for which it is known.

Carlson Hospitality (parent to Radisson Hotels and Resorts) takes the Four Seasons approach one step further by putting critical information directly into the palms of its management team with its proprietary MACH-1 (Mobile Access to Carlson Hospitality, Version 1) portable EIS. The system uses Compaq's iPAQ handheld device running Microsoft's Pocket PC operating system. The system communicates with the company's core systems such as Curtis-C (central reservations), Harmony (property management system based on Fidelio), and CustomerKare (data warehouse) to gather key performance data. It is expected that the system will soon feature completely wireless transmissions for real-time access to data and be made available to all key hotel managers and corporate executives throughout the company. With such a system, it does not matter where a manager is, he/she can always know what is going on and when his/her input or intervention is required. Thresholds (floor and ceiling values) and specific events can be programmed to raise red flags or alert managers of changes (either good or bad) in status to key measures. If the changes are positive, managers can be notified so that they give praise where it is deserved. If the changes are negative, the system can warn managers of the gravity of the situation so that an intervention plan can be developed. Perhaps in the future, artificial intelligence will be used to provide, and in some cases carry out, suggested courses of action, much like advanced yield management systems work today in turning rules on and off as situations dictate.

In both of these examples, an EIS is being used to help managers stay on top of things and monitor the health of the business. These EISs serve as information portals, providing a consolidated and unified view of the data, complete with drill-down capabilities, querying options, and other sophisticated analytical and modeling tools. *What-if analysis* and *scenario-building* functionality (forms of data modeling under situations of changing variables or assumptions) further assist in discerning patterns and cause-and-effect relationships in the data. These systems shift the data reporting from lagging measures to leading measures, allowing managers to become proactive rather than reactive, to take action and prevent problems—long before things spiral out of control and become irreparable. As previously stated, open systems and better systems integration are making such access to data possible. This is a real blessing to management companies that operate multiple properties under different brands with different core systems. With this technology, they now have a way to quickly and automatically consolidate the data without the need to re-key them, making it possible to conduct comparative analyses between current, budgeted, forecasted, and historical information.

7. THE IMPORTANCE OF INFRASTRUCTURE

In order to achieve value from technology, a firm must have an appropriate, capable, reliable, and solid, yet flexible, technology infrastructure in place. Like a building's foundation, the technology infrastructure is the base upon which all technology applications are built. Simply put, the technology infrastructure is *everything* (i.e., people, technology, business processes, and organizational culture) necessary to support the flow and processing of data and information. It determines a firm's capabilities or limitations. A poor, ineffective, or inappropriate infrastructure will undoubtedly cause problems for the firm, namely, inhibited growth, unrealized potential, service delivery failures, and uninformed decisions. All of these are undesirable and could be catastrophic to the firm. Although most of the infrastructure remains behind the scenes, its failure will quickly bring it into the forefront. Therefore, managers must not underestimate the importance of infrastructure and must not skimp in this area. Such shortsightedness almost always causes heartaches and growing pains at a later point in time. Instead, managers should pay close attention to the selection, building, and ongoing maintenance and updating of the firm's IT infrastructure. This is not to say that the entire infrastructure has to be purchased at once; it should be scaleable, adaptable, and purchased as needed.

The infrastructural elements are discussed throughout this book and will be explored in greater detail in the next chapter. Of particular note are the systems' architecture (hardware and software design, operating systems, and programming languages), network topology and communications protocols, the databases, data warehouses, data mining tools, intranet, security, systems procedures, organizational culture, and human elements. There is a broad range of systems in use within hospitality firms to run operations, link with suppliers and allied partners, and share data throughout the organization and across its value chain, the collection of all of the direct, indirect, and support functions, from supplier to customer, necessary to drive revenues and firm profitability. It is important for systems to be able to talk with one another, that is, share data back and forth with each other as business needs dictate. This sharing can only be achieved if the systems in use are able to talk the same language, which requires defining software, hardware, database, and communications standards at the onset. The data network then becomes the glue that connects various systems together. The databases are the underlying storage cabinets that house all data collected, and, in turn, allow users access to these data through queries, reports, and data sharing with other systems. As one might suspect, successful use of data between systems requires common language, terminology, and formats. In the previous chapter, data warehouses, megastorage houses for large volumes of complex data, and data marts, subsets of a data warehouse with specialized groupings of data, were introduced. These are both powered by sophisticated databases, and when data mining, querying, and reporting tools are applied, the data contained within can be ordered, processed, and analyzed so that key patterns can emerge to provide insights and guidance as to how to grow and better manage the business through new product and services offerings, pricing strategies, marketing campaigns, etc.

Arguably, what is described here represents an idealistic state. Unfortunately, the hospitality industry is far from attaining such a state, given the number and complexity of systems used today and the widespread use of older, outdated technology (i.e., legacy systems). Consequently, applications called middleware are used to assist in the integration—or at least communications—between disparate systems.

The Internet, with its ubiquity and common standards, opens up many doors to providing access to data. Many hospitality systems are becoming Web enabled, that is, connected to the Web for data sharing and reporting. Using virtual private networks (VPNs, Chapter 4), employees can access their systems and data in a secure manner from anywhere, so long as they have an Internet connection. Internally, the company intranet becomes the information portal and gateway to the organization's key systems for those who have been granted access privileges. Security is a critical, yet sometimes overlooked, element of the infrastructure, especially when it comes to wireless technologies and applications. Data are corporate assets, and like any other important asset vital to a firm's success and competitive advantage, they should be protected. Access should be limited to only those who need it, when and where they require such access. Firewalls, passwords, and encryption, among other things, are all part of the security infrastructure. Finally, when looking at the technology infrastructure, managers should not overlook the organizational culture and humanistic elements (including support network) that play such vital roles in the attitudes towards and usage of IT throughout the firm. Although it may not be necessary for hospitality managers to fully understand the technical ins and outs of their companies' IT infrastructure, it is essential for them to know the physical capabilities and limitations of this infrastructure. It will define what is and what is not possible.

8. SUMMARY

In an information age, competition is based on information, the time it takes to acquire this information, how the organization and its employees act on this information, and how soon they act. The possibilities and applications for an EIS and DSS are virtually endless. Think about how they can extend resources and enhance the bottom line of a hospitality organization. To manage the business by the numbers, information technology and a good technology infrastructure are required. A performance measurement and monitoring system are ideal applications for these tools, which should become a standard component of every organization's technology applications portfolio, with appropriate access provided to key managers. These tools are great assets for managers, but they do not replace the need for good, strong, intelligent managers. The systems can process the data, but someone still needs to interpret the results and make the decisions.

Because information is perishable, timely access is critical, and since the quantity of information is often excessive, tools are needed to help filter out the noise from the substance. An EIS and DSS are key tools in a firm's business intelligence arsenal. They can offer different views of data, drill-down capabilities, and powerful analysis and reporting tools to help interpret meaning from the data, thereby reducing the time involved in analyzing data and the level of statistical knowledge required by managers. To provide value, these systems must provide meaningful information for a well-defined set of measures and managerial questions so that managers can quickly address the issue(s) at hand. These systems must also allow some customization to meet user preferences and job needs. A more effective and productive manager, someone who is constantly in the know and armed with up-to-the minute data, can spread himself or herself further across the organization and make better (i.e., fact-based versus gut-based) decisions. By being more informed, managers are in better control of their environment. They can, therefore, better coach their employees and raise the level of accountability for all departments, teams, and managers around the resort. To a large extent, management can now be done on an exception basis, but one must keep in mind that an exception does not necessarily have to imply a negative situation or identify an underachiever. It can also be used to recognize positive results, star performers, and factors contributing to the organization's success. Remember, the power is in the information and your ability to interpret and apply that information at the *right* times in appropriate and ethical manners.

Leading strategists suggest that the key to winning the future is to develop industry foresight and to stake a territorial claim before anyone else. Following this advice, however, is not as easy as it may sound, especially when you take into account how quickly things change in the era of high-tech. IT applications are essential in helping to wade through that voluminous data to uncover trends, patterns, and meaning, but remember, technology is not enough. It is how you (and your staff) use the technology and the information it yields that will make a difference. Learning to ask good, intelligent questions, having the systems in place to be able to answer these questions, and knowing how to interpret and apply the answers are important and required traits for hospitality managers. Knowledge, not location, is the key competitive determinant in the digital economy. Moving forward, the playing field and rules of engagement will be quite different than what has been seen in the past. New business models will emerge, especially as the Internet, intranets, and wireless technologies gain in both capabilities and in presence in the industry.

9. CASE STUDY AND LEARNING ACTIVITY

Measurement Before Management

Richard Sperry works for a major hotel management company. His corporate office has decided that his talents, honed as the head of strategy for the brand, need to be targeted towards the northeastern sector of the United States. This region has forty-five hotels and is presently the corporation's weakest performing region. Of particular concern to his boss is the ability of one of the competitors in the region to respond to market forces more readily, leaving the company at a major disadvantage. One competitor in particular always seems to have its finger on the pulse and adjusts its room rates perfectly to meet shifting demand seen in the region. Its package deals constantly meet with high approvals, and its owners couldn't be happier.

Having been burnt from the many "if you buy it, they will come," computer solutions offered by many vendors in the dot.com era, management is skeptical of purchasing new systems. Fortunately, Richard has a history of solving problems with little increased spending due to his ability to manage and use information effectively. Management is in clear agreement that the company is presently at a competitive disadvantage. Rather than react to every new offering a competing property may introduce to the marketplace, Richard and his boss concur that the best strategy to compete is to better use information to build a solid foundation of smart business practices blended with quality service offerings. The following five goals have been established and will be used as the basis of measuring Richard's performance over the next year:

1. Increase revenue by 5 percent
2. Increase occupancy percentage by 6 percent
3. Increase Guest Service Index (GSI) scores to 3.5 (on a scale of 1 to 5, with 5 being the most satisfied and 1 being the least satisfied)
4. Decrease food costs by 5 percent
5. Reduce employee turnover by 15 percent

Current Systems

Luckily for Richard, each hotel recently upgraded its technology applications portfolio. Currently, each property shares a similar network infrastructure and common operating system. High speed Internet access is available at all properties on personal computers running Windows XP Professional. Software, despite being upgraded, has not been standardized throughout the company. Among the forty-five hotels in Richard's region, there are three different property management systems, four different restaurant point-of-sale systems, and three different database architectures in use. Additionally, word processing, spreadsheet, and other productivity software differ from property to property with a mix between Microsoft Office Professional and Lotus SmartSuite. Browser software is equally divided in the company between Internet Explorer and Netscape.

Current Procedures

Report compilation and dissemination requires each hotel's night auditor to fax weekly flash reports to the regional office where the numbers are entered manually into a spreadsheet so that a consolidated report for the region can be prepared. Comment cards, the sole measurement for GSI scores, are mailed to the corporate office each week. The corporate office compiles the scores to create the GSI index and then mails a printed report to the regional office each month. The food and beverage director submits bi-weekly purchasing histories and nightly sales data to the on-site controller who compiles the data and faxes a series of reports to the regional office. Each month, the regional office faxes a series of summary financial and operating reports to the corporate office and each property in the region detailing actual performance versus budget and year-to-date statistics. These reports are then reviewed by the general manager and become the subject of discussion in executive committee meetings at each hotel.

Richard has some great ideas for a new strategy. He knows that he has to be able to measure what he is about to manage. Our learning activity is based on that theme.

Learning Activity

1. What are the key problems facing Richard Sperry and his organization as described in the above scenario? If you were in Richard's shoes,

how might you go about addressing these challenges? What would be your strategy and why? Be sure to provide appropriate justification and a specific (i.e., detailed and measurable) action plan.

2. Before any action is taken, what managerial measures must be implemented for the company's five goals, and how should these be implemented? What procedural changes are required at each property and at the regional and corporate offices? How should these changes be introduced, and who should lead the change effort?

3. Would any of the data require access restriction? If so, who should have access, and to which data?

4. Evaluate the technology applications portfolio and infrastructure for Richard Sperry's company. What are its strengths and limitations? In what ways is technology being used effectively? Where is there room for improvement? What changes would you suggest and why?

5. If you were to design a balanced scorecard approach for measuring and monitoring performance and the overall health of the organization for Richard Sperry's company, how would you go about it? Where would you start? What issues might you face, and how can you overcome them? What would your proposed balanced scorecard look like?

10. KEY TERMS

Balanced scorecard	Executive Information System (EIS)	Lagging indicators
Critical success factors	Flash reports	Online analytical processing (OLAP)
Data hierarchy	Information asymmetry	Predictive analysis
Decision Support System (DSS)	Knowledge management	Red flags
Drill-down		Scenario-building
		What-if analysis

11. CHAPTER QUESTIONS

1. What are the characteristics of and differences between data and information? Why is it important to distinguish between the two, and how can data be converted into usable information?

2. Why do hospitality managers feel a sense of information overload? How can they cope?

3. As a hospitality manager in an information economy, what are the important traits for you to possess? What information would you consider essential to perform your job? How would you use this information?

4. What are the core IT infrastructural components to a company's information systems and why are they so important? What roles can the Web and intranets play?

5. Is information the basis of competition in today's marketplace? Can information provide competitive advantage? If so, how?

6. What are the issues associated with data collection of which a hospitality manager should be aware? How can hospitality organizations improve the quality of their data?

7. What would you consider to be an ideal balanced scorecard for a hospitality organization? What measurement categories and measures would you use and why?

8. What are the differences between an executive information system (EIS) and a decision support system (DSS)?

9. How is IT raising the bar of accountability, changing the way we manage operations, and contributing to performance of employees and the firm as a whole? How do we, as managers, know what questions to ask and where to find their answers?

10. What are knowledge management systems, and how do they differ from a series of databases? Why do organizations need them (in other words, what are the driving forces; what are the primary applications; and what's their business value), and how do you tangibly measure their benefits?

11. Why should people share information? How does sharing information change its value? What are the ethical considerations involving the use of data and information that managers should take into account? Why are these important?

12. How can hospitality organizations create processes and information technology infrastructures for more effective management and for enhancing performance and productivity? What is required? What challenges might exist, especially culturally, technically, and organizationally?

12. REFERENCES

Gates, Bill (with Hemingway, Collins). 1999. *Business @ the speed of thought: Using a digital nervous system.* New York: Warner Books.

Kaplan, Robert S., and David P. Norton. 1996. *The balanced scorecard: Translating strategy into action.* Boston: Harvard Business School Press.

CHAPTER ELEVEN

Strategic Hospitality Technology Investment

CHAPTER CONTENTS

INTERVIEW

Mike DiLeva is the head of Unisys' Hospitality division. He began his career in hospitality in the early 1990s. After launching a successful casino marketing program, he joined a small dot.com company, finished his MBA, and then joined Unisys.

Q: Mike, thanks for taking time out. Can you tell us about your background?

A: Sure. I started in the hotel business in the early 1990s more or less by default since the economy was in a downturn and the hospitality business was the only place offering opportunities at the time. It proved to be a blessing as I really took to the industry and wound up spending a decade there, specifically on the casino hotel side of the business. It was during that time that I really came to appreciate the significance of technology and the impact it can have on a service industry like hospitality. For example, during a business downturn caused by the expansion of our property, I and a few colleagues put together a casino marketing program that relied heavily on technology to identify new customers and deliver specific rewards to that group. The program was an overwhelming success and ultimately got patented. Shortly thereafter the dot.com boom occurred and I realized that we were at the dawn of a new era that would be as socially and economically influential as the Industrial Revolution and I wanted to be a part of it. I was in graduate school at the time and leapt at an offer to join a small dot.com named PCRoomLink that was an early advocate of in-room computer systems. About a year after that transition, I finished my MBA and with the technology and hospitality experience, moved to Unisys, which was known for networking and system integration.

I viewed it as a tremendous opportunity since Unisys has a strong transportation division, strong operating systems, and solutions such as customer loyalty systems for airlines around the world. The company was looking to leverage its expertise in travel into a new arena. Clearly hospitality is perfect since it's a lot like transportation in terms of dealing with perishable inventories, narrow margins, and high guest-service standards. Unisys is used to solving issues associated with those challenges and wanted to enhance its existing technological resources with someone that understood the operations of the hospitality business.

Q: Someone with industry experience?

A: Exactly. Someone who could say to the technology people—this is what the hotel business really needs. So that's how I got to where I am today.

Q: How do you like it?

A: I love it. It is a wonderful industry. Unisys is now entering the market with an in-room Internet product since that's the biggest technology issue right now, but we do plan to expand our offerings into other areas such as customer loyalty and customer relationship management systems as well as video on demand.

Q: Video on demand, are you teaming up with anyone there?

A: We are not adverse to teaming but right now we have acquired technology that we're introducing to the market on our own. In-room entertainment is really the "next big thing" aspect of the industry that is ready to be re-invented. The analog pay-per-view model is slowly dying and I've heard an awful lot of lodging executives complain about the service levels currently being offered by the major players. If you look at the overall model in room entertainment, the "free to the hotel" pay-per-view model was really the start of what became the fatally flawed "free to the hotel" Internet model. There was this view that future cash flows would be so enormous that they would support free installation, revenue sharing, and free televisions. Now after 10 years, 10 years in which profits have been non-existent, that model is ready to collapse. Technology continually evolves and the entire industry is looking to move to a digital platform. Unfortunately, because of the legacy environment as well as the lack of a financial incentive, there is a re-luctance or inability to invest in new systems or platforms. For video-on-demand, even though we want to partner with new players, the current environment makes it difficult to join forces without also assuming the baggage associated with the difficult legacy environment. The flawed "free" pay-per-view model is no different than what became the flawed "free" In-ternet model. For a business model to be sustainable in the long run and to deliver value to guests it has to offer value to both the hotel and the sup-plier and it can't be one-sided in terms of risk or reward.

Q: Okay, what if we take that one step further? If I'm a hotelier, how should I look at hospitality technology for strategic or competitive advantage?

A: The first step is to look at technology more strategically. Fortunately, that's already happening. I think in a macro sense, you are seeing a lot of com-panies where IS would once report to the CFO because it was viewed merely as a cost center. Now, however, IT is reporting through marketing, with the thought that IT can enable a market differentiation or product ad-vantage to make it more customer responsive, or through the CEO, which obviously elevates it in terms of perception, prestige, and responsibility. Another trend is to see more technologists incorporating higher-level busi-ness skills. Tim Harvey, for example, the CIO of Hilton started out as a pro-grammer, but along the way became an analyst and then obtained his MBA. He really understands the business issues that apply to technology. In gen-eral I think you are seeing that companies recognize that technology needs to be looked at a lot more strategically and it is not just how can it save me money, it's how can this give me a leg up on the competition?

Q: So, do you see IT moving from more of a cost center to a profit center?

A: I wouldn't necessarily say it is a profit center because I think that puts an undo expectation on what IT should be. That still looks at it as very compartmentalized. IT needs to be a horizontal resource that permeates throughout the entire company. You are right. It definitely was a cost center, that's why it reported through the CFO.

Q: Do you think you can use occupancy and RevPar as a benchmark as to how well you are doing with your technology?

A: I don't think the metrics on technology are going to be any different than they are in the hotel business in general. I mean the industry is evaluated on occupancy, ADR, and RevPar. I think that if technology contributes positively to those areas then technology is successful. I'll give you a great example. A company that I think is doing a very good job with in-room technology is Wingate Inns. Cendant had a vision that this mid-market brand will appeal to business travelers and it recognized that business travelers needed high-speed Internet access. So it wove that into its product offering and marketed it properly. So now if you are a guest of a Wingate hotel you get complementary high-speed Internet access included in the room rate. The cost is already incorporated, as is every other amenity in the hotel from the gym to the swimming pool, into the room rate, so you don't worry about charging for it when it's used—it's an amenity. Because Wingate has woven it into its business practices and marketing positioning, Wingate's usage is 15 percent and growing dramatically. What's the impact? Well, in a service business, guest satisfaction is always a key metric. Benchmarking the industry guest satisfaction rating for their brand, the industry average in terms of guest perception of value is 57 percent while Wingate's is 74 percent. So when you look at technology strategically and weave it into all of your business practices you really have some dramatic impacts on some of your key metrics and performance evaluations.

Q: How about recent hospitality graduates? What are some of the things they should be aware of or keep their eyes on when they start making purchasing decisions?

A: I think the walls between IT, operations, and marketing will really be broken down. I think too often there is a real conflict there. If I were a young IT professional in the hospitality industry, I would talk to the marketers and operators and, even more importantly, talk to the customers. Ultimately it all comes down to the customer. What does the customer want? If you are a technologist, don't allow yourself to be captivated by the what ifs or by the whiz-band tech product du jour such as checking in via a PDA when there are far more pressing issues such as what are my guests struggling with and how can technology be used to solve that. I think that is really a better way to go.

1. INTRODUCTION

Making a purchasing decision relative to a strategic investment in corporate information systems is very different than a consumer technology purchase. When people buy consumer technology, they often tend to start any discussion about which alternative to purchase with a question along the lines of "Which one is best?" The natural follow up to this is "How much does the best one cost?" followed quickly by "How much do the other ones cost?" And so goes most of the selection process when it comes to buying anything from MP3 players to automobiles.

As technology consumers, people are programmed to think of quality and functionality as being somehow related, and, at the same time, they equate "the most functionality" with "the best." Although there may be a great deal of validity to this type of thinking when it comes to purchasing MP3 players, it is often misplaced in the world of business-based information systems. This is because when it comes to acquiring technology for your hotel, restaurant, or any other business, it is not nearly as important to get "lots of functionality" as it is to get "the right functionality for your business."

2. REDUCING EXPENSES AND INCREASING PROFITS

The single most important thing to remember when you think about strategic investments in hospitality information technology is that these investments must generate a positive *return on investment (ROI)* just like any other strategic corporate purchase. In the past, many technology vendors and professionals have tried numerous arguments for why technology investments cannot be measured against a quantitative yardstick for ROI. These arguments are all weak at best and more often simply the result of laziness and ineptitude. This section will discuss ROI in its most simplistic terms, and then in a more detailed manner.

One thing to always remember is that in order for an information technology system to generate a positive ROI, it must either reduce costs or increase revenue in some quantifiable way. If a hospitality professional never remembers anything about detailed ROI calculations or information system minutia, he or she can always fall back on this most basic premise. If an information technology system is worthy of the investment required to implement it, the proponent of that system must be able to quantify in a demonstrably objective manner the approximate value of specific savings (i.e., decreased expenses) and/or increased profits that the system will generate.

If you always think about strategic technology investments in terms of increased profits or decreased expenses, you will tend to make better purchase decisions. The problem is that quantifying cash flow based on a system's purported functionality takes time and effort for which many people do not have the skill or aptitude. It is not in the scope of this text to make you an expert in performing such calculations personally, but the following precepts should provide you with the knowledge necessary to make someone else (i.e., the system vendor's salesperson or your accountant) perform an accurate and objective analysis for you.

Decreased Expenses

Decreased expenses, or cost savings, are generally the first element of *payback* or when the purchase actually pays for itself either through new revenue or cost savings those systems try to achieve. Whenever the discussion of decreased expenses begins, business managers have a habit of thinking immediately of staff reductions. This is not completely unwarranted in hospitality because staffing is usually one of the largest "controllable" costs. In restaurants, labor can be anywhere from 20 to 35 percent of total revenue. In hotels, when the *fixed costs* associated with property depreciation and other fixed asset depreciation and maintenance are excluded, staffing is usually the largest single cost element. Information systems are very often used to make manual processes more efficient or automate labor-intensive tasks, and labor costs are one cost element that needs to be considered when assessing information technology investments.

Implementing information systems that provide increased productivity can certainly lead to dramatic reductions in labor costs. However, decreased expenses associated with new information technology can come in many shapes and sizes, and labor is not the only place operators can save money from new information technology.

- New technology can decrease the cost of maintaining systems. For instance, newer computer platforms that are more reliable, perform better, and have higher availability of cheap repair parts and labor can significantly reduce the cost of hardware maintenance contracts.
- *Recipe management software* can help operators develop recipes that use even quantities of bulk ingredients and therefore reduce food costs by eliminating waste. However, this may not be a solution for higher end establishments who need quality ingredients.
- Periodic maintenance systems for kitchen equipment, HVAC, and other fixed assets can significantly reduce the operating costs of these systems.
- Power control systems designed to monitor electrical usage and turn lights off when a room is vacant or cool buildings earlier in the day can significantly reduce electrical power consumption costs.

There are two important things to remember when looking at potential cost savings provided by an information system:

- Fixed costs don't usually go down (that's why they are called fixed).

• Each hotel, restaurant, and club has a unique cost structure.

Every corporate entity in the world has fixed and variable costs. Many times in hospitality, fixed costs are associated with guest service requirements that are not negotiable based on the organization's market position. As a result, a system may be capable of reducing the labor required to perform certain tasks, but may not generate any savings as a result.

For instance, imagine that a vendor can clearly demonstrate that a system reduces the time required to perform some task by 50 percent (from 6 labor hours to 3 labor hours). On the surface, this reduction would mean that the system saves $8/hour multiplied by 3 hours multiplied by 365 days per year, or a total of about $8,750 per year (plus overhead and benefits). If the system only cost $10,000, this would appear to be a great deal, or would it? What if your hotel is a small, high-end property and you always have two people on duty at night because guests expect immediate attention twenty-four hours a day. Or maybe it is a low-end hotel in a very bad neighborhood and you always have two people on duty at night for safety reasons. Now imagine the task in question is performed by the night shift crew, which is otherwise unoccupied for the majority of its shift. In this scenario, even though the system can be clearly shown to reduce labor requirements, because the cost of maintaining the night shift is a fixed cost, and because those resources are not 100 percent utilized in the existing scenario, it is possible that implementing the new system could result in a $10,000 investment with no appreciable cost savings (and therefore a negative ROI).

Increased Gross Profits

There are two important concepts to remember when analyzing a system's potential to increase gross profits.

• The assessment must include only increases in gross profit, not *gross revenue*. Gross revenue is total sales. Gross profit subtracts expenses or direct costs from gross revenue. Therefore, expenses from the new purchase must be considered.
• The assessment must be limited to only those gross profits that are directly attributable to the new system and would not be achieved without the system.

Take particular note of the fact that this section is captioned "Increased Gross Profits" and not "Increased Revenue." All too often technology purchasing agents focus on revenue enhancement, probably at least in part because that is how vendors advertise. In fact, in a properly prepared ROI calculation, revenue only exists in the supporting detailed data. The actual top line ROI calculation is only concerned with increased gross profits.

When analyzing investments, remember that *gross profits* are equal to gross revenue less direct costs. If we use gross revenue in our ROI assessments, potential investments will look much more favorable than they actually are. This is an important point to remember because vendor advertisements for systems rarely include a complete ROI calculation, but very often highlight "increased revenue." It is not uncommon to hear someone say, "I installed this new system and my sales went up X percent." The problem with this line of reasoning is that although it is appealing on the surface to say revenues are going up, without knowing the full cost of generating those revenues, it is impossible to determine if the system was a good deal or not.

For example, assume the cost of implementing a new spa management system is $20,000. To objectively determine whether the new system would help book $50,000 per year in additional spa revenue, you would need to look at the details. If the spa is staffed internally and generates a 50 percent gross margin on every treatment sold, then the $25,000 first year return makes the purchase decision very easy (assuming all of the projections are verifiable). However, if the spa is run on a contract basis with a 10 percent royalty on total sales, the annual payback of $5,000 may or may not justify a $20,000 investment (depending on the cost of capital and other factors). Although this example is obviously oversimplified, the concept holds true for all forms of potential increased revenue. You must convert incremental gross revenue projections to incremental gross profits before you can assess the potential value of a new information system.

3. SYSTEM EXAMPLES

Different types of systems can generate various forms of revenue for an establishment. Depending on what the system is designed to do, information technology can result in higher unit sales volumes or increased gross margins.

Yield management systems can generate higher gross margins on room revenues while *restaurant menu management systems* can generate higher gross margins on food items by substituting less costly ingredients or by using historical sales data to accomplish the following:

- Develop more effective pricing strategies (e.g., menu mix)
- Create a more effective menu mix
- Schedule employees more efficiently
- Improve functionality for offering and controlling promotions (e.g., buy one get one or happy hour pricing)
- Process credit cards more efficiently
- Improve functionality for cross-marketing other services to existing customers (generate coupon for other company-owned restaurants)

- Increase covers or average checks through the implementation of the new system (and by how much)

When analyzing the potential revenue increase, remember to attempt to identify an increase resulting only from the implementation of the new system. Any forecasted revenue increase due to other reasons, such as a change in the market, must be excluded. This is especially difficult if you plan to monitor the system benefits after conversion because additional revenue attributed only to the system is very difficult to quantify.

4. CASH FLOW AND COSTS

There are many formulas for calculating specific cash flow relative to different types of investments, and a good technology investment can and should be reduced to a financial investment equation before a purchase decision is made.

$$ROI = (\text{Increased Profits} + \text{Decreased Costs})/\text{Investment}$$
all cash flow must be adjusted for time and the cost of capital

There may be additional costs associated with operating the new system. These could include the following:

- Hardware/software maintenance due to automating a manual system or an increase over the old system
- Additional labor due to a short-term decrease in productivity after conversion (to be added to the up-front cost since it typically affects costs only during the first year)
- Costs of converting any exhibiting or historical data
- Costs of interfacing the system with other existing applications or devices
- Communication costs
- Consulting services

There are a number of different things to consider when determining the total cost for a new system. The projections should include all costs associated with the project including purchase price, implementation, and training. Some examples might include the following:

Application software	Workstation operating system
Network operating system	Cabling (cost of cable and cost of
Workstations	installation)
File server	Printers
Uninterrupted power supply (UPS)	Backup system
Network training	Application training

Shipping	Hardware training
Consulting services	Furniture (new, replaced, modified,
Additional payroll during training	or constructed)
and conversion	System selection costs

Although hard cost savings are the numbers that most companies focus on when determining whether or not to move forward with a new IT project, there are other intangible or "soft" benefits that need to be considered as well. These might include benefits such as improved guest service, employee morale, or image in the marketplace. Although they cannot be included in the calculation, they are very important factors that need to be taken into account. Some examples include the following:

- Better morale from use of a more user-friendly system
- Overall improved productivity from a more efficient system
- Improved job retention rates due to higher overall job satisfaction

5. SYSTEM SELECTION PROCESS

Although the details of how to specify and select an information system are beyond the scope of this chapter, a discussion of the basic system selection process is necessary to fully understand how IT investments are made. The system selection process described here has nine steps. Although many of these steps can be performed in parallel, it is important that each is performed and that step 1 be completed before any other step in the process begins.

1. Verify/develop the conceptual design for the enterprise
2. Define functional and system requirements for the component application(s)/create organizational consensus on the requirements
3. Compile a request for proposal (RFP)
4. Develop a vendor short list
5. Solicit proposals
6. Assess proposals against criteria
7. Visit reference sites
8. Have vendors provide demonstrations
9. Final selection

Verify/develop the conceptual design for the enterprise   Selecting a particular application (POS, PMS, CRS, or anything else) without having first reviewed the long-term IT strategy for the entire enterprise is like buying a pair of suit pants without knowing if you have a jacket, tie, or shirt that goes with them.

They may be the best pants you've ever bought, but if you can't wear them with anything you own, you've effectively either forced yourself to spend money on items you hadn't planned to purchase or wasted whatever money you spent on the pants. So it is with information systems—each application should fit into an overall plan designed to effectively leverage your use of information to create additional shareholder value.

The world of information capture (collection), processing, storing, and reporting can be, and should be, divided along the same lines as functional operations within the enterprise. One example of how to do this is to divide all your business functions into a matrix, as shown in Figure 11-1.

A soon to reopen hotel might purchase many systems that require integration with existing hardware and infrastructure. The hotel wishes to integrate as much of the existing architecture as possible with the new purchases. What requirements of the system and captured data would integrate with what you already have? This is the endeavor of the matrix. Some of the fields have been filled in to serve as a guide in helping you tackle the remaining fields.

All too often, the critical first step is ignored. This is especially true when outside consultants are brought in to assist or when insiders from a single department or business unit perform the selection without interdepartmental involvement. It is absolutely critical to ensure that this first step is performed completely and with a solid look toward future operational and competitive requirements. Additionally, knowing your business today is unfortunately not enough. The successful purchaser will have an eye towards the future. Notice the "Retail Operations" section under "Associated Data Capture Requirements"; you do not know all the data fields to be captured that may be needed in the future, so you leave some room by requesting that certain fields be left blank and able to be named and used at a later date. Not all vendors will allow forward looking requirements; however, it is vital to negotiate "in" what you can. As an operational efficiency and cost saving measure, all systems and matrix-oriented decisions should follow this forward looking thought process. You could thank yourself one day for the right decisions you made years ago and avoid having to purchase a "whole new" system.

The end-product(s) of this first step should, at a minimum, include a list of component applications that will be required to create the entire enterprise's information infrastructure, and a solid idea of the system architecture (including communications backbone) that will be used to host and integrate each of the component applications.

Define functional and system requirements for the component application(s)/ create organizational consensus on the requirements Once a long-term-strategy and architecture for the entire enterprise have been developed and agreed upon, the task of selecting a particular component application can begin in earnest. Although the top level or basic functional and system requirements for each component application should flow from the conceptual

Functional Area	Specific Capability Requirements	Associated Data Capture Requirements	Involved Systems/Technologies
Unit operations: Front Office F&B Housekeeping Reservations Engineering			Entire hotel network
Retail Operations (ie., gift and pro shop)	Standard POS capabilities plus CRM	All relevant fields captured by credit card data with the addition of number of purchases to date and additional preference fields left blank to be named and utilized at a later date	None, however integration with the PMS is needed
Human Resource Management	Live updates on the Web—a must in addition to standard features	All relevant fields from I-9 IRS forms with the addition of property and department-specific fields.	Payroll (electronic data interchange)
Financial Management and Control			
Communications			
Decision Support			Revenue, yield management, and CRM

Figure 11-1. Purchasing a new system requires proper planning. A matrix can help keep information organized.

enterprise design, the detailed list of requirements necessary to properly evaluate alternative applications must be defined separately for each system. There are several key strategies that are worth employing during this step:

- Don't let management pick the new system. Create a "system selection team" and solicit both input and active involvement from the people who will actually have to use it. It is always best if you can select several "informal leaders" early in the process and win them over as "champions" of the new system by involving them in the selection process.

- It rarely makes good business sense to automate inefficient processes. More to the point, many of the system selection processes are often hampered by the identification of "requirements" whose only purpose is to preserve some non-value-added function within the organization. A key element of any system requirements definition process is the ability to objectively analyze the processes the system is designed to support and ensure those processes are designed as efficiently as possible.

- Ensure involvement from multiple departments or business units within the organization (even if it appears as though only one unit is really affected or "owns" the system).

- Clearly define exactly what you need, or you will never be able to accurately or objectively compare which vendor's application is best suited to your business. You should not let your staff begin any serious conversation with any single vendor until you have developed a list of specific requirements.

- Most organizations purchase any type of application once in a long while and then use/amortize it for several years. As a result, the level of knowledge of what is available is relatively low. It is worth while to attend a trade show or seminar or spend some time doing research (in-house or with a consultant) so you have an up-to-date perspective of what functional capabilities you should legitimately expect from your new system.

- As you speak with internal staff about "requirements," remember to keep expectations in check. There are systems and vendors available that will do anything you want, but everything comes at a cost. When you start thinking about adding "customization" to a packaged system so that you can meet everyone's "requirements," you add to the cost of the system.

One approach to defining and building consensus about requirements uses the following steps:

- Speak to colleagues and read articles about systems that have been recently installed in business units similar to your own. Use this research to identify common features expected to be in any system.

- Refer to your own enterprise system design documents to identify minimal system and functional requirements ("show stoppers") that you know in advance any system you select will have to have as a minimum.

- Speak informally with one or more vendors (preferably at a trade show or seminar where you can see many vendors' applications in a short period of time), and develop a list of features and functions that appear to be of value for your business.

- Combine all of the preceding to create a "master requirements list." You can then use this master list as a group facilitation tool when you start to meet with members of your selection team.

- When meeting with members of your team, allow them to "think out of the box" and identify new functionality or features, but remind them constantly that everything comes with a price tag and the "perfect system" they want may not exist.

- Each requirement identified by the group should be prioritized, either relative to other requirements, or against some absolute scale. Many people prefer using a scale of 1 to 5, where 5 is a show stopper, 3 is a legitimate need with the potential to add some value, and 1 is a desire with little or no chance of impacting system implementation.

The final output of these steps should be a complete and prioritized list of specific functional and system requirements for the component application.

Compile a request for proposal (RFP)   If a solid enterprise-level strategy and conceptual design have been complemented by a set of clearly defined component application functional and system requirements, compiling an **RFP** should be relatively simple. Please refer to the RFP appendix for a detailed model. There are several elements worth noting for inclusion:

- Never sign a contract that includes "customization" on a fee basis. If the system you are purchasing cannot meet all of your organization's requirements "out of the box," then your vendor should provide a firm fixed-price agreement to make the necessary modifications.

- Place all of your system and functional requirements in a numbered outline, matrix, or some other format that forces each vendor to address each requirement specifically and discreetly.

- Always make the vendor include a clearly defined timetable for customization and implementation. Ensure the proposed contract documents include a process for remedy if the vendor does not meet the proposed delivery schedule.

- Make each vendor specifically address such support issues as training, help desk, and remote and local software maintenance.

- Make each vendor provide both a historic and forward-looking build schedule. The historic build schedule should include a notation as to whether builds released during the previous twenty-four months were released on schedule or delayed. Make each vendor supply a specific statement as to whether future builds are included in maintenance costs.

- Make each vendor supply cost information using the same format (provided by your company in the RFP). This prohibits vendors from "burying costs" in different places and thereby making your selection process more difficult.

Develop a vendor short list   Developing a vendor short list can be both the easiest and the most short-sighted step in the system selection process. It can be the easiest because you can simply make a list of several systems that you have seen in advertisements and know about. It can be the most short-sighted because you may feel tempted to include any one of the many new and vastly improved products that enter the marketplace every day. Good places to start for lists and further information in this industry are the vendors listed with the AH&LA and the HFTP organization as well as *Hospitality Upgrade* magazine.

Developing a short list of vendors *before* sending out a request for proposal (RFP) is an important element of the system selection process for any organization that purchases multiple systems. The reason is that if you constantly ask a long list of vendors to spend their time and resources responding to RFPs and proposing systems they have little chance of being selected to provide, your organization will lose the credibility necessary to exact complete and earnest responses from multiple vendors.

There are several rules of thumb that people often refer to in the vendor selection process, but in the end, all of them are rules of thumb, none are cast in stone, and "rules" can never take the place of good old-fashioned research.

One approach to narrowing the field of potential vendors that seems to work well uses the following steps:

- Refer to one or more well-maintained databases of systems like the one you are selecting. (A caution on databases and buyer's guides: the vendors listed in them often fund these guides. There may be several good vendors that do not appear in the guide you are using; therefore, it is important to use either multiple guides or a comprehensive database that does not rely on vendor advertisements for funding.)
- Use the databases to identify a list of vendor systems most likely to match your organizations system and functional requirements.
- Send a *request for information (RFI)* to those vendors that you think are the most suited to your needs. (The purpose of an RFI is to provide vendors a low cost, low effort means to provide you just the information necessary to know if they should be on your short list.) Some basic questions that should be included in an RFI refer back to some of those "rules of thumb" such as the following:
  - Can the vendor provide a list of reference installations similar in size and operation to yours, and is the vendor willing to provide a point of contact at each?
  - How long has the vendor been in business and can the vendor demonstrate his or her company's financial stability? (Financial

stability and time in market should not be sole determining factors for the nonselection of any vendor, but they are elements of risk that stakeholders should be aware of in advance of making a selection decision.)

- Use RFI responses and interviews with reference installations to narrow your list of vendors to five or fewer vendors who appear capable, responsive, and responsible.

Solicit proposals   Soliciting proposals from good vendors is not as easy as you might expect. Vendors with good systems are in high demand and their ability to hire and train additional technical staff is limited by a global shortage of skilled information technology personnel. As a result, writing detailed proposals and estimating the cost of significant "customizations" require the allocation of valuable people who could be working on other (profitable) projects.

You should therefore not expect good vendors to answer detailed RFPs in an unrealistic time frame. This often requires more advanced planning than most organizations are able to muster. It is not unrealistic to include an eight-week period for vendors to respond to your RFP. This is not because it takes eight weeks for a vendor to write a complete response. More often, it is because it takes four weeks for a vendor to determine that your project is worth dedicating the necessary resources to pursue and to ask all the additional questions and clarifications needed to answer your RFP accurately.

Assess proposals against criteria   Two critical elements of this phase are objectivity and sensitivity analysis.

One approach is to simply start by using the functionality matrix developed during the requirements stage, and ask each member of the selection team to grade each response on a scale of 1 to 5. It is important to make each individual grade each proposal independently. The purpose of independent evaluations instead of a group evaluation in a large meeting is two-fold. The first problem with group evaluation is that some of the people will not read all of the proposals thoroughly. The second problem is that some people will allow their own perceptions to be changed without reason.

Eventually, however, the entire team should meet to discuss the results of the individual evaluations and attempt to reach a general consensus on the merits of each vendor's application relative to the specific criteria identified in your RFP. The important point during this meeting is to gain consensus on each specific functional requirement before allowing the conversation to veer toward "whose proposal was best." In this respect, it is often of value if the manager responsible for the selection process has somebody collect and compile all the individual evaluations from team members in advance.

Depending on the size and complexity of the project, the use of simple spreadsheets or complex decision support tools can be of great value. For smaller projects, it is easy to lay out individual evaluations, calculate average scores, and visually see how consistent various team member evaluations were.

For larger more complex projects, it may be appropriate to aggregate scores by category of requirement and then determine the average score and standard deviation for each category of requirements.

For smaller projects, placing the average scores in the same spreadsheet as priority for each requirement will quickly generate an objective score for each vendor's proposal. For larger projects, it may be helpful to use a decision support tool that allows you to build a requirements model and then perform sensitivity analysis on your results. The sensitivity analysis allows the selection team to see what the impacts of various requirement prioritization and/or scoring decisions are on the model's outcome. This is very helpful because it allows you to avoid lengthy discussions about decisions that do not change the model's outcome.

Visit reference sites   No matter how close or lopsided the results of your proposal evaluations are, you should always visit at least one vendor reference site for each of your top choices. In addition, you should speak at length with several others via telephone if you don't have the time or resources to visit them.

It is important to bring your prioritized requirements matrix with you when you visit or call the vendor's reference installation sites and to have the same group of people make each visit or phone call.

In addition to seeing if the system truly does all the things you need it to do, some questions you should ask the people at the reference site are the following:

- Did the vendor install the system in accordance with the schedule laid out in the proposal, and if not, was the delay caused by the vendor or the customer?

- Has the vendor supplied the system in accordance with a reliable schedule?

- Have software and hardware maintenance fee increases been reasonable and predictable?

- Does the vendor provide reliable support in terms of help desk availability, on-site hardware service, and other factors? How often does the customer spend extended periods of time on hold, or wait a day and a half for "4-hour" on-site service?

It is important to visit at least one installation site that is similar to yours. It is acceptable if one site is similar in size and another is a similar type of operation. If, however, the only reference installations the vendor can provide are for enterprises either significantly smaller or those that do completely different things than yours, you ought to consider the additional risk involved in migrating and/or scaling a system from one business to another.

Have vendors provide demonstrations   The key to vendor demonstrations is to ensure that you do not buy a system based on the appearance or sales skills of the person presenting the demonstration. The reality in most instances is that the company purchasing a new system is replacing an old, much less functional system. As a result, a good salesperson could make almost any vendor's application look incredibly functional and robust to a room full of operators who have been working with the proverbial "bearskins and rocks" for several years. It is important to remove this element of subjectivity from the equation.

The simplest way to make vendor demonstrations more useful and informative is to confine the vendor to a script. A favorite is the ice skating analogy:

- Each vendor has 40 (80 or 120 depending on the complexity of the system) minutes to walk you through a series of functions that you have scripted out (based on your RFP and functional requirements document).
- Following the 40-minute compulsory presentation, each vendor gets an additional 20 (40 or 60) minutes to provide a freestyle explanation of what makes his or her solution uniquely suited to your business.

By making the vendors stick to a tightly written and consistent script, you can be sure that each member of the team has the opportunity to personally verify that the vendor's system does in fact perform all of the functions identified in your requirements document. In addition to making sure you will receive what you think you are buying, this element of universal team verification and "buy in" is often critical to a successful rollout.

A note on vendor demonstrations: Don't ask a vendor to spend the time and money necessary to come to your site and perform a demonstration if you have not determined that this vendor has a viable and competitive alternative for your application. If you have narrowed the field to two vendors that you believe are head and shoulders above the competition in terms of being perfectly suited for your business, you should not ask other vendors to do demonstrations.

Companies will often have policies requiring the comparison of at least three systems to ensure competitive pricing. This is not a bad policy, but analyzing three alternative proposals does not mean making a vendor you have no intention of selecting spend thousands of dollars to do a demonstration.

Final selection   Assuming that the vendor's demonstration verifies the information presented in his or her proposal, the final selection process is a foregone conclusion. In cases where the demonstration reveals weaknesses in a particular vendor's application that were not evident (or simply glossed over) in the proposal, final selection is less easy.

If you have more than three good candidates that came out of the proposal analyses (scoring) stage and only one was eliminated during the vendor demonstration, then you might choose to reconvene the selection team to discuss the other alternatives. In the end though, no matter how many selection committees are formed and how much input is received, the manager responsible for the system selection process has to be both willing and able to make a decision.

The final note on system selection is not much different than the final note on buying a car: You have to be willing to walk away. All too often in this business, you find yourself driven by the lure of "being one step ahead of the competition," by the dull whine of Wall Street for "any kind of news," or simply by employee complaints to jump into system acquisitions that do not make sense. During the past ten years, businesses within every vertical market segment have scrambled to increase capital spending for information technology, often with very little real increase in shareholder value or corporate productivity. We now see software prices either stagnating, or in some cases decreasing, as rapidly as hardware prices. If the system you want is not available today at a reasonable price, wait twelve months and try again. It's better to have done the analyses twice and made a good investment, than to have done the analyses once and made a poor one.

6. IMPLEMENTATION

Now that you have purchased the correct system, a proper implementation procedure needs to be adopted whether it is hardware or software. There are ten steps.

1. Choose a project manager from your existing staff. This may or may not be the person who headed up the selection process. As hard as it may be, this must be a capable person who must be relieved of daily duties and given the lead to serve as your liaison with the vendor's project manager. This person is now the boss and your lifeline to the project's implementation. The project manager will take charge of the remaining steps in cooperation with your entire staff.

2. Set a schedule. This covers coordinating and confirming the specific delivery of the product and associated dates and any needed supplemental items. The contract and vendor schedule needs to be understood. What may be a good date for the vendor may not be for you. Implementation should be done at off hours and off peaks so as not to affect business operations. Weekend nights are often a good time for business hotels, whereas restaurants might want to find a slow weekday. Resorts can adopt a new system during off seasons as can sports arenas and convention centers.

3. Establish a training system. Before tackling your own property, send a select group of staff from various departments to your vendor's site for initial training. From there, develop a training schedule for your property. When will it occur? For how long? What compensation will be given? How about perks? Training can be both a nice break from the daily grind and a chore. Try to make it as comfortable as possible.

Training in the hospitality industry is often an afterthought due to high turnover. However, the greatest system in the world is useless if no one knows how to use it. Training needs to be taken very seriously or else all of the careful analysis up to this point can go up in smoke.

4. Meet with the vendor and exchange notes on steps 1 through 3. Resolve any issues to date and request specific information from the vendor on what to expect from the system and related elements during the upcoming time period. Communicate these facts to all involved to keep them in the loop.

5. Stop and analyze. This may seem like a good step to skip. However, you are approaching the point of no return—the implementation phase. Is everything and everyone ready? Has a contingency plan been put in place? An example may be paper records and systems. Likewise, a good rule of thumb is to contact all the stakeholders in the company and remind them in the next few days you are adopting a new system and apologize in advance for any unwelcome occurrences.

6. Start implementation in *one* department. This entire department must adopt the new system. Old ways of doing things replaced by the new system must be discarded. The system must be totally embraced by all. Those in this first department will serve as additional trainers on the new system and importantly play the role of "cheerleaders" for future departments. These are the people who can spread the word that "it wasn't so bad." Keep in mind that change is difficult and that people are creatures of habit. It is important to win allies early.

7. Stop and analyze. Has the new system affected the processing power of any in-place systems? For example, oftentimes new software may take up precious processing power of the CPUs involved to the detriment of other applications. Take care in monitoring all of the systems. It may surprise you that even the climate control systems may have to be fine-tuned to accommodate new additions. Your model for the new system's implementation is being set. Human comfort and settings deserve proper attention, particularly if the system is to be used for long hours.

8. Move on the next department. With all the expertise and experience gained to date, the next department is usually easier. The important component here is to monitor the communication of the system between these first two departments. Is your network being adversely affected? For example, complex database queries of your entire customer database or large print jobs can tie up a network. Additionally, the connection to your outside network needs to be tested.

9. Stop and analyze again. Again? Yes, the third time is the charm and is critical since enterprise or companywide implementation is next. You are about to turn your whole location over to a new system (if

your whole property is involved) and want to make sure that everything is okay.

10. Rollout the system propertywide.

Following these steps is safe and efficient. Oftentimes business requirements and the fast moving nature of this industry can truncate some of the above processes. Stay with these steps as best you can to avoid problems.

7. SUMMARY

Judging by the amount and different types of technology used in the hospitality industry and presented in the previous chapters, it seems that every current and future manager must have a solid technological knowledge base. However, just as important, a manager must understand business. During the dot.com era in hospitality, many purchasing decisions were based on "neat" features and functionality of a proposed system under the assumption that future profits would one day appear. During this period, owners were often scared that if they did not have the current technology, their customers would go elsewhere. Many purchases refused to bear fruit. Now, those in charge of making purchases have gone back to basics. Advancements in technology are still respected; however, business considerations come first. Simply put, any new system needs either to increase revenue or reduce costs. Understanding and utilizing financial metrics and definitions such as return on investment (ROI) and differing cost and profit structures are again the norm for management.

Hospitality is a fast-paced industry where wants and needs of any new purchase often boil down to "something that works." Given the capabilities and price tags of solutions available in the marketplace today, more understanding is necessary. In reaching a determination on the potential purchase, a detailed system selection process is needed. From the beginning of the process where exact needs are established, to site visits of the system in use at the end of the process, all steps along the way are crucial and related. This is equally important in the implementation stage where analysis and testing are done along the many steps before it is committed companywide.

With understanding, proper usage, and analysis of the particulars presented in this chapter, the next technology purchase can be a successful one.

8. CASE STUDY AND LEARNING ACTIVITY

People + Process + Product = Success

By Michael DiLeva,
Director, Hospitality Solutions, Unisys Corporation and
Edward F. Nesta,
President, E.F. Nesta and Associates

Meeting guests' need for technology following the dot.com bust requires a return to the basics. Hotels have traditionally been slow to adopt new technologies, particularly when compared to their travel industry peers such as airlines and car rental companies. So it was particularly opportune in the 1990s when a myriad of venture-capital fueled Internet companies emerged to help the industry to meet travelers' demand for high-speed Internet access (HSIA). These companies installed and managed a complete turnkey HSIA solution free-of-charge and even offered properties a share of the revenues from guest usage. What seemed like a match made in heaven, however, quickly soured as guest utilization rates hovered in the low single digits and the HSIA providers, lacking the revenues to support their huge capital investments went bust—leaving hotels soured and guests unable to connect.

So what happened? Some pundits say it was a product with a poor value proposition. Others point at the overall business process, which had the solution operating as a stand-alone entity as opposed to an integrated offering or property amenity. And still others point to a hotel staff that had little training and little incentive to support or promote the solution. Who's right? Actually, all of them are correct. People, process and product are all required to create a positive guest experience and it's simple algebra to note that if you remove one of the variables, the entire equation no longer adds up. The introduction of HSIA in the hotel industry is an enlightening case study on the need to focus on all three of these key components.

For example, following the demise of the majority of the leading in-room HSIA suppliers, it was theorized that hotels would be able to recognize the missteps of the past and refine their HSIA offerings. However, with the exception of a few chains, most hotels in the early days of the 21st century are still disappointed with their HSIA results and travelers are still grumbling over the lack of high-speed Internet access that enables them to do things that they've accepted as commonplace, such as communicating with their office and clients via e-mail, conducting Net meetings, participating in Web-based training, listening to their favorite music online, and checking the current trading price of the stocks in their portfolio.

Why the continuing poor results? When you scratch the surface, you'll usually find that one of the three Ps is missing. For example, the most obvious thing in need of a fix was product, so most hotels began turning to more established technology companies to supply the solution, resulting in a more stable product that provided guests with better service and functionality suited to their needs. But product alone is not a panacea. A new hotel in the Midwest, for example, contracted with a Fortune 300® company and installed a state-of-the-art solution but did little to market HSIA to their guests, nor did they train their employees—the people component—on how to promote the solution or how to recognize guests carrying laptop computers at check-in (who would be most interested in using inroom HSIA).

The theory of "if you build it, they will come," may have worked for Kevin Costner in the film *Field of Dreams*, but for hotels a better theme may be "if a tree falls in the woods and no one is there to hear it, did it make a sound?" In other words, it makes perfect sense that guests are unlikely to order room service if a menu is missing from the room or if the operator answering the phone is unaware that the hotel has a kitchen. For successful HSIA deployment, as much time needs to be spent on employee training and guest marketing as is spent on providing high-speed data lines, establishing network monitoring of key infrastructure components, or installing a broadband backbone.

So is this all just theory? Has anyone actually put it all together? For an example of a successful strategic deployment of HSIA throughout their properties, one need only look at Starwood Hotels and Resorts or Cendant's Wingate Inns brand. Starwood, for example, took a methodical approach to HSIA, building a sound business model first, before jumping into the technology. They also spent countless months developing a compelling marketing message, creating collateral materials that delivered that message to the guest in a high-profile fashion, and ensuring that employees were well versed on the availability of the solution and how to inform guests as to its availability. They're already reaping the rewards of a focus on people, process, and product.

Wingate Inns is another success story. Rather than inserting HSIA as a "bolt on" service like others in the industry, Wingate developed a strategy that integrated HSIA into their overall market positioning. It became a key amenity that was indistinguishable from any other component of their offerings and the results are spectacular. In the August, 2000 issue of *Hotel Business*, Wingate Inn, Atlanta-Buckhead, Georgia, David Smith noted that "on weekdays, when we cater primarily to business travelers, the percentage of guests using our high-speed Internet access (at the Atlanta-Buckhead location) comes to roughly 75 percent. And once they do use this service, the guests have shown they're likely to come back for another stay with us." That article went on to note that "Smith credited this high degree of guest satisfaction as one of the main reasons why the hotel's occupancy has been running ahead of projections."[1]

So while some hotels languish with 2-5 percent HSIA utilization rates, Wingate has noted that "High-speed Internet usage increased at the brand's properties to 12.7 percent in February 2001 from 7.75 percent in May 2000"[2] and the company recently projected that utilization will hit 25 percent in 2002.

The bottom line is that a single focus on people, product, or process will not allow for success. After all, a tired old roadside motel with even the friendliest staff and the finest service can't compete with a new, upscale four-star property. And the most luxurious new-build won't succeed either if they have a staff that cares little about serving their guests. Whether it's implementing a new guest technology like HSIA or examining how to adapt to the entry of a new competitor into your market, hoteliers need to focus on all three factors—people, process, and product.

Learning Activity

1. How important is your vendor's financial health to your decision to purchase from the vendor? Explain.

2. What are the three Ps?

---

[1]Technology Challenges, *Hotel Business Magazine* (special edition), August 2000.
[2]*Hotel & Motel Management Magazine,* 7 May 2000.

3. Why should understanding business practices come before technology purchases?

4. Was Wingate correct in making HSIA standard in its room offerings? Should Wingate have made it a separated amenity? Explain.

5. How can technology lead to higher occupancy rates in hotels?

6. What staff members should be trained on HSIA?

7. How would you judge if the HSIA endeavor was a success or not? List at least three criteria.

9. KEY TERMS

Fixed costs	Recipe Management Software	RFI
Gross profits		ROI
Gross revenue	Restaurant Menu Management System	Yield Management System
Payback		

10. CHAPTER QUESTIONS

1. What is the difference between a RFI and a RFP?

2. What are the nine steps of system selection?

3. What are the ten steps of implementation?

4. How would you further the ten steps of implementation to multiple sites?

5. How do you calculate ROI?

6. What is the difference between a fixed and variable cost?

7. Name three factors to be cautious of in system selection.

11. REFERENCES

Brueggeman, William, and Jeffrey Fisher. 2001. *Real estate finance and investments*. 11th ed. New York: McGraw-Hill/Irwin.

Horngren, Charles, Gary Sundem, and William Stratton. 2002. *Introduction to management accounting*. 12th ed. Upper Saddle River, NJ: Prentice Hall.

Taylor, Bernard W. 2002. *Introduction to management science*. 7th ed. Upper Saddle River, NJ: Prentice Hall.

White Paper

HOSPITALITY INDUSTRY TECHNOLOGY INTEGRATION STANDARDS

When Property Management Systems (PMS) were initially developed, the primary object was to replace the laborious task of manually posting all charges to guest accounts. Before the advent of the computerized PMS, creating a blank ledger sheet (folio) when a guest checked in to a room initiated this process. The folio would then be placed in a file (bucket) by room number. Additionally, those accounts to which a posting was permitted, but were not guest folios, were placed in the front or the back of the bucket. These were known as "city ledger" accounts, because typically they were set up for local business to which direct billing was permitted.

Each transaction that was to be charged to the guest's room was posted individually to the correct folio. The folio was extracted from the section in the bucket, which had been set up for that room and placed in the posting machine. The previous balance, the category of the transaction, and the transaction amount were then entered. The posting machine printed the transaction, adding the amount to the total, and printed the new total on the folio. It also accumulated the category totals, which were then printed at the end of the day. When it came time to post the nightly room and tax charges, the folio for each room was pulled, updated, and returned. Control totals were run on the folios with much regularity. The night audit function consisted of ensuring that the total of transactions plus a previous control total would add up to a new control total.

The computer changed all this. The need to individually post the nightly charges was eliminated, as the process could be done automatically. Control totals were easily accomplished, and the task of the night auditor was no longer an all night task.

The laborious task of posting individual transactions still existed, though, because of the amounts which needed to be entered for guest charges like phone calls. Even the earliest phone systems used a printer to log each phone call. These phone calls then had to be rated (with the hotel's mark up) and entered onto the folio.

The earliest interfaces where developed by taking the output to the printer (typically a serial device) and simultaneously transferring that data into the PMS. The PMS then calculated the rate for the transaction and posted the amount to the guest folio automatically. The interface had to be written to take the exact output of the printer and parse the data into data elements (or fields) which could then be used to calculate the length of the call, the number called, whether it was a local or long distance call, etc. The PMS then used a look up table to determine the amount that should be charged to the guest.

These interfaces were extremely unreliable. Often the connection would be lost, the data scrambled, or data lost completely. There was no method by which the transaction could be validated. The phone system was unaware that its data was going anywhere other than just the printer. It was up to the PMS vendor to write the interface and to create as robust a connectivity as was possible.

This, however was the birth of the serial interface. Since one of the earliest standards which was set within the computer industry was the EIA RS232 Serial standard, almost all computers had the ability to receive and transmit serial data. There were some problems with the character sets which were used internally within the computer systems. A translation could be easily accomplished both into and out of the computer, so a standard ASCII (American Standard Code for Information Interchange) character set on a serial port became the de facto standard for communication between computers and from external devices to computers.

Even a somewhat unreliable automatic posting was far superior to a very unreliable hand posting of the phone charges. Soon, both the phone system vendors and other device vendors started creating output specifically to be posted to the folio by the PMS. As each vendor created its mechanism to post data, it created its own set of data elements and communication methods. While ASCII standards exist for transmissions, not all vendors implemented them completely or in the same way. Some vendors believed that they could do better, and created methods which required special acknowledgments by the PMS. Eventually, each vendor created its own specifications, and the PMS vendors had no choice but to program to each individually. One common thread prevailed, in that the serial ports were used to communicate between the devices and the PMS.

Today, we are living with this legacy, but the computer world is changing. Serial ports are no longer the preferred method of communicating between computers. We have entered a world of networking, and networks are now the de facto standard for communication.

The network environment does a number of things that are far superior to the serial ports. While the original serial ports were severely limited in their speed (usually to 240 or 960 characters per second), networks work at a minimum speed of 100,000 characters per second.

You will typically see the speeds quoted in baud (which is bits per second, where each character requires 10 bits). That is why you see 2,400 baud or 9,600 baud as the speed ratings for serial devices. Serial is also limited in the distance between devices without an amplifier. This is because the serial protocol requires electrical pulses to be sent along a line and the length of the line increases the resistance to those pulses. Also, all the validation of data and assurance that the data arrived correctly must be done within the programs that send and receive the data. There is no standard for this validation. Typically, the transmitting system will send a message that is appended with a value that somehow represents a check digit (typically known as a CRC or cyclic redundancy check). The receiving system then performs its own calculation and compares that to the received check digit. If these are not the same, it then must send a message to request a retransmission of the data. Again, this is not a standard, but rather a method that must be agreed upon by the sending and receiving systems.

The standard method of writing a serial interface program is to create a task that monitors the serial port for data. When data is received, this triggers the appropriate processing event. The interface program captures each character that is received and continues to build a record until the agreed upon end of record character is received. All data validation and data parsing must be written into the monitor program.

The network, on the other hand, accomplishes all these checks and validations automatically. The data sent from one system to another is bundled into packets, and these packets are sent to the destination system. If the packet is garbled, the network software requests a retransmission without the knowledge or intervention of the application software. In other words, the network assures that the data gets there correctly. Additionally, with the inclusion of telephone services, the network can extend through the world. All security and connectivity is taken care of in the network operating system. Whether the protocol it is IP, IPX, or SNA, the involved parties need only agree on the protocol. Currently, TCP/IP (Transmission Control Protocol/Internet Protocol) is the standard for forming the packets and transmitting between computers.

A single network connection will allow any number of devices to interact with a computer, while a dedicated serial port is required for each external device. Serial connections are no longer considered fast enough, reliable enough, or flexible enough to be an acceptable method of communication, yet our existing legacy connections continue as serial interfaces.

No matter what the method of connectivity, it is necessary for the two parties to agree on the data elements that are going to be exchanged. One of the things that is evident is that there are only a finite number of data elements (or fields) which are represented within the hotel environment. Unfortunately, there are no standards within the industry as to these elements. For example, something as simple as a guest name could be represented in many different ways. You could have separate elements for first, last, title, etc. or you could have a single field which is populated with last, title, first. If you include the potential problems with international names, the problem is quite complex. If you consider the data elements necessary to represent the address, the problem becomes a monumental project. Since there is no standard, the systems typically have to convert data to communicate with another system. The general method is for the external device vendor to make the definition, and for the PMS to be programmed to the device manufacturer's specification.

Something as seemingly simple as a room number can be represented in many different ways. Is it purely a numeric? Is it alphanumeric? How many characters should it have? Is it left justified? Are their trailing spaces, or trailing nulls? Each system has set its own specification and no industry body has attempted to set a standard which may be used globally ensuring that data will be consistently represented between systems.

Not only are there no standards for the data elements, there are also no standards as to the data element types. Some systems use short integers, some use long. Some use dates as strings, some use dates as integers. Some dates are based on number of days from January 1, 1900 or some other date, others from the year 0. The method used to avoid these conflicts is to convert all data to string values and create a fixed length record where each field starts at a specified character and ends at a specified location.

In order to create a usable standard, the data elements and the types of data must be standardized. All of this could (and should) be done for any type of communication standard.

It is clear, however, that the serial interface cannot be the standard of the future. We have evolved into a world where networking is the only acceptable method for establishing connectivity between systems.

Proliferation of interfaces

At any given time, there are dozens of vendors providing Property Management Systems to the hospitality industry. In addition, there are many new devices being introduced into the hospitality market with the intent to provide additional guest services. These new devices and services do not fall into previously defined categories. Internet services, travel services, in-room fax services all require interfaces to the Property Management System (PMS) to fully automate these services. The propagation of new devices and the amount of effort required by a PMS vendor to write a new interface cause many new vendors to be shut out of the market. If the vendor cannot convince the PMS providers to build an interface, no hotel will buy that product. No PMS vendor will write an interface without funding by the device vendor or the customer. Even then, the time necessary to complete and test the interface may make the project not feasible.

In the past, devices were generally grouped by function and previous efforts at standardization were oriented toward attempting to create standard message formats for that class of devices. For example:

- Point of Sale Devices that are primarily used in restaurants
- Telephone Management Systems which turn the phone on or off in a room
- Telephone Call Rating Systems that establish the charge for a call
- In-room Movie Systems that allow a guest to view a pay-per-view movie
- Minibar Systems which dispense soft drinks, liquor, or food items
- In-room Facsimile Systems that allow a guest to send or receive from a room
- In-room Computer usage
- In-room Internet connectivity

Each of these device classes was considered as separate, but when you analyze the messages necessary to interface each of these devices, there are only a few functions that cover all the devices:

- The device must be able to test a room or guest for authorization to charge
- The device must be able to query for which folio is associated with a guest
- The device sends a charge to be posted to a guest folio
- Some devices must be notified when a room is occupied or vacated
- Some devices may allow housekeeping and maintenance to send messages
- Some devices may allow the guest to review the current folio
- Some devices may allow the guest to initiate a checkout

There is no reason that these functions cannot be used by all the device classes that may need to use them. Therefore, by creating reusable functions rather than device class messages, it is possible to minimize the number of specifications necessary between the devices and the PMS or Food, Beverage and Retail Management Systems (FBRMS).

Recently, new devices have been introduced which do not fall into existing device classes or categories. However, the messages necessary for these new classes are in fact handled within the functions that are already specified for other device classes. A new device may merely adhere to already existing function specifications and require no additional programming on the part of the PMS vendor to accommodate it.

The result is that rather than defining a specification for each class of devices, we can instead analyze all the functions that all devices must accomplish. This considerably reduces the number of standards which must be written and maintained, and makes the acceptance of new device classes a moot issue.

In an attempt to address these specifications, the American Hotel and Motel Association has initiated the Hospitality Industry Technology Integration Standards (HITIS) project. The goal of HITIS is to identify those functions that are used by all the various devices and to standardize the implementation of these functions.

In addition to the identification of the functions that must be available to devices, the HITIS committee believes that it is important for a common data dictionary to be developed. This would allow all systems to use the same structures for things like room numbers, names, addresses, etc. All standards would then include only those data elements that have been identified as part of the data dictionary, and all vendors could rely on those data elements being supported by all HITIS compliant systems.

While we do not minimize the impact that these common data definitions and functional specifications will have on legacy systems, it is the goal of HITIS to create standards that will be used going forward. No intention exists to compromise the standards because of legacy systems.

Those vendors who do not wish to modify their existing systems to meet HITIS standards simply will not reach HITIS compliance. Those vendors who do create new releases of their software which adhere to the HITIS standards will likely find their costs of maintaining their interface library significantly reduced, and their product more widely accepted by the hotel customers.

Data Element Standards vs. Object Standards

In a **data element standard,** the communication between systems is accomplished via messages. Each message has some identifying text within its data. The identifier establishes what type of message is being sent. Each message is processed as a discrete action. As a specific example, the Micros Point of Sale serial interface has the following general format:

Start of Header Character (SOH)

Message Identification (representing the physical unit sending the message)

Start of Text Character (STX)

Data

End of Text Character (ETX)

Checksum (4 characters plus another end of text character)

End of Transmission Character (EOT)

Within the data block, the first two characters represent the type of message that is being sent, and the balance of the data block represents the specific data for that message. The message consists of a series of fixed length fields as they have been defined by Micros. The SOH, STX, ETX, and EOT are single bytes defined within the ASCII character set. Each message type has a different format.

If the receiving system does not calculate the same checksum as it receives from the POS system, it must request a retransmission of data. Some logical number of tries will be accomplished before the system reports an error. In the event of an error, the vendors must agree as to what will be done.

The **object standard** is in many ways the same as the data standard, but relies on the network to perform the communications between processes or between systems. An object is a piece of compiled or interpreted code that provides some service to the rest of the system. In effect, the program on a computer is using a procedure or subroutine (object) which resides somewhere else. Whether that object is local (on the same machine) or remote (on another machine somewhere within the network) does not matter to the program which calls the object. It is up to some underlying management program to determine where the requested object resides and to set up and carry out the communication with that object.

To better understand an object, equating the components of the object to the serial messaging will help.

In an object standard, what was referred to as a message is now referred to as a method. Rather than sending a message, the sending system initiates a method, which causes the transaction to be processed.

The data elements from the serial example are referred to as attributes in the object, and the call that is made to the object includes the required attributes.

Rather than stacking the data in one long string, the individual data elements are kept atomic and the data associated with the attribute remains linked with the attribute. No parsing of data is necessary on the receiving side, and there is no necessity to send or calculate a checksum.

Each message type is reflected in a separate method, so no ambiguity may exist as to what type of message has just been received.

All of these occur at a level that is above the communication verification, because the communication is accomplished by the transport layer (the network) over which this connection occurs.

The object may be called from within a program on the same system, in which case the transport layer may be in memory or on the internal bus. The object may also reside on another computer, in which case some additional process must be in place that allows computer A to know about the existence and availability of the object on computer B. There are a number of ways in which this computer to computer object registration may be accomplished.

In the early part of this decade, the Object Management Group established a standard for client server integration. This standard is known as Common Object Request Broker Architecture (CORBA).

It should be noted that the term "client–server" does not necessarily mean that one system is the client and one is the server. It only means that one system initiates the call, while the other completes the action. A system may act as the client in one case and as the server in another. This is true even in the case of the serial model.

CORBA is currently endorsed by almost all of the major computer industry suppliers. The one notable exception is Microsoft. Microsoft created its own standard known as COM (Component Object Model). This standard would allow the creation of modules that can be used from a program to communicate and interact with an encapsulated process. Expansion of this architecture to multi-processor environments is known as Distributed COM or DCOM.

A recent cooperation between Microsoft and the Object Management Group has resulted in an agreement that creates a common definition allowing CORBA and DCOM objects to interact. The new specification defines how

COM and CORBA objects will interoperate and defines support for object interaction among networked COM/OLE and CORBA systems.

With this interoperability in place, it will be possible for a vendor to create an object based interface that will work in all computer environments, giving the hotel far more flexibility in the selection of guest service and data collection devices. The PMS vendor will write a small library of HITIS compliant objects that may be called by a device vendor's HITIS compliant program. The PMS host (server) will ensure that the requesting device (client) is authorized to use the object (authentication) and then allow the device to implement those methods that are required.

PMS vendors will likely continue to charge an interface fee for the library of objects which it supplies, but if a hotel wishes to change its device vendor, there is no need for the PMS vendor to be involved. In this way, a device which is no longer being supported, or which no longer meets the needs of the hotel, may be replaced with a more current or state of the art HITIS compliant device without additional programming on the part of the PMS vendor. New device vendors need only create HITIS compliant systems and their devices can be integrated into the hotel PMS environment without the necessity of paying for or waiting for a PMS vendor to complete the device interface.

HITIS represents a significant contribution to the future of information technology within the hospitality industry. As with any attempt to create and implement standards, there will no doubt be reluctance and hesitation, but the overwhelming benefits to the industry are clear. PMS and FBRMS vendors will be able to concentrate on the capabilities of their core software, and device vendors will be able to sell their systems to any hotel with a HITIS compliant PMS. Hotels will no longer be locked into the finite list of interfaced devices from their PMS or FBRMS vendors, and new device vendors will be able to create systems that can be much more readily accepted by their potential customers.

CORBA

CORBA is a widely supported standard method for implementing objects within a heterogeneous computer environment. Following is an excerpt from the OMG Web site:

The Common Object Request Broker Architecture (CORBA) is the Object Management Group's answer to the need for interoperability among the rapidly proliferating number of hardware and software products available today. Simply stated, CORBA allows applications to communicate with one another no matter where they are located or who has designed them. CORBA 1.1 was introduced in 1991 by Object Management Group (OMG) and defined the Interface Definition Language (IDL) and the Application Programming Interfaces (API) that enable client–server object interaction within a specific implementation of an Object Request Broker (ORB). CORBA 2.0, adopted in December of 1994, defines true interoperability by specifying how ORBs from different vendors can interoperate.

The (ORB) is the middleware that establishes the client–server relationships between objects. Using an ORB, a client can transparently invoke a method on a server object, which can be on the same machine or across a network. The ORB intercepts the call and is responsible for finding an object that can implement the request, pass it the parameters, invoke its method, and return the results. The client does not have to be aware of where the object is located, its programming language, its operating system, or any other system aspects that are not part of an object's interface. In so doing, the ORB provides interoperability between applications on different machines in heterogeneous distributed environments and seamlessly interconnects multiple object systems.

In fielding typical client–server applications, developers use their own design or a recognized standard to define the protocol to be used between the devices. Protocol definition depends on the implementation language, network transport, and a dozen other factors. ORBs simplify this process. With an ORB, the protocol is defined through the application interfaces via a single implementation language-independent specification, the IDL. And ORBs provide flexibility. They let programmers choose the most appropriate operating system, execution environment, and even programming language to use for each component of a system under construction. More importantly, they allow the integration of existing components. In an ORB-based solution, developers simply model the legacy component using the same IDL they use for creating new objects, then write "wrapper" code that translates between the standardized bus and the legacy interfaces.

CORBA is a signal step on the road to object-oriented standardization and interoperability. With CORBA, users gain access to information transparently, without them having to know what software or hardware platform it resides on or where it is located on an enterprises' network. The communications heart of object-oriented systems, CORBA brings true interoperability to today's computing environment.

COM FUNDAMENTALS

The Component Object Model defines several fundamental concepts that provide the model's structural underpinnings. These include:

- A binary standard for function calling between components
- A provision for strongly-typed groupings of functions into interfaces
- A base interface providing:
    - A way for components to dynamically discover the interfaces implemented by other components
    - Reference counting to allow components to track their own lifetime and delete themselves when appropriate
    - A mechanism to uniquely identify components and their interfaces
    - A "component loader" to set up component interactions and additionally in the cross-process and cross-network cases to help manage component interactions

Binary Standard

For any given platform (hardware and operating system combination), COM defines a standard way to lay out virtual function tables (vtables) in memory, and a standard way to call functions through the vtables. Thus, any language that can call functions via pointers (C, C++, Small Talk®, Ada, and even Basic) all can be used to write components that can interoperate with other components written to the same binary standard. The double indirection (the client holds a pointer to a pointer to a vtable) allows for vtable sharing among multiple instances of the same object class. On a system with hundreds of object instances, vtable sharing can reduce memory requirements considerably.

The extension of this model to a multiple computer environment is known as DCOM (Distributed COM). From Microsoft's documentation:

MOVING TO A DISTRIBUTED SYSTEM

Ken Bergmann, Microsoft Developer Network Technology Group

These articles cover issues that are raised when the boundaries of an application that is based on the Component Object Model (COM) are extended beyond the desktop to include objects on different computers.

COM in a distributed environment (DCOM) extends COM to support communication among objects on different computers. In a nutshell, DCOM is simply COM with a longer "wire"; it works natively with TCP/IP and the HTTP protocol to provide an "object glue" that will enable business applications to work across the Web.

DCOM enables interobject communication on a LAN, a WAN, or even the Internet. DCOM is included with Microsoft® Windows NT® 4.0 and is available as a free upgrade for Microsoft Windows® 95. DCOM will also be available for the Macintosh® and all major UNIX platforms in early 1997. DCOM is a replacement for OLE Remote Automation.

Moving to a distributed system adds to the design process such issues as remote procedure cost, bandwidth, security, and remote registration. The article Overview of DCOM Development Issues, although targeted to a C11 developer audience, is recommended reading for all COM developers.

When you develop an object transaction model for Distributed COM (DCOM) applications, consider that remote-procedure calls are expensive when compared to in-process calls. It is good practice for distributed object transactions to absorb the cost of packaging object properties into a single variable for transfer over the wire and then unpacking those properties on the other end, in order to avoid the cost of multiple remote-procedure calls. Read Distributed Services in the Corporate Benefits Sample and The Corporate Benefits Sample Transaction Model for an application of these principles to the Corporate Benefits Sample COM servers.

The Information Revolution in Hospitality:

A Guide to Intelligent Marketing 2000–2020
by Cindy Estis Green

Cindy Estis Green, Pegasus Business Intelligence, Pegasus Solutions, Inc., has more than 20 years of hospitality industry experience. Green spent seven years with Hilton International in both corporate marketing and operations positions. In her last assignment with Hilton before starting her own company, Driving Revenue, she served as general manager of a 400-room full service hotel. Her experience ranges from small 100 room properties to large international operations.

As director of marketing for the National Restaurant Association, Green developed her skills in the direct marketing area with an emphasis on direct mail and telemarketing; she had success fine tuning customer profiles and identifying the best prospective targets for new business. While with Hilton International in corporate marketing, Green served as director of market research and marketing information systems. Her expertise extends to the area of database marketing and analysis. She developed several major state-of-the-art systems for Hilton International, which improved the level of information available for marketing decision-making. She has done analysis for many types of hotels and destinations by taking actual guest usage information and developing profiles of target groups. This approach to market research, combined with traditional qualitative and quantitative methods, has proven to be extremely successful. Green is one of the few consultants in the travel/hospitality industry specializing in data mining.

Green has developed and implemented marketing information systems for individual properties as well as international networks for corporate use, including involvement in the design team for Hilton's reservation system. She has substantial experience in related areas such as pricing, yield management, and strategic marketing, which tie in to the database work through the various systems which were developed under her supervision. These approaches are now part of the Pegasus Business Intelligence toolkit since Driving Revenue, Green's company, was acquired by Pegasus Solutions in 1998.

The hotel industry is capital intensive in its financial structure and has a Byzantine complexity in its management and ownership relationships. It has recently become dominated by public ownership and, therefore, now reflects the additional impact of the world's stock markets. This development and an overall availability of financial resources have sparked the merger and acquisition frenzy that is resulting in a consolidation to fewer large companies and a reduction in brands. Many companies are striving to build critical mass to improve the value of the company, gain cost efficiencies and show growth for Wall Street in North America or the City in Europe.

All of these factors are the setting for the industry's move through the threshold of this millennium. The next few decades will be heavily influenced by the already fast paced worldwide changes in technology and communications. These environmental issues will impact hotel executives both internally in their own companies and externally as these factors change the travel behavior of the consumers in the industry's various market segments. These issues will cause different approaches at the chain and brand level, others at the unit level. They will require changes in the organizational structure as well as changes to compensation and incentive plans. These issues will echo loudly for the industry in the next 20 years.

Where will the pressure points be for marketing management from 2000–2020? There are many, but this article explores those most dependent on marketing information:

- Distribution Strategy
- The Use of Market Share in Marketing Strategy and Business Assessment
- Revenue Development and Yield Management

Each section outlines details of the changes anticipated and the ways in which marketing executives can prepare to sharpen skills, acquire information, and ready themselves for the new environment. Each section also includes a reference to the marketing metrics appropriate to measure results or performance for that discipline of the marketing mix.

DISTRIBUTION STRATEGY

Historical Perspective

There have long been intermediaries in hospitality marketing channels. The traditional one is the travel agent. There were retail agents who dealt with consumers directly and there were wholesalers who created travel packages, including hotel stays. The wholesalers also pre-purchased blocks of hotel rooms (without a plan to package them with air or other travel products) and resold them to agents with direct consumer contact. In some parts of the world, travel was dominated by this intermediary-driven supplier of hotel rooms (e.g., Europe in the 1970s and 1980s).

By the end of the 1970s, the travel agency channel was supported by the global distribution systems (GDS) provided by the airlines to facilitate airline bookings. Hotel booking capability was an add-on along with car rental. Travel agencies found electronic booking less costly to their operation and began to insist that all products be available for them through these channels. In the early 1980s, GDS volume was less than 5 percent of all reservations and by 1999, it had grown to over 20 percent. There were two major players: Sabre from American Airlines and Apollo from United Airlines, and several small ones such as System One from Eastern, PARS from TWA, and Datas II from Delta. The total number of GDS terminals used by travel agents was fewer than 100,000 in 1983, generating under two million reservations, and was 565,000 in 1999, generating almost 40 million reservations.

Why Is Distribution Important?

Use of intermediaries is important to marketing in two crucial ways:

1. It greatly affects all decisions in the marketing mix, including pricing, promotion, sales, and packaging through its impact on marketing costs and relationships.

2. It creates a mutually dependent commitment between participants through an infrastructure that is not easily changed and would be expensive to re-create. It becomes a part of the service delivery structure that the customers become accustomed to and trained in using.

The dangers, of course, are that all members of the distribution "food chain," from consumer to hotel, may have vastly different goals that can harm one or more members while helping one or more. Some channel participants may not respond to consumer needs equally well and hurt the hotel's business prospects as a result.

In the hotel world, there was an early concern that the airline systems did not have a primary interest in offering hotel booking capability through their GDS systems. It was a necessary evil to the airlines. In order to accommodate the travel agent demands and be where the bookings were, hotel chains had to build expensive interfaces to each of the major GDS systems. For small chains or independents to compete, they had to hire third-party central reservation providers who collectively operated like the larger chains and built the same interfaces.

Airlines wanted to receive a fee for each hotel booking, travel agents received their usual commission, and the hotels had to recover costs from the investment in the interfaces. While voice reservations were expensive, electronic bookings were a close second. The result was a collective of hotel chains that decided they would have more power together than individually to negotiate desirable functionality in the GDS systems to support their shared intermediary, the travel agent. They also decided, as a cost-saving measure, to collectively build a technical "switch" to link all central reservation systems to all airline reservations systems. The company created in 1988 to take the onus off each chain's reservation department to build and maintain individual GDS interfaces was called The Hotel Industry Switch Company © (THISCO).

In 1994 the next major change in distribution occurred when the Internet welcomed Hyatt as the first hotel chain to go online using a company called TravelWeb. This Web site was started by THISCO to provide hotel booking capability for all hotels and chains. In the last five years since this event, total hotel bookings on the Internet have gone from two million dollars per year to a half billion dollars per year. By 1996 Marriott, Hilton, and Hyatt each had their own chain-specific Web sites. Avis Rent-a-Car developed interfaces to the GDS systems and started selling access to their switch which now, as a Cendant company, has about 20 percent of the hospitality electronic reservation volume versus THISCO (now called Pegasus Electronic Distribution) which has about 65 percent. The balance of the volume is in direct connections to a few GDS systems created by several large chains who decided it was cheaper, given their high volume, to connect themselves.

Current Situation

What does this mean today? In 2000 more than one in five of all reservations are electronic (GDS and Internet combined) and 10 to 12 percent of the total electronic bookings originate from Internet sites. While only 1 to 2 percent of all bookings is quite small, the Internet volume is increasing exponentially each month. And the Internet is affecting many other functions such as customer communication, access to better information and a strong embrace by the consuming public and businesses for a myriad of purposes.

Consumers are going online in droves. However, travel agents are still the prime intermediary; the Travel Industry Association claims they represent just over 20 percent of all hotel bookings worldwide. They still use the GDS systems, but there are some big changes underway. The now independent GDS companies (most have spun off the airlines) are providing Web capability, such as corporate intranets, for the agents to replace the legacy GDS technology. Some are starting Web sites like Travelocity (from Sabre) and 1 Travel (from Amadeus) to serve the consumer markets with the ability to book all travel products (air, hotel, car). In the old distribution model, the travel agencies maintained the customer relationships and the GDS vendors managed the connections between suppliers and distributors. In the new model, the same vendor on the Internet can manage both. In response to this change, the GDS companies have started to acquire sites with direct customer contact so they join the rush to dominate the new Internet channel before the old GDS technology is eclipsed by it. For example, Galileo's plan following the purchase of Trip.com is to launch a consumer travel portal.

The GDS vendors are also providing hotel booking capability to new Web sites with no other means to get hotel central reservation connections. Virtual

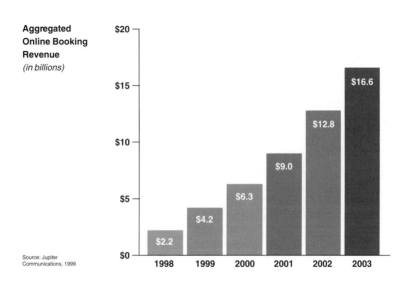

Aggregated Online Booking Revenue (in billions)

Source: Jupiter Communications, 1999

travel agencies like Preview Travel (now owned by Travelocity), HRN, and Expedia.com have sprung up to offer online-only service to consumers. More than 60 major hotel companies have initiated a significant Web site presence that includes real-time room booking capability; this number is growing daily. Travel agency originated bookings still incur a commission to the hotel supplier. Now, rather than a GDS fee and a fee to deliver the reservation to the central reservation system (CRS) in addition to that commission, there is a flat fee or commission for the originating Internet site and the CRS delivery fee.

What had looked like the ultimate inexpensive channel of distribution proved more complex to develop and maintain and has clearly become anything but inexpensive. More importantly, this venue is growing in leaps and bounds. To keep this in perspective, however, it is important to realize that electronic bookings are still significantly less costly than voice reservations and the pressure is great to grow electronic volume and shrink traditional voice volume.

Since the Internet is clearly the media for the explosive growth ahead, it is important to review the types of channels that are emerging and indicate the impact of each main category as it relates to marketing or distribution strategy.

The typical new travel Web site is like TravelWeb or Travelocity in which existing room inventory and existing rates (from the GDS or the CRS) are offered in new venues. Some offer comprehensive travel offerings, others offer hotel rooms only. Some are general portals to an inventory that exists elsewhere (such as CNN or Yahoo), others are specifically travel destinations (such as Preview Travel/Travelocity.com and Expedia.com). Then there are the Onward Distribution Portals that are merely another way to get to new international markets such as Recruit, an Asian portal that converts existing Internet content into Kanji for the Japanese Internet's version of CNN, Lycos, and the plethora of Japanese-only travel sites. While it is confusing to have so many new venues for business, from a hotel marketer's point of view, there isn't much to do that is different regarding its room inventory or its maintenance. Once you have a strategy for onward distribution to assure you are tapping all sites that will deliver value to you, you may just choose different rate or room types to meet the needs of each user base.

Some sites demand a greater attention to the rate issues. The emergence of "auction sites" such as priceline.com or Expedia.com's Price Matcher service and "distressed inventory" sites like lastminute.com or lastminutetravel.com require considerable thought to pricing and the impact of rates on yield management decisions. Discount sites, such as HRN and Travelscape will also be effective distribution channels to fill need periods and will require more attention from the industry's revenue managers. But the inventory still comes from the same places, not requiring new maintenance or any real changes to the distribution channel chain.

There are some sites that are coming online that may attempt to bypass components of the existing distribution chain such as HotelBank.com in Scandinavia. This site is trying to bypass the GDS systems by allowing corporate travel managers to tap direct CRS inventory through a Web browser interface.

While this is limited, and it could only be successfully done by a vendor that has a critical mass of hotels to satisfy the needs of the corporate accounts, this model could have a more resounding effect on the distribution landscape.

Another new innovation worth tracking is a site like All-Hotels.com. This site is a traditional model of a travel site (with independent hotels as a target) in terms of handling rates and inventory, but it plans to provide the added value of collecting user preferences in order to match the user to the appropriate hotel based on preference criteria. It further plans to build a database of guest preference information that a hotel can purchase and offer added services to hotels to provide satisfaction and other customer relationship management after a guest stay for ongoing dialogue.

In summary, there are four main categories of Web sites for hotel bookings:

- property/brand specific (e.g., hyatt.com)
- mega-travel generalists (e.g., TravelWeb, Expedia, Travelocity)
- niche (e.g., golf, corporate—usually addressing one market segment)
- rate-driven sites (e.g., auction, distressed inventory and discount/wholesaler type)

Each type of site requires different treatment for rates and inventory management and has very different revenue and distribution implications. Participation in all sites is not only likely but for many hotels essential to maintain a presence in the new distribution marketplace.

Distribution Strategy for the Future

The strategic issues to hotel chains are (1) the costs of distribution and (2) anticipating how to be where the bookings are.

It is expected that within five years electronically delivered reservations will constitute over 50 percent of all bookings and in fewer than ten years, this number will be upwards of 75–85 percent. There is pressure on suppliers to move away from commission-based pricing. There is a move toward travel agent development of consumer Web sites supplemented by new revenue sources such as sale of peripheral products (e.g., travel clothing, insurance). There is a tendency for heavier usage of chains' branded sites. This is motivating chains to spend more money on expensive consumer advertising to drive traffic to their sites. This pattern will give tremendous bias to the chains with the deepest pockets to build the Internet as a channel. While there are large numbers of brand-sensitive customers who choose hotel rooms by brand and would be attracted to a Web site that is brand specific, there are also many customers who prefer to "shop" around in the general or in the price-oriented travel sites. As of 2000, it appears to be evenly split with 50 percent in each category. Most forecasts point to the absolute volume increasing and the percentage of general Web sites to outpace brand-specific sites. Whatever the split in

Web site preferences, there is a huge growth in Internet bookings that is partially displacing voice calls and GDS bookings.

The least understood challenge of the future is grasping what role the Internet will play once the dust settles on mergers, acquisitions, and fallout from new Web sites. The executives charged with distribution must manage a Web strategy with two components: (1) management of one's own hotel chain site and (2) management of those elements that are part of a hotel chain's "onward distribution." There is a high cost involved in maintaining a presence in many of the dozens of Web sites offering a combination of non-travel content with hotel bookability, including such well-known names as AOL and CNN. Some of these booking sites piggyback on the databases and booking capability of the larger players like Expedia.com or Travelocity/Preview Travel in a way that is transparent to the end user. If all these sites are to include booking capability, how do you maintain hotel information, rates, and inventory in dozens of sites? How do you keep up with all the new sites that are literally starting daily? This extensive distribution network using the Internet is being referred to as the travel industry's Alternate Distribution System (ADS) meaning it is an alternative to the GDS or direct calls to central reservation offices.

Onward Distribution Is Crucial

The database maintenance required to support the ADS network is an expense to each hotel chain. It will cost a chain to "do it yourself" or the chain will opt to pay an intermediary to maintain a central database of descriptive hotel information that gets updated once and gets distributed to all sites instantly. Further, it is more efficient if the rates are not in a database separate from the central reservation system, but merely available in a "seamless" connection by opening a window into the current rates as displayed in the CRS. One opts to hire someone to research the plethora of new sites or one pays an intermediary to research and handle all technical connections to be sure reservation delivery needs are met.

Independent hotels with a Web site can enjoy a significant benefit when they take advantage of technology that links their Web site to their property management system or uses a Web-based reservation system like Synxis. If a property can avoid maintaining a duplicate inventory (on the Web and in a local PMS) this can be a desirable route. This distribution option carries relatively low reservation delivery costs and the opportunity to demonstrate a high level of customer service in the booking process that helps level the playing field with chain hotels. However, this option does not address the onward distribution needs of a property. The independent properties must also make their Web site known to the Internet consumer and this is not an easy or inexpensive feat given the cacophony of messages on the Web. So, while this option can be a viable component of an independent hotel's Internet strategy, it must be used in conjunction with other actions.

The most efficient way for a small hotel group or independent to be in most sites for onward distribution and minimize maintenance costs is to utilize a third-party reservation provider. It would be unrealistic for an independent hotel, even with a full-time Web manager, to keep up with the offerings and arrange connections to every viable Web site. So, while third-party providers such as Pegasus Solutions/Utell, Lexington, and VIP used to look like expensive distribution channels that were often criticized by subscribing hotels for not delivering enough volume, they are now playing a much more crucial role. They are, in many cases, managing the implementation of the complete distribution strategy for participating hotels. In conjunction with their connectivity vendors (e.g., Pegasus), they are maintaining a presence in key Web sites as the sites become viable.

The Questions About Travel Agencies

Another challenge of the next ten years will be to work with the newly emerging roles of travel intermediaries and the fast-growing tangle of

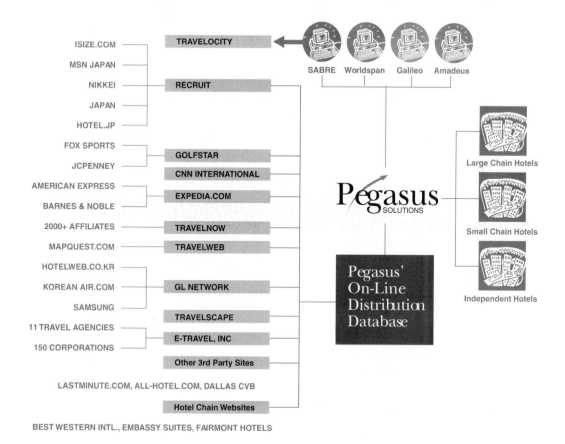

communication media to the consumer. Will travel agents become consultants and move from commission-based compensation to fees for service? What other revenue streams will they cultivate? Will all commission-based agencies have to be online to survive? How will the online-only travel agency sites differ from the traditional travel agencies? Will they become mega-aggregators of all types of travel products or will they select specialized niches to dominate? Will there be one central database of hotel information maintained for the industry to support each chain's onward distribution needs or will each chain have its own approach? Certainly the industry will gravitate to the most cost-effective method to handle all of these options.

New Technologies

Another major change to the reservation distribution picture is being driven by speech recognition technology. Even today, tests are being done to automate the most straightforward reservations like those made into room blocks for conventions or corporate rates. These reservations can be handled by a telephone switch and an automated system from the initial call to delivery at the hotel. This method will certainly grow as it represents a major reduction in costs from a labor-intensive voice reservation. Hotel chains will encourage consumers and all third-party bookers, like corporate travel planners and travel agents alike, to use the less expensive electronic media. Then they will apply pressure on the various components of the electronic distribution chains to reduce costs further in those channels consumers and bookers find easiest to book. A handheld device that transmits via satellite to make reservations through the Web is an example of another technology in the pipeline that will facilitate and lower distribution costs.

Groups, Meetings, and Tours

There is a demand to have meetings, conventions, and tour operator business travel through the same electronic distribution pipeline that previously had been exclusively used by individual commercial and leisure travelers. Web-based booking systems for groups are plugging into the distribution channels and bookings are being automatically carried directly to hotels bypassing the need for manual rooming list re-entry and delays in room pickup counts. In addition to the rooming list and reservation relay systems, meetings business is the focus of another category of Web site in which RFPs and bids from hotels are exchanged. These sites do not participate in the reservation-handling component of the booking, but rather deal with the exchange of information necessary for hotel selection and contract negotiations related to meetings. While some sites have links to automated sales and function books for online availability checks, most are in the early stages of development and are performing a fairly complex and customized process.

Hotel Branding

Due to all the variations in ownership and management structure: branded hotel chains, management companies, investment companies, franchise companies—some publicly traded, some privately owned—these issues will have a different bearing on each. For instance, would a management company managing multiple brands, want to initiate a Web site and introduce the management company brand (in addition to the brand names of each of its branded hotels e.g., Sheraton, Hilton, Marriott) to the consumer? Is it worth paying the high cost to develop brand name recognition through various distribution channels when the branded chains are already doing it and charging for it through their management fees? Consumers and travel agents will more easily locate all the hotel options in a given city, determine suitability for a given traveler, and book chain and independent hotels alike. So how will brand awareness and brand loyalty change since distribution may no longer be the same point of differentiation it has been historically?

If the chain's central reservation facility may not be the dominant source of business it once was to its franchisees and management company hotels, can the chain command the same prices to provide it? There are other services that were typically provided by a brand, a hotel chain, or a franchisor that are being effectively replaced or challenged by newcomers on the Internet. In addition to the important reservation processing function, sites to help hotels purchase goods at volume discounts, inventory management of a hotel's assets, and the imminent onset of widespread Web-based property management systems are all publicly available Web services sold on a transaction basis. Can every hotel benefit from these new services without having to pay the fees to a brand or flag? Will hotels just be replacing old technology and services with new or will the overall expense and benefit dynamics be changing to be as dispersed as the new distribution network is? Will consumers still relate to the brand of hotel or will they relate more to the brand of the delivery system that handles all but their night's stay? These will be the crucial questions of the next five to ten years that will require serious strategic planning by senior management.

Forecasting the Future

Since so much of the total lodging revenue industry-wide is booked through the use of direct sales resulting in contracts, (i.e., corporate transient travel or meetings) the largest opportunity in the near term for the Internet channel will be in the leisure or non-contracted business segments. Both traditional and online travel agencies have moved aggressively into this space to address these categories of business. Companies like Expedia.com and Travelocity are dominating today in the online agency category but traditional agencies such as Uniglobe, American Express, and Rosenbluth are making great strides. They offer the convenience of "one stop shopping" to the consumer so the end user need not search the Web from hotel site to hotel site. This aggregation of travel product is a great advantage to all. Those who are brand or property loyal can go directly to the sites they know.

So where does this leave the hotel chains or the independents who are rushing to build and market their own Web sites?

From the 2000 viewpoint, with a squinted eye to the future, it looks like there will be a different impact on chains than on independent hotels. Hotels need to seriously consider what the Web will do for them. Will it bring incremental new business, become the primary venue for the sale of distressed inventory, or just provide a new and hopefully a lower-cost distribution channel? Though the benefits may be a blend of all three based on any company's business mix, a Web plan needs to be integrated into the overall marketing strategy. And while the "travel superstores" are likely to have the edge over branded hotel sites for generating booking volume, these brand-specific sites will also be an essential building block in the marketing plan of a hotel company.

Although hotels' branded sites currently measure their success based on booking counts, they may ultimately prove more useful to support customer information gathering and for retention purposes rather than for customer acquisition. Those marketers who use their branded Web site as a communications tool to engage in dialogue with their customers are likely to gain the most benefit from this particular channel.

On the other hand, these travel superstores may be able to cast the widest safety net possible to capture the sale of otherwise unsold inventory. Some agencies and superstores sell specialized and higher-end niche products like adventure vacations or specific recreational offerings that will help fill another business category for the leisure-oriented higher-end properties.

While chains may smooth out their business by better filling need periods, independent hotels may gain more incremental new business (as a proportion of their total) than the chains. Through this channel, a hotel can raise its awareness level to a much greater degree in the leisure and small business segments than ever before. But success will depend not on the property's individual Web site initially, but on the distribution strategy it undertakes. Independent hotels will expand their reach dramatically by including themselves in key aggregator travel sites (like Expedia, TravelWeb.com, or American Express) and in specialized sites that match the hotel's offerings.

Being "where the bookings are" will be the mantra of all hotel entities although chains and independent hotels will approach this differently. No hotel property or chain will generate enough bookings through its own site to rival the bookings it receives through its central reservation 800 number service or third-party agencies (online or traditional). All hotels will still need a presence in all channels.

Larger hotel companies will be able to leverage their size and geographic dispersion to participate in many more venues to sell distressed inventory. By utilizing third-party travel providers and co-operative promotional partners who share a similar customer base, chains can add lift to their promotional investments. The airlines are building a sound Web foundation that may prove to attract a wide and well-qualified audience. The relationships with hotels for online promotions are not as mature as those related to the frequent traveler joint programs. For instance, an airline's "weekly special" e-mail may reference a partner car rental company or hotel chain by name, yet few include corresponding special rates at hotels within the cities being promoted.

Customer Service Is Where the Web Will Take Hotels

All hotels, however, will begin on a "level playing field" when it comes to customer service and personalization. The techniques made famous by Amazon.com (which Internet specialists call collaborative filtering) have not yet been applied to travel. Gathering key customer preferences and using that information to generate more sales through better customer service is the formula. The pre-sale, post-sale and ongoing dialogue with customers in the travel sector is yet to be defined. This function can apply to all market segments: leisure, business, meetings, group and tour. Whether bookings can be made easily through the Internet or not, this channel can provide the basis for a retention plan that dwarfs that of the traditional frequency programs dominated by miles for dollars.

It is the execution of this function, which is so easily facilitated by the technology and communications network of the World Wide Web, that will likely determine the ultimate winners in electronic distribution.

Marketing Metrics

The kind of information the hotel chain and unit level marketing executive will need to effectively measure success in this new environment will be more detailed than ever. The basic need is to track volume shifts by distribution channel and to measure market share relative to competitors for each. There are definite implications for revenue managers. It will not be enough to track the business by rate and value but it will be necessary to account for associated costs of each channel when optimizing the revenue stream.

Volume Production Through Each Channel of Distribution (GDS, ADS)

Which series of Internet venues are being touched as part of each transaction?

It is rare that all business will come from one or two Internet sites. As the Internet appeal grows, the business will continue to be fragmented and it is essential to identify the growing sources and trends through each.

- These data must be matched against corresponding costs to get a clear picture of the value of each channel of distribution.

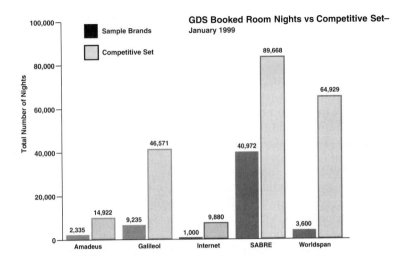

Differing fees based on the channel structure and connectivity of each will cause some channels to be more attractive than others.

- Market share information will indicate what volume each GDS, Internet, and travel agent venue is delivering relative to your competitors.

These data must be tracked with a frequency that matches your volume. If there are dramatic high-volume changes, it must be examined more often during those high-growth periods.

Geographic Origins and Destinations of Business

Where is the business coming from and where is it being booked into? Which cities are getting it? Which states and countries are getting it? Where are the travelers located? Which originating cities are producing the highest volumes by GDS, ADS, and travel agency?

Travel Agency Information

Which agencies are booking into which destinations? What is your market share of each agency? Each consortia (i.e., group of affiliated agencies)? Which agencies are booking your competitors and not booking your hotel(s)? What is the relative value of each travel agency or consortia to the recipient hotel(s)?

Customer Information

Which customers represent those most likely to book? What are the essential pieces of information needed to properly service these customers? What are the appropriate categories of customers so they can be grouped for more targeted messages? What information are the customers willing to share in exchange for better service? How can this information be applied to improve retention in the corporate and meetings segments?

RECOMMENDATIONS FOR MANAGING DISTRIBUTION CHANNELS

(1) Measure the costs and revenue of each distribution channel today.

If you don't already have a baseline measurement on your company's relative position in each channel create such baselines as soon as possible. Quantify your full cost per reservation and the overall annual cost. Likewise, know your current revenue per distribution channel. Understand the growth trends, watch them regularly, and explore the reasons for changes when they occur. Investigate the mechanism for affecting changes such as promotional opportunities and increased shelf space—be sure you can always quantify the results of your actions. The GDS systems and Internet sites may offer new screens or participation in corporate intranet development. Stay abreast of these developments and participate as appropriate for the type of business you want to control through this channel. Ensure your participation is commensurate with the value of the business you expect to be delivered.

(2) Conduct periodic risk assessment on each channel of distribution.

Understand which ones may be eclipsed by a new player or a substantial development in an existing one. Mergers, acquisitions, and implementation of new technology will cause constant change in the distribution channel landscape in the next five to ten years. Understanding how these developments will affect each hotel company's business will be crucial. This knowledge will be shared at industry events and through associations such as HEDNA and HSMAI and its Executive Forums. Each hotel company needs to be more proactive and to play out scenarios on each change. It will not be good enough to "keep abreast" of changes, but rather crucial to completely understand the impact the change could have in the context of the company's business volumes through that channel. Management companies that depend on multiple brands to deliver reservations to an array of hotels in the group must work with executives managing the reservation systems for each of their brands to be sure the approach taken by each brand toward each distribution channel will serve their hotels well.

(3) Consider the impact on your brand.

Assess if you have a clearly defined brand promise. If your brand is largely defined by the basket of services you provide your franchisees or owners, such as volume purchasing discounts and reservation access, then you still have a substantial amount of work to do to establish a brand identity. If you feel threatened that a Web site will "own your customers," then you likely do not have a fully developed brand strategy. There are marketing image and operational issues that need much further definition and, even more challenging, will require a method to ensure consistent execution at the unit level. The impact of the distribution channel management on your brand is really only the tip of the iceberg, but it should be the lightening rod to get each company to closely examine its brand strategy.

(4) Understand how to take advantage of the native environment of each distribution channel.

Treat each distribution channel individually as you make decisions about the products and rates you sell through it. Consider the nature of each Internet venue and each GDS. The user base varies considerably. If, for example, one GDS has a strong user base in Europe and those markets are not significant feeder cities for your hotels, then the attention paid to that GDS may vary greatly from one which dominates in North America where your volume is sourced. Similarly, don't try to fit the GDS rate structures into the Internet environment. Where there is more flexibility, be sure to change your offering to avail yourself of these options.

Consider the user base. In 2000 Internet users are largely consumers; GDS users are largely travel agents. The Internet is ideal to initiate dialogue with your customers. Therefore, focus on the customer types most likely to engage in dialogue. If the leisure and direct consumer market is who you get through the Web, build your image (in the form of products, rates, communication/promotion) to address that audience. If GDS remains predominantly oriented to the corporate market, beef up corporate offerings. If travel agents are being used increasingly for specialized, complicated bookings, such as customized packages or high maintenance customers, make it easy for that type of customer to use you.

Make sure the Web sites you are in can handle the rate, room types, descriptive text, graphics, and management of other key reservation functions you want to sell there. That means they are capable of displaying the product properly, including graphics, and maintaining the product offering so the information is current and can transmit the reservation and all the changes to it in an efficient and timely manner. If the Web sites cannot do that, work with the third-party provider (such as Pegasus Solutions, Inc. or your central reservation provider) to help get the Web sites upgraded so they can support your needs. Many of the Web sites powered by the GDS systems are constrained by the limitations of the legacy GDS technology that supports them.

"Friction free" should be a goal for each channel of distribution and part of each hotel company's marketing plan should include a well-thought-out plan to make each distribution channel as open and smoothly functional as possible for the type of bookings your hotel(s) attract.

(5) You will need to document a Web distribution strategy which addresses the two main points of management of your Web site and management of your onward distribution.

- Management of your own Web site includes among other things: design/ look and feel, its short- and long-term goals, its development plan, booking capability, a research plan to examine the site visitors' usage and perceptions, and a plan to develop and exploit links to and from your site.

- Management of an "onward distribution" plan that examines how your inventory and hotel information will be distributed onwardly to all the Internet sites you want to be in. This includes connectivity, reservation delivery, inventory maintenance, and an ongoing plan to research what is happening on the Web that could affect your business favorably and not. Management of rates and room inventory as appropriate for each of these many Web sites will be a more complex job than the already demanding one performed by the industry's revenue managers. Their jobs and the systems they depend upon need to be expanded so they can track and act upon the new wider range of distribution channels.

(6) Document a Web communication strategy that is tied closely to a data collection and market research plan.

Once the distribution channel landscape settles down into a known network of third-party providers, the Internet (through a hotel or chain's own Web site) will most likely be a hotel's or hotel chain's core vehicle for customer service and retention. There may be more opportunity to generate incremental revenue through retention programs than by bearing the cost of a new business acquisition, particularly for hotel chains. Independent hotels have a greater opportunity to find new customers through this growing channel. But, like the larger hotel companies, they will also rely upon larger travel generalist Web sites with a critical mass to reach out and find new customers or customers to fill need periods. In order to address requirements for customer service and retention, a communications plan will be necessary. This plan should include a promotional plan to get users to visit your site along with the plan for on- and off-line dialogue with your hotel guests and customers and with prospects visiting your site. It should also include the communication plan to be applied online in other sites, and the strategy with complementary partners through Web site design and e-mail-type correspondence.

Web site navigation and links to/from other sites becomes essential to examine and refine since customer visits for information will always outpace bookings. The cooperative partnerships with complementary vendors (travel and merchandise) can be more extensive with the communications alternatives made possible by the Web. Collection of customer preferences will be essential to build a communications strategy.

Remembering that the Internet, more than anything else, is the place for virtual meetings of like-minded communities of people, the communications strategy needs to articulate how you plan to (a) get the attention of and (b) talk to those who share your hotel(s) as a common interest. You will need to have a market research plan that defines the data to collect and defines how you plan to use those data to improve customer service and facilitate dialogue for that Holy Grail of marketing: owning the customer relationship.

THE USE OF MARKET SHARE IN MARKETING STRATEGY AND BUSINESS ASSESSMENT

Historical Perspective

There was little mention of market share and marketing strategy in hotels in the 1970s. There was more demand than supply, little competition, and hotels took orders for business that they "cherry picked" for appropriateness to their own operations. There were few marketing executives and almost all effort was placed on coordination of sales. A spurt in hotel development in the late 1970s and 1980s changed all that. Learning to compete was a new skill for hotel companies. All the marketing techniques that were in vogue and becoming more sophisticated in the mature consumer products, retailing, and financial services industries were brand new to the hotel community in 1980.

The technology infrastructure within hotels at this time was based largely on accounting and the beginning of reservation and check-in/out facilities through the installation of property management systems. Central reservation systems were in their infancy and most hotel chains had multiple regional reservation centers. Since there was no need for marketing information at the time these systems were developed, there was no provision made for it. Statistical reports from either the accounting (back office) or property management (front office) systems were aggregated financial statistics for overall hotel performance. All geographic information was for all types of business on a combined basis.

The realization of the absence of marketing information in system development arose in the mid-1980s when hotels needed to become more knowledgable about their customer bases. There was tremendous competition for every type of customer and for the first time, the customer was "calling the shots" in the new demand-driven atmosphere. Understanding what type of business a hotel chain received, by hotel and overall, became critical. Understanding where each customer type came from and guidance on where to go for more was essential. The concept of planning revenue and marketing expenses by market segment was just being introduced. They were called marketing plans but they were more like tactical sales plans with revenue projections. Hotels with large airline crew bases had heavily skewed geographic origin information based on the unimportant origins of individual members of airline flight crews. The source data were rendered entirely worthless without segmentation capability. Some hotels had virtually no management information reporting.

Why Is Business Mix and Market Share Management Important?

Gaining market share has long been considered the road to riches for businesses. The businesses with the greatest market share will be the most profitable. This concept was quantitatively proven 25 years ago through the Profitability Impact of Marketing Strategies (PIMS) and documented on numerous occasions in prestigious journals like *Harvard Business Review.* Whether it is still considered the sole variable related to profitability in today's fragmented niche-oriented economy or not, it is certainly still considered an essential metric for managing annual plan results and for assessing overall business prospects.

There are many types of essential marketing information control tools such as:

- sales analysis
- expense-to-revenue ratios
- profitability by region, customer, account, distribution channel and all its variations
- efficiency of market mix by type: e.g., sales staff, advertising, sales promotion, distribution, promotional type (e.g. frequency programs) and
- marketing effectiveness overall.

Market share is the one measure that has been almost entirely absent from hospitality marketing planning and management. The main reason is that the source numbers are not available in one central place and/or not generally shared. There has been one major database of hotel performance information available in the United States, but it is once again, based on aggregated accounting figures for a hotel overall with no direct application to marketing by market segment.

How can you measure market share? The standard market share measures used in consumer products and shown in the current aggregated hotel terms are:

1. *Competitive Set or Served-Market Share*
   Your chain's or hotel's room nights and revenue as a percentage of those hotels or chains that either serve the same customers or those reached by the same marketing effort. For example, if Sample Brand has 100,000 room nights and the hotel chains that serve the same customers in the same markets have 500,000 room nights, Sample Brand has 20 percent competitive set market share.

2. *Relative Market Share (to top three competitors)*

Your chain's or hotel's room nights and revenue as a percentage of the combined sales of the three largest competitors. For example, if Sample Brand has 30 percent of the market and its three largest competitors have 20, 10, and 10 percent. Sample brand has 75 percent (30/40) relative market share.

3. *Relative Market Share (to leading competitor)*

Your chain's or hotel's room nights and revenue relative to your single largest competitor. If your competitor has 100 percent and you have 5 percent more, your relative market share is 105 percent. That is, if your competitor has 100,000 room nights and you have 110,000, you have almost five percent more of the total market share than your nearest competitor (10,000/210,000).

Current Situation

The new property management and reservation systems have been built with some consideration for marketing needs. There is still a constraint in these systems that prevents them from serving as marketing information systems. They are designed for fast transaction processing to satisfy check-in and check-out needs. Their data formats are technically designed to handle transactions with a guest as efficiently as possible. These structures are different from the formats used for full marketing analysis (refer to section on Revenue Development) that would demand data to be stored in different ways. Notwithstanding, there has been a great step forward in the ability to separate basic performance measures like room nights, average rates, percentage of room nights and revenue by market segment. Typical market segments used by hotel chains are corporate business traveler, government, weekend leisure guests, conventions, corporate conferences, and tour series. Hotels are now able to examine their own business and measure actual revenue against budget by each type of business or market segment.

In the more forward thinking hotel chains, marketing planning is done by deciding which types of business are most profitable and which are expected to be easiest for a hotel company or unit to acquire. A plan is designed each year by looking at each market segment and for some, each corporate or group account, to decide what they can expect to achieve in business volume that year. The part of this equation that is not generally available is the ability to determine what the overall market potential is for each type of business. In consumer products companies like Procter & Gamble, there is an exact accounting for the units sold of each type of toothpaste and each type of laundry detergent in every geographic region and each retail outlet. When an assessment is made, it is clear what the market share is by product, by region, and many other variables. Hotels have not yet reached that level of sophistication in marketing control tools.

How Will Hotels Measure Market Share Tomorrow?

There is a move for the major hotel chains to be more interested in pooling information like the consumer products companies. Living in the complexity of today's fast-moving environment, often with constantly increasing pressure for profitability due to the widespread public ownership of the hotel chains, will necessitate the usage of market share measures to drive improvements in profitability.

In order to make these statistics useful in hospitality terms, there are several additional variables that need to be introduced.

First, the concept of market share by market segment and channel of distribution is essential. It will require all the above generalized market share measures to be cast by market segment. This will have the greatest impact at unit- and regional-level marketing. These are operational marketing measures. But, in the hotel industry, unit level is the lowest common denominator. Marketing success must occur there to support and take advantage of the strategic programs and distribution venues that are developed and implemented on a corporate level. When finance-driven merger and acquisition activity cannot be used to increase a hotel chain's profit, success will rely upon profitable hotel management, one unit at a time. Many of the major chains involved heavily in acquisitions from the mid-1990s have now shifted focus to running profitable hotels since opportunities for acquisition have dwindled.

Second, there are major differences in capacity and hotel configuration even within the same basic hotel types. These variables must be factored into the equation. Given two hotels in the same location each has 200 rooms but one has 15,000 sq. ft. of function space configured into a ballroom and several breakout rooms, and the other has two small banquet-type rooms, the business mix possibilities will be widely different. The market share of each type of business will be incomparable due to differences in their meeting-related business. The overall expectation of potential financial performance of these two properties may also be different.

Market share will no longer be the simple arithmetic figure it was viewed as before. It will be a combination of (1) customer penetration by account, (2) customer spending share, (3) average rates by type and (4) all weighted by capacity constraints, including function space, recreational facilities (golf, spa) and other significant drivers of demand. It will be necessary to view market share in the context of the underlying business potential—and this may require a more complex calculation than in the past to derive.

Impact on Business Valuation

The collection of market share data on a property level will facilitate corporate and investor-level determination of business value. These demand statistics by type of business combined with supply variables for each city and region will be invaluable to the development and financial community. The expectation of

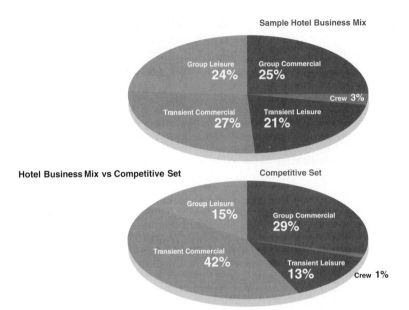

Sample Hotel Business Mix

Group Leisure 24%
Group Commercial 25%
Crew 3%
Transient Commercial 27%
Transient Leisure 21%

Hotel Business Mix vs Competitive Set

Competitive Set

Group Leisure 15%
Group Commercial 29%
Transient Commercial 42%
Transient Leisure 13%
Crew 1%

profitability for each unit in a chain and for a chain overall will be better assessed by building models of potential based on accurate segment-specific supply and demand variables. Scoring systems already exist in the industry with more limited variables to address basic profitability potential. These systems allow for a chain to determine if they are performing at par with their competitors. It also allows for a more objective assessment of competitive set. The sample on the following page reflects revpar potentials between competitive properties based on a weighted scale taking into account location, chain affiliation, size of hotel, and overall annual revenues.

Currently, most competitive sets used for aggregate market share statistics such as revpar, occupancy and average rate are devised by the properties themselves. Once a valid supply and demand model is established in the hospitality industry, competitive sets will be created based on relative scoring and customer input rather than exclusively based on decisions by hotel management. Further, competitive sets are not often relevant for one hotel at an aggregate level; they are only meaningful if they are market segment-specific. On a corporate basis, they can be used to compare chains with similar product types.

How Market Share Can Impact Marketing Strategies

While business strategies are wide-ranging and include financial and operational components, some typical defensive marketing strategies are to be the Market Leader, Market Challenger, Market Follower and Market Nicher. Some examples will illustrate how market share is applied when choosing a market strategy. Clearly, a Market Leader is most concerned with maintaining or growing market share. Coke employees know market share the same or better than their stock price. In the hotel world, the Market Leader will most often be the target of every competitor.

Market Challengers are companies like Colgate (to P&G's leader), Pepsi (to Coke), and Ford (to GM). In the hotel arena, it would be Radisson and Starwood (to Marriott). Market challengers pursue market share by directly attacking, using a backdoor strategy (like Timex using mass marketing against traditional jewelry stores), or by gobbling up the smaller competitors and niche players (like many beer companies did). These companies have proven they can move market share by utilizing clever product innovations, becoming better at service delivery, or various other methods. Other than share price, market share is usually their most watched statistic.

Market Followers can be very profitable with a stable number two or three position. A study documented by marketing guru Phillip Kotler citing a *Harvard Business Review* report indicates that numerous companies with half the market share of the leader had a five-year average ROI that surpassed the industry median.

Being a follower does not necessarily mean Market Followers are passive in their roles. They may move more quickly into new markets, change service offerings to be more tailored to customer needs. The keys to their success are market segmentation and focus on ongoing research and development to identify new innovations more quickly. Guarding their position to make sure they do not slip in their market share is crucial for players in this role. Because of

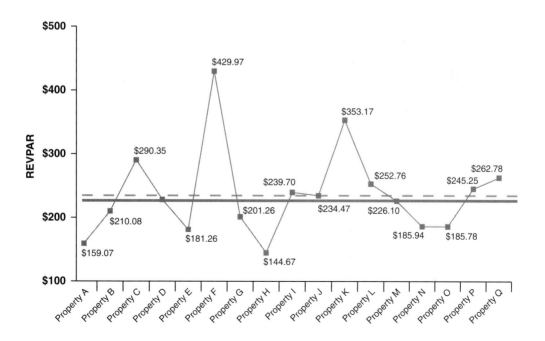

Hyatt's size relative to some larger competitors, it has successfully employed this strategy.

Market Nichers may be smaller firms but they can fragment individual markets. They must be ever conscious of market potential. Participating in a market with a nicher can be difficult on a mainstream product. For instance, Ian Schrager hotels in New York City and Los Angeles or Wyndham's Grand Bay Hotels & Resorts are very much niche players. The appeal of their uniqueness is impossible for a large chain affiliated hotel to match. Usually their segments are very specialized and they are at greater risk of losing large pieces of a market because of it. On the other hand, nichers can be very effective because they are focused on the type of business for which they excel at servicing. Managing market share to understand what portion of the overall market potential they will control will help in understanding what a more mainstream hotel can accomplish. Likewise, a niche hotel or company can become more realistic about its own potential.

How Do You Interpret Market Share Shifts?

Interpreting market share is also a consideration. There are several mitigating factors that require a more complex consideration to this assessment.

1. A negative change in the environment that causes a general downturn in business will not always affect all hotels equally. For instance, during the Gulf War, those hotels in London who were better equipped to handle wholesaler business (which was all that was available) had less of a drop in market share than those who had entirely built business around the commercial traveler markets.
2. A hotel company or unit with greater than average opportunities should have greater increases in market share than those with lesser opportunities. Larger chains with a very strong brand identity should not be judged to be doing well if they are just holding the lead as market share leader. If a hotel has superior facilities for meetings business, it should be continually growing its share in this market segment. Maintaining leadership in absolute terms will not be acceptable.
3. If a new brand or new hotel enters a market, all other hotels will not necessarily lose share equally. Also, it would be expected in a static market that a hotel or chain would lose share. This does not necessarily mean the company or hotel is under-performing in its market.
4. If there is a conscious effort to change business mix by dropping lower profit margin customer groups (e.g., airline crew, government), the unit's market share will drop but it may not be a sign of declining performance. It may only be a temporary lull while the property ramps up with higher margin replacement business.
5. Market share is best used as a trend figure. Short-term fluctuations are normal and expected. For instance, a few large meetings that may

only be in one or two hotels at the unit level may sharply alter a hotel's market share that is not participating in the meetings business. Widespread renovation efforts or new building spurts may also understandably impact chainwide market share without cause for alarm in overall performance. In this example, it would be essential to understand the cause of the anomaly.

RECOMMENDATIONS FOR MANAGING MARKET SHARE

(1) Start examining all statistics by market segment.

For the marketing of hotel operations, stop looking at aggregated financial statistics like occupancy, average rate, and revpar to manage the marketing effort of your hotels. These statistics do little to help a sales and marketing team direct specific efforts to improve results. That is, look at the types of business within each operation such as corporate, group, and leisure. It is the building block of market segments that forms the basis for a hotel's revenue. Compare your production by market segment against your competitive set in each hotel market. Use associations such as HSMAI and AH&MA to be neutral organizers of these data. Prevail upon those industry-based association leaders to work with the larger companies to initiate a concerted effort for improvement in the quality of data available for sales and marketing use.

In most branded or flagged hotels in the industry, approximately 30–50 percent of an individual property's business is controlled by corporate or branded programs such as the central reservation system, travel agency consortia and national account management, distribution channel management (including Web sites), corporate frequency programs, and branded advertising campaigns. That means between 50–70 percent of a hotel's business is controlled locally through contracted corporate deals, group, meetings, and local leisure business. The local hotel must exercise control whenever possible and there must be market share metrics available to help local management judge when they have succeeded.

(2) Developers need to conduct feasibility studies by business mix and understand exactly how much corporate, leisure, and group business there is to be had in the trading area of a new hotel.

Hotel configurations should reflect the anticipated demand by type of business. While there are always limitations imposed by lot size, shape, and corresponding architectural design, a hotel should be ultimately built to match market demand. Some new builds or renovations can stimulate new demand in an area, but here must be a baseline of knowledge on how much business already exists. Then, a realistic assessment can be made of how much more a new hotel can bring.

Given the explosion in public ownership of hotel branded companies, REITS, and management companies, it is likely the investment community (which expects a higher level of analysis than the banks that finance local unit development) will impose the requirement on hotel developers to develop future revenue projections by market segment.

(3) Market share by market segment will be a necessary addition to the market potential models that are developed.

The financial and operational assessment of existing hotel companies and chains is generally based on various formulae for return on investment. The time horizon for performance review is generally one year at a time to operators and three to five years to investors. While public ownership is shortening the time horizon to the quarterly financial result level, there are still significant improvements to be made to assessment of company-level performance.

More sophisticated techniques need to be employed such as the one used by Paul Slattery of the London office of the investment banking firm of Dresdner Kleinwort Benson. Taking criteria such as brand equity, hotel size, location type, reservation flow, market share, and other variables, a scoring system can be applied to individual hotels within a group and combined to determine overall value of a hotel company. Due to the tendency for many hotel companies to be decentralized with many different ownership and management arrangements, their value must be assessed by summing the value of each individual hotel in the group.

Furthermore, *potential value* of a hotel group can be determined in a similar fashion. Applying these same scoring models, a hotel company or prospective investor can identify when a hotel group is undervalued by comparing current performance against its potential based on its score.

These scoring models require market share by market segment as a crucial component to assess potential. Performance above or below a benchmark for a competitive set is all relative to the business available in the area and the physical configuration of each property. Further, brand reservation strength and other factors need to be incorporated.

REVENUE DEVELOPMENT AND YIELD MANAGEMENT

If *yield management* is effectively optimizing revenue by managing the flow of business through the distribution pipeline, *revenue development* is concerned with making the pipe larger, enhancing and facilitating the flow of business through it.

Historical Perspective

Hotel companies have always employed revenue development techniques to find new business and to get more business from existing clientele. Due to the previously discussed reference to a lack of competition prior to the 1980s hotel building boom, the methods utilized were not as creative as they will become in today's and tomorrow's world. The primary communication methods were image-oriented print advertising, rack brochures, and direct sales staff available to take orders for hotel rooms and catering. Roadside properties would manage street signage and develop relationships with tourism-oriented rest stops on main thoroughfares nearby.

Yield management in hotels is the science of optimizing the yield from the flow of revenue coming through the pipeline. Given capacity constraints, get the most revenue by choosing the highest-rated business to fill the available space. This requires the ability to predict demand of all rate levels of business to layer in the highest rates available given demand levels for each day in the future.

While this was happening in airlines since the late 1970s, it was introduced to hotels initially through sales automation that was meant to control the booking of groups, conventions, meetings, and tours. This was in the mid-1980s. The focus was on analysis of group profitability to assess revenue less direct expenses for each component of a group stay, including rooms, food and beverage, and other revenue. The early systems were able to provide some pricing guidelines to sales managers so they could sell more profitable groups and decline those with lower yield. It was a great innovation to factor catering revenue into the total picture when assessing a group's value to a property.

The property management systems, usually responding to user demands, started to develop some built-in rudimentary systems to help give hotel-level managers the ability to build historical demand patterns for comparison to business-on-the-books statistics. There were no predictive algorithms built into PMS systems. Concurrently, corporate level reservation staff would typically scan hotel's availability controls to spot check for appropriate rate or availability restrictions given historical patterns of demand. Some developed their own Lotus 1-2-3 models. Others worked manually.

Revenue Development and Yield Management: How Important Are They?

Probably the single most important controllable variable in day-to-day marketing operations will be revenue development and yield management. While distribution channels, frequency, and other corporate programs provide the infrastructure for a chain's marketing operation, once in place, the incremental differences will be driven by the chain's ability to constantly improve revenue. Cost savings can be a tactic employed as a one-time measure to improve profitability but ongoing incremental benefits possible through cost-saving strategies are limited. The pressure, particularly on public companies, will be tremendous to continually improve profits through revenue growth.

Customer relationship management (CRM) is the latest buzzword in the move toward improving a company's intimacy with its customers. This is the

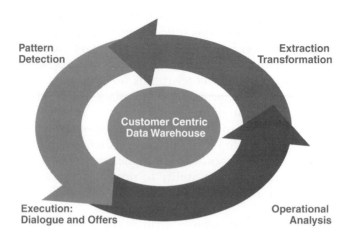

natural evolution from the mass marketing of the last few decades to a closer type of communication that closes the distribution gap between the service provider and the customer. While distribution channels are becoming more and more transparent to the user (i.e., hotel guest), customers expect the hotel chain to know them and will reward those that do with more of their business. There is a relationship between how well a hotel chain knows a customer and how much interractivity exists in their relationship. As the need to know customers better and to create more of a dialogue with them grows, there is a greater need for a CRM or customer relationship management system. In the model on the following page, the four quadrants represent approaches that combine relative measures of knowledge about customers with levels of interractivity. The hotel industry is recognizing the need to move up on these continuums in its quest to differentiate itself to key customer groups. Data warehousing technology will support this business requirement.

The CRM cycle calls for marketers to identify their target markets, differentiate their offerings and message, communicate to selected customer groups, and to then customize based on the feedback they get. A 1997 Coopers & Lybrand study shows that the top three benefits from CRM cited by actual experience in the respondent companies were:

- enhanced targeted marketing
- improved customer segmentation
- increased customer retention

Yield Management is becoming widely practiced in hospitality to enable the industry to improve revenue by applying microeconomic principles to the availability of rates. This discipline is now used in most industries in which capacity is limited and there is lead time for purchase.

In the 1982 bestseller, *Megatrends,* John Naisbitt, predicted the need to not only find a way to deal with the uncertainties of today's marketplace, but also to find a way to predict the future. To be able to anticipate what was going to happen and to plan for it, to maximize resources you have and to maximize revenue from those resources is the goal.

An excerpt from *Scorecard,* the revenue management quarterly, tells us that the main rule of economics today is that you can no longer depend on cost-plus pricing. The power of determining price has shifted from the provider to the marketplace, fueled by the consumer's new "value" mindset, and direct access to a wide range of competitive choices. Today, the concept of price-based costing has driven massive change in the way companies are viewing their internal business and production processes. This publication points out that revenue management, in some form, will be a central and essential core competency in every company, and that consumer profiles will be derived from the universe of consumers in every category, rather than the traditional tiny fractional samples. The individual responsible for revenue management will hold a senior executive post in each major company and the work of this function will be the center of all revenue generating activities and will micromanage all resources to produce the greatest amount of revenue possible.

HOW WILL REVENUE DEVELOPMENT AND YIELD MANAGEMENT CHANGE IN THE FUTURE?

Revenue Development

Methods for revenue development will address the time-honored need to get and keep customers. This will include new techniques for prospecting, retention programs, sales extensions, and cross-selling. Hotel chains are beginning to pursue data warehousing technology to develop better customer profiles.

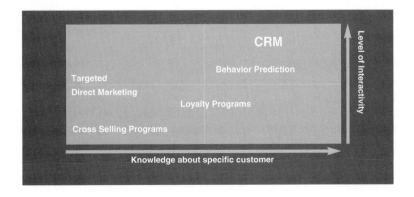

These systems are being applied to improve prospecting so the marketing dollars spent can generate greater revenue returns. They are being used to supplement chain-wide frequency programs so unit-level customer service and local recognition programs can be employed.

Hotels are utilizing new high-tech data mining techniques such as Golden Nugget Maps™ to help identify prospects in areas that are new markets for the hotel or the chain.

The map indicates areas that have been fully penetrated (dark grey), those with a lot of potential and some penetration (medium grey), those with a lot of potential and no penetration (light grey) and those to be ignored (white).

These so-called "golden nuggets" are the geographic markets that are ripest for prospecting. The map shows the hotel has not tapped these areas for business, but from its consumer profile, it appears that it could have a high percentage of qualified prospects. While this type of data mining technique will not guarantee success, it will greatly limit the risk of wasted promotional spending.

Recognition and improved guest service are being utilized equally by large and small chains to gain a more stable loyalty from its guests. Reward-based loyalty programs will continue to grow but the pot cannot continue to grow richer or all chains will lose the ability to cost-effectively retain their most frequent customers. Now that hotel companies have started to examine business levels hotel-by-hotel market segment-by-market segment, it is clear that there are important types of business that are not influenced by the corporate frequency programs. The race for guest loyalty will be won by the hotel companies that have the discipline to deliver guest service consistently, not necessarily those with the richest rewards. It is an area that allows small and large companies to compete on equal footing. The bias built by reward schemes and brand name awareness can be quickly diffused by more effective use of the new distribution channels and more dedicated efforts to give personal recognition and develop dialogues with desirable customer groups.

There will be a move to more personalized marketing, not necessarily to one-to-one, but rather to marketing to small likeminded clusters of customers who have similar traveling needs. Managing this effort will require technology, but this is already affordable today. Those companies that will succeed in this environment will market smarter by using information more intelligently. Developing customer clusters and planning promotions against them will be the basis of the new methods utilized. Less direct sales and more direct marketing. Not necessarily using direct mail, but through the Internet, e-mail, telephone, and through more focused local media. The move will be from market segmentation to micro-segmentation. The computers will support this effort and communication breakthroughs will make this crucial customer information readily available at the point of sale or point of guest contact.

Breakthroughs in wireless technology will further enable this process. There will be a move from "broadcasting" messages to "narrowcasting" mes-

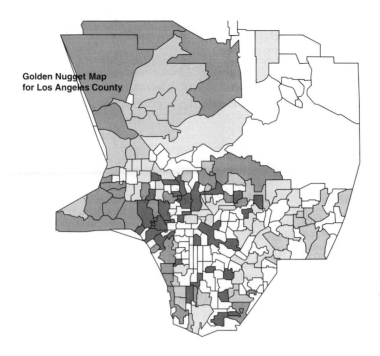

Golden Nugget Map
for Los Angeles County

sages to a much shorter list of individuals who have indicated an interest. This is called "permission marketing" and involves asking the consumer to "opt in" to participation in a marketing program or series of customized offers.

Hotel chains will need to get full buy-in to make this approach a "way of life" in their organizations with support and understanding by operations, finance, and marketing to make it work. The building of customer relationships and the accompanying loyalty will not be "in your face" methods, but rather a series of transparent, silent, hassle-free systems that simplify reservation making, getting the room ready, providing for special needs. The Internet will become an important part of the infrastructure in getting the information to and from customers to assure their needs are met and the process is smooth and hassle-free.

MARKETING METRICS FOR REVENUE DEVELOPMENT

Typical statistics that will be used to measure success in revenue development will be related to customer spending patterns, relative valuation by micro-segment, and development of lifetime value analyses to begin predictive modeling of important customer groups. Anticipating products to be purchased, appeal of promotional offers, and matching micro-segments to need periods will drive the information needs to support the modeling efforts. Typical micro-segments might be Midweek Seniors, Season Switchers, or Commercial Weekend Getawayers.

- **Revenue Generated for Every Marketing Dollar Spent**

  If the marketing budget is $1 million and the revenue generated is $5 million, this metric would be $5. This number must be compared to other numbers in a competitive set for relative comparison.

- **Lifetime Value per Customer**

  The revenue contribution for each customer over the years they are utilizing a hotel or chain must be shown as a cumulative total. If a guest has had 20 stays in a property over a three-year period, his/her total revenue would be the baseline. Then direct promotional costs to acquire and retain this guest along with direct operating expenses would be deducted from the revenue. The ultimate statistic would be the customer's lifetime value.

- **Average Spend per Stay by Revenue Center by Micro-segment**

  Once the clusters or micro-segments are established, all revenue generated for each stay is added together and divided by the number of stays. If a segment has generated $1 million in a given time period and represents 2,000 stays, the average spend per stay is $500.

- **Typical Arrival/Departure Patterns by Micro-segment**

  Each micro-segment will have a typical arrival and departure pattern by day of week. While all 49 combinations can be examined, hotels will be more interested in grouping these arrival/departure pairs for more realistic action. Matching micro-segments to need periods by day of week and key arrival/departure groupings will be essential to maximize revenue opportunities.

- **Revenue per Available Customer (Revpac)**

  There is a limited universe of prospects for each product hotels will sell. There may be only 3,000 households who have the appropriate income and travel profile to utilize a particular property or chain. Using this finite group as the 100 percent potential, it will be essential to measure what revenue is being generated out of the total possible. Quantifying the universe of prospects will become a new science. Even today, this is possible utilizing data mining tools based on geo-demographics in the consumer markets.

- **Attrition Analysis**

  Examining those customers lost to your properties will be as important as examining those you get to come back. Look at the profiles of those lost and be sure to look at patterns of those you are losing. Gather market research information from them to overlay on their last stay data to find out why they left you and where they are going now.

YIELD MANAGEMENT

Since so much of the reservation flow in hospitality is moving toward an electronic medium, the opportunities for yield management are much more promising. The single-image inventory enjoyed by centralized airline systems will soon be found in hospitality. Once all rooms sold through all channels are controlled centrally, the improvements will be enormous.

The cost of distribution has seldom been factored into the yield management equation, and yet, these costs are significant and directly related to the reservation process. Should a channel of distribution be given little or no inventory access if they are a higher-cost type of business than another channel given similar rate levels? While there have been moves in crude ways before to restrict GDS reservations that carry high costs, it is never a scientific method. Now, with a fast track to single-image reservation inventory, the systems will have to calculate costs as well as revenues within the predictive models. Overall demand levels for competitive sets and similar hotels will have to be built into algorithms to more accurately gauge relevant demand flow for future periods.

Very complex and customized technology is being developed by most chains to build decision support models to help the increasingly more sophisticated revenue managers generate higher yields on their business volumes. The major chains are investing in multi-million dollar systems and supplementing the technology with training at appropriate points in the process. The kind of information that will be useful in this world will be reviewing future revenue streams by day of week, by distribution channel, and by market segment all relative to your competitors or similar hotel types. Comparisons to the same patterns in previous periods with known outcomes can be helpful.

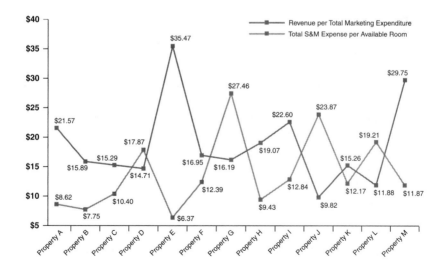

The main complication to yield management is coming from the growth in the Internet-originating reservations. Many new sites with limited ability to display all rates or all room types are emerging. Those with a business model built around a price-oriented purchase such as priceline.com or those selling distressed inventory like lastminutetravel.com will seriously challenge the yield/revenue management systems. Determining what rates should be sold and how to manage inventory in so many new and far-flung channels of distribution will not be a complete change to existing yield systems, but will make them more complex.

MARKETING METRICS FOR YIELD MANAGEMENT

- **Average rate by day of week by market segment**

    One of the most crucial measures for hotels with the perishable commodity of a hotel room is the revenue generated on a day-by-day basis for each source of business. Hotel management need to effectively manage each day individually in order to optimize their revenue.

- **Revenue per available room by day of week**

    It is extremely useful to track your revpar against your competitive set based on differences in each day of week. The Thursdays you have struggled to develop may be consistent with much of your competitive set.

- **Market share by segment by day of week**

    Knowing how each market segment fares on each day is the essence of effective yield management. Overall performance is good to know, but cannot be acted upon without the knowledge of the underlying production in each type of business that constitutes the revenue base.

- **Your hotel's business volume vs. your competitive set for future days (citywide pace)**

    Knowing how much business a hotel has on the books for future periods is important, but even more valuable is knowing how much business is on the books for one trading area, or for one competitive set. What do you have? What is booked overall in the area and do you have your fair share of future bookings?

- **Future volume of business by distribution channel by arrival day of week**

    Just as hotel management wants to track its overall business volume by day in the future, it would also benefit from volume by distribution channel. This will allow the assessment to be done by day of week taking into account the costs of each channel.

- **Net value of each market segment (revenue less distribution costs) by channel of distribution**

Due to the high cost of distribution discussed in the first section of this report, it is necessary for the hotel to consider these costs when assessing the value of each unit of revenue.

RECOMMENDATIONS FOR REVENUE DEVELOPMENT AND YIELD MANAGEMENT

(1) Build a strategy for Customer Relationship Management that addresses every aspect of your relationship with customers.

Look at your account management systems, property-level guest-history functionality, corporate-level loyalty programs, promotional campaign management methods and overall plan for learning what you need to know about your customers.

Look at how your customer knowledge can be utilized to improve guest service, guest retention, and new business development. Try to make it as easy as possible for those at the point of contact (reservations, front desk, and sales staff) to have the information necessary at the time they need it. Try to give these staff members an understanding of how to use the customer knowledge to either improve guest service or guest retention. Be sure you have a method in place to measure guest service and guest retention so you know when your delivery systems are working and when they are not. Make data analysis and the application of the business intelligence you gain seamless to the operational staff and the customer.

Consider how you will use the Internet in implementing Customer Relationship Management (CRM). While the focus of Internet for hospitality marketers has been on its implications for distribution, the ultimate focus will be on creating cyber-communities of consumers with similar interests. Hotels can leverage this environment by building CRM strategies for the Internet. Communication with its customers before, during, and after a stay will be commonplace. Confirmation of needs, solicitation of travel preferences, satisfaction, and future travel planning will be the nature of the dialogue on the Web. It is this dialogue that will cement relationships and form the basis for a new form of customer loyalty. The results of this dialogue will be stored in back-end data warehouses for use in marketing analysis and tactical marketing programs.

Staying current with the explosive growth in communication improvements will be essential. Breakthroughs in wireless technologies will facilitate the move from "broadcasting" to "narrowcasting" messages to individual customers through many new mediums such as personal digital assistants (PDAs), cell phones, and all successive technologies that emerge. "Permission marketing" will be the watchword of the future in this communication plan. Rather than sending many messages to those a vendor thinks are likely to be interested in an offer, they will only be sent to those who specifically choose to participate by opting to be on a distribution list.

Don't confuse data mining with Customer Relationship Management. The former is the data management and analysis toolkit used to understand customer profiles and assess tactical results, the latter is about engaging your customers in a meaningful and mutually beneficial relationship. Data mining is a necessary function in the CRM process, but it is not CRM. The scope, planning, and range of processes and systems affected by CRM are much more complex than the single component of data mining. Think about ways to "CRM-enable" your operational systems. Examine property management systems, reservation systems, Web sites, customer service, front desk, and all related customer contact processes. Use data mining to help focus the efforts on the appropriate customer groups and to analyze results of iniatives undertaken. Use direct mail, direct e-mail, and other personalized communication vehicles to communicate with customers. Use market research to understand what is important to your customers and use task forces of line managers to improve processes so customer preferences are consistently delivered.

(2) Consider cost of distribution when assessing the relative revenue produced by each channel of distribution.

Use data on your hotels' customer base and look at the future business on the books for your hotels' and their respective competitive sets. While measuring your business by market segment is already a major step forward for most hotels, there must be the added layering of distribution channels for management to properly determine relative value of each type of business and, on a micro level, on each customer.

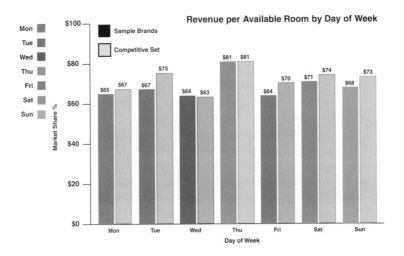

Use your yield management tools to assess revenue but also apply costs since distribution costs are such a significant part of assessing the value of each type of business.

Re-assess the impact of the Internet, particularly how your yield management methodology changes to handle the discount, auction, and distressed inventory sites. The landscape is getting considerably more complex for pricing and inventory management. Be sure you consider the volume of each channel of distribution and the perception given to the consuming public by participation in each. Will they remember they got a great rate on somenew-travelsite.com, or that they stayed in a Sheraton? What portion of your bookings will be by consumers who have learned that waiting to make bookings can be a really good deal? You will need to build the answers to these questions into intelligence on each strata of bookings to fill your hotel(s) so you can make decisions that optimize your revenue.

(3) Channel your resources against business based on the benefit they deliver.

Measure the benefit of each type of business relative to potential demand—not its absolute benefit. Assess what you receive compared to what is available in your marketplace. Create measures of potential demand based on patterns of demand by each type of business you are tracking. Stratify your customers and choose those you want to engage in an in-depth relationship. Don't assume that those who participate in card-based loyalty programs are the only "good customers" worthy of your personal communication. There are heavy travelers who are not loyalty card users. How many stay in your hotels?

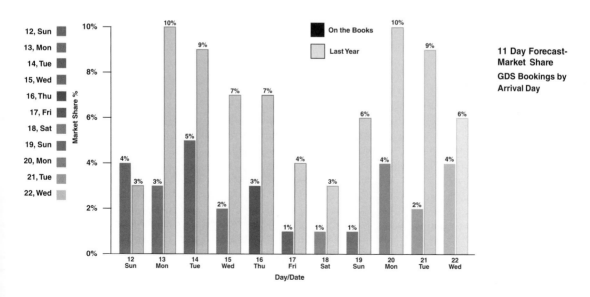

Use all media, including your Web site, direct mail, in-hotel communication, and loyalty card vehicles (e.g., e-mail) to communicate with your selected group of customers. Developing active relationships with a two-way dialogue will maintain loyalty. There will be a lot of competition for engaging in this dialogue so it will take some effort to get it right. Most companies have not yet perfected this except within their frequency/loyalty customer base and it is limited compared to the way it will be in the future. A hotel will need to anticipate customer needs, facilitate all steps in the interaction to be hassle-free, and deliver on personalized needs in a very consistent manner. This will require corporate- and hotel-level participation to get this right along with considerably better technology than is utilized currently in most hotels. Seamless links will be required between reservations, Internet sites, property management systems, customer service delivery systems, and other communication systems such as a direct marketing database. Because of the requirement to deliver personalized services consistently, the base of customers who will benefit must be carefully selected and the revenue they deliver with corresponding acquisition costs carefully scrutinized. A backend data warehouse with data mining tools will be essential for all required analysis.

In the development of revenue management methods, whether they are yield or customer relationship management in nature, the hotel marketer will need to consider the crucial question of who owns the customer? The point of contact that becomes favored by the customer to get information about a product or its pricing, and the way in which the customers choose to interract with the product/service deliverers will strongly impact any hotel or chain's ability to "own the customer." The organization that succeeds most in developing the best primary relationships with its customers will enjoy the benefits of higher revenue and a more secure revenue stream.

Understanding the Complexities of Hotel Global Distribution Systems and Channels

UNDERSTANDING THE HOTEL GDS

The concept behind GDSs is to deliver a product (in this case, a perishable product) to the marketplace quickly, reliably, and cost-effectively for purchase anywhere in the world by any interested party in order to win market share, build customer loyalty, and generate revenues. Within the hotel industry, however, there is no universal definition as to what constitutes a GDS. Traditionally, the term evolved from the airline industry and is often used to refer to the airline reservation systems used by travel agents to connect with hotel central reservation systems (CRSs) and book hotel accommodations for their clients. This chapter takes a much broader perspective, defining GDS as the entire network of people, systems, technology, and distribution channels used to help a hotel sell its products and services. What follows is a more in-depth discussion as to the various components comprising GDS to create an Internetworked environment.

Evolution of GDS in the Hotel Industry

The definition of a global distribution system for hotels evolved from the airline industry. Throughout the 1960's and 1970's, the airlines introduced automated central reservations systems commonly referred to as CRS. American's SABRE and United's APOLLO (now part of Cendant's Galileo) were the two largest. Over time, access to these systems was extended to travel agencies as a way of increasing bookings and reducing overhead. Airlines recognized as early as the mid-1970s that it was cheaper for them to process travel agent reservations electronically (i.e., via computer) versus over the telephone. (Coyne, 1995) As these systems grew in power and reach, they began selling seats for other airlines and forming global alliances with other airlines and travel-related services. They expanded their coverage to include hotel accommodations, rental cars, cruises, travel merchandise, and more. Thus, they became generic, broad-based travel-reservation systems. (Emmer et al., 1993) In return for their services (listings and reservations processing), they charged transaction fees for every booking or sale processed. Hence, they became global distribution systems, where global referred both to international reach and breadth of product offerings. Following suit, the hotel industry began adapting this terminology. With increased emphasis being placed on a global marketplace as the result of increased focus on international trade, travel, and financial markets, it seemed only logical to rename these systems as global distribution systems. Despite this new vision, the focus has mainly revolved around the CRS, which is only one component, albeit an important one, of a hotel GDS.

A hotel GDS is comprised of six core technologies: the hotel PMS, the hotel CRS, a universal "switch" (e.g., THISCO or WizCom), airline GDSs, the Internet and intranets, and a telecommunications wide area network (or WAN). The integration of these various technologies allows hotels to distribute information regarding their rates, availability, and facilities to travel intermediaries and consumers throughout the world. Each of these technologies provides an access point to hotel information and a potential point-of-purchase. It can be said that to achieve competitive advantage, a hotel must have access to the most points of distribution possible at the least cost and provide the complete and accurate information in a seamless manner. To attain this state, several sophisticated automated links or interfaces are required, which integrate these heterogeneous systems and architectures.

Guests Are the Central Focus

To put things into proper perspective, please refer to Figure 1, which illustrates the multi-faceted dimensions of a GDS in the hotel industry. At the heart of this diagram are the guest and all of the information related to the guest. This is a guest-centric model. After all, the guest is the mainstay in the hotel business,

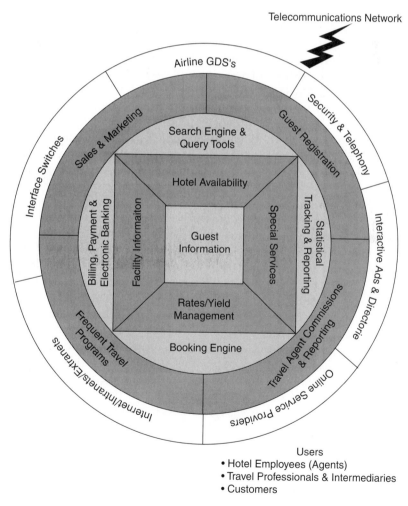

Figure A 1. Understanding the Hotel GDS

something that sounds obvious but is sometimes easily forgotten. Since the guest is the primary purpose of a hotel's existence, it makes sense that he/she serves as the focal point of the distribution system and strategy. Guest information goes beyond the basics of name, address, dates of stay, and method of payment. It must also include guest preferences and guest history. When combined with dates of stay and room request data, this information comprises what is commonly referred to as the guest name record (or GNR).

Building and Shaping a Knowledge Base

With respect to guest information, the goal should be to build a usable knowledge base that will allow hotel service employees to provide a unique, personalized experience. The GDS becomes the central repository and distribution vehicle for this knowledge. The reservations process is often the first encounter with a guest and the primary collection point of vital guest information. This information will then feed subsequent phases of the guest life cycle, namely registration and the guest stay. Therefore, it is incumbent upon the hotel to accurately collect this information up front and subsequently communicate this information to all service delivery points and personnel responsible for providing these services. Each future encounter throughout the chain of interaction with that guest should then call upon and add to this knowledge base so as to provide a more holistic experience of the guest and to create a more extensive understanding of the customer and his/her needs and preferences. By using advanced database technology, this information can then be queried, analyzed, and distributed to all associates in the organization. It is no longer limited to one or two employees who have developed a close personal relationship with the customer. In the end, it is the service received and experienced that will make the overall difference and form the lasting impressions on each guest. Since the reservations process is one of the earliest stages in the guest life cycle, it is the logical starting point to begin collecting guest information.

For repeat guests, the basic information can be retrieved instantly, thereby shortening the process and advancing the level of the exchange to one of greater meaning. Once this information has been collected, it can be shared with each subsequent encounter, thereby reducing the need for basic information exchange and improving the accuracy of service delivery. The nature of these later encounters can also move to the next level—that of more personalized service and richer information exchange. This newly acquired guest information can then be incorporated into the hotel's knowledge base, complementing what already is known. As the cycle continues, the organization reflects a true learning culture.

A GDS collects and distributes reusable information to all service points within the organization. It can also extend the reach of the organization by sharing this information with external entities providing services as an agent of a particular hotel. Businesses require information and knowledge of how to use this information to be competitive. As such, content and access become the two most critical conditions of success. (Vogel, 1997)

A fundamental principle of communication theory is that a network's potential benefits grow exponentially as the number of interconnected nodes increase. (Quinn et al., 1996) Another basic tenet of communication theory is that as communication flows become relatively more convenient, more powerful, and less expensive as the result of new mediums, traditional means of communications become less convenient, less powerful, and more expensive to operate. (Noam, 1997) Both of these maxims apply to a GDS. First, its value increases exponentially as the number of people connected to it increase, and the more information is shared, the more valuable it becomes. Second, through the use of information technology, communications are faster and cheaper than via more traditional means such as by telephone, which is being displaced by newer, cheaper forms of communications such as electronic data interchange (EDI). In most cases, electronic transactions are preferred over less efficient means of communications such as telephone, fax, or electronic mail.

Hotel/Facility Information, Rates and Availability

The next level in the GDS pertains to information regarding the hotel (i.e., property-level data): its facilities, services, rates (rate plans), and availability (room status). Some of this information is static, such as a hotel's address and number of rooms. Other information, such as availability and rates for a given date or date range, is more dynamic, changing frequently during the course of business. The situation becomes more complicated when yield management and pre-negotiated (contract) rates are considered. Managing the currency of information and disseminating this information in real time to all parties and systems in the distribution network becomes an awesome challenge. This is why the proper GDS linkages and infrastructure are vital to one's competitiveness. In essence, the GDS provides each hotel with "shelf space" or market access. How the hotel is indexed, displayed, and subsequently sold will depend upon to which distribution channel(s) a hotel subscribes.

Accessing information about a particular hotel is an important part of the guest shopping experience. This information is critical in the marketing process of a hotel. It also plays a crucial role in setting guest expectations regarding service levels that he/she will likely experience during the actual hotel stay. It is this information that often differentiates between competing hotels. In addition to rates and availability, guests typically want to know directions or how far a property is from a particular location like an attraction, airport, or office park. They also want to know about various room types and amenities (e.g., views), the availability of special services and facilities (e.g., recreation), and what types of events might be featured in the local community during their stay. For many hotels and resorts, the types of service requests are often quite involved due to the many epicurean tastes of their guests and the uniqueness of many of the rooms.

Generally speaking, the more unique a hotel is and the higher level of services it offers, the more complex and time-consuming the reservations process will be. A large number of room types complicates the inventory and selling processes. By creating room types that capture unique room attributes, a hotel can then inventory these attributes and sell them upon request. Thus, there is a higher reliability in guaranteeing that the requested room features can be met. This creates added complexity in selling, yielding, and managing the hotel's room pool than if generic room types are used. In most hotels, it is easy to describe, sell, and substitute a generic king-bedded room. However, in a luxury hotel for example, there are many more dimensions that must be considered such as the decor of the room, the view, its history, etc. Also, for specialty hotels, luxury hotels, and resorts, the types of services requested tend to be more intricate; for example, arranging limousine service, helicopter transport, or a sailing excursion. It is not uncommon for a reservation agent to arrange golf tee times, dinner reservations in one of the hotel's dining facilities, or theater tickets, etc. at the same time the room reservation is made. Thus, the reservation system's capabilities must be extended beyond the reach of hotel rooms and include booking capabilities for all services and facilities offered at a particular resort or luxury hotel. The level of departmental interconnectivity required is higher than that for other hotel segments.

Making information available in a usable format is challenging, particularly when the information must be distributed to the extended sales force (e.g., travel agents, Internet users) via the airline GDSs or to reservation call centers using a chain's CRS. First, this information must be collected and checked for accuracy. Second, it must be organized and put in some meaningful and usable format. This requires that the data are accessible and searchable. It also requires that the information itself is standardized and displayed in a uniform format. For years, hotels have struggled to fit a multitude of rates, room types, and other information into a format compatible for airline GDSs. Often, this compromises the value of the information, making it difficult for a particular hotel to describe and convey the value of its uniqueness or charm. Finally, it must be distributed to all selling points in the distribution network. This includes reservation call centers, hotel sales/reservations associations, travel agents, Internet users, etc. The information must be distributed to anyone, anywhere, and at any time where a reservation can be made—and it must be kept current. The latter stages are often where the difficulties lie due to the complexities of managing multiple distribution channels, many of which require significant manual or human intervention and oversight.

Because of the reliance on older technologies, airline systems, which were originally designed to sell seats on airplanes versus hotel rooms, the amount of "space" allotted for descriptive information and unique property or room attributes is minimal. Moreover, the format in which it is displayed is limited to plain text and is hard for a reservation or travel agent to read, process, and effectively communicate to a guest in a short period of time. Finally, search criteria are limited to only a few qualifiers, making it relatively difficult to discern one property from the next. Information may, and often does, go unnoticed. If information is not properly communicated, it is possible that guests may request and be promised accommodations that a particular hotel cannot meet. This is an all-too-common occurrence. Thus, the overall usefulness of this information is diminished as a result of inadequate technology. Consequently, an over reliance on airline GDSs can lead to more commodity-like positioning, where tangible aspects such as price and location are the basis of product differentiation versus amenities, attributes, and service levels.

Despite their global market reach and deep penetration in the travel agent arena, airline GDSs can clearly be restrictive for hotels because of the way attributes and distinguishing features are displayed and sold. The dynamics of selling a hotel room are different than those for selling an airline seat. There are many more complicating factors, features, and variables, especially when group sales and packages are involved. Therefore, the amount of information needed to complete a sale is greater, particularly as product uniqueness increases. This is one of the many reasons why the Internet holds so much promise for the industry. While airline systems are powerful, use sophisticated technologies, and extend the reach of the hotel industry globally, they can constrain how hotel rooms are displayed, described, and sold. The software used for these applications is complex, dated, and difficult to change. Although these programs work well in the airline industry, they lack important support for the hotel industry.

Tracking and Managing Room Availability

Historically, a hotel's inventory was managed directly at each property. Rooms were then allocated to the various channels (e.g., airline GDSs and hotel CRSs) under an open and close statusing system. Each distribution point only had access to a subset of the hotel's inventory. The approach was mostly manual and required a high degree of maintenance and oversight, and as the number of distribution options increased, so did the complexity of managing a hotel's inventory. If not properly managed, which was often the case due to imprecise forecasting, this approach led to over- or underbooking, two equally unattractive situations. Moreover, consumer confidence in the process was eroded. They were sometimes denied rooms when rooms were available; other times, they were promised rooms when there were none to be had.

Tracking and managing room availability is a fundamental function of a hotel CRS and, therefore, of a GDS. Since rooms (which are a perishable commodity) are the primary products being sold, accurate inventory is paramount. With multiple people selling rooms for multiple properties in multiple locations simultaneously, managing room inventory becomes a daunting chore, especially if the GDS lacks the automated links to provide last-room availability and seamless integration (called Type S connectivity) with each selling point in the network. The process is confounded by the need to simultaneously manage and control several dimensions or attributes (e.g., room type, rate, package, market segment) in order to yield the highest possible revenue for a given night. While most hotel reservations systems can manage multiple dimensions, they are unable to manage them concurrently. As a result, hotel room inventory is subdivided into what is referred to "buckets," which are defined based on the single-most important attribute (e.g., room type) or combination of attributes (e.g., non-smoking king). This approach is limited because it requires rooms to be allocated and because it presupposes that a guest always fits into one of the predefined categories. If not, manual manipulation of the system is required in an attempt to satisfy all of a guest's requests. Additionally, to honor group commitments, many systems require rooms to be pre-blocked (at least by room type) even before definite reservations are received. Consequently, the reservations system will deduct these rooms from the total available supply rather than treat them as an integral part of the hotel's complete inventory.

More sophisticated reservations systems allow further subdividing of the available inventory in each "bucket" or category along a second dimension (e.g., rate) to provide greater control (namely limits, either minimums or maximums, and fences) and interchangeability of room types. For example, either a king-bedded room or a double-double room can accommodate a single traveler requesting a generic room for one night, depending upon availability and demand. In these cases, the system will accept the reservation and adjust the total available inventory appropriately to avoid overbooking without forcing the depletion of a specific room type. These systems also provide the ability to block rooms based on multiple attributes without having to assign a specific room number.

Today's reservations systems are complex, require tight integration with all systems involved in the distribution process, and must be able to manage multiple rate categories simultaneously for multiple hotels. Hotels set up rate scales (typically highest to lowest rates) based on various conditions such as room type and market segment. Each point on the scale is known as a rate category, which can be managed individually with its own set of booking rules, selling restrictions, and inventory limits. The yield management function is involved with defining these different rate categories, setting the various price points, and opening and closing them for sale. This is a dynamic process. Therefore, it is important to have all systems involved in the distribution process linked for the real-time exchange of rates and availability data. For example, rate category A may represent a hotel's rack rate, the highest rate ever charged for a room. This rate category would always be open because no one would ever want to turn away guests who are willing to pay full price. At the opposite end of the spectrum may be rate category G. Included in this category might be rates that have limited availability; for example, the employee rate. Because these generate little revenue, they may be offered in limited supply so that the hotel can generate a profit. This is why travelers are sometimes unable to use travel award certificates even though a hotel has availability. It has availability, just not at the rate requested. In between would be rate categories established for loyal corporate accounts and affinity groups (e.g., AAA and AARP).

Complex algorithms are required to effectively manage, control, and optimize inventory (i.e., open and close availability, set rules and restrictions, etc.) within the reservations system, and then it is incumbent upon the hotel's revenue manager, through its GDS, to ensure that these rules, restrictions, rates, and availability are populated throughout all channels that comprise the GDS. It should be noted, however, that even with these complex algorithms in place, limitations do exist which require manual shifting of inventory to rectify the situation. It would be ideal if there were a "one-button" or automatic update process within the revenue (yield) management system to send all distribution channels and systems like CRS and PMS the latest changes, but, unfortunately, this will take some time to realize. Open systems and standards must first be put in place, but this is an important goal for which we should strive, as it will greatly facilitate inventory management and distribution. Through effective control of room inventory comes increased profitability.

Interfacing and the Drive Toward Seamless Connectivity

Over time, the linkages between a hotel's property-based systems (i.e., PMS) and its chain's GDS and between the hotel GDS and the airline GDSs have improved.[1] However, not all chains have the GDS technology infrastructure in place to support seamless connectivity. Therefore, these organizations must continue to manage multiple sets of books. Because multiple sets of books are still being maintained throughout the distribution network and not always properly synchronized, credibility issues still remain, and hoteliers feel the loss of control over their inventory because they have been "victimized." Their current technology limits their capabilities and creates frustrations that have been eliminated in more technologically-advanced organizations. With more advanced, automated linkages between core systems, much of the manual, human oversight is eliminated, and access to last-room availability is provided to the major points in the distribution network.

The current trend is to move toward seamless connectivity or a single-image inventory, where a travel agent or other member of the extended sales force can "look" directly into and book within a hotel's CRS. (Vallauri, 1995) The industry's current emphasis has been on developing seamless connectivity between a hotel's CRS and the airline GDSs. Emmer et al. (1993) predict that one day, the focus will shift to building seamless access directly between airline GDSs and hotel PMSs. Using the approach of seamless connectivity, a travel agent or other member of the extended sales force is granted access to the same set of information and last-room availability that had typically been restricted to internal sales associates. In effect, this eliminates the need for multiple sets of inventory books, creating a single-image inventory. Since each point in the distribution network has access to and is quoting from the same set of infor-

---

[1] See Vallauri (1995) and Coyne and Burns (1996) for a discussion on the different levels of GDS interfacing: manual, Type B, Type A, and Type S seamless connectivity.

mation, credibility in the process is greatly improved. Instant confirmation numbers (generated by the hotel company's CRS) can be provided, and each hotel company has control over how its properties are displayed and the types of information regarding facilities and services are provided. Complete integration of a hotel's property management system (PMS), CRS, and the airline GDSs is a fundamental tenet to provide travel agents and other external sales agents (including customers who book directly from the Internet) with the ability to book last-room availability right down to the individual property level.

Lack of seamless interfaces and a single-image inventory can prove counterproductive, and in the words of Emmer et al. (1993), suicidal. First and foremost, it is an impediment to delivering consistent, high quality customer service. Without this capability, travelers or travel agents are not necessarily guaranteed access to accurate and timely information. Rates and availability may be obsolete. As a result of misinformation, a hotel or third-party selling rooms on its behalf can unwittingly turn down business when rooms are available or oversell a hotel when rooms are not available. Either situation leads to frustrated customers. For example, a hotel distribution channel may report no availability in the system when, in fact, rooms are available. In this example, hotel room availability was never updated and became unsynchronized with the master inventory. Second, restricted access to inventory and rates creates inefficiencies in the distribution process. It causes the development of a hierarchy with an associated degree of bureaucratic processes. Third, the inconsistencies in rate and availability between distribution channels can lead to distrust and a tainted reputation. Finally, incomplete data necessitate additional steps by the guest or travel agent to fill these informational voids. This typically requires accessing one or more of the hotel's other distribution channels. As a result, the distribution channels are taxed unnecessarily, driving up the cost to maintain them and service the customer. By providing seamless access and a single-image inventory, hotels can reduce their overhead, streamline the process, increase their bookings, and reduce human error. (Emmer et al., 1993)

Yield Management Ramifications

With the advent of yield (revenue) management systems, the rate and inventory management functions become even more complex when utilizing multiple distribution points. In the past, hotels would set their rates seasonally. Other than perhaps for a few special events, a hotel's rate structure was fairly static throughout each season. Introduce yield management, and the dynamics change exponentially. Today, it is not uncommon for a hotel chain to change its rates multiple times throughout the day, based on availability and occupancy projections. Magnify these changes by the number of hotels in a chain, and the volume of rate changes is in the thousands. If the industry adopts dynamic or real-time pricing models (Davis and Meyer, 1998) where rates change continuously like a stock market based on supply and demand, consumer bidding, and other variables, the volume of rate changes would be even more substantial and result in exponential growth. Regardless of the scenario, to be effective, each rate change must be communicated to every distribution channel in the system, as soon as it occurs. This is a daunting task, but with the aid of information technology and a capable technology infrastructure, the update process can be done in a very timely and efficient manner.

Rate management must also take into account the hundreds of pre-negotiated (i.e., contract) rates, numerous affinity rates offered to those who qualify, and total, unconstrained demand. To maintain control over discounting, rate decisions historically were often made at the property level. Today, however, the model is shifting since this is not always feasible, especially when trying to provide more convenient access to customers and travel agents alike. In an interconnected world, rates and availability must be made available to everyone in the distribution network. If not, the problem becomes one of rate integrity. Consumers will lose trust in some channels in favor of others, or worse, they will seek alternative options. To offset this negative image, many hotel companies have introduced "best available rates" (or BARs) programs whereby the rates quoted at any given time are the lowest possible for which that guest qualifies at the time of the request. While this has helped to reduce some of the customer anxiety associated with rate shopping, it has not fully rectified the problem. Guests continue to contact multiple points in the distribution network, searching for the lowest possible rates and verifying the accuracy of rates quoted. This excess shopping overtaxes the distribution channels, consuming valuable time and resources that could be devoted to selling versus validation. Furthermore, it makes it difficult, if not impossible, to capture, categorize, and analyze turndowns (i.e., denials and regrets) across multiple points of distribution, an essential ingredient for calculating total, unconstrained demand for yield management. (Orkin, 1998)

Despite such limitations, the GDS offers several tools to revenue managers. Its automated linkages to a hotel's yield management system ensure that information on the books as well as historical data are accurately and timely fed into the yield management's optimization routines.

After the yield management system has calculated the appropriate forecasts, it can optimize the availability, determine the appropriate rates, and set the selling restrictions and recommended strategies in the reservation system. The rates must then be shared in a timely manner with every channel in the distribution network to enable equal access to travel agents, call center reservation agents, hotel employees, and Internet users alike. Real-time uploading of rates, availability, and selling restrictions is an important GDS function, now that yield management has become commonplace in the industry. Automatic rate uploading is also important with the group sales process for responding to requests for proposals from various groups, travel agents, or wholesalers looking to buy large blocks of rooms. Seamless connectivity, as discussed previously, can alleviate many of these situations and thereby provide booking agents with the best possible rate available given a set of criteria at that moment in time, anywhere in the system.

The requirements for real-time access to rates, availability, and hotel information placed on hotels by customers, travel intermediaries, and the industry itself present some technological dilemmas that must be addressed. In order for hotels to optimize speed and performance of their reservation systems, it is necessary to maintain data in multiple locations. In an online world, distributed databases are a fact of life because people want instant access to everything, whenever and wherever they want. Because of the complexities associated with large databases, it would be incomprehensible for a single database to process all queries and related transactions. Consequently, in order to streamline searches and reduce the amount of processing by a single system, data are distributed to multiple systems and databases. For example, airline GDSs and switches contain a certain amount of hotel information, typically static data but not always. This allows these systems to process initial queries. For example, when a traveler accesses an Internet Web site and searches for all hotels with availability in a given city for a given date range, the query can be processed quickly (i.e., in real time) by searching a database maintained by the Web site engine. Conversely, if the search engine had to check each individual hotel database for which this Web site represents to see if these conditions can be met, the search would take infinitely longer. The compromise that hoteliers make is a trade-off between data redundancy and speed. The data redundancy increases the management burdens because if data are not accurate, customers will be misled. The result will be either oversold rooms or lost bookings, neither of which are attractive alternatives. To overcome this dilemma, hotel organizations must eliminate duplicate data where possible by trying to reduce data redundancies. When not possible, hoteliers must provide database updating and synchronization at routine intervals. Additionally, to enhance real-time access, hoteliers need to ensure high-speed data networks and high performing computer processes and databases to enhance the overall speed of their systems.

The goal should be seamless access to rates, availability, and information to all channels in the network unless otherwise advertised. For example, airlines and some hotels are using the Internet to offer deep discounted fares and rates that are only available via this channel. They do this to provide an incentive to their customers to use a lower-cost booking channel. This approach works so long as all channel operators/users and the customers themselves know what they must do to find and secure the best possible fares or rates. Some hotel companies, however, have resisted this approach in favor of rate integrity. From a guest service perspective, they favor quoting the same rates and availability information from all channels in the network. One approach is not necessarily better than the other. However, each company must set its strategy and understand the consequences. For example, will special discounts offered only on the Internet create more confusion and questions than bookings? The goal should be to find ways to increase bookings and overall yield.

By effectively managing the distribution channels, a hotel can provide incentives to direct customers via those channels that require less overhead to operate than other, more costly ones. Too many special rates and discounts offered to small audiences via specialized channels can be cumbersome to manage, both for a hotel and for a guest. Under such circumstances it may be necessary for guests to use multiple booking channels to shop for and then subsequently book accommodations. For example, a hotel may offer a particular company or group of individuals (e.g., an affinity group) a certain percentage discount off any available, published rate. To shop for the lowest rates, it may be more advantageous to go to the Internet. However, this channel may not accept the corporate account number or a group affinity code to honor the discount. Therefore, a telephone call to another channel may be required to see that the discount is appropriately applied. Use of multiple channels to book a single reservation can add unnecessarily to the overhead of the booking process.

A growing trend in rate management that may help to alleviate some of the problems cited above is the use of "net" rates. With net rates, the hotel provider negotiates rates with various third-party sales agents. These rates represent the lowest rate a hotel will accept on a given day for an available room and for a specified room type. It is then incumbent upon the travel agent to add his/her travel commission if he/she so chooses. Using this approach, hotels can open their availability to all channels. The booking method and the relationship between a hotel and the booking channel will determine whether or not the booking can receive a commission. This approach ensures that travelers are always getting quoted the best possible rates, given their room requests, dates of stay, and preferences. However, it poses new ethical dilemmas for travel intermediaries. If a traveler requests rate and availability information for a hotel which lists rooms available on a net basis (i.e., they are non-commissionable), will the agent honor the guest's request and book his/her reservation or will the agent try to persuade the guest to select an alternative room type or hotel in order to receive a commission? One would hope that a guest's interests are always placed first. The implications for a traveler are twofold. First, a traveler must select reputable agents and build a trusting relationship. Second, a traveler will need to shop agencies to see which one has the best relationship and negotiated rates with the travel provider of choice. Here again, the focus is on aggregation. The top volume producers are likely to have the advantage and negotiating clout.

The central issues when looking at rates and availability information are where this information should be stored and where control over the master books should be maintained—at the property or at some central location. Traditionally, this control has been held at the local or property level. However, chains are increasingly favoring a more centralized approach, with input and override capabilities from the local level. Hensdill (1996) suggests that with single imaging, centralized inventory management is the logical approach since it provides a single point for rate dissemination. Additionally, she envisions centralized yield management. The type of centralization to which Hensdill (1996) refers relates mostly to centralized processing and management. Yet, the implications are more far-reaching than she implies. What if the large chains decide to yield by city or by region versus by hotel? Some of the leading chains with a significant operating base and products representing multiple product lines in a given city could reshape the entire competitive playing field. The debate here should focus less on where the data reside; this point becomes inconsequential as long as all points in the distribution network have concurrent access to the same information.

By linking revenue management systems with the hotel GDS, seamless access to rates, restrictions, and selling strategies becomes more probable. In turn, this improves consumer confidence in each channel and lessens the number of inquiries received by each channel from those shopping rates or seeking confirmation of the rate(s) already quoted. The even bigger and far-reaching potential of better channel management, however, is the ability to yield by *profit* as opposed to revenue. Instead of simply managing yield based on revenue, one can now consider the possibilities of factoring in the acquisition costs of business. This new approach to yield would allow hoteliers to strengthen bottom-line performance rather than top-line performance by being even more selective in the business it selects when they must decide between displaced room-nights.

Critical Technologies: The Search and Booking Engines

Underlying the GDS components described above are two critical technologies: the search engine (or querying tools) and the booking engine. With the advances of the Internet, it is easy to see how essential a fast and reliable search engine is to quickly wade through volumes of information. A search engine is not just for the Internet-based distribution channels. It plays a vital role in all channels where a guest must find appropriate accommodations given a set of criteria (e.g., location, vicinity to attractions, price range, amenities, types of recreation), personal preferences, and company travel policies (if applicable). The GDS must provide tools that allow customers and end-users alike to navigate quickly and find the accommodations that meet the requests at hand, within a hotel, a product line, a chain, or even among a group of competing hotels featured in the same travel booking system (e.g., Orbitz, Expedia, or Travelocity). The robustness of these search tools becomes more important as the discriminating features between hotels become fewer and as guests' needs become greater. The booking engine is the vital link to convert a prospective customer into an actual customer. After the appropriate accommodations have been found, the booking engine allows the guest, agent, or reservations associate to process the booking and update the inventory throughout the GDS network.

Sales and Marketing with GDS

Sales and marketing is another key aspect of the GDS network. Traditional views of a reservation system and its agents have focused on order taking processes. While this is one component of the activity, the central elements are sales and marketing. The reservations staff is and should be viewed as part of the hotel's sales force. Likewise, the GDS should be viewed as a sales tool, not just as an order entry device. The sales and marketing component becomes more obvious when one considers group sales and the role of the sales office in attracting and booking groups and conventions, maintaining leads, and managing correspondence and sales contracts. Here the dynamics become more complex, as the GDS is frequently required to match the availability of sleeping rooms with that of meeting and convention space, recreational facilities, and destination amenities and activities. Additionally, a GDS must facilitate a hotel's ability to analyze and respond to requests for proposal (RFPs).

Important components of the GDS include the sales forecast book and the function book (diary). The GDS manages and reports on availability and rates as well as group ceilings, cut-off dates, pick-up rates (i.e., booking pace), attrition, etc. It also bridges the sales department with the rooms and reservations departments and helps to eliminate duplicate transactions or needless handoffs. Upon acquisition of a group contract, rooms must be reserved and blocked, using the group rooming list to build individual reservations for each member of the group. Real-time access to room availability, rates, cut-off dates, and selling strategies is just as important with the sales office as it is for travel agents. The GDS becomes a tool that helps them determine whether business should be accepted or declined. Built-in "what-if" tools, modeling capabilities, historical data, and knowledge can provide the necessary decision support in real time. If decisions are not properly made, the hotel's REVPAR may suffer.

Heretofore, much of the attention placed on electronic bookings under the umbrella of global distribution systems has been geared towards transient guestrooms rather than on meeting space and group sales. Fortunately, however, this is changing as chains look to advance their capabilities and level of automation to support group sales and conventions. These areas offer significant opportunities for hotels to enhance their lead-tracking capabilities and service levels, not to mention maximize revenue opportunities. There is no question that the group sales, meetings, and conventions functions are more complex than the reservations function for transient sleeping rooms. The number of variables and the amount of information that must be exchanged are far greater. For example, in arranging meeting space, one must consider the types of meetings, the space requirements, room layout, menu planning, amenities, rate structures, billing, rooming lists, and more. Because airline GDSs and universal switch companies have not geared their products to enable the selling of such services and due to the lack of standards in this area, the development of centralized sales and marketing systems has lagged behind that of reservation systems.

Opportunely, this is changing. Several hotel chains have implemented centralized sales and marketing systems that allow agents to sell meeting space and group rooms within their respective organizations. While traditionally focused on lead generations and referrals, these organizations are being transformed into full-service booking centers. The marketplace offers several products to support these functions including products from Micros/ Fidelio (Fidelio Sales and Catering), National Guest Systems (Miracle), New- market International (Global Delphi), and SABRE Decision Technologies (En- vision/Function Book).

Via the Internet, new tools are emerging to help meeting planners shop for and book convention and meeting space. These tools aid in shopping desti- nations and facilities, issuing requests for proposals, and finding special deals (hot dates). These new tools are a welcome relief to meeting planners who typ- ically spend countless hours and develop frustration when planning meetings and conventions. As an illustrative example, consider a large, international company that would like to plan its annual sales and marketing meeting for ap- proximately 500 associates. This company's preference would likely be to hold its meeting in a major metropolitan city offering a wide variety of entertain- ment and recreational facilities, not to mention a destination that would at- tract the widest number of participants possible. Naturally, the company would be looking for the most affordable accommodations possible, given its set of re- quirements. For the meeting planner assigned to coordinate all of the arrange- ments for this event, the planning process is rather daunting. The list of possible cities is endless: Paris, Barcelona, Seoul, New York City, etc. The chal- lenges include finding hotels and meeting space that can accommodate a group of this size for the given dates and offer the various recreational facili- ties and amenities desired by the group, coordinating transportation, etc.—all within an acceptable price range. As one might suspect, the combinations and permutations of planning such an event are overwhelming given the level of de- tails and the number of variables that must be considered (e.g., sleeping rooms, meeting space, catering, transportation, recreation). The process is even more complicated if the company is flexible on the dates of its meeting in order to achieve better rates.

The above example represents a significant opportunity for hotel GDSs. Hotel companies that can facilitate such shopping, planning, and bookings will be able to differentiate themselves through increased service. A sophisticated hotel GDS should allow meeting planners the opportunity to enter a list of pa- rameters and preferences for a given meeting. The system, in turn, would pro- vide a listing of hotels and rates that match the guidelines, dates, and specifications entered. It could even suggest alternative dates and locations that would fill off-peak demand and offer clients better rates. In the end, clients will have a smaller pool of options, thus allowing them to shop in a more timely and efficient manner. The amount of time and the cost of shopping are drasti- cally reduced.

In return for such convenience, clients will appreciate the ease in which they can do business with a hotel company, which will likely become the ba- sis for building a long-lasting relationship. For hotel companies, developing such capabilities offers tremendous opportunities for building competitive advantage. Competitive advantage can come through developing customer loyalty as well as through new opportunities to win new business and maximize revenues. Consider a large chain with multiple convention and resort hotels that might be eligible for such business. With a sophisticated hotel GDS in place, the hotel company could quickly and easily assess the business opportunities and determine which facility or facilities could meet the client's needs, and provide the most profitable opportunities for the hotel company.

With a well-connected GDS, work can now be completed closest to the source of activity, thus providing better and timelier service to the customer and creating an end-to-end transactional environment. After all, this is the fundamental purpose of a GDS and the main tenet of the hospitality business.

The Extended Sales Force

The hotel property reservations and sales force is augmented by a number of entities. For chains, reservation call centers, regional and national sales offices, and sister properties/brands are logical extensions of the sales force. These agents are equipped with the tools, technology, and know-how to cross-sell any number of brands, products, and services within a given hotel company as well as share leads, referrals, turndowns, and overflow demand.

Another natural element in the global distribution network for the travel industry is the travel agent and other intermediaries such as corporate travel planners, wholesalers, consolidators, bucket shops, destination marketing organizations, convention and visitors bureaus (CVBs), etc., or in the case of large groups and conventions, incentive houses and housing bureaus (organizations that work with large conventions to plan and book lodging accommodations and process the rooming lists). Accordingly, a travel intermediary is anyone or any organization that plays a role in influencing a travel purchase decision or in booking the actual reservations. There is a certain amount of discretion exercised by these intermediaries when selecting or assisting in the selection of hotel accommodations for their clients. The travel agent, for example, provides a useful service to hotels by marketing their facilities and booking accommodations for those who wish to stay there. In turn, they expect compensation in the form of commissions, typically 10% of room revenues for each reservation booked.

Other entities that should be considered as part of the extended sales force include Internet search engines, Web portals, online booking services, travel clubs, auction sites, and bidding services. These play important roles in the matchmaking processes and are gaining popularity and usage.

Electronic bookings are inherently less expensive to process than bookings made over the telephone because they reduce the labor required and eliminate the costs incurred when using a toll-free number. Thus, hoteliers should place greater emphasis on establishing electronic networks and the digital infrastructure required to promote and facilitate electronic bookings. Hotels that can drive up the number of electronic bookings can substantially decrease their overhead.

Travel Agent Commissions

Timely and accurate payment of these commissions has been known to improve travel agent loyalty. Therefore, many of the larger chains have developed and implemented centralized applications to track, report, reconcile, and pay travel agent commissions. Although this may be viewed as more of a support service, it is included here as part of the GDS system because of its overall influence and significance in the travel booking process. To work successfully, the GDS must track travel agent activity by IATA number. This includes reconciliation between expected room-nights versus actual room-nights, since reservations can be canceled, extended, or shortened. Proper and timely administration of this function reduces unnecessary overhead researching reservations after-the-fact and matching them with guest folios. In the end, a centralized travel agent management system provides a valuable service to an important marketing arm of the hotel. Slow payments and inaccurate tracking of travel agent bookings are commonly raised concerns by travel agents. (Schulz, 1994) For example, if a reservation made by a travel agent is modified at a later date by another distribution channel or at the time of registration, the travel agent may not receive credit for channeling the booking to the hotel. By using automation to rectify these problems, hotels can maintain positive relationships and ties. As a result, the travel agent distribution channel can be a rewarding and lucrative one for a hotel by filling rooms that might otherwise go unsold. Travel agents, when used correctly, can be an effective sales force for hotels, not an adversary as many hoteliers view them. (Schulz, 1994) However, this channel also requires careful oversight so that commissionable rooms are not displacing higher-margin rooms coming from noncommission-able channels.

Other External Linkages

A GDS must also provide linkages to various external systems such as electronic banking, and airline frequent travel programs. Online billing, banking, and electronic funds transfer are growing trends. Corporations are seeking ways to control and reduce travel and entertainment expenditures. As part of this new wave of cost-consciousness, they are turning directly to the suppliers to provide detailed reporting on their company's purchase activity. Furnishing this transaction history, summarizing it, and presenting it to client organizations in a meaningful format will become new sources of value-adding services and strengthen the customer-supplier alliance that is so commonly sought after by customers in this competitive environment. Corporate intranets will help to provide this detail and electronically bill large organizations in regular intervals for all travel that has occurred company-wide. Billing transactions can then be electronically matched and verified against employee expense reports. Companies could then streamline their accounting and accounts payable departments and submit a single check, or better yet, make an electronic payment each month to their hotel supplier(s) of choice. This level of automation would also streamline the accounting process for a hotel, ensure faster payment, and reduce float.

The Internet model of commerce (e-commerce) is adding to the speed in which electronic payment is becoming an acceptable alternative. In the traditional model, a GDS must be able to authorize credit card accounts to guarantee reservations. In some cases (e.g., advance purchase), the purchase occurs at the time of reservation. Therefore, the GDS must be equipped to handle an electronic credit card settlement. In the future, as electronic payment and usage of smart cards grow, a GDS will need to be equipped to handle full settlement and funds transfer with various forms of electronic currencies. A GDS will also need to be more adept at dealing with and converting foreign currencies, thus emphasizing the global nature of the industry. This means that reservations should be quoted in a guest's native currency (or the currency of his/her choosing) while taking into account the appropriate, up-to-date currency exchange rates.

Frequent travel points are quickly becoming a new form of currency, thanks in part to new promotions by credit card companies, telephone companies, and others. Affinity cards allowing consumers to earn points for travel have mushroomed. Hotels have long maintained relationships with airline frequent travel programs to help build and earn customer loyalty. Staying at hotels often earns guests bonus mileage on their airline carrier of choice. Therefore, hotels must include membership information for each of their guests in their guest history and profile systems. Managing these relationships, the various promotions, and the awarding of points requires strong technological ties between the hotel company and the participating airline. The GDS provides the vital linkage. It must store the appropriate rules and bonus promotions and forward guest account information to the selected airline program when points have been accrued as the result of a hotel stay. Successful links require that a hotel's GDS communicate and pass the necessary information to and from the hotel property management system. In turn, the GDS must be able to forward this information reliably to each participating airline program. Equally important is a growing demand for guests to have the ability to check account balances, redeem points, and request room upgrades instantaneously during the reservations process. In order to meet such demands, a GDS must have the proper real-time linkages to a frequent travel system.

Airline GDSs

Fundamental to today's hotel GDS strategy is connectivity to the many airline GDSs because they provide access to the travel agent market and because they are increasingly being used as the backbone, information source, and booking engine of many Internet travel booking services. In short, airline GDSs are a prominent source and distributor of hotel information (e.g., rates, availability, etc.), which is supplied to them by the participating hotels.

Through consolidation, the number of primary airline GDS vendors (i.e., dominant, global players) has been reduced to four: Amadeus, Galileo, SABRE, and Worldspan. Each vendor is vying to control the world's supply of airline seats, rental cars, and hotel accommodations. As previously mentioned, while the hotel industry has enjoyed a large degree of success through airline GDSs, this technology is unable to fully and properly represent hotels and their unique attributes. After all, these systems were initially designed to sell airline seats, which have very different and far less complex characteristics than hotel rooms. Other problems include outdated technology (these systems date back as much as 30 years), inflexible programming languages, costly maintenance and administration, complex and expensive interfaces, time-consuming updates, and rising transaction fees. Hence, hoteliers are growing increasingly dissatisfied with the capabilities of airline GDSs, and in an age of direct marketing customized to each individual consumer, the airline GDSs are showing their shortcomings. However, many obstacles preclude the development of a replacement system, including cost, technical expertise, and market penetration. Since airline GDSs continue to hold a lock on distribution, play a critical role in reaching key markets, and are used as the primary booking engine for so many distribution channels today, their use will likely continue for years to come, even though in some situations they may be bypassed.

Universal Switches

Universal switches are communications devices that essentially translate, convert, and exchange information between hotel systems (CRSs or PMSs and airline GDSs). Today, these switches help to level the playing field, providing all hotels, independent and chain-affiliated alike, with equal access to the airline GDSs, without the need to develop and maintain multiple, costly interfaces to each airline GDS. The marketplace features two switch providers: Pegasus Systems' THISCO and Cendant's WizCom. These vendors provide competing services, and their universal switches have become among the most vital components in the hotel GDS strategy because they provide hotels with universal access to airline GDSs, travel Web sites, and more. They provide a cost-effective vehicle in which hotels can be represented and sold via multiple distribution channels, complete with last-room availability—without the need to develop new interfaces for every new distribution channel that emerges.

As the number of distribution options grows, connectivity to these switches becomes more valuable. For example, Pegasus' TravelWeb and WizCom's TravelWiz are logical extensions of the services these switches provide. Both are Internet booking services that are connected to their respective switches to provide consumers with online hotel booking capabilities. With a switch in place, hotels need only develop and maintain (note: these could be outsourced, if desired) one interface to the switch of choice. The switch provider will then develop and maintain all linkages to external systems. Although there are still subscription fees, transaction costs, and interfaces to be maintained, the overhead is significantly lower than maintaining separate links to each of the airline GDSs, Web booking services, etc. Additionally, the switch vendors help provide more leverage for the hotel industry when trying to negotiate for added functionality in each airline GDS. Because of the connectivity they provide, the switch companies are quickly becoming one of the most influential and strategic components in a hotel GDS network.

Enter the Internet, Intranets, and Extranets

Throughout this chapter are references to the Internet, company intranets, and extranets as growing parts of the hotel global distribution network. These entities and the assorted technologies they use (e.g., search engines, filtering tools, multimedia, push technology, software agents, etc.) are among the fastest growing components of the hotel GDS environment and offer the most potential for reshaping how the distribution network reaches its constituents. Hotel property management systems and reservation systems are becoming "Web-enabled" to support Internet bookings without having to rely on intermediary systems like airline GDSs and switches. These tools offer new alternatives for bypassing traditional GDS players, and they provide anytime, anywhere access to reservation services. Reservation channels that bypass airline GDSs and travel agents provide streamlined access and reduce transactional overhead. With the use of open standards, the Internet also has potential for serving as a company's wide area network (WAN) that connects multiple sites (hotels, call centers, offices, etc.), intermediaries, and customers. Taking advantage of the Internet's communications and networking capabilities will enable hotels to further reduce their operational overhead.

Electronic commerce is not a new concept. It has been around for some time. What is new, however, is the increased attention on electronic commerce because of the role of the Internet. The Internet essentially provides a cost-effective infrastructure for communications, standards, and a set of tools necessary for businesses to take advantage of electronic commerce, either business-to-business (B2B) or business-to-consumer (B2C). What was once affordable by only large organizations is now attainable by small companies and individual hotels. Expensive, private data networks between two companies can now be replaced by the Internet, a public access information highway, thereby enabling electronic commerce between any organization and consumer with access to the Internet.

The Internet and the lodging industry are considered to be a good match for each other for the following reasons cited by Chowdhury et al. (1997) and Wada (1997):

1. The Internet communicates rich content extending beyond room rates and availability. Pictures, video, maps, and more assist hotels in proactively selling their products. These sites are more than just order-takers.

2. The majority of consumers book their own lodging accommodations rather than relying on travel agents.

3. Internet booking sites are targeting the customer directly rather than travel professionals. Thus, these services are making it easier and more convenient to shop and book travel. Plus, they are complementing their Web sites with additional tools, information, and services to ease the travel planning process.

4. The Internet supplements booking services provided by reservation agents at call centers.

The Internet covers the entire gamut of lodging accommodations. Not only does it provide information and booking services for all of the traditional lodging segments (i.e., budget to luxury), but it also provides access to bed and breakfast establishments, country inns, hostels (youth and elder), cruises, campgrounds, timeshares, and even home exchanges. The geographic regions covered are just as expansive, ranging from major metropolitan areas to some of the most remote locations known. This adds to the richness of content available and makes the Internet the most comprehensive source of travel information, anywhere in the world.

Many hotel companies are aggressively pursuing use of the Internet to market their properties, disseminate information, correspond interactively and instantaneously with their customers, and extend their booking channels. They are frantically trying to figure out the critical success factors of the digital economy, what have become commonly and collectively known as the C's of the Internet world: *content, community, commerce, customization, convenience, context, connectivity,* and *critical mass*. To many, the Internet represents an economically appealing opportunity for redefining their fundamental business model. The goals are to enhance the customer value proposition, to establish customer intimacy, and to build guest loyalty by taking advantage of one-to-one marketing opportunities and by creating enriched, personalized consumer shopping experiences through the use of collaborative filtering tools and non-intrusive software agents that track users' behavior to learn their interests and tastes. The benefits to the consumer are individually targeted promotions, suggestive selling, and tailored experiences when interacting with company personnel or when paying a visit to its Web site.

Business-to-business commerce over the Internet also presents attractive business opportunities and is being spurred by the rise of intranets and extranets. These technologies offer hotels vast potential in reducing the dependency on travel intermediaries and airline GDSs. They also offer great promise in cutting distribution [channel] costs and overhead while building customer loyalty and switching costs.

To the consumer, the Internet is a powerful, convenient, and invaluable tool to explore destinations and shop for travel accommodations. To many, it is quickly becoming an indispensable resource. It provides a wealth of current information and resources (e.g., maps, currency conversion, travel advisories, weather forecasts, frequent travel account balances, calendar of local events, and more). With the click of a mouse button, consumers can easily compare hotel properties, rates, and travel destinations. Graphics and multimedia tools allow visual inspection of the accommodations, facilities, and surrounding area so guests know what to expect before they arrive. The Internet is widely used by consumers to hunt for travel bargains, and with push technology and smart agents, comparison-shopping and bargain hunting become almost effortless. Electronic monitors of rates and fares (sometimes called e-savers) notify consumers via electronic mail. There are even sites available where consumers can specify their price threshold or participate in an on-line auction and bid for travel accommodations. In other words, consumers dictate the prices they are willing to pay. What the Internet means is that consumers are more in control of the purchase process and are more informed—which may equate to more demanding. Increasingly, the trend points towards the potential for dynamic pricing or what Davis and Meyer (1998) call real-time pricing models, where price fluctuations occur constantly and instantaneously much like that of a stock market where prices are driven by the volume of trading. If successfully adopted in the hospitality industry, this could take revenue (yield) management concepts to a whole new level.

For hoteliers, these developments may provide attractive alternatives for selling distressed inventory, boosting occupancy levels during off-peak times, and providing consumers with inexpensive, low-risk trial usage opportunities, but if successful, they will likely change the dynamics of customer-supplier interaction and the way room inventory is managed, controlled, and sold. More sophisticated software applications will be required to monitor and allocate room inventory to these emerging distribution channels.

Despite the limitations of today's technologies (e.g., modem speed, software user-friendliness, etc.), millions of people are accessing the Internet and booking travel. With more advanced features, better organization, and faster performance, all of which are promised as part of Internet2 and its complement the Next Generation Internet (NGI),[2] the number will only skyrocket.

Agenting Transactions and Relationship Management

The Internet is bringing a sense of reality to the "virtual enterprise." It is also giving rise to agenting transactions and relationship management. In a sense, it is a preview of what is yet to come. The convergence of personal computers, telephony, the Internet, television, other forms of media, and feature-rich software will ensure that new forms of electronic commerce take shape. By providing universal access to information, the Internet has the potential to transform commerce, from marketing to consumption. Enhancements in personal digital assistants, smart agent technology, information appliances, wireless communications, and interactive television will fuel new forms of

[2] For further information regarding these developments, please refer to *http://www.internet2.edu.*

commerce. Moreover, the consumers' quests to redefine price-value relationships (i.e., higher quality at lower cost, delivered faster and more customized) for the products and services they buy will not only require but demand new forms of commerce and new channels of distribution—all of which require technology to deliver. Tantamount to this new paradigm created by the Internet will be an increased focus on transaction-based economics, where fees are charged for actual usage, sales, bookings, leads generated, etc.

Chat Rooms, Discussion Groups, and Bulletin Boards

Another component of the Internet that should not be overlooked is the Web's word-of-mouth capability. One should not underestimate its ability to amplify people's feedback, both positive and negative, and its ability to outlive traditional forms of communication. Some companies routinely monitor these forums to gain valuable customer feedback and insight as to customer/market needs. They also monitor these forums for references made about their companies or products and provide "damage control" when necessary.

Discussion or "chat" groups, news groups, and bulletin boards create a sense of community and build loyal followings. From a consumer's perspective, these forums provide precious insight that enables them to make more informed purchase decisions. The information garnered here can guide consumers in the selection of a hotel product or company just as easily as it can steer them away from one that resulted in a negative experience for someone else (even if the people have never before met). For example, Amazon.com uses these forums to advertise and build hot links to its electronic bookstore. With this approach, the company can customize reading lists for each special interest group because their demographics are well-defined. The result: discussion groups provide and generate leads and referrals for Amazon.com. In the future, smart agents, or as Tapscott (1996) refers to them, "knowbots" or simply "bots," will automatically read, evaluate, and filter the content of these discussion groups and use it to feed the selection and decision criteria for each and every purchase decision.

Internet Service Providers

Extensions of the Internet are the online service providers such as America Online, EarthLink, MSN, and others. These services provide users with easy access to travel booking services through alliances and connectivity to key travel databases, many of which are powered by airline GDSs.

Intranets and Extranets

One of the fastest growing markets for electronic commerce is the business-to-business marketplace via intranets talking to each other to comprise an extranet. Business-to-business transactions are rising in volume via the connectivity of multiple intranets in what have become known as extranets.

Leading many of the new developments in intranet development and online travel is computer giant Microsoft. In July of 1996, Microsoft formed an alliance with American Express, the largest travel agency network in the world with travel bookings in excess of $15.1 billion (US), to provide an online booking service for corporate travel. ("American Express and Microsoft," 1996) The goal of this alliance is to embrace Internet and intranet technology to revolutionize how corporate travel is booked. According to American Express, 66% of its corporate customers will likely use Web-based interactive booking by 1999. (Christensen, 1997) The American Express/Microsoft product, called American Express Interactive, will help companies control travel expenditures, the third-largest controllable expense in most companies, by enforcing corporate travel policies and making pre-negotiated rates accessible to all company associates. The product provides business travelers with a fast, convenient, and secure method to book travel accommodations consistent with corporate travel policies and guidelines directly from their personal computers. At the same time, the system will provide better control, expense management, and increased savings to companies who choose to implement the system.

The possibilities for using the Internet are many and limited only by one's imagination. In time, the convergence of telephony and computers will enable real-time transmission of voice and video using the Internet to communicate with anyone in the world, regardless of what type of telephones or computers are used on either end. While holding a conversation, the users can continue to surf the Internet, download or transfer files, and watch videos. This research explores at greater lengths the many developments, capabilities, and services available using these technologies as channels for distribution.

Supporting Entities and Technologies

The hotel GDS model would be remiss if it did not include various support entities. Underlying the entire GDS model is an intelligent telecommunications and security infrastructure that makes it all possible. This formidable and sophisticated infrastructure must maintain a high degree of reliability, offer high-speed throughput, and provide secure transmissions. With the convergence of computers, telephone, and televisions, these networks must be able to concurrently handle large volumes of multimedia traffic. This infrastructure includes the telephones, cable, routers, firewalls, encryption, and the networks that allow for the secure exchange of data, voice, and multimedia to sell and market the hotels. Traditionally, these networks were private networks, built and supported by each organization or outsourced. Today, they also encompass public networks like the Internet. These networks, in and of themselves, are extremely complex and include a number of devices from telephone switches, satellite dishes, and networks to computer monitors (to track network traffic), security devices, and more. All combined, these components comprise the information superhighway for the organization. They must be intelligent to route traffic via the fastest and most cost-effective path possible. They must also be smart enough to reroute traffic in the event of a network or system outage, and they must be secure to limit access to only authorized individuals and entities. The intelligence built into the network ensures its reliability, security, and operability without a lot of human interfacing. While most of the network functions are behind the scenes, they are critical to the success of the GDS model.

Telecommunications, Telephony, and Networking

There are also a variety of telephony products, services, and components that are used to make reservation call centers more productive and efficient. Most visible is the toll-free number, which until recently was country-specific. Today, toll-free numbers are global, allowing a single number to be advertised worldwide. Call centers use automated call distributors (ACD's) which route calls to available agents, sometimes even at other hotels or call centers. They also provide meaningful reports regarding agent productivity, talk time, and total time spent waiting in the queue (i.e., hold time). Caller ID is another form of telephony service that can benefit the reservation process by helping to recognize a caller and retrieve his/her travel profile and most recent reservation before the call is answered. These are just a sampling of many of the telephony components that comprise the hotel GDS environment.

Another support component of a hotel's GDS network is marketing media and collateral: advertisements (print, television, radio, billboards, Internet, etc.), promotions, and directories. Traditionally, these elements would likely have been omitted because they were unidirectional, print-only media. However, in today's interactive, electronic world, the distinction between these forms of marketing collateral and online booking systems becomes blurred. Now, they are instrumental in alluring customers to booking venues. For example, electronic "click-it" advertisements or directories on the Internet can easily and transparently be connected to online booking services. Therefore, they are no longer considered outside the realm of the GDS network but rather an integral part of it.

Statistical Reporting and Data Mining

Statistical tracking, reporting, warehousing, and data mining represent additional support functions. A hotel GDS has become instrumental as a primary feed for systems such as these that support aggregate or consolidated reporting. While their functions may not necessarily serve the day-to-day operations of the business, they do provide hotels with vital information regarding the demographics of their customers, their buying habits, their individual preferences, and the method of booking. For most hotel companies today, these technology components represent some of the hottest in the industry because they help organizations better understand their customers, group them into like segments, service their needs, and optimize their margins based on consumer types and segments. In the end, they can support relationship building that is requisite for one-to-one marketing. In many instances, the reservations process is a guest's initial contact with a hotel. It also serves as one of the primary information collection points in the guest life cycle. Therefore, it is compulsory for each hotel to ensure accuracy at this phase in the guest life cycle since the information collected here feeds all subsequent phases and ultimately builds the data warehouse. Successful data mining will only be as reliable as the quality of the information entered.

The People Element

Lastly, the component that has been missing in the model until now is people. People—and soon their technological counterparts like smart software agents and voice-activated response systems—are an essential component of any hospitality business, and the GDS model cannot function without them. People categorically refer to the obvious users of the system like a hotel's reservations staff and the reservation agents at the central call center. People also refer to the extended sales force such as travel agents, wholesalers, representatives at sister properties/products, CVB staff, etc., and of course, people refer to the not-so-obvious, the customers themselves.[3] Traditionally, customers would not be considered as users of the GDS system. Their use of GDS services and interaction would be indirect through travel agents or hotel reservations staff. With the Internet and other forms of online booking, customers are now part of the sales force. They are booking hotel rooms for themselves, their families, their associates, and their friends just as a travel agent would do. They can also instantly communicate experiences, both positive and negative, to hundreds and thousands of people with a few keystrokes and the click of a mouse. Therefore, they must be factored into the GDS network much in the same manner as any other system user or agent. In summary, anyone who has access to the GDS has the tools and knowledge to carry out a transaction. In essence, each and every person is now an "expert" in nearly every sense, just as a travel agent, corporate travel planner, or hotel reservation agent.

The GDS as an "Ecosystem"

From the model depicted in Figure 1, it is now possible to understand just how vast and complex a hotel GDS really is and why it is such an important component to a hotel's IT portfolio. Because of its reach and interdependence upon so many other systems or entities, it is appropriate to describe a hotel GDS as a business ecosystem. (Moore, 1996) It provides the infrastructure or, as others (e.g., Davis and Davidson, 1991; Tapscott, 1996) have coined, the "infostructure" that will become one of the main driving forces for competitive

---

[3] Customers can also refer to delegates or people representing guests who coordinate and book travel accommodations on their behalf such as an administrative assistant, a family member, etc.

advantage in the hotel industry. The hotel company must build relationships and key alliances, vertically and horizontally, in order to establish a successful GDS environment and digital network to sell rooms, meeting space, and other hotel amenities and recreation. It is possible and sometimes desirable for one or more components to be outsourced. This decision, however, is subject to many factors (such as resources, core competencies, and values) and must be made on a case-by-case basis. Because of the very nature of the GDS network, it is clear that many components have virtual linkages.

DEVELOPING A FRAMEWORK FOR HOTEL DISTRIBUTION CHANNELS

To better understand which distribution channels are available and how a reservation flows through the distribution network, it is helpful to build a model. Building models is a useful way to illustrate and depict the flow and process of a reservation. On the surface, making a reservation seems like a relatively straightforward and simple process. Behind the scenes, there are many confounding factors and intermediaries. Thus, in reality, the process is quite complex, at least from a technical point-of-view. Defining such a model is no easy task due to the many variations and idiosyncrasies that can result. Thus, any model that is depicted results in a necessary compromise between simplicity, accuracy, and generalizability. (Weick, 1979) The models presented in Figure 2 and Figure 3 are no exception, yet they are valuable tools for documenting the many approaches a guest has in making a reservation, the possible points of failure, and the number of entities involved—each of which expects some benefit or fee for the services it provides in the booking process.

Needless to say, building a classification scheme appears to be a most difficult challenge. This is due to the number of different perspectives one can use to study each channel; the many variables that must be considered; the combination of distribution channels that may be used to shop for the best available rate for any single booking; and the various outsourcing models, partnerships, and strategic alliances that are presently used to provide these channels. In practice, one typical approach to categorizing guests is based on the type of traveler or the purpose of travel, namely corporate/business, leisure, or group/convention. However, when trying to apply this classification scheme to the various distribution channels used, it becomes clear that there is no direct alignment because the technology and channels used by each category are not mutually exclusive. The same holds true when trying to categorize travelers based on industry classifications of expense management: corporate-managed, self-managed, or unmanaged. Finally, classifications of distribution channels by how a guest chooses to book hotel accommodations (e.g., via a travel professional or using a do-it-yourself approach), by person doing the booking (e.g., guest or some delegate such as an administrative assistant, spouse, friend, or colleague), by channel focus (e.g., brand service, mega resource such as a one-stop shopping service,

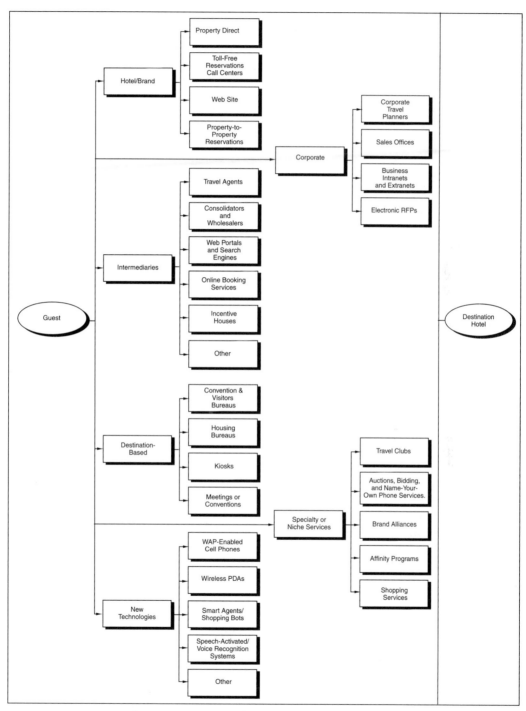

Figure A 2.   Types of Hotel Distribution Channels

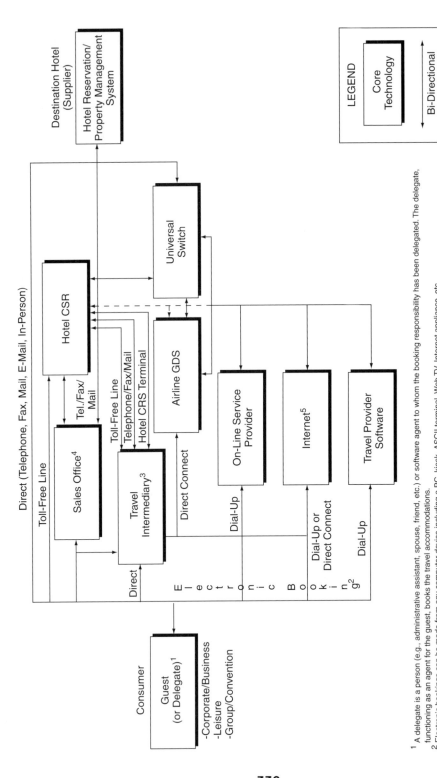

Direct (Telephone, Fax, Mail, E-Mail, In-Person)

Figure A 3. Hotel Distribution Channels Schematic

1 A delegate is a person (e.g., administrative assistant, spouse, friend, etc.) or software agent to whom the booking responsibility has been delegated. The delegate, functioning as an agent for the guest, books the travel accommodations.

2 Electronic bookings can be made from any computer device including a PC, kiosk, ASCII terminal, Web TV, Internet appliance, etc.

3 Travel intermediaries include travel agents, corporate travel planners, travel wholesalers, consolidators, bucket shops, destination marketing organizations (DMOs), convention and visitor bureaus (CVBs), etc.

4 Includes local, regional, and traditional sales offices.

5 Sister technologies such as corporate intranets and extranets are also included here.

330

discount service, or niche-focused service), or via the technology used (e.g., telephone, fax, computer, wireless device, etc.) provide no clear-cut answers either. Thus, gaining a complete understanding of hotel distribution channels continues to remain a perplexing matter.

Developing a taxonomy for hotel distribution channels or being able to segment customers by channel—or perhaps by experience desired—is an outstanding topic for subsequent research. Although it is beyond the scope of the present study, it is an important topic that will likely gain significant interest and be the subject of great debate over the years to come. The value of understanding and classifying distribution channels from a practitioner's perspective is better, more effective distribution channel management. In other words, a taxonomy of distribution channels could provide hoteliers with meaningful insights as to where they should distribute their products (i.e., what channels should be used to market, distribute, and sell inventory), when and how these channels should be used to maximize their effectiveness and booking potential, and how companies should invest in and market these channels. A better understanding in each of these areas would help hoteliers better understand channel management, especially the costs and contributions (i.e., revenues) of each distribution channel and the services sought by consumers. From a researcher's perspective, this knowledge would shed additional light on how consumers book hotel accommodations, how they view the booking process in relationship to the core service delivered (i.e., the hotel stay), how they evaluate the success of the booking process, what services they seek, what motivates them to use the channels they do, how they value the consumer-provider dyad, and how the concept of hotel brand is valued.

In understanding the booking process, it is important to consider the fundamental mechanics behind it. First, there is a hotel that provides rooms (i.e., supply) to a customer (guest) who is in need of hotel accommodations for one reason or another. This represents the demand. The distribution channels are what match the demand with the supply. The basic approaches are categorized in Figure 2. While there are many ways in which a guest can shop for hotel accommodations and reserve rooms, the primary methods can be summarized by six major categories. These include hotel/brand, corporate, intermediaries, destination-based, specialty services, and new technologies.

For many travelers, a specific hotel property, hotel company, or a brand name often drives the decision as to where they should stay. In such cases, information is obtained and reservations are made by contacting the property's reservations office or sales staff directly (either in person or via telephone, electronic mail, mail, or fax), by calling the company's toll-free reservation center, by accessing the company's Web site, or by contacting an affiliated (i.e., sister) property. In many situations, it is not uncommon for a guest to use a combination of these methods and others described below to gather information and complete the booking process.

In the case of corporate travel, travel arrangements are generally governed by corporate travel policies and sometimes pre-arranged contracts with one or more hotels or chains of hotels. Oftentimes, business travel is coordinated through a corporate travel office by professional travel planners or agents. At times, lodging accommodations are made via a hotel organization's local, regional, or national sales office, and increasingly, companies are turning to intranets and extranets for electronic access to availability and bookings and enforcement of company travel policies. Another growing trend for corporate travel is the use of electronic RFP (request for proposal) services which automate and streamline the corporate hotel bidding process for contract rooms, volume and rate agreements, and large groups or conventions. The reader should note, however, that not all corporate travel is booked using one of these approaches. Any of the other methods noted in Figure 2 may also be used; thus, underscoring the difficulties in creating a taxonomy or typology for hotel distribution channels discussed earlier.

Another popular method of booking travel arrangements and hotel accommodations is with the help of travel intermediaries. The most common of these is the travel agent, who provides expertise and consultation concerning various destinations, packages, travel excursions, experiences, and lodging accommodations as well as access to rates and availability information. Travel wholesalers and consolidators represent other forms of intermediaries. These entities buy lodging accommodations in bulk and then resell them to others, typically travel agents. Generally, they are bundled or packaged with other travel arrangements such as tours. Incentive houses are yet another type of intermediary. These organizations assist in planning and coordinating arrangements for large meetings and events. Among their roles are the selection of hotel accommodations, the negotiations for room rates, and the booking of reservations. With the popularity of the Internet, a host of new intermediaries have surfaced, ranging from online travel agents and consolidators to Web portals, search engines, and mega services providing one-stop shopping. Web portals and search engines can play an important role in matching the consumer (demand) with a hotel or hotel company (supply). Some may handle the actual booking process, but this is typically done through an online booking service under a hosting or co-branding arrangement, an alliance or partnership between the Web portal or search engine and a booking engine or online booking service. The intermediaries listed above are just a sampling of the major players. As the result of new technologies, new forms of intermediation will likely arise as well as new intermediaries themselves.

Destinations are another popular method driving travel. Some tourism experts consider destination as the primary reason all travel exists and as the determinant for all travel arrangements. Under these situations, a consumer typically has a particular destination and experience in mind but needs assistance in finding lodging accommodations at the chosen destination. While it is possible to contact travel agents and hotel companies directly, these consumers may seek assistance from convention and visitors bureaus (destination marketing organizations). Many of the more sophisticated convention and visitors bureaus now have electronic booking capabilities for area hotels in their communities and extend these capabilities to their Web sites as well. Customers may also call upon housing bureaus to make their hotel reservations if the purpose of travel is to attend a large conference or convention, particularly if the event is citywide. At times, convention and visitors bureaus function as housing bureaus. Other times, separate, third-party organizations are hired by event planners and conference organizers to process all of the lodging requests for the event's attendees. If guests are already in transit, they may use an information kiosk if one is available along their travel route or within the destination city to select and reserve their hotel accommodations. In effect, destination-based services function much like travel intermediaries and could be construed as such. However, because of the emphasis placed on destination as the primary motivator of travel or determinant of lodging needs, destination-based services warrant special distinction.

In recent years, there has been a growth in specialty services and niche players that play important roles in the booking process and in capturing specially targeted audiences. These services, too, could be categorized as intermediaries since they serve as middlemen in the relationship between customers and hotel providers. The Internet has popularized many of the newest players in this category. These include travel clubs (e.g., Cendant's Travelers Advantage); auctions, bidding services, discounters, and name-your-own-price Web sites (e.g., priceline.com, Hotwire.com, TravelBids), and shopping services that shop and compare rates and availability from multiple sources (e.g., The Trip.com's intelliTRIP). Affinity programs describe a new form of referral service seen on the Internet. Perhaps the most visible is Amazon.com's Associates Program. Under this program organizations enroll and act as referral agents by providing links to Amazon.com in exchange for a commission on all sales that were referred by the associated Web site. Affinity relationships are growing in importance for capturing special niche markets, Web communities, and individuals seeking specific experiences. Other forms of specialty services include brand alliances (e.g., the oneworld and Star alliances in the airline industry) that are forming among companies to share customers and leverage products and services.

The new technologies category is a catchall for emerging technologies and distribution channels. These include wireless, hand-held devices and WAP (Wireless Application Protocol)-enabled cell phones, voice driven systems, and automated shopping agents (bots) powered by smart agent technology. Once these become popular and adopted by a critical mass, they should be reclassified into a more specific category.

The schematic in Figure 3 depicts the various entities, interrelationships, and the flow of information involved in the hotel distribution process. As the reader will quickly note, this chart is significantly more complex than the illustration in Figure 2 because of the many different combinations of channels that may be used to shop for lodging accommodations and complete one booking. These complexities further illustrate the difficulties one encounters in trying to develop a concise classification schema. Nevertheless, these diagrams are important first steps in gaining an appreciation for the complexities involved and in building a more complete understanding of hotel global distribution channels.

It is important to note that each component of Figure 3 represents a potential point of failure, a potential cost to the hotel, and an opportunity for some outside entity to learn more about one's guests and possibly begin developing separate relationships with them—which could result in conflicting guest loyalties—or possibly having guests "stolen" away without noticing until after it is too late! Because a GDS represents a mission-critical application to a hotel (i.e., a primary source of revenue), one should take the necessary precautions to ensure reliability, uptime, and service levels from each component and system provider in the GDS network. One should also focus on the information flow to ensure there are no bottlenecks and that each channel is synchronized with accurate and current rate and availability information.

The Hotel Distribution Channel Schematic

The chart shown in Figure 3 has many facets. The left-hand side of the chart depicts the consumer (or guest), whereas the right-hand side of the chart illustrates the supplier, the destination hotel. While the consumer in a hospitality setting is typically referred to as a guest, it is important to note that in the case of the reservations booking process, the guest is not necessarily the person making the booking. Oftentimes, this responsibility is delegated to someone close to the guest such as an administrative assistant, a spouse, friend, or colleague, who may or may not be sharing the accommodations. In the not-to-distant future, it is conceivable that this responsibility will be assigned to a software agent.

The purpose of travel and type of travel can vary. Typical classifications are corporate or business travel, leisure travel, and group/convention travel. Also, the person paying for the accommodations can vary. It may be the guest himself/herself; it may be an employer; or it may be some other party such as a client. The bolded boxes around hotel reservation/property management system, hotel CRS, airline GDS, universal switch, and Internet represent the critical technologies, key databases, and access points supporting the distribution process. Generally, every other component illustrated serves as a front-end to one of these core technologies.

It should be noted, however, that the Internet itself is a compilation of a multitude of technologies and services. Consumers can find lodging accommodations via a number of different search strategies: using a search engine, going directly to a hotel company's Web site, finding a destination marketing organization online, or booking via one of the many online travel services. The Internet is often a front-end to other systems, namely airline GDSs. This is the case of many of the Internet travel booking sights like Expedia, Travelocity, etc. Over time, though, this will likely change. Evidence exists today which shows the Internet as the primary booking engine. Such is the case with

WORLDRES.com. Also, one should note that the Internet, as depicted here, includes its sister technologies such as corporate intranets and extranets.

All of the lines indicate linkages between one or more of the various entities. The double arrows imply that communications are bi-directional. For example, a guest requests accommodations on a certain date and then receives confirmation as to whether or not his/her requests can be met. Rates and availability (inventory) should be updated and disseminated to all distribution points concurrently. The desire is for instant or real-time communications. Anything short of this results in lower quality guest service and the possibility that a guest may have time to shop elsewhere. Thus, fax, mail, and electronic mail reservations are among a dying breed since they do not offer interactive, real-time communications. Instead, more emphasis is being placed on more interactivity through Internet bookings and travel agents with online access via airline GDSs.

Many of the traditional forms of booking required manual and human intervention, whereas the newer forms are fully automated, with the reservation data being transferred from the point of entry to the hotel PMS without the need for re-keying. This automation improves accuracy and speed while reducing the cost of operation. The most effective channels are those that provide seamless access to a hotel's rates and inventory availability. Anything short of this results in inconsistent information and a greater likelihood of over- or underbooking.

The dotted line between airline GDS (and Internet-related options) and hotel CRS implies that this linkage may not be required, as is the case if a hotel or hotel company relies on one of the universal switches to provide this linkage. This represents significant savings to smaller companies who cannot afford to develop and maintain interfaces to each airline GDS. In the future, it is possible that the airline GDS could disappear from the model altogether if the bypass theory proves viable. There is a current movement in the industry to find ways to extend the distribution network without reliance on the airline GDSs. THISCO is one company aggressively pursuing this mission by establishing direct links with corporate intranets and travel agents. While the long-term ramifications of this are positive to hotels, it is still unclear if the industry can remove the stranglehold that airline GDSs have wielded over the industry for so long, especially since they are at the heart of so many booking services available via the Internet.

It is not necessary that a hotel participate in all of the distribution channels illustrated in Figure 2 and Figure 3. The decision as to which channel to subscribe is a strategic choice and should be made in the context of the co-alignment principle: allocating resources to those channels that will likely yield the highest cash flow per share. This decision should only be made after the organization's distribution channels, sources of business, and marketing mix are fully understood. On-going analysis and audits should be conducted to verify that the chosen strategies still hold true given changes in the marketplace. It is also necessary to evaluate the information being disseminated and the selling strategies being used to determine that they are consistent across distribution channels, accurate, and aligned with the organization's marketing strategy.

Some points for further contemplation with regards to the model in Figure 3 include:

- *Competitive Advantage*—Achieving competitive advantage with distribution channels requires more automated links, links of higher quality, and links that are cheaper to maintain and operate than those for competing hotels. "Shelf space," visibility, and consumer convenience are important dimensions. Additionally, choices are necessary so that customers can select the booking method(s) most accessible and appropriate for their needs and comfort zone.

- *Data Ownership and Security*—With increased reliance on outside entities to process and transfer key customer information, hotel companies must be willing to share access to what traditionally have been considered proprietary data. Guests, on the other hand, are concerned about privacy and the security of their credit card information. Additionally, more electronic linkages creates greater vulnerability or risk. Therefore, more emphasis must be placed on creating secured systems with encryption, firewalls, and other technologies. Data at risk include:
  - Guest Data and Profiles
  - Hotel Availability, Rates, and Operating Statistics
  - Selling Strategies
  - Credit Card Information
  - Consumer Buying and Spending Habits

- *Guest Ownership*—The booking process is an important relationship opportunity between a hotel and a guest. Key guest data is collected and codified within the company's systems. Because this is an opportunity to get to know a guest better, it should be an activity closely monitored and controlled by a hotel. If others are allowed to play an active role in the booking process, it can diminish the relationship building between the hotel and its guests. Moreover, it can relinquish this opportunity to others, who may relish in the opportunity to build better relationships and then mine those relationships to their own advantage. If a hotel is not careful, it could find itself losing customers due to increased influence or leverage by intermediaries.

- *Control of Room Inventory and Selling Strategies*—As more and more outside entities look to book hotel reservations, control of room inventory and enforcement of selling strategies become more difficult. With "virtual" organizations becoming more commonplace, hotels will need to learn new management techniques, form alliances, and make greater use of information technology to help them maintain control and data integrity without discouraging these outside entities from booking at their hotels, inhibiting the booking process, or adding to the overhead costs. Further, it is likely that these outside entities will require compensation for their services (if they have not already done so) and will attempt to leverage volume to gain higher compensation.

- *Synchronization in Real-Time*—The goal of distribution channels is to expand the hotel sales force. This can only be done effectively if every distribution point is sharing the *same* information regarding rates, availability, and restrictions. Telecommunications and database replication and synchronization technology can help to ensure data reliability by providing the same information to multiple distribution points concurrently.

- *Risk of Service Delivery Errors*—The complexity of the distribution channel paths, the reliance on external sources, and the distance of these sources from the hotel can increase the likelihood of errors:
  - Inaccurate or Incomplete Information (Rates, Availability, Hotel Information, Spelling of Guest Name, or Preferences Recorded in Guest Profile)
    - Lack of Knowledge Regarding the Product
    - Reservation "Not In Order" at Time of Check-In
    - Guest (e.g., Frequent Travelers) Not Properly Recognized
    - Over/Underbooking
    - Technology Failures (Downtime)

- *Cost to Maintain Computer-to-Computer Links and Multiple Distribution Channels*—Developing and maintaining computerized interfaces to multiple, heterogeneous systems is costly and resource-intensive due to complexity and frequent, systemic changes. Additionally, the costs associated with the multiple points of distribution and the various technology paths required are eroding a hotel's profit potential. Hotels should:
  - Choose which distribution channels are most cost-effective for them to support and focus their resources accordingly.
  - Provide incentives to customers and travel agents to direct activity to those channels that are most cost advantageous and would allow the hotel company to realize the greatest profit potential. Some examples of approaches being tested to influence consumer behavior include:
  - Frequent Traveler Points
  - Random Contests (e.g., Radisson's "Look to Book" Program)
  - Discounted Rates or Fares
  - Special Promotions

- Faster Travel Agent Commissions
- Disincentives or surcharges for using channels of higher cost (e.g., Delta's failed experiment with surcharges for reservations not booked via its Web site)
  - *Cost of Travel*—With continued emphasis on cutting costs, corporations are increasing their efforts to control corporate travel and entertainment costs. Many organizations are implementing software, using corporate travel planners, or establishing agreements with large travel agencies in hopes of obtaining better rates while enforcing corporate travel policies. These travel entities continue to play an important role in the booking process. Additionally, hotels are increasingly being asked to provide companies with information regarding the spending habits of their employees and electronic expense reports. This adds a new dimension to the bi-directional flow of information between the hotel supplier and the customer (or his/her employer).

REFERENCES

Chowdhury, Seema, Bluestein, William M., and Davis, Kara. (1997, June). Entertainment & technology: Leisure travel on the web. *The Forrester Report, 1* (3), 1–16.

Christensen, Eric. (1997, April 21). Intranets provide privacy, profit. *Hotel & Motel Management,* 31–33.

Coyne, Robert. (1995, July 24). The reservation revolution. *Hotel & Motel Management,* 54–57.

Coyne, Robert and Burns, John D. (1996, April 22). Global connectivity. *Hotel & Motel Management,* 28–30.

Davis, Stan M. and Davidson, Bill. (1991). *2020 Vision: Transform your business today to succeed in tomorrow's economy.* New York: Simon and Schuster.

Davis, Stan M. and Meyer, Christopher. (1998). *Blur: The speed of change in the connected economy.* New York: Warner Books.

Emmer, Rita Marie, Tauck, Chuck, Wilkinson, Scott, and Moore, Richard G. (1993, December). Marketing hotels: Using global distribution systems. *Cornell Hotel and Restaurant Administration Quarterly,* 80–89.

Hensdill, Cherie. (1996, September). GDS bookings on the rise. *Hotels,* 82.

Moore, James F. (1996). *The death of competition: Leadership & strategy in the age of business ecosystems.* New York: HarperCollins Publishers, Inc.

Noam, Eli. (1997, September–October). Why the Internet will be regulated. *Educom Review, 32* (5), 12–14.

Orkin, Eric. B. (1998, August). Wishful thinking and rocket science: The essential matter of calculating unconstrained demand for revenue management. *Cornell Hotel and Restaurant Administration Quarterly*, 15–19.

Quinn, James Brian, Anderson, Philip, and Finkelstein, Sydney. (1996, March–April). Managing professional intellect: Making the most of the best. *Harvard Business Review*, 71–80.

Schulz, Christopher. (1994, April). Hotels and travel agents: The new partnership. *Cornell Hotel and Restaurant Administration Quarterly*, 44–50.

Tapscott, Don. (1996). *The digital economy: Promise and peril in the age of networked intelligence*. New York: McGraw-Hill.

Vallauri, Didier. (1995, October). GDS connectivity altering travel business. *Lodging Hospitality*, 51.

Vogel, Peter. (1996, July). Know your business: Build a knowledgebase. *Datamation* [On-line]. Available: http://www.DATAMATION.com/PlugIn/issues/1996/july/07know2.html.

Wada, Isae. (1997, July 7). Research firm: Online caps will backfire on carriers. *Travel Weekly*, 1, 41.

Weick, Karl E. (1979). *The social psychology of organizing* (2nd ed.). Reading, MA: Addison-Wesley.

XYZ Property Point-of-Sale RFP

Proposals in response to this Request for Proposal (RFP) are due by close of business on . . . .

CONFIDENTIALITY STATEMENT

This document, its enclosures, attachments, and all other information, spoken or written, made available in regard to any information herein, are confidential and proprietary property of The XYZ property. Any disclosure or reproduction of the above referenced information in a verbal, written, photographed, photocopied, electronic, or other manner, without prior written consent of an officer of XYZ property, is prohibited. Even then, those so authorized may only use the information consistent with the consent and only for purposes of addressing the goals, objectives and requirements contained within this document. All copies of any portion of this document must include this Confidentiality Statement.

Extreme care should be taken in the methods and locations used to review, discuss, and store this document. By receiving this document you assume full responsibility as outlined in this Confidentiality Statement and agree to be bound by all interpretations thereof. Unauthorized disclosure of the information contained herein as described above, or as a result of eavesdropping of any type, will be your sole responsibility and punishable by the fullest extent allowable by law.

Table of Contents

Section E: Operating Environment
Section F: System Response Time
Section G: Equipment Configuration
Section H: Physical and Environmental Requirements
Section I: Implementation & Training
Section J: Documentation
Section K: System Upgrades
Section L: Contracts
Section M: System Costs

I. INTRODUCTION

A. Scope

Property XYZ is seeking a feature rich Point-of-Sale System (POS) that will support the operational requirements for the food & beverage outlets as defined in this Request for Proposal (RFP). This RFP provides the necessary information for you to prepare a proposal and also provides background information about XYZ. The purpose of the RFP is to effect the successful negotiation, execution, and consummation of a definitive agreement between Property XYZ and appropriate bidder(s) to provide XYZ with a Point-of-Sale System.

B. Objectives

To select a full-featured POS System that will address not only the standard POS requirements, but also the many unique operational needs of a full-service resort like XYZ. At a minimum, the final solution must:

- Provide a quick, simple, and straightforward solution for entering and tendering guest checks using touch-screen technology.
- Be a user-friendly system that is easy to learn and requires minimal training.
- Provide management with effective controls for day-to-day management.
- Provide comprehensive, timely, and accurate information.
- Provide comprehensive and flexible reporting and inquiry capabilities.
- As much as possible, maintain a paperless system for record keeping.
- Function using hand-held devices for all pool-side outlets.
- Provide operational flexibility to meet the day-to-day challenges and procedural adjustments typical of a new opening.
- Be fully functional with all staff properly trained by opening day.

Although price is an important factor in this process, XYZ places great importance on the quality and dependability of the products reviewed. To determine the quality of systems proposed, emphasis will be placed on the following factors:

- Stability and soundness of the programs (i.e., full-featured, robust, and proven reliability)
- System integrity and security
- The vendor's reputation for quality hardware, software, and service with existing customers

C. Property Overview

Insert as much detail about your property here. Include physical layout, number on staff, target market, etc. For our purposes, XYZ is a restaurant in a 500 room hotel with a pool and golf course. Management also runs a second hotel which needs a POS in its restaurant.

D. Project Schedule

The following dates reflect estimated timeframe for POS selection, contract negotiation, and installation for the vendor's use in planning responses. This information is subject to change by XYZ.

Dates	Action
5/27/2003	RFP Sent to Vendors
6/17/2003	RFP Received Back
7/15/2003	Decision Made by Owners
9/1/2003	Contract Signed
9/13/2003	Equipment Ordered
11/15/2003	Installation and Training, site 1
12/15/2003	Grand Opening site 1
6/1/2004	Equipment Ordered, site 2
81/2004	Installation and Training, site 2
10/1/2004	Grand Opening, site 2

E. Bidding Guidelines

The bids and proposals in response to this Request for Proposal should comply with the following guidelines:

1. All areas of consideration must be answered concisely, following the directions outlined under each subheading. All statements must be supported with concrete examples or explanations. Ambiguous statements such as ". . . all reasonable support" are not acceptable.

2. Vendors who wish to provide information that is not addressed in the RFP are encouraged to do so as an addendum to the proposal. We realize the approach of each potential vendor will be unique. We have therefore attempted to present the specifications in general terms. Points that we feel are essential, however, are presented in detail.

3. Vendors are encouraged to provide any additional information, insight, thought, and ideas on how the vendor can help XYZ succeed with this project.

4. XYZ reserves the right to introduce additional factors not contained in this RFP in order to obtain the most suitable solution. After submitting a proposal, each vendor must be prepared to have the operational aspects of their proposed system reviewed in detail by XYZ representatives. A portion of this review may be requested without vendor presence.

5. Questions regarding any information herein should be directed to the project manager from XYZ. **Vendors must not contact any XYZ employees directly.**

6. Vendors judged to be the most qualified to fulfill XYZ's requirements will be invited to visit for further discussions. This meeting will include a demonstration of the proposed system. At this time, each bidder must be prepared to elaborate upon and clarify its written proposal.

7. XYZ plans to make their initial selection within 30–45 days following the final vendor demonstration meeting.

8. Failure to comply with any of the RFP response requirements may subject a proposal to rejection.

9. **Each vendor must be prepared to include any or all statements made in their proposal in a contract for systems and services, or as an addendum to that contract.** Acceptance of proposals from any source in no way obligates XYZ to the vendor. Furthermore, such acceptance is not a guarantee of any type for current or future business relations. XYZ reserves the right to accept or reject any and all proposals, in whole or in part, at any time.

10. Each proposal must be signed by a duly authorized officer of the submitting company.

11. Two (2) copies of the response to this RFP must be received at the project manager's office, one (1) hardcopy along with one (1) softcopy, by the date on the cover of this document. Refer to the cover page for complete address information.

12. Any vendor selected to provide systems to XYZ will be required to present an insurance certificate as proof of liability covering the full scope of their work, for at least $1,000,000.

13. Each vendor submitting a proposal must be a direct national representative of the manufacturer, or the actual manufacturer. (If you elect to submit the RFP through your local dealer, please specify the name, address, and number of the dealer chosen to service XYZ)

14. XYZ requires that vendors provide access, via a software escrow agent, to any applicable software source code, in the event that vendor is no longer able to provide effective support or to continue enhancing the product. Please indicate how this would need to be handled.

15. XYZ reserves the right to adjust the Project Schedule dates at its sole discretion.

16. The vendor's costs for proposal preparation, demonstration and testing will be the sole responsibility of the vendor.

II. VENDOR INFORMATION

The following information must be supplied by each vendor:

A. General Information

Respond to all questions detailed in "Appendix A–Vendor Questionnaire."

B. Financial

Provide a copy of your latest annual report or audited financial statements including the balance sheet, income statement, and statement of cash flow. As with all information in your response, this data will be held in confidence. Please note that a "call my banker" type response is not acceptable.

C. Experience

Provide a brief background on your company along with major milestones in the company history.

D. References

Provide a list of customers with a similar configuration, preferably local or regional, using the proposed system along with the list of modules currently in use. Please provide at least two of these references for installations completed in the last year. Please also provide a list of similar installations currently in progress.

Please provide the following for each reference.
- Company name
- Company address
- Contact person (management)
- Company telephone number
- Description of system and use
- Date of implementation

E. Literature

Please attach any additional information that describes your product. Describe what is unique about the proposed solution and what sets it apart from other proposals.

III. GENERAL REQUIREMENTS

The following areas detail some of the general requirements to be considered in the identification of the new POS for XYZ:

A. Network Operating Environment

While the network operating system will not drive the purchase of the POS system, a graphical environment (GUI) using Windows XP at the server with Windows 2000 or XP at the workstation is the preferred approach. It is critical that vendors should propose the most stable and robust environment for their system with a proven track record. This includes Unix or any form of thin-client. All POS terminal locations will be cabled with either Enhanced Cat-5 twisted pair or fiber (still to be determined). The current plan for connecting the networks at the two locations, the Country Club and the Hotel, includes T3 data communications lines.

Server Configuration:

The POS configuration must include the necessary components to ensure that at no time will the system at either location be inoperative in the event of a communications failure between the two locations. For those systems that support continued use of the POS terminal while communication with the server is down, a single server at the hotel is an acceptable configuration. For those that do not, a server will be required at both locations (note *"Section E. Consolidated Reporting"* for this configuration). The property management system, however, will operate off a single server at the Hotel and the POS systems at both locations must interface to the PMS.

XYZ will be looking to the vendor for assistance with the hardware and networking requirements including:
- Providing specifications for all hardware including terminals, printers, file server and any other necessary peripherals.
- While XYZ is considering sourcing hardware from a third party, those POS vendors that sell hardware are encouraged to submit hardware prices as well.
- Upon completion of the installation, MIS personnel must be thoroughly trained on all aspects of system maintenance.

B. Device Requirements

Proposed POS terminals should be a pc-based flat-screen active-matrix PC POS terminal with integrated credit card reader. Should be durable, environmentally sealed (protected from spills), and as much as possible, scratch resistant. Receipt printers should be thermal in the front-of-house, and dot-matrix in back (for two color). Due to frequent electrical problems in the southern Florida area, surge & UPS protection is critical.

C. Modules

The following POS modules and general functionality are required by XYZ
- Basic F&B POS functionality in the revenue outlets as defined in section IV–FUNCTIONALITY REQUIREMENTS
- Handheld use for certain outlets
- Comprehensive package tracking (through interface with the PMS)

XYZ will also require the following modules/applications:
- Restaurant Management System (RMS) to include:

- Cash management and reporting
- Management reporting
- Inventory & Purchasing
- Report generator
- Retail POS for retail outlets

XYZ is also considering the following applications:
- Frequent Diner
- Table Management
- Menu Management
- Restaurant Reservations
- Minibar

Note: As outlined above, XYZ will be selecting numerous F&B related applications outside of just POS. We realize all vendors will not be able to propose all applications. At a minimum, interfaces with each of these will be required.

D. Interfaces

A very critical component to the POS system will be the interfacing with other hotel systems. Vendors must clearly define the functionality available with each interface:

Depending on the modules being proposed, the new system must provide the following interfaces. Where applicable, vendors currently being considered are listed. Others may be added or removed as necessary.

For all interfaces listed below, vendors must provide:
- A detailed description of the features and functionality supported by the interface.
- A listing of those systems to which an interface is already available and installed.

Where applicable, the above information should be provided even for those applications being proposed (such as inventory) as XYZ may still decide to purchase the POS system from one vendor and the other system from another.

1. *Property Management System (PMS)*

   Due to the resort nature of XYZ along with the extensive offering of activities and food & beverage, package tracking will be critical. Any systems that offer enhanced interface functionality to include package handling should provide detailed functionality description. On the average, packages are expected to account for approximately 50% of the daily occupancy.

   PMS Vendors currently being considered include:
   - Encore
   - HSI
   - Micros Fidelio
   - MAI
   - MSI

   LANmark
   Jaguar
   Version 7.1
   HIS

- Resolutions   Guest View
- Springer-Miller Systems   SMS|Host

2. *Credit Card Processing*

A single credit card processing system will be used property-wide that
has yet to be determined. The selection of this system will be driven by
the selected property management system vendor.

3. *In-Room Entertainment*

Interface will be necessary to allow for room service ordering directly
through the in-room entertainment system in the guest room. Vendors
currently being considered include:
- LodgeNet
- On command

4. *Minibar*

If an interface is available with any minibar systems, provide system
names and functionality.

5. *Golf Tee Time*

If an interface is available with any tee time systems, provide system
names and functionality.

6. *Purchasing/Inventory*

7. *Menu Management*

8. *Reservations*

9. *Table Management*

10. *Accounting*

This applies to an interface with Purchasing.

11. *Golf cart GPS*

Ability to interface with golf cart GPS system to enable food & beverage ordering while on the golf course. Designed to allow food prep
prior to arrival between the 9th and 10th holes.

When planning the interface installations, the vendor must:
- Give The XYZ project manager adequate advance notice for all tasks
  where the hotel is responsible.
- Vendors must insure that all interfaces will be up and running on the
  each of the opening dates.
- A permanent backup plan must be in place by go-live so that no post-
  ings are lost in the event of a system problem.
- Backup procedures must be detailed in writing.

E. Consolidated Reporting

Due to the unique layout of XYZ, with two separate locations, there are specific reporting requirements that must be supported. Each outlet must be
able to report individually, each location must be able to report individually
and consolidated reporting including both locations must also be available.

IV. FUNCTIONALITY REQUIREMENTS

Please respond to all questions in "Appendix B–Functionality Requirements." While completing the questionnaire, keep in mind all information detailed in sections I through III of this proposal.

For section on "Tracking and Reporting," report samples should be provided.

For other sections, screen captures should be provided as necessary.

To help us better understand your solution, please feel free to add additional descriptions or details as necessary.

If you are able to supply any of the other modules currently being considered (i.e., table management, menu management, reservations, frequent diner, minibar, or retail POS) please provide functionality descriptions for those modules. Provide any screen captures that may help to describe functionality.

V. PROPOSAL FORMAT

All vendors must follow the format described in this section when completing and submitting proposals for consideration. Each section of the proposal must be clearly labeled and separated by an index tab also lettered and labeled as indicated in this section.

The required sections for vendor responses include the following:

A Vendor Information

B Scope of Proposal

C Requirements Matrix

D Sample Reports and Screen Layouts

E Operating Environment

F System Response Time

G Equipment Configuration

H Physical and Environmental Requirements

I Implementation and Training

J Documentation

K System Upgrades

L Contracts

M System Costs

Section A: Vendor Information

This section should consist of the responses to the questions listed in *"II–VENDOR INFORMATION"*

Section B: Scope of Proposal

This section of the proposal should be a concise statement of the relevant factors in the vendor's approach to supplying hardware, software, support and other key elements as each applies to XYZ's requirements and objectives. Briefly describe the proposed system, highlighting major features, functions, and any areas of potential non-compliance with RFP requirements.

State the modules which you are proposing in response to this RFP. Describe the methods that you will use to insure compatibility with the other systems we will be interfacing to.

Section C: Functionality Requirements

This section should consist of the completed requirements form in *"Appendix B–Functionality Requirements."*

Section D: Sample Reports & Screen Layouts

In Section D, include sample reports and screen layouts.

Section E: Operating Environment

Section E should begin with a description of the proposed operating environment incorporating the requirements as described in *"A. Network Operating Environment."* Vendor proposals should describe the specific version of the operating system that would be installed with the proposed system. Indicate how long the vendor applications have been operating on this version of the operating system in a live environment. In addition, please provide the following information:

> *Languages/Development Tools:* Indicate the programming languages used to develop your system. State what other tools are used in developing your system.
>
> *Database:* Describe the file organization/database structure supported by your operating system.

Section F: System Response Time

Based on vendor experience, please indicate the following response times assuming a hotel and F&B configuration similar to XYZ, that has been operating and accumulating data for one year:

> *Credit Card Approval:* Indicate the wait time for a credit card approval from the time of the card swipe assuming your recommended method of data communications is in place.
>
> *Back-up:* Indicate the backup time for daily, weekly and monthly backups.

Daily Processing: If applicable, indicate the processing time required for the end-of-day process.

System Startup: In the event of a system failure, indicate the time for the system to be up and fully functional from the time the server powered up.

Section G: Equipment Configuration:

In Section E, please detail specific information <u>including itemized cost</u> for *all* of the hardware that you are proposing referring to *"B. Device Requirements"* for device types and quantities. If you are not proposing hardware, please indicate the same specifications for equipment that would be required to run your application.

Where applicable, please make sure to include the following information:

File Server(s): model number, speed, memory size, hard disk capacity, and configuration. Include size and model of monitor.

Storage: type (disk, tape) model number, cost, and capacity.

Note: The new system must include the bidder's recommendation for either hardware redundancy or fault tolerance. If the hardware proposed is to be redundant, the recommended hardware configuration should specify all redundant components and their quantities required for redundancy.

POS Terminal: model number, speed, memory size, network card, and hard disk capacity. Include size and type of touch-screen monitor along with information about cash drawer.

Printers: model number(s), speed, size, and required accessories. Please indicate which printers will be connected to the network and those that would be "slave" printers.

Modems: indicate the number and type of modems necessary for the proposed configuration.

Other Hardware: Please provide the necessary details for any other recommended hardware including network hubs and uninterrupted power supplies.

Section H: Physical and Environmental Requirements

In this section, present an outline of technical and pre-installation assistance your firm will provide. Also explain what is required but not provided by your company and how it is normally accomplished.

List all site preparation information including server space requirements, any special mounting methods required, special power requirements (including any need for isolated power circuits), and the number and type of required data communication lines. Please include information on cabling requirements along with electrical, architectural, and other special concerns. Indicate the maximum distance which all peripherals may be located from the computer or control unit.

In addition, describe any environmental requirements for the proposed system, including air conditioning, humidity control, power supply, etc.

Section I: Implementation & Training

The following table details the staff training requirements for each of the two phases:

Phase I			Phase II		
Department	Staff	Management	Department	Staff	Management

Based on these staffing levels (which only includes staffing numbers for employees that will require system training) and the two opening phases as outlined in Property Overview," please provide detailed information on the proposed training process for XYZ including:

- A sample installation schedule using a calendar without dates
- Total number of training hours for each phase
- Number of vendor trainers required for each phase

Include the recommended number of days for the following:

- Network installation
- Network training for MIS personnel
- Interface installation
- On site post-conversion support

Please also provide the total cost for all implementation and training services outlined above. Using the following format, summarize the assignments, responsibilities, when due and associated costs, where applicable, for implementing the proposed system. Systems must be fully functional on the dates outlined in "Property Overview." Add any factors not listed in the implementation schedule which are relevant to a successful implementation including detailed customer responsibilities.

Tasks	Assigned to	Time
XYZ	Vendor	

Section J: Documentation

Provide a list of the user and system operating manuals that will be provided. In addition, please include a copy of the table of contents and index for each. Please state if technical writing assistance will be provided to document XYZ specific policies and procedures relating to your system. This could include any necessary interface procedures, emergency network procedures and any necessary checklists (such as night audit or Front Office management procedures). Indicate your policy for documentation of system enhancements or upgrades, how the user base is updated, how often, etc.

Section K: System Upgrades

In this section, please provide the following information regarding software upgrades:

- Are new releases with improved and additional functionality provided on a regular basis? If so, how often?
- How would your company handle system upgrades for an installation of this size?
- What kinds of additional training and implementation services are provided for new releases and at what cost?

Section L: Contracts

In this section include samples of all contracts related to your proposal. Include hardware, software, service, support and supplies contracts and any information needed to assess the scope of each.

Section M: System Costs

In this section, please include all costs associated with the project as defined in this RFP. Provide the complete itemized cost for each hardware and software component of the proposed system. Include unit cost, extended cost, quantity discount scales, and total cost for each item. Also indicate the length of time quoted prices are valid.

Please make sure to include the following:

- All applications, modules, and interfaces
- Network operating system
- Other required utilities
- Programming—Hourly/daily rate for programmers, consultants and any other individuals that may be necessary if specialty programming is required
- Installation—Itemize all installation costs
- Other Costs—Itemize any other related costs not already listed

Index